BEHAVIORAL CHANGE
IN AGRICULTURE

Concepts and Strategies
for Influencing Transition

BEHAVIORAL CHANGE IN AGRICULTURE

Concepts and Strategies for Influencing Transition

Edited by J. PAUL LEAGANS
and CHARLES P. LOOMIS

CORNELL UNIVERSITY PRESS | *Ithaca and London*

First published 1971 by Cornell University Press.
Published in the United Kingdom by Cornell University Press Ltd.,
2–4 Brook Street, London W1Y 1AA.

International Standard Book Number 0-8014-0648-X
Library of Congress Catalog Card Number 73-157150

PRINTED IN THE UNITED STATES OF AMERICA
BY VAIL-BALLOU PRESS, INC.

Contents

Preface

Structuring agriculture so that it feeds a nation and is an instrument of economic growth is a central problem today in a hundred countries around the world. The agricultural portfolio is generally conceded to be one of the most complex in any government. What is the proper arrangement of ends and means? How can it be created? Once created, how can it be made to function effectively on a continuing basis? The answers given by governments to these questions affect two-thirds of the world's population directly, and all of its three and a half billion people indirectly.

This volume explores these and related questions. The intricate threads it contributes to the fabric of a growing knowledge about the agricultural modernization process in traditional societies are from the researches and personal experiences of many international scholars in several disciplines. Even though the current body of knowledge related to the immensely complex phenomenon commonly referred to by the term "agricultural development" may be described as in its infancy, or at best its adolescence, its impact is tantalizing: it forces the hands of those of us who are trying to research the problem with more precision, to understand its nature, and to formulate more promising designs for accelerating innovation in low production areas of the world.

The mechanism for identifying and weaving the threads into the pattern described in the following chapters was a recent international conference held at Cornell University organized around the topic: "Concepts and Strategies for Behavioral Change in International Agricultural Development." The central objective of the conference was to glean fundamental concepts from the several disciplines and subject areas having high relevance to influencing behavioral change associated with agricultural development in low producing areas of the world, to analyze these concepts, and to indicate their implications for strategy. This primary content was incorporated in eight basic papers which were critiqued by specialists who also supplemented the primary papers with numerous concepts and suggested strategies drawn from their own wide research and experience.

The design of this volume has several unique features. First, the focus is on the human behavioral variable at both the macro and micro levels. This emphasis assumes that behavioral innovations are needed not only by those at the farm level, but also by government leaders and others functioning at the macro level, who must create the environment necessary to encourage innovation by the ultimate decision maker—the farmer. Emphasis on the human element also stems from accumulating evidence that the blueprints for agricultural development advanced in the literature to this time deal largely with nonhuman variables—physical, economic, biological, and technological—hence, they tend to overlook the significance of the human behavioral element in the entire process. Yet the human variable is the ultimate determinant of both the quality and speed of progressive innovation. The usefulness of emphasizing the human element as a dependent variable is suggested by many writers in this volume, as they recognize the importance of orienting their material to reflect the overall human dimension rather than merely confining it to their own disciplines. This effort led to improved communication among those representing different disciplines in the conference.

Second, the authors of this volume reflect the current trend from discipline-oriented to problem-oriented approaches to change. They recognize the immense complexity of the agricultural development process and assume that the known range of dependent, independent, and intervening variables, affecting both the quality and speed of innovations in the agricultural enterprise, transcends the capacity of any single discipline, basic or applied, to supply the required technology or to create the optimum conditions for its utilization. Implied by this assumption is the need to develop and maintain a better balance between basic and applied researches and to bridge the gaps often existing between them. Similarly, a closer fit is needed between the biological and social sciences. Consequently, the conference brought together prominent agricultural researchers and technologists, political scientists and administrators, economists and sociologists, social psychologists and educators, theorists and practitioners with competencies in the various dimensions of agricultural modernization, to pool their points of view, to examine their findings in relation to the known requisites of modernization, and to report the results for international examination.

A third feature of this treatise is a continuity, which ranges from the identification of relevant concepts in the various subjects, across a continuum of analysis and specificity, to a synthesis of strategy implications for decision-making. The contributions are organized into five parts following an Introduction (Chapter 1) designed to provide a theoretical orientation to the entire volume. Part I focuses on complementaries in macro and micro approaches and thus provides a framework for the remaining units. Part II is oriented to technology and its utilization and hence analyzes the technical subject matter with which behavioral change in agriculture must relate and the educational process of promoting its utilization. In Part III the economy and the polity are analyzed in relation to each other and to the process of agricultural development. Social science and development is the focus of Part IV, which treats human behavior as a dependent variable in the change process. The final part, "Synthesis: Concepts and Strategies," consists of four chapters designed to identify and relate primary concepts and their implications for strategy enunciated in the previous chapters. Special attention is given to the social sciences, the agricultural sciences, and the administrative sciences.

Each part is prefaced by an Editors' Introduction designed to orient readers to the subject, to provide a rationale for viewing the relationships of the part to other parts of the volume and to the agricultural modernization process.

Because of its increasing usefulness as a tool for analysis and synthesis of complex phenomena, an attempt was made in organizing both the conference and this volume to utilize "systems analysis." The selection of this approach assumes that the agricultural development process as a whole constitutes a "system," and that it functions as a whole because of the interdependence of its elements. In this sense, this volume analyzes many of the elements of an infrastructure essential to development of the agricultural enterprise. The use of systems theory is illustrated in Chapter 1.

Extending throughout the volume is the premise that central and state governments must assume the primary tasks, not only of creating supplies of applicable technology and related production requirements, but of effective extension of modern age science to all people who can benefit from its use. This goal calls attention to the fact, not always recognized and understood, that usually there exists a significant time-gap between the availability of scientific discoveries and their widespread application by the ultimate utilizers. One of the most profound recent discoveries about the process of agricultural modernization is that the laissez-faire approach will not do the job, that leaving agriculturists to their own initiative and resources is not enough, and, conversely, that external environmental intervention is necessary through the use of modern technical, physical, economic, social, educational, and political inputs.

The universe of focus is intended to include farmers, professional agriculturists, government, business, and political leaders as the central actors in the drama of agricultural modernization; physical, political, biological, economic, social, technological, and educational variables in the environment must be manipulated so as to set a stage conducive to achieving the human behavioral patterns required.

The special effort in this volume is not to formulate "recipes" for solving specific problems, but to identify basic concepts or clusters of ideas which may serve as "anchor points" useful to decision makers at both the macro and micro levels in formulating strategies for transforming tradition-oriented agricultural systems to modern ones. Hence, the ideas advanced are intended to be suggestive and exploratory rather than prescriptive and exhaustive.

The conference which provided the basic materials in this volume was sponsored by the International Agricultural Development Program, College of Agriculture, and the Committee on Structural Change and Modernization, Center for International Studies, Cornell University. Grateful acknowledgment is expressed to the Ford Foundation for major financial support of these programs. Adequate recognition of all the people who contributed to the planning and conduct of the conference and to the preparation of this volume is not possible. Some of them who made major contributions are recognized in the section titled "Contributors."

Special thanks are extended to many who were largely in the background. Kenneth L. Turk, Director of the College of Agriculture's International Agricultural Development Program, encouraged the proposal from the beginning, advised the conference planning committee, and arranged the financial requirements. Douglas Ashford, Director, Committee on Structural Change and Modernization, Center for International Studies, served on the conference planning committee and made financial arrangements to assure the publication of this volume. Dean Charles E. Palm, College of Agriculture, and Helen L. Wardeberg, Professor and Chairman, Department of Education, followed the entire effort and facilitated its every administrative need.

Others who took much time from their regular duties to advise the senior editor in designing and conducting the conference were Harold R. Capener, Professor and Head, Department of Rural Sociology; Marvin D. Glock, Professor of Educational Psychology; George C. Kent, Professor and Head, Department of Plant Pathology; and John W. Mellor, Professor of Agricultural Economics. Douglas Pickett, Research Assistant to the senior editor, was an indispensable aide in handling details of arrangements. Equally helpful were Mrs. Lynn Bauerle and Mrs. Angela Mesmer who skillfully typed the extensive materials related to the conference and the revised drafts of this volume.

Finally, deep appreciation is expressed to my friend and colleague, Charles P. Loomis, for joining me in the editing. His insights into editorial problems and his contributions to the Editors' Introductions were indispensable. Responsibility for the integration and synthesis of the papers comprising this volume, as well as for editorial shortcomings, remains, of course, with the editors.

J. PAUL LEAGANS

Cornell University

BEHAVIORAL CHANGE IN AGRICULTURE

Concepts and Strategies for Influencing Transition

1. Introduction

That little is known about how to start and facilitate modernization of traditional societies has been the claim of critics of both the communistic and the noncommunistic efforts at modernization. Millions have been spent, say the critics, but little has been learned. Although we must admit that there are no manuals available, we will not agree that nothing has been learned. Of course, it is not easy to communicate what has been learned, and it is especially difficult to communicate to audiences at different levels of sophistication. It is not easy to lay out specifics for the agents of change themselves—extension educators, public health officials, government leaders, and other macro decision makers—and for those people and groups whom the agents hope to change—farmers, managers of cooperatives, and so on. It is even harder to communicate to various scientists who specialize in the analysis and study of the basic principles concerning the change involved in moving from traditional agriculture such as that of India to that of such western societies as the United States and Canada. As we have worked with these various audiences, we have found that the so-called "change agent–change target" model has certain advantages both in communicating what has been learned about the modernization process and in generating hypotheses to be tested.

In any discussion of change, particularly planned change, it is convenient to differentiate what is called the "target" system from the "change agent" system. The change agent is the person or organization attempting to introduce or effect a change; the target is the group or individual at which the change is aimed. For example, if an agricultural extension service in a given community or village is attempting to organize the rice growers there into a one-variety rice production community, the extension service is the change agent system and the community involved is the target system. The supervised loan illustrates a simple example of the change agent–change target system.

In the supervised loan, the loaning agency from either the private or the public sector designated as the creditor is the change agent. The individual or plurality accepting the loan and, therefore, becoming a debtor, whether this be a family, a cooperative, or a community, is the change target. The process whereby supervised loans are made illustrates several concepts which are important for an understanding of change agent–change target systems.

As the supervised loan is made, two status roles are created: the creditor and the debtor. These status roles, like others such as teacher, physician, agricultural agent, or banker, define what is expected of the incumbent. In this case, the debtor enters a contract agreeing to follow certain improved practices and to repay the loan. The creditor also under contract agrees to make credit available to the debtor at lower than normal interest rates and to provide supervision and other assistance. As the two status roles are established, a process of great importance for the analysis of social change is also established— "systemic linkage." The creditor or change agent system comes to be linked to the target or debtor system, so that in some respects the two systems function as one. Systemic linkage may thus be defined as the process whereby one or more elements of at least two social systems are articulated in such a manner that the two, in some ways and on some occasions, may be viewed as a single unit. However, it is important in this connection to note the provision, "in some ways and on some occasions." In general, in pluralistic societies such as ours, the actors or members of change agent and change target systems both maintain boundaries. The family or other plurality receiving a supervised loan does not merge with and become the property of the bank or the loaning agency in a totalitarian sense. "Boundary maintenance" may be defined as the process whereby the identity of the social system, be it target or agent, is preserved and the characteristic interaction pattern maintained.

Traditional societies and subsystems of societies usually are characterized by strong boundary-maintaining processes. Sometimes these are supported by powerful sanctions. The American Old Order Amish farm families in Pennsylvania subject any member who becomes linked with a change agent system (by adopting a new device such as an electric fence or an automobile) to what is called the *Meidung*. This sanction results in all members of the sect avoiding and refusing to speak to or to have anything to do with the adopter. The term "sanction" refers to the rewards and penalties meted out by the members of a social system for inducing conformity, achieving goals, and maintaining boundaries.

"Goals" are what the members of either the change agent or the change target are attempting to achieve. Presumably when the members of the change agent system and the target system attempt to achieve goals which satisfy the members of both systems, systemic linkage and change is facilitated. Thus, in the case of supervised loans to farmers, both the loaning agency and the farm family are interested in the goal of increased income. Goals, however, must be achieved in accordance with agreed-upon prescribed rules. The rules which set out what is acceptable and unacceptable are the "norms" of the social system.

Both organizations and members vary in the influence and/ or power they have on one another. "Power," a most important component of social systems of all kinds, is defined as the capacity to control others. It is important to differentiate legitimatized power, designated as authority, from nonlegitimized power, which may be called coercive force. When the police officer makes a routine arrest, the physician prescribes a regimen, or the agent of an organization which has made a supervised loan insists that the creditor follow a practice specified in the loan agreement, the power involved is legitimized in the status roles and hence is authority. Examples of coercive force are robbery and rape.

The manner in which power is articulated between agent and target systems is of great importance in the analysis of planned change. The manner in which the robber, the revolutionary, the dictator, the policeman, the physician, the teacher, the creditor, and others, exert power and/or influence leads to the process of evaluation and, so far as applicable to members, resulting rank, status, or prestige. This rank, status, or prestige of an organization, a status role, or an individual represents the value the specified component has for the system involved. It is important to note that although the wealthiest and most prestigious change agents are usually the most powerful, these qualities do not necessarily have to coincide. Thus, one of the most remarkable characteristics of the ranking system in India, the caste system, has been the ability of the highest caste, the Brahmins, to achieve the most prestigious position without in all instances being the most wealthy or the most powerful. In many cases Brahmins have been relatively weak both politically and in terms of worldly goods but seldom lacking in respect and honor.

Typically, wealth is composed of scarce nonhuman resources which permit system members to attain objectives. "Facility" is defined as a means used within the system to attain the members' ends. The facilities for attaining the goals of a farm family may be machines, medicine, livestock, land, buildings, or bank accounts. Often the chief objective of the agent is to change and improve these means and their use. The systemic linkage between change agent and change target may be dependent upon various facilities. For instance, diffusion studies indicate that those farmers who use radios and reading materials are earlier adopters than those who do not use these communication facilities.

In terms of the various concepts defined and used above, the supervised loan, which constitutes a linkage between the loaning agency or change agent system and the borrowing debtor, places emphasis upon *facilities* or the capital outlay advance, the *norms* specified in the contractual relationship under which the loan is granted, the common objectives or *goals* of both loaning agency and debtor; and the *sanctions* available to the change agent. The most important and powerful sanction permits the change agent or creditor to refuse to renew the loan if the debtor does not adopt improved practices and methods and otherwise conform to the norms of the contract.

Although only two of the authors (Kenneth Parsons and Charles Loomis) specifically recommend use of the supervised loan to further agricultural development, it illustrates the two most important processes in the strategy of change; namely, systemic linkage and boundary maintenance. These processes can be best understood in terms of the critical concepts and elements we have reviewed: goals, norms, power, sanctions, status roles, and rank. Although the authors do not give equal emphasis to these concepts, all use the ideas they represent. The concepts, used in reference to and as organic parts of the change agent–change target analysis of change, provide means for indicating and explaining both similarities and differences in the presentations. More importantly, they make it possible to provide an integrated presentation of the strategy of change required for agricultural development.

Part I, which deals with power and a form of systemic linkage symbolized by the term "complementarities," puts special emphasis on very general goals, power relationships, and overall comprehensive strategy and tactics of change. Although micro systems and modest efforts are not ignored, it is effectively argued in Part I that such broad macro concepts as efficiency in organizational operation and honesty in all important dealings, whether these involve marketing farm products, building roads, or extending credit, are extremely important for agricultural development. In brief, agricultural development is not merely making two blades of grass grow where there was only one before. Agricultural development, thought of in these broad systems terms, requires an extremely complicated strategy in which an optimum form of the interrelation and use of facilities, status roles, and application of power is attained.

In Part II, the strategy of relating the change agent to the change target system is considered from a position "above the battle," so to speak. From this lofty and abstract position, consideration is given to whether or not the technology and facilities needed in so-called underdeveloped areas are already available so that it is sufficient to recommend that educators in status roles such as those of extension agents, salesmen, agriculturalists, and so on, be employed as many claim. This latter judgment is rejected. But likewise, the recommendation of some that all resources for agricultural development be invested in applied regional research is likewise rejected. An in-between position requiring that technology and facilities be adapted to each target system but that also effective agricultural extension organizations, here called change agent systems, be established to implement the achievement of regional knowledge centers is recommended.

In Part III, the economy and polity as components of society are considered and the importance of the norm of "freedom of choice" on the part of all actors, especially agriculture producers, is stressed. Also, the importance of establishing the optimum form of systemic linkage between change agents in the government and the peasants and farmers is considered.

In Part IV, social scientists who are more or less at home with the concepts just reviewed, consider how agricultural development should be planned and studied. In the final segment of the book, Part V, "Synthesis," the junior editor undertakes in Chapter 10 a more complete articulation of the use of the change agent–change target systems as he develops them with a full range of concepts in the Processually Articulated Systems (PAS) model to round out the discussion and provide an integrated treatment of planning and studying change. The other summary chapters are likewise brought into focus through this form of analysis. In addition, the simplified version of the model presented in subsequent introductions to each part will, we believe, assist readers in interrelating the approaches of various authors.

PART I

COMPLEMENTARITIES IN MACRO
AND MICRO APPROACHES

EDITORS' INTRODUCTION

In chapters 2 and 3, by Arthur Mosher[1] and Karl Deutsch, there is no specific mention of either a change agent system or a change target system; both authors, however, take for granted the concepts of social system and systems analysis. Mosher's chapter, organized around "The System of Agricultural Development," designates eight elements, most of which are aims or objectives resulting from what we have called systemic linkage. Deutsch, also taking the systems model for granted, feels that human systems improve not by degrading, but by building up the human components.

It is difficult to conceive a broader target system than that discussed by Mosher. He suggests that, in addition to farmers, behavioral changes must be achieved by many others in order for agricultural development to occur. These include merchants and bankers, manufacturers and distributors of agricultural commodities, politicians and governmental administrators, research scientists, teachers, financial authorities, and others constituting a broad spectrum of behavioral changes

[1] At a 1959 conference on technical assistance held at Cornell University, Arthur Mosher said, "Attitudes and values of the professional agent of change as expressed in personal behavior are a vital part of agricultural development, he needs to understand and to accept emotionally the unique role he is to play." Irwin T. Sanders, ed., *Interprofessional Training Goals for Technical Assistance Personnel Abroad* (New York: Council on Social Work Education, 1959), p. 94.

essential to agricultural development. Mosher specifies three broad categories which compose the change targets: farms, agri-support facilities, and agri-climate, including among other things, the influences of what we have called norms in the change agent–change target model.

The essence of the linkage which he would require for the development of the agricultural society may be specified as *multiple complementarities.* Eight "elements" or essential pre-requisites, sequences, and feedbacks, which he specifies for development are presented in succinct form. They include goals to be achieved by the change agent system in collaboration with the target systems, such goals as upgrading the quality of land, creating and strengthening a progressive rural structure, and developing an adequate supply and timely distribution of farm supplies and equipment with superior technology developed from research. That these goals and others are to be achieved by what we have specified as systemic linkage is indicated by what Mosher describes as requirements of effective development, namely, continuous assessing and reassessing of the potential of regional rather than country-wide development. The dynamics of the linkage is given by arrangements, through research, to achieve a constantly changing farm technology.

The scope of the linkage process in the relation between change agent and target systems is illustrated by Mosher's view that once the agri-support operations and agri-climate are functioning effectively, farmers will be able to help themselves. He has stated elsewhere that a good start would be a first class "ambassador" for agricultural development in each capital city, a lobbyist among legislators, administrators, and university personnel, to help identify the kinds of behavioral change that are going to be necessary in their countries. Thus, as Mosher views the change target, it is not the farm family alone, as in the supervised loan example, which must be the focus of attention. The broad spectrum of changes necessary for agricultural development includes "agri-support" activities and changes in the "agri-climate."

If Mosher were to take the position of the "agricultural ambassador," thus becoming the change agent, the target system would be viewed in a special way. To the "system" approach he would apply "multiple complementarities" with the eight essential prerequisites. It is important to note, however, that the whole society is not the target. The highest priorities are given to the infrastructure, which includes agricultural extension education and credit, research and technology, and supplies and equipment.

Underlying Mosher's discussion is what may be called central place theory and integrated community development. The first four items listed among his eight priorities or "elements" all take place territorially, that is, within a region. Apparently, in this region, villages and towns in which emerging centers are located will not be randomly arranged. Although Mosher does not explicitly say so, they will be hierarchically related to one another and provide the farmer with services in accordance with well-known principles by which trade and service centers are organized in small villages, towns, and cities. The farmer, in using these centers to dispose of his products and make purchases, will follow certain principles. Presumably the change agent, whether it be an arm of the federal government or the "agricultural ambassador," will consider emerging growth centers and stress the importance of integrated development, or what Mosher calls "optimum complementarity." Agri-support activities will prosper in the presence of a favorable agri-climate, and supporting infrastructures will be encouraged by institutionalized freedom and incentive. In the broad spectrum of behavioral changes essential to agricultural development, agri-support activities, necessary for farm production, and the agri-climate, within which the farmer and these activities operate, must be furthered. Obviously on such a broad front the change agent must be concerned with all components of systems but especially the element of power.

The use of power in agricultural development is discussed in Chapter 3 by the noted political scientist Karl Deutsch. As he deals with the factors necessary for inducing change into the target system, he stresses the importance of vigor, health, and willingness to change on the part of members of this system. He suggests reserving one or two years' supply of emergency food stores for every target country to provide people with a future for which to work. As a crucial factor in overcoming resistance to change he suggests that the change agent assume some or all of the risk involved, so that members of the target system can free themselves from risk and work for improvement.

Deutsch has written elsewhere that change agents such as military governments or other forceful users of power, such as those frequently described in developing Communist countries, cannot apply force without "cost." Thus, the application of force costs in the sense that it requires manpower. Such use of power has other disadvantages. For Deutsch, the military government or Communist use of force is inflexible; he recommends a power which will not break. The military government is "gross power . . . [and], thus power not to have to learn." The ideal use of power by a change agent would be that coming from "the self-transforming organizational system." Presumably such change agents would be so sensitive to the needs and reactions of the change target that they would have a built-in form of adjustment to these needs and reactions. Not unrelated to this consideration of power is currency or social capital. A change agent may apply power, which always costs, in such a manner that the power of the change agent is augmented rather than reduced. Various health and other similar programs which meet the expressed needs of the people, carried on and advanced by change agents, may strengthen these change agents and make it possible for them to make expenditures or exercise force on less popular activities. Thus, even though health programs may increase replacement rates of the population faster than the food supply increases during the period which they are advanced, they may be functional. They may create confidence of the people in the change agent so that later certain less popular programs, for example, some devised to increase food production, may be introduced.

The reader should keep in mind the theme of achieving optimum complementarity in the infrastructure in the macro environment through the ideally constituted change agent. If both expressed and implied linkage of the various change agents with the change targets are considered as they are discussed, the change agent–change target analysis will assist in relating later presentations to these broad treatments. Likewise, as the ideal of the "self-transforming organizational system" as a change agent which exercises power, and in the interest of the target is considered, it can be related usefully to the topics of later chapters.

2. *Agricultural Development*

ARTHUR T. MOSHER

The behavioral changes that are essential to agricultural development are not confined to farm operators nor even to rural people as a whole. It is true that agricultural development does require many and repeated behavioral changes among farmers, but it also requires appropriate behavioral changes by sellers of farm supplies and equipment, buyers of farm products, and bankers or other credit agencies. These are still mostly rural people, operating in towns and small cities, and the extension services in some American states, at least, have included them in their clientele. But even beyond these groups, there are many others, in any society, within which behavioral change is a requirement if agricultural development is to come about.

It is helpful in analyzing the requirements for agricultural development to distinguish three broad categories of activities and influences. One of these is farming itself. Farms are the places where all of the components of agricultural production are put together. Some of these components are inherent in farms themselves: the chemical nutrients of soils, exposure to solar energy, the moisture provided by rainfall and irrigation. Others are provided by the farm operator: the performance of the tasks of husbandry and farm management. But still other components of progressive farm production are provided by widely scattered activities elsewhere in the economy: fertilizers, agricultural chemicals, implements, fuel, electricity, and specially produced and distributed seeds. Farmers put all of these together in the processes of farm production and it is in this sense that farms can be considered the assembly lines of a dynamic agriculture.

Farms can only be operated efficiently at constantly rising

production levels (or even at the same sustained level if purchased inputs are utilized) in the presence of a set of what we may call agri-support activities. These are not farming, but are essential to progressive farm production. They include the industrial and commercial activities of mining or manufacturing, processing, and distributing fertilizers, or producing and distributing improved seeds, of manufacturing and distributing agricultural chemicals, of manufacturing and distributing farm implements and other equipment, of collecting, transporting, storing, and processing farm products, and of managing farm credit. Agri-support activities also include a set of noncommercial activities: research to develop a constantly improving farm technology, extension services to help farmers develop appropriate knowledge and skills, and education and training to provide the skilled technicians needed by all of these agri-support activities.

If farms are the assembly lines of agriculture, then farming localities within which farmers have ready access to all of these agri-support activities are the factories. To make such localities possible a full range of agri-support activities becomes as important as competently managed farms.

The third component of progressive agriculture is what we may call an appropriate agri-climate. The agri-climate is made up of all of those influences and "rules-of-the-game" within which both farming and agri-support activities must operate. It is composed of social values and forms of social organization that flow from the general culture of the country or region. It includes the impact of legislation with respect to land ownership and tenancy, the incidence of various types of taxation, the nature of the political and administrative processes, the degree of influence of farmers in political decision-making, and the degree of concern of the existing political elite or of the general citizenry about economic development in general and agricultural development in particular. It includes the rate of industrialization in the country as this affects both the off-farm domestic demand for farm products and the amount of nonfarm employment available, the extent and terms of trade of foreign demand for farm products, and the relative prices of farm inputs and the products of farm production.

Farms are essential to a progressive agriculture. They can support development only in the presence of a full complement of agri-support activities. Both farm and agri-support activities will prosper and be increasingly productive only in the presence of a favorable agri-climate. Behavioral changes are necessary and important throughout this entire structure. It is not farmers alone who must change the ways in which they think and act in order for agricultural development to occur. Nor is it enough for behavioral changes to characterize merchants and bankers in towns and small cities. The attitudes and behavior of manufacturers and wholesale distributors are involved whether they are handling essentially agricultural commodities or not. Similarly, the behavior of politicians, governmental administrators, research scientists, teachers, the urban electorate, fiscal authorities, and budget bureaus is involved also.

A Concept of Agricultural Development

What is meant by "agricultural [1] development?" The term represents a cluster of at least six related but separate concepts. First, it may involve agricultural expansion. This occurs when additional land is brought into agricultural production, utilizing additional labor and capital instruments without a change in "the state of the arts" of farm production or agri-support activities. It was largely expansion that characterized American agriculture throughout the nineteenth and early twentieth centuries. It was expansion when Filipino farmers moved into Mindanao and Javanese settlers into southern Sumatra.

Second, agricultural development may take the form of increased production per acre of cropland or per head of livestock. It is this process for which I personally prefer to reserve the term agricultural development. It involves primarily a change in the nature or quantity of purchased farm inputs, or changes in the productive capacity of the land, or changes in crop and livestock management practices, or, more fre-

[1] Throughout this chapter, the words "agriculture" and "agricultural" are used in their normal American meanings related to the production of crops and/or livestock, on farms. They include both agronomy and animal husbandry. They exclude forestry and fisheries.

quently, some combination of these. That type of change has been prominent in the United States since World War II; it has been important in Japan since early in this century, and has recently become so in Taiwan, Western Europe, and parts of Pakistan and India. Sometimes agricultural expansion and development have been concurrent, as in the recently irrigated regions of northwestern Mexico. More frequently, expansion has been followed some years later by development, as in the canal colonies of the Punjab.

A third member of this set of concepts of development is agricultural growth, here meaning the total growth of agricultural production in a particular national economy, whether resulting from expansion or development. But do we mean growth in physical quantities or in terms of market value? From the standpoint of statistical measurement it has to be in value terms for there is no other way in which to combine the physical quantities of such disparate products as characterize farm production. If total production is expressed in terms of market value, however, how is a situation characterized in which physical production is rising, but due to falling world prices (reflected domestically) the composite market value of farm production is stationary or declining?

The fourth concept of agricultural development is a situation characterized by rising value of agricultural products per agricultural worker.[2] In one sense, that concept seems to be the one most pertinent to the ultimate objective of all production activity, since the total goods and services that mankind

[2] "Agricultural worker" normally means "farm worker" and it may be best to stick to that definition. However, since a progressive agriculture requires a full set of agri-support activities, both commercial and noncommercial, all adequately manned, and since these agri-support workers are needed only in relation to the nation's farm production, it would be logical to include them as agricultural workers in any calculation of product value per agricultural worker. Those manufacturing farm inputs that could be exported might be excluded from the calculation, but certainly all of those who distribute farm inputs domestically, who purchase farm products and move them to central markets, who engage in agricultural research, extension, credit, and teaching are really part of any country's agricultural labor force since without them farming can only be worthwhile when it is wholly for the subsistence of farm families and uses no purchased inputs, and without farming there would be no need for agri-support activities.

can consume depends on the total that it produces, and the total that can be produced depends on the average production per person. For a particular country having an appropriate natural and climatic base for agricultural production, increasing production per worker may be an important part of increasing the total value of economic production.

A fifth concept of agricultural development is that of rising income per person employed. The attraction of that concept grows out of the very legitimate desire to see those who operate a nations' farms enjoy a rising material level of living. However, so many questions of terms of trade between farm and nonfarm prices, taxation policies, population growth, and the availability of nonfarm employment are involved in determining the level of farm incomes (and the purchasing power of these with respect to nonfarm-produced consumption goods and services), that rising incomes per person employed in agriculture is unlikely to provide a useful concept for stimulating development at early stages of the commercialization of agriculture.

The sixth concept, that of agricultural transformation, refers to the normal long-run phenomenon, as a national economy rises in productivity, for workers to be shifted out of agriculture into other types of economic effort. Development, in this context, consists of a decline and disappearance of the predominance of agriculture in an economy. It always involves a decline in the proportion of a nation's labor force engaged in agriculture. After a point at which further agricultural expansion is not economic, nonfarm employment opportunities are increasing faster than the size of the labor force, and substantially full employment exists, it involves a decline in the absolute size of the labor force in agriculture, as well. Such agricultural transformation is not inconsistent with rising income per agricultural worker. It may or may not result in a decline in total farm output, depending on whether or not the productivity of agricultural labor, in value terms, rises faster than the decline in the size of the agricultural labor force. Within this concept, agricultural development is consistent with declining total agricultural output. In this case, development consists of whatever changes in agriculture are consistent with maximum over-all productivity for the economy as a whole. The agriculture of a country might well be "developing" in the very process of disappearing.

The most straightforward and useful of these six concepts of agricultural development are the first two: agricultural expansion, in the sense of extending widely accepted technology to the cultivation of additional land, and agricultural development, increasing the output per acre of land by appropriate changes in farm inputs and practices. Each of these concepts is highly useful in planning programs to accelerate agricultural growth, particularly at early stages of commercialization. Programs to accelerate expansion are different from those to stimulate development. In some regions, one or the other is indicated by the state of knowledge about improved farm practices, the degree of availability of off-farm employment opportunities, the rate of population growth, and other factors. In other regions, both processes can well be pushed simultaneously.

Each of the other four concepts is useful for particular purposes: agricultural growth, despite its ambiguities, is a useful indicator of over-all progress being made in a nation's agriculture. Rising product value per worker, and rising income per worker are useful concepts with respect to various types of analyses. The same is true of agricultural transformation. None of these last four concepts, however, is as useful in identifying the discrete, specific activities that may need to be undertaken or strengthened in order to accelerate agricultural growth as are the concepts of expansion and development.

Acceleration of Agricultural Development

How can agricultural development be accelerated? Some of both agricultural expansion and agricultural development comes about through what one might call "autonomous" changes in behavior in response to changes in the natural and human environment. Some changes in the environment have impacts on human behavior with respect to agriculture that are wholly incidental or concomitant; they are by-products rather than planned effects. The Mormons moved west in pursuit of religious liberty and contributed to American agricultural expansion in the process; they gave no thought to and had no interest in statistics of agricultural growth. Similarly, when any region becomes wholly settled and cultivated but population keeps on growing, the expansion that may result is not an activity undertaken overtly to enhance over-all agricultural production; it is an autonomous reaction to changed conditions that incidentally results in agricultural growth. When farmers in Java begin to dam small streams and build irrigation channels in order to grow two crops of rice instead of one as population increases, they are engaging in autonomous agricultural development. In these and other ways agricultural expansion and development frequently result from human response to environmental changes without being sought primarily for themselves.[3]

There are ways in which agricultural expansion and development can be purposefully accelerated. An important feature of these various approaches is that the elements are not mutually exclusive categories. Each tends to concentrate on a single aspect of a complex phenomenon. Such concentration is essential in the operation of specific programs to spur agricultural development, but it should not become the basis for formulating over-all strategies, because of the tendency to neglect certain equally essential elements.

One of these approaches puts emphasis on technological change with respect to farm production. It concentrates on the undeniable fact that research on plant breeding, pest and disease control, and soil fertilization are basic to agricultural development. Without plants continuously modified genetically to resist disease, respond to fertilization, adapt to differing microclimates, and yield products of specific qualities and amounts, agricultural development cannot proceed. Engineer-

[3] It may have been one of the shortcomings of the measures we have undertaken in our various forms of technical assistance or foreign aid that we have tended to canvass our domestic public efforts overtly to accelerate agricultural expansion and development without giving adequate attention to some of the autonomous forces that have influenced these changes in our own government. Just as scientists have recently turned to studying the mechanics and chemistry of the operation of the eyes, ears, and brain to get hints as to how the function of these can be synthetically duplicated, it might pay us to give more attention to autonomous changes in the history of our own economy for the hints these might give as to effective forms of purposeful activities to accelerate desired types of change.

ing research to develop the tools, implements, and draft power units to carry out constantly changing farm technology is also basic.

Another formulation of the acceleration of agricultural development puts the emphasis on economic profitability. One form of this is very closely related to technological change: the idea that what we need, primarily, in order to achieve agricultural development is to discover and purchase a more profitable set of new "income streams." Another form is an emphasis on creating a pattern of farming localities each offering local agri-support services that, taken together, enhance each farmer's opportunities and incentives for more productive farming. This is the "agricultural infrastructure" argument. Still another economic approach to development gives specific attention to land tenure arrangements as these effect farmers' economic incentives as well as the distribution of political power. Another economic emphasis is to urge a revision of credit availability—and particularly to find a way to get farmers out from under their present load of indebtedness—on the assumption that that obstacle must be cleared away before other important aspects of agricultural development can be available to farmers.

A third major focus is the necessity for agricultural education and training through schools, colleges, and extension education, including youth clubs. This approach is based on the argument that changed patterns of farming, of agri-support activities, and of sound public policies and administration can only come into being as individual persons gain new insights and new skills to provide both specialist competence and broad general understanding.

A fourth approach to accelerating agricultural development is to improve the capacity of the land to support increased production. Activities to that end include irrigation, drainage, land grading, and erosion control. These activities may accelerate agricultural expansion where they are applied to lands not previously cultivated, or agricultural development where the land is already cultivated but higher yields or multiple cropping can be made possible by improving the quality of the land.

The fifth approach is different in that it is a commodity approach. It takes two forms. One form is to select one crop for which a favorable market demand exists and for which prior research has identified feasible means of substantially increasing production and then to concentrate all efforts on the spectrum of changes, whether in research, extension, credit, or marketing arrangements, that may be needed in order to achieve increased production of that one crop. The other form is to select one or several crops for which a satisfactory market demand exists, set targets of increased physical production of each, estimate the requirements of different farm inputs needed to meet the output targets, and then take steps to have those inputs, in proper quantities and at the right times, made available to farmers.

Other approaches might be added but we have reviewed enough of them to enable us to see that each of these approaches embodies a particular validity, but few competent students of agricultural development now take the position that any of the above approaches, pursued alone, will be sufficient. The impulse to try to find a panacea, a short cut, a single-emphasis approach to agricultural development, is a strong one and grows out of the urgency of the need for expansion and development in many countries. But the problem is too complex; it is an example of what can be called a "systems" problem, one of many facets, with multiple complementarities, essential prerequisites and sequences, and many feedbacks. We are coming closer to being able to describe this system in ways that can be applied operationally without overly complicated means of analysis and allocation.

Elements in the System

One element in the system of agricultural development is a continuous reassessment of regions of differing agricultural potential within a country. Regions of immediate high potential, where both existing land quality and locally verified research results are adequate to provide the natural and biological base for immediate increases in the production of one or more crops, are the indicated places to concentrate on providing local agri-support services. Regions of future high potential, where soil and climatic conditions appear favorable for increased production but where either land development or adaptive research must come first, are the places to concentrate on such development and research. Regions of low potential, where technological break-throughs that are not now predictable must precede substantial agricultural improvement, are the places to be bypassed for the time being. The delineation of these regions of differing agricultural potential must be continuously reassessed, since the results of research and land improvement keep moving their boundaries, as does the success farmers may have had in moving their farm practices nearer to the economic limit made possible by previous research and other developments.

A second element is the creation of a progressive rural structure. This means the complex of rural facilities and services—largely agri-support activities—that brings each farm assembly line within the "factory" of a fully equipped farming locality, and that provides transport and communication networks to tie these agricultural factories into the total national economy. A progressive rural structure is composed of an identifiable set of facilities and services among which complementarities are very high and the sequence in which they need to be made available is quite definite. For greatest efficiency roads should come first. Local verification trials and the strengthening (or creation, where necessary) of market towns at suitable intervals, each to serve a farming locality of appropriate size, should come next. Providing extension services and production credit should follow. With all of these facilities established, their regular operation and constant upgrading to meet changing conditions becomes a continuing part of the agricultural industry of the country.

Not only is there a logical sequence in which these facilities and services of a progressive rural structure should be established, there are also optimal norms with respect to the location and strength of each. These may vary with circumstances, but coefficients such as miles of road per thousand acres of cultivated land, distance between market towns, number of farmers per extension agent, etc., can be established and applied to the process of planning and implementation.

The third element in the system is the achievement of a constantly changing farm technology. This is agricultural research, provided that term is interpreted widely enough to encompass informal experimentation, field trials, and even "tinkering" as well as highly disciplined, carefully controlled research. It is research in these various forms that discovers (or develops) the specific varieties of crops and livestock, plant and animal protection practices, fertilization practices, and farm management practices that can lead to higher productivity. Research is also important with respect to agri-support activities.

The fourth element involves measures to secure and distribute adequate supplies and equipment embodying the new technology developed by research. In includes the manufacture or importation of fertilizers, pesticides, and implements; the production of improved seeds; and the timely distribution of all of these. This task involves both technical aspects related to the production and distribution of each form of equipment and problems of pricing, foreign exchange management, and import regulations to make it economically feasible for these services to be rendered adequately.

The fifth element is activity to upgrade the quality of the land wherever physically feasible and economically desirable: irrigation, drainage, liming, and leveling or terracing. Farmers frequently do a considerable amount of this on their own farms. Pioneering homesteaders sometimes engage in it on a small scale in opening new lands for cultivation. Most of the work, however, must be carried through on too large a scale for individual farmers, particularly with respect to irrigation works and drainage systems. Yet there are many areas where it is precisely these activities that are required in order to convert regions of future potential into regions of immediate high potential.

The sixth element is adequate attention to the production incentives of farmers. Provision needs to be made in any program for giving explicit attention to farm prices for both products and inputs, and to land tenure and credit arrangements as these bear on farmers' incentives. To give attention to farm prices does not necessarily mean to manipulate them artificially. It may mean to engage in research related to ways of decreasing total costs of production of particular crops or to encourage farmers to shift away from farm enterprises for which price relationships are unfavorable. In some cases it may involve explicit attention to cultural factors that inhibit the effects of market prices.

The seventh element is the education and training of agriculturally related technicians of many types and varieties: research workers, extension agents, credit agents, practicing veterinarians and engineers, agricultural officials, statisticians, seedsmen, teachers, and analysts of agricultural and economic development.

Finally, we must add a public administrative framework and machinery for executing the public activities that must always be part of any progressive agricultural industry. A progressive agriculture is always partly private and partly public. It cannot be otherwise. The management of individual farms is usually more efficient when it is private. Commercial agri-support activities are privately managed in the United States but publicly managed in certain other countries. Even where they are private, certain public activities (such as policing standards of weight, measurement, and quality; establishing public market information services; and enforcing fair trade practices) are essential. Agricultural research, the training of agricultural technicians, the administration of extension services, the planning of large-scale land development programs, the maintenance of roads and highways, are always public activities to one extent or another.

Insofar as possible the above eight elements should be mutually exclusive. Complementarities among them abound, and side effects of each that relate to others, but substitutability should be slight. Also, each element represents a distinctive type of human activity related to agricultural development. Taken together, the elements of the system are largely parallel to the requirements for effective organization and implementation of a program to spur agricultural development. They lend themselves reasonably well to a process of planning that results in a solution indicating rather explicitly who needs to be responsible for doing what in order to implement the plan.

The eight elements involve many implications for behavioral change. The most obvious are the behavioral changes of farmers. The specific changes in farming practices are easily identified: where farmers get their seeds, how they plant, how they irrigate, how they control pests, etc. These changes involve elements of knowledge, skill, and self-confidence. But many other behavioral changes of farmers are important, particularly at early stages of the commercialization of agriculture. Farmers must learn increased reliance on "probabilistic" knowledge as conveyed in research reports, production and price projections, and other statistical information. They must shift from selecting farm enterprises on the basis of family consumption needs to increasing participation in the market. They must move from reliance on the inputs furnished by the farm and the family to spending increased amounts of money each year on purchased production inputs. They need to alter their concepts of credit away from those associated with borrowing to meet seasonal consumption needs to include the productive uses of credit to meet the costs of purchased farm supplies and equipment. They must make more frequent shifts from one farm enterprise to another in response to shifts in product and input prices and to new cultural practices offering different cost and returns relationships.

But when we turn our attention to the commercial and noncommercial agri-support activities that are integral parts of any progressive agricultural economy, we see that equally numerous behavioral changes are involved. Merchants must learn new techniques of handling farm inputs and products. Research workers must learn new techniques of analysis, new habits of cross-disciplinary cooperation, new criteria for deciding what problems to tackle, new patterns of central and regional experimentation and local testing. Policy makers must gain a deepened understanding of interrelationships between activities within agriculture and between agricultural and other parts of a national economy. Administrators must learn new techniques that, without sacrificing discipline, encourage and release the abilities of their subordinates, and new habits of interagency cooperation that serve the joint objective of agricultural development. Planners must learn to design programs that vary in different parts of a country to fit regional differences in development potential, and they must learn to plan in terms of achieving a versatile structure for a progressive agriculture in which the product-mix is highly flexible and constantly changing. Behavioral change is an integral aspect of almost all elements in the agricultural development system.

We must keep in mind whether we are primarily concerned about strategy implications for behavioral change in agricultural development or about strategy implications for extension services.

When the emphasis is on the former, we should remember that changes in human behavior come about without the intervention of change agents as well as with it. Farmers, within limits set by cultural values, respond to price changes. They learn from each other. Societies make adjustments to technological change; they adjust to demographic changes; they alter their values under the impact of new ideologies. Purposeful efforts to bring about behavioral change are superimposed on these ongoing "autonomous" behavioral changes.

With respect to agricultural development, the behavioral changes that are needed are multiform. Some of them can be among the overt purposes of school and college education, of extension education, of in-service and on-the-job training. Some can be achieved by creative administration that encourages initiative and innovation among subordinates. Some occur concomitantly as an important side effect of opening new lands to cultivation, installing irrigation systems, making farm inputs or new sources of credit available locally, building and maintaining roads and highways, installing telephone lines, or extending mail delivery services. It is only in the context of awareness of all of these types of influence that we can meaningfully discuss strategy implications for behavioral change related to agricultural development.

When the emphasis is on strategy implications for an extension service, a different set of factors becomes important. Extension services usually deal (at least at early stages of the commercialization of agriculture) only with farmers and farm families. They cannot be expected to bring about the wide variety of behavioral changes that are needed elsewhere in the society. And we must at least question whether behavioral change should be the sole objective of an extension service. To accept that assumption would be to abandon completely an earlier concept of the role of extension, that an extension agent ought to do, or urge others to do, whatever needs to be done in rural areas to increase agricultural production or farm incomes, that no one else is doing. Under that concept an extension agent could legitimately cull or caponize chickens whether in the process he was teaching farmers to do it or not; he could act as a broker in lumping together the needs of different farmers for limestone and then himself place the order for carload lots; he could arrange for the purchase by a farmers' organization of a seed-cleaning machine and manage its operation pending such time as commercial companies began offering satisfactorily pure and standardized seed. There are places today where, in addition to encouraging behavioral change, extension workers should either provide, or stimulate someone else to provide, some of the other local agri-support services on which development depends. Extension also has a role with respect to planning, to make sure that the varying needs of different farming localities receive adequate attention.

The roles of behavioral change and of an extension service are neither mutually exclusive nor are they identical. Concepts of agricultural development have strategy implications for both.

3. Developmental Change: Some Political Aspects

KARL W. DEUTSCH

Much of the research on the themes of agricultural development and behavioral change is thorough and explicit but misses one detail—the people who work in agriculture, the rural population. We read about "agri-support" and the "agri-climate" and these are valuable concepts, but what can we learn about "agri-population," the people who actually live on the farms or in the villages? One difficulty arises immediately. In our American experience we think of farmers as employers or entrepreneurs who use large amounts of machinery and small numbers of farm hands. But in parts of the South, they are more likely to be family farmers, and in most of the rest of the world, they are chiefly peasants.

Development Begins with People

The American farmer is the descendant of a "city slicker." The people who left England in the seventeenth century came from towns. They came not as peasants, with many ancestors who had all followed village traditions, but as nontraditional farmers willing to change their tools every few decades.[1] In the nineteenth century indeed, every generation of American farmers did change the shape of its tools, and many farmers were willing to give up the stony acres of New England, showing none of the peasant's proverbial attachment to the soil, and move to the more fertile fields of other parts of the United

[1] See Siegfried Giedion, "Four Changes in American Tools," in *Mechanization Takes Command: A Contribution to Anonymous History* (New York: Oxford University Press, 1948).

States. We find that these qualities of pioneering, expansionism, and technical innovation were balanced with a city person's disregard for the conservation of resources—both forestry and land.

We also find, as some historians have pointed out, that the German immigrant farmers in Pennsylvania behaved quite differently. They stayed in Pennsylvania. They conserved the soil. They cherished every tree, and they built beautiful villages in the Pennsylvania Dutch country where their descendants still live. The Japanese in California were a still more striking example of what happens to an agricultural situation by importing a population with particular qualities—physical, mental, cultural, and economic.[2]

But there is an important factor even simpler and more basic than the technological and economic habits of the rural population, and this, too, though it may not sound political, is so in fact. This basic dimension is the health of the population—its mortality, morbidity, and blood count. These add up to the politics of life and death.

A survey by the Sinha Institute in India in 1962 showed that in three sample villages, picked by random, almost all of the families had heard about the Japanese method of rice culture. They knew in reasonable detail what it was all about. Some had been informed by extension agents, others by government officials, still others by the radio or by neighbors, but practically none of them was using the new method. And one of the major reasons given to the interviewers of the Sinha Institute was that the Japanese method of rice planting, which produced about twice as much rice per acre as the Indian method, required much more physical labor, and the Indian villagers said they just did not have the strength.[3] The Indian Hematological Survey found that village women in India have approximately one-third fewer red blood corpuscles than women of that age, build, weight, and size ought to have. The Indian

[2] Carey McWilliams, *Factories in the Field: The Story of Migratory Farm Labor in California* (Boston: Little, Brown, 1939). See especially chapter 7.

[3] Interview with Dr. Jha, Sinha Institute of Social Research, Patna, Bihar State, India, Jan., 1963.

villagers' report of greater susceptibility to rapid fatigue is
borne out, it seems, by medical data.[4]

The economists' proverbial complaint is that if you have a
land reform program and give land to the country population,
the first thing these unenlightened people will do is to eat
more and therefore diminish the amount of farm produce
available for the cities or for export; this expectation is probably quite realistic. It may be that the first infrastructure of
agriculture may need to be in the stomachs of the village
population. They may first of all have to eat enough to have
the strength which an American or European farmer has for
their day's work.

The susceptibility to illness or mortality exacts a very heavy
toll on the village economy. A villager whose wife recently has
died in childbirth is unlikely to concentrate all his efforts on
increasing agricultural productivity. A family that expects
every second of its children to die before the age of two is
hardly persuaded to postpone immediate gratifications for distant goals. In order to have a puritan ethic, an ethic of working for the future, people must first believe that they have a
future. A puritan ethic requires a reasonable life expectancy.
These considerations clash with the theory of some demog-
raphers and anthropologists that we ought to postpone public
health measures in developing countries in order to avoid a
rapid growth of population; after all, the more people who
stay alive, the more must divide the income.[5]

The health and vigor of the country population is one of
the preconditions for agricultural development and, in the
long run, also for political stability. A government that brings
a high expectation of life to the villagers would have at least
the testimony of our American founding fathers that life,
liberty, and the pursuit of happiness are the most basic and
fundamental things people want their governments to facilitate.

One of the most effective ways for government to achieve

[4] Interview with Dr. Chaudhuri of the Hematological Survey, India
Statistical Institute, Calcutta, Jan., 1963.

[5] The suggestion has been made repeatedly. I heard about it first from
Dr. Margaret Mead at a lecture at M.I.T. in the early 1950's.

long-run popularity would probably be to provide the fundamental essentials of public health—drinkable water and edible food in appropriate amounts. We might seriously consider whether it would be better, in the interests of the free world, *not* to keep developing countries "on a short tether," so that in case of crop failure they would be at the verge of famine, and therefore presumably more responsive to the suggestions of diplomats from more affluent countries. On the contrary, it might be better for the stability of the free world to build up systematically one or two years' supply of emergency food stocks in every country in the noncommunist world in whose political stability we are interested. This different kind of statesmanship would involve a change in our own agricultural policy, so as to increase rather than limit our own food production, but it could be very important if one were to separate in the world's poorer countries the problems of agricultural development from those of sudden famine.

Risks of Innovation

A political theory of the rise and decline of certain kinds of innovative behavior, based on some historical cases, is useful. In the irrigation cultures of ancient Egypt and other countries, it appears that population increased as agriculture increased, and it seems reasonable to infer that population eventually grew to the maximum number that could be fed with the available food. Irrigation itself, of course, once had been an innovation, and so was its extension, until all lands that could be were irrigated, and all obvious improvements in agricultures had been made. Further improvements and innovations apparently were not seriously attempted. Once a traditional agriculture, irrigation-based or otherwise, has reached this maximum, it encounters a gross disproportion between costs and benefits of all further innovation. Any innovation that succeeds would only give people a slightly better meal. This is desirable, but the immediate reward is marginal. Every innovation that fails, however, will kill some people.

It follows that in traditional cultures that have moved up to the very limit of subsistence, further innovations promise very modest and marginal rewards, but swift and terrible risks which are intensely salient. To this degree, it becomes a mechanism for teaching its people to fear and distrust innovation.

Such well-founded distrust, based on the processes of anti-innovative social learning, may exist in some countries in our own times; and agricultural development will have to break its grip. This may require not exhortation but insurance— the public underwriting of some risks of innovation. Consider what might happen in a country or a district where one could tell the population, "We want you to try this new method, but we guarantee you at least the same income and at least the same food supply even if it should fail." The new crop method might be more dependent on rainfall, or on some other uncertain condition, and if the population is sure that no deprivation that could be blamed on the new experiment would seriously hurt them, they might be willing to innovate. American university professors, whose salaries do not depend at all on the success or failure of their research innovations, are an innovative group. When we do not risk our subsistence, we are quite bold.

Motives for Innovation

This leads us to the broader question of the motivation of the agricultural population. The first aspect is their time perspective. Are they willing to work for distant goals? Are they willing to postpone some of their gratifications, small as they may be? As has been pointed out above, their life expectancies and the reassurance they receive from the government are here of prime importance.

The second aspect related to motivation might be the agricultural population's work habits including diligence, accuracy, and the maintenance of implements, as well as over-all care of material objects. One extreme counterexample is that of the Havasupai Indians who were given a Ford tractor which was carried down on muleback to the bottom of the Grand Canyon, and reassembled there. For one season, it plowed beautifully all of the Indians' fields, but then it was left standing out in the rain and turned to a heap of rusty metal.[6]

[6] Communication from Ralph Patrick, Department of Humanities, M.I.T., in the early 1950's.

The obsession which every user of iron tools must develop about protecting them from rust and the neatness and care which are basic to so much of modern civilization often date back centuries in some of the countries that made the transition to modern agriculture successfully. Compulsive neatness in Japanese culture goes back at least to the Middle Ages. German diligence can be traced back to the second half of the seventeenth century when, after the Thirty Years' War, the landlords of East Prussia, the Junkers, introduced what is called *Gesindezwangsdienst*. This was the compulsory service from all the people on the estate who had to spin, weave, and otherwise be productive during the long winter months, and who were taught to feel guilty if not diligent according to their conscience. Today, work has become a German form of psychotherapy, and some people say, a German intoxicant.[7] There is a striking difference between this compulsive behavior and what we find in the "poverty cultures" of rural populations and the urban poor in various parts of the world.[8] An important point was, of course, that the Prussian taskmasters stayed on their farms; the nobleman lived on his estate, he looked after it, he talked to his employees. The Russian, the Austrian, the Italian landlord did not. There is an obvious difference in the degree of leadership that goes into the teaching of work habits. Some oppression, it seems, is compatible with their inculcation; abandonment is not.

A third characteristic of the agricultural population influencing motivation is the ability to organize. Although this may be the ability to organize under authoritarian patterns, including the familiar patterns of discipline, reliability, punctuality, and diligence, autonomous patterns of work in small groups are perhaps more crucial. Edward Banfield describes the work habits and social culture of the inhabitants of a small village in southern Italy, and he reports that the local villagers were almost totally unable to cooperate. They would not trust each other. When an American suggested they should

7 See S. A. Burrell, and Karl W. Deutsch, eds., *Backgrounds for Community,* forthcoming; and Henry Wallich, *Mainsprings of the German Revival* (New Haven: Yale University Press, 1955), especially pp. 328–343.

8 Oscar Lewis, "The Culture of Poverty," *Scientific American,* 216, No. 16 (Oct., 1966), 19–25.

get together for a station-wagon emergency ambulance service to the nearest hospital, his suggestion was turned down on the grounds that they were sure that whoever was entrusted with the gasoline for the ambulance would steal it. When he suggested the local priest, he was told he too would steal it. The villagers were convinced that nobody was ever to be trusted outside the narrow circle of one's family. This was "amoral familism," as Banfield described it, an almost pathological inability for mutual trust which can be quite serious in the development of a community or a region.[9]

Evon Vogt describes a group of Texans who moved into New Mexico to raise pinto beans.[10] They overinvested, had far too many tractors and too much farm equipment which was idle most of the time. Given a small government grant to build a high school for the children of their own community, they built the walls up to one floor; when the grant ran out, they stopped working and refused to cooperate. Not surprisingly, they did not become very prosperous.

Another settlement in this same area, growing the same kind of pinto beans, did better. These were Mormons. One of the most striking experiences one can have concerning the character of a population is to drive across the Utah state line from Nevada. The last town in Nevada is a scene of peeling paint, tattered buildings, and broken windowpanes, all dusty and undermaintained. Five miles across the state line, one comes to Haven, Utah, irrigated and green, where every house is freshly painted, and everything clean and well maintained. The whole community showed a degree of care that would have put Denmark or Switzerland to shame. And one could see here, within a few miles of each other, two communities in which a radical difference had been made in a similar environment because of the culture which people had brought with them.[11]

[9] Edward G. Banfield, *The Moral Basis of a Backward Society* (Glencoe, Ill.: Free Press; and Chicago: Research Center in Economic Development and Cultural Change, University of Chicago, 1958).

[10] Evon Z. Vogt, *Modern Homesteaders: The Life of a Twentieth-Century Frontier Community* (Cambridge, Mass.: Harvard University Press, 1955).

[11] For a discussion of Mormon social institutions see Thomas O'Dea, *The Mormons* (Chicago: Chicago University Press, 1957).

Responses to Modernization

The different character of populations has an important effect on their responses to the processes of social, economic, and political modernization. Some basic concepts for analyzing such responses have been suggested by Masao Maruyama, the leading political theorist of Japan.[12] Many political systems can be characterized by the two parameters of the ways in which most individuals in them respond to the process of modernization. One parameter Maruyama calls "centrifugal

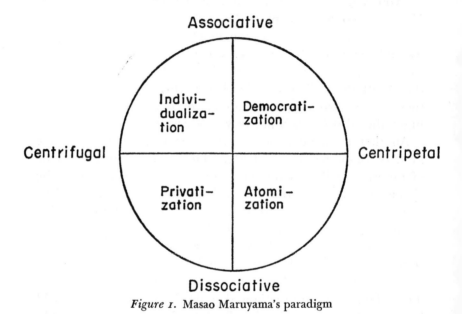

Figure 1. Masao Maruyama's paradigm

versus centripetal" (see Figure 1). Does a political system tend to organize most things toward and around one single political center? Or does it tend to decentralize politics and administration wherever possible; and do regions, districts, and special groups all try to get as far away from the central government as they can? The second dimension he calls "associative versus

12 Masao Maruyama, "Patterns of Individuation and the Case of Japan: A Conceptual Scheme," chapter 14 of *Changing Japanese Attitudes toward Modernization*, Marius B. Jansen, ed. (Princeton, N.J.: Princeton University Press, 1965), copyright © 1965 by Princeton University Press, Paradigm A, p. 495 and material from pp. 489–531 in paraphrased form.

dissociative" social and political behavior. The population of some countries includes many individuals with associative behavior, that is, with a high capability for founding and managing autonomous groups. By contrast, people in another kind of country include a much higher proportion of individuals with dissociative behavior, that is, showing a low autonomous group-forming capability.

With these four poles, representing only two dimensions, Maruyama characterizes the United States as highly "individualized," that is, moderately centrifugal but highly associative, a country made up of joiners with very high capabilities for forming and running autonomous groups. Switzerland, which is also high in associative behavior, is even somewhat more centrifugal, and is in the same category as the United States in Maruyama's scheme. Great Britain belongs in a different category, which Maruyama calls "democratized." Its people are highly associative, with a very high capability for creating and maintaining autonomous groups, but with a preference for doing many things through a single capital city and a central government. In the same "democratized" category we may add Sweden. Regardless of the contrast between the centripetal political cultures of Britain and Sweden, and the far more centrifugal political cultures of the United States and Switzerland, all four countries have succeeded in developing political democracy combined with economic progress. The high associative political capabilities of their combined populations were decisive for the outcome.

Dissociative political behavior patterns of individuals, by contrast, make the success of democratic institutions unlikely, but they are not incompatible with considerable economic and technical progress. Maruyama distinguishes two such dissociative patterns in response to the strains of entering modernity. "Privatization" is dissociative and centrifugal; privatized individuals care neither for governmental action nor for the goals and efforts of autonomous groups. They mainly care for private and personal interests, which may range from the simple pursuit of careers or wealth to more differentiated interests in art, science, religion, or personal relationships. A political system in which privatized individuals predominate is relatively easy to govern, as long as the government calls for only limited efforts and support by the people. The political coherence and performance of such a system are likely to be relatively low among the different types of modernizing countries. This system most nearly resembles a premodern traditional society, most of whose population distrusts the central government, avoids forming any voluntary new groups, and remains preoccupied with its traditional local groupings and affairs.

The second kind of dissociative political behavior forms the last type of response to modernization in Maruyama's scheme. Here, individuals again are unable or unwilling to cooperate in forming autonomous groups to pursue common interests. But although they distrust each other, and perhaps themselves, these persons trust the state. They rely on the central government, identify with it, and readily support it, both against outsiders and against those in their own midst who become suspected of nonconformity. Individuals who respond in this manner Maruyama calls "atomized." Such people are the raw material of totalitarian politics. They "oscillate between overpoliticization and utter apathy," and they are "most susceptible to charismatic and authoritarian leadership." They feel helpless and alone without a central authority and ideology to give them security and reassurance, but under central leadership, they are capable of great efforts and sacrifices, as well as of vast cruelties and errors.

Much of the political style and system of a country will depend on which of these four particular types of responses of individuals to the general experience of social mobilization (or "individuation," as Maruyama calls it) will predominate in a particular country at a particular time. Since such individual responses may change, the successive predominance of different types of responses may produce different stages in the political development of a country. Thus, much of the political development of Japan during the twentieth century is seen by Maruyama as a "pendulum movement" between dissociative periods, in which atomized and privatized individuals prevail in politics, and centripetal periods, where atomized individuals are prominent but where these are joined and balanced or reinforced by democratized ones. This contrasts with the experience of some other countries, where individualization—the creation and maintenance of autonomous groups, and the free choice among them—has formed the pivot of politics, with the back-and-forth swing between privatization and democratization accounting for the major variations. The politics of still other countries might be centered on privatization, modified at times by individualization and group autonomy, and at other times by atomization and excursions toward totalitarian behavior. Finally, we might consider the possibility that politics in some countries may center more nearly on the democratized style of behavior, combined at times with group autonomy and individualization, but also swinging at other times toward a strong admixture of atomized and near-totalitarian responses.

Such considerations raise the question of whether it is possible for a developing area that is highly decentralized and rich in privatized individuals to move directly into centralized or federalized government, or whether the path of development first would have to go through a stage of atomization and authoritarianism, or else through a stage of pluralistic decentralization and group autonomy.

Models of Change

It is important to consider here the ability of the population to learn and to change their perceptions, to break and to change their own habits, to change and to increase their own capabilities and performance.

The political and economic modernization of the developing countries creates a potential demand for models and agencies of change. In the 1930's, many academic people wrote studies about cooperatives, and many government studies were made about cooperatives in the days of the New Deal. After 1945, a fair amount of money was given to encourage studies of the entrepreneur.[13] After World War II, the entrepreneur

---

[13] See Joseph Schumpeter, *The Theory of Economic Development: An Enquiry into Profits, Capital, Credit, Interest, and the Business Cycle,* Redvers Opie, trans. (Cambridge, Mass.: Harvard University Press, 1934). See also Harvard University Center in Entrepreneurial History, *Change and the Entrepreneur: Postulates and Patterns for Entrepreneurial History* (Cambridge, Mass.: Harvard University Press, 1949); Seymour Harris, ed., *Schumpeter, Social Scientist* (Cambridge: Harvard University Press,

became academically and politically fashionable, and since the late 1950's and 1960's he has been the darling of our programs. Many support programs now deal with finding out how to find an entrepreneurial type in the villages of Ruritania or Blankistan; in fact, we are trying to find entrepreneurs in all developing countries.

However, when one develops agriculture mainly by trying to find an entrepreneurial minority, these men may well turn out to practice the early entrepreneurial creed of nineteenth-century Manchester—"Every man for himself and the devil take the hindmost," or government charity take the hindmost, as the case may be. The result of their practice may well be a pattern of agricultural development with a large degree of displacement of the poor. The entrepreneur makes more money, and when his less efficient neighbor is in trouble, the entrepreneur lends money to him with interest, and soon there is rural indebtedness and usury. There arise rural moneylenders who may or may not be the brothers-in-law of the local landowners. Eventually, there emerges a well-to-do elite which will, with luck, innovate, improve, and do all the good things entrepreneurs can do. If the country is not so lucky, they may not do them. But in either case the poor get poorer, and they also grow more resentful. Again, with luck, they become displaced and move to the big cities. They are a headache for the government in such places as the poor suburbs of Caracas and Rio de Janeiro, or the Villa Miseria on the outskirts of Buenos Aires. The slums and shanty towns of two-thirds of the world are, among other things, memorials to the effects of the unbridled entrepreneurial spirit.

To be sure, the poor are not only displaced from the countryside by entrepreneurs and market forces; they are quite often pulled by the attractions of the city, or pushed by the miseries of village life. But sometimes the development of entrepreneurial patterns in the villages has the effect of weakening village solidarity, making life harder for the poor and displacing them. If the government is lucky, these uprooted people go to the cities and join the slum-dwellers. If the gov-

1951); Karl W. Deutsch, "Joseph Schumpeter as an Analyst of Sociology and Economic History," in E. N. Saveth, ed., *American History and the Social Sciences* (New York: Free Press-Macmillan, 1964), pp. 64–79.

ernment is less lucky, they are likely to join the political opposition, or even the guerrillas, and a serious security and stability problem in the country may result.

With very good luck, of course, most of the poor in the cities will be employed under conditions which they find tolerable. If there is vigorous industrial expansion, as in Japan between 1870 and 1900, the people displaced from the villages are reemployed in the cities quite quickly, and this may actually be very good for industrial development.[14] In Egypt, on the other hand, over a period in which 10 per cent of the population moved out of agriculture, only 1 per cent of the population moved into industrial employment, which means that 9 per cent of the population moved into the statistical limbo of the underemployed or casually employed.

If reemployment of the displaced rural population is not fast or attractive enough, one must expect that entrepreneurial development will be accompanied by major social struggles. This happened in France before the French Revolution. It happened in England in the Chartist period (1830–1850) when there was a certain degree of working-class radicalism. It happened in Russia when there occurred, from the 1890's onward, a vigorous rural entrepreneurial development of people the Communists later called "tightfists" or kulaks.[15]

It might perhaps be quite desirable, therefore, to study cases in which habit-breaking, innovation, and learning have occurred in less competitive or disruptive ways. It is easy to recall cases of a more cooperative development which combined rural economic progress with greater community solidarity and more stable politics. The first was the transition of medieval Switzerland from grain to pasture agriculture and the long-distance export of cheese, which involved a radical change in land use and in production habits. After the breaking of aristocratic and landlord power, this transition was achieved by the Swiss through an ingenious and interesting combination of collectively owned pasture land and individually owned

[14] Nobutaka Ike, "Taxation and Landownership in the Westernization of Japan," *Journal of Economic History*, 7 (Nov., 1947), 160–182.

[15] See Karl W. Deutsch, "Social Mobilization and Political Development" in *American Political Science Review*, 55, no. 3 (Sept., 1961), 493–514.

stables and cattle; the combination turned out to be singularly successful. This strikingly modern combination of cooperative solidarity and national monetary calculation for distant markets occurred at the end of the Middle Ages and at the beginning of the Renaissance.[16]

Danish farmers changed their habits in the nineteenth century. They responded to cheap American grain, not by demanding tariffs to keep it out, but by raising hogs to which they fed the cheap grain and exported the bacon to England. The Danes soon did spectacularly well in a situation which impoverished farmers in East Prussia and Ireland.[17]

What happens when there is a massive input of extension services, agri-support, and training? It might be worthwhile to examine the Coimbatore region in India, which looks spectacular when you have flown over miles and miles of country scarred by soil erosion, and suddenly see areas which are contour-plowed, full of little tanks and water reservoirs, and generally kept with what seems, to a layman at least, an extraordinarily high level of care. One is told outside of Coimbatore, only half jokingly, that "they all have pots of money there," and that all farmers there are rich. One major reason for the region's conspicuous prosperity seems to be that there has been a college there teaching agriculture for two generations, so that these farms are now run in part by the children of the first graduates—a second generation of farmers who themselves have had more modern courses at the college. The experience of this region might suggest more studies of rural cooperatives, adult education, and combinations of entrepreneural and cooperative patterns which need not be rigid alternatives.

All these things lead back to one central question—what kind of people with what kind of habits are engaged in agriculture—and what, if anything, can change how many of their habits at what speed? A first answer seems to be that governments, politics, and ideologies are the most powerful devices

[16] See Karl W. Deutsch and Hermann Weilenmann, *United For Diversity: The Political Integration of Switzerland* (New Haven: Yale University Press, forthcoming).

[17] Charles P. Kindleberger, "Group Behavior and International Trade," *Journal of Political Economy* (February, 1951).

known to change the characteristics of a population. They cannot always do so, but political regimes, particularly if united with religious or ideological movements, have brought about some spectacular changes. Islam, Mormonism, Communism, Puritanism, Calvinism, Lutheranism, and Shintoism as modified during the Meiji restoration, all have been remarkably effective in changing the characteristics of large populations.

Allocation of Risks and Costs

Governments and ideologies can command and exhort, but social and economic institutions can provide more continuous and ubiquitous organizations and rewards. All these may relate directly to the question of agricultural incentives and costs, as mentioned in much of the literature of agricultural development. But though the term "land tenure" occurs often in such writings, the ugly words "landlord" and "land rent" appear much more rarely, if at all. In the discourse of political scientists, however, the word "landowner" probably cannot be avoided. We cannot make him discreetly disappear in some "land tenure pattern." We cannot ignore the question of how much land rent is superimposed on the physical and technological costs of producing income.

After the American Revolution, when the American farmers had driven landlord Sir William Pepperell out of the Maine coast, it still cost just as much to raise crops in Maine. But since nothing more had to be paid to Sir William, the production costs of American agriculture had become slightly less. Something similar had happened in the Hudson Valley where the patroons' farms were expropriated, and in the Mohawk Valley where the Loyalists had major holdings.[18] In many countries and at many times, land reform has meant the expropriation of landowners, in particular absentee landowners, with or without compensation. In estimating the probable effects of land reform, or of avoiding or postponing it, one must differentiate between land rent paid for ownership and managerial services which command a price. Many a good landlord may combine in his own person the roles of an owner who takes a moderate amount of rent and of a manager

18 Charles A. Beard and Mary R. Beard, *The Rise of American Civilization,* one volume ed. (New York: Macmillan, 1930), p. 293.

who earns a good deal more for real managerial services on his estate. But if we divide the two functions, then it often may be possible that land rent for owners, particularly in countries emerging from chieftainship or some form of quasi feudalism, could be wiped out at no particular economic loss.

The controlling considerations may rather be political. Would a class of landholding elite have the capability of producing so much civic strife and political resistance that the costs of fighting them would be higher than the costs of compensation? Usually, privileged classes are fairly well organized, they have respectable political and military capabilities and experience, and it is generally more reasonable to compensate them if at all possible. Most of the European land reforms since 1789, of course, have involved some real redistribution of land, often wiping out the old feudal type of land rent and its various successors.

But, if a scheme for land reform is to be evaluated, with or without compensation, two simple questions arise. What percentage of agricultural land actually has changed hands or title? And, by what percentage have the actual payments of the peasant, either per acre or per unit of crop, been reduced under that title? Payments could have remained unchanged or even increased in the form of new taxes or debt payments for compensation to the old owners, or in the form of interest payments to new creditors. For in some countries, land reform compensation has been financed by burdens put on agriculture itself, usually on a twenty-year, prorated basis. This means quite often, as in the pre-1914 Russian case, that a peasant who previously had to pay in the name of property to his landlord now has to pay in the name of indebtedness. And since debtors do not love their creditors, this frequently makes for little more political stability than the original state of affairs which land reform itself had been intended to cure.

On the other hand, if the country is prosperous, the markets in the cities for farm produce are good because industry is growing, and payments are moderate, then this tactic works well, as it did in nineteenth-century Germany and Austria. Perhaps a better way of financing land reform would be to put it on the general tax revenues of the country as a whole. That is, if the inequality of land ownership is a major burden on the productivity and stability of agriculture, it could be argued that it is in the national interest, particularly in a predominantly agricultural country, to have the financing of land reforms paid from the economy as a whole, and not have it re-enter on the cost side in the incentive structure of agriculture where it could only work as a disincentive.

Another possibility, particularly for very poor countries, could be for governments to finance the compensation of their landowners internationally, either through the United Nations or bilaterally in cooperation with a friendly major power. In either case, compensation would be financed in part through the taxpayers of the rich countries of the world.

A question, which in a traditional political system is resolved more or less automatically in line with the relative power of the interest groups concerned, is whether the taxes are mainly put on the rural areas, or whether they come from the outside, or whether they are put on the luxury consumption sectors, import sectors, and the commercial sector. Ordinarily in politics those who have power can escape burdens and those who lack power must bear them. In the political push and pull of many a country, the major power-holding groups, such as the army, the importers, the main seaport and city interests, and the landowners, all of whom have more power than the peasantry and the village population, resolve most political problems on the backs of the villagers. It would be interesting to consider, insofar as the United States has political influence in some of these countries, whether it would be possible to reallocate the distribution of burdens in the less affluent countries so as to lighten the strain upon those sectors of the society that are most likely to prove productive in the reasonably near future, and to put more of the burden on those sectors which, in any case, are not likely to make much of an additional contribution to the gross national product.

Government and Infrastructure

Government administration and political capabilities enter intimately into the general infrastructure of agricultural development. For example, agricultural development has a transport infrastructure which begins with roads and with the allocation of means of transportation. One could, of course, allocate most jeeps to the army for a war, and then have no automobiles available for doctors. But one would imagine that eventually allocations could be modified.

These are political problems. The political structure will decide how much transport, how much health, education, knowledge, mechanical or electrical energy, and how much water for wells and irrigation will be available in the villages. Seed and its quality are political. In many ways, Kwame Nkrumah's overstatement, "Seek ye first the political kingdom," was a dangerous half-truth, but let us not forget the half of it which is true.

The political or government sector is only one, but indeed one of the most crucial sectors of the whole system. It is the control sector. This leads to a few technical questions. What is, and what should be, the size of the government sector in a developing agricultural country? In the poorest countries for which we have data, the government revenues near the end of the 1950's were about 13 per cent GNP, as in Pakistan at that stage of its development. In the most highly developed noncommunist countries, as in Sweden, the total revenues of the government, the public enterprises, and the social security system, amounted to 52 per cent of GNP. Between these two countries, Pakistan and Sweden, there is a range of sizes of government sectors. In many of the world's advanced countries, the total government sector, including national or federal, state or provincial, and local or municipal governments, runs to around 30 to 35 per cent of GNP. West Germany's public sector about 1960 was between 41 and 44 per cent, depending upon details of bookkeeping, and West Germany is renowned for having a favorable climate for private enterprise. An advanced country thus can have a government sector of over 40 per cent, as has West Germany, or of just 40 per cent, as has France, and foreign investments and gold bars may still keep coming in. Another country can have a government sector of 17 per cent of GNP, as has Brazil, and many a local businessman with a little money may take it out as fast as he can.[19]

In the United States, the public sector in the late 1950's was

[19] Bruce M. Russett, Hayward R. Alker, Jr., Karl W. Deutsch, Harold D. Lasswell, *World Handbook of Political and Social Indicators* (New Haven, Yale University Press, 1964), Table 16, p. 64.

about 27 per cent of GNP, and with the help of the Vietnam War, it could go up to perhaps over 30 per cent. This is a relatively small public sector for a highly advanced country. Economists like John Kenneth Galbraith have commented upon the contrast between widespread "private affluence" and "public squalor" in our "affluent society," and the relative neglect of many aspects of such matters as education, transportation, low-cost housing, poverty, and race relations has caused increasing concern.[20]

About one-third of public expenditures usually is military, but a modern state tends to spend more than half of all its budget on nonrepressive activities. In this sense, Marx, Engels, and Lenin are not realistic for our time. In the nineteenth century, most government expenditures, indeed, did go to the armed forces and the police, and Ferdinand Lasalle claimed that the Prussian constitution had exactly three fundamental articles—infantry, cavalry, and artillery. But the modern welfare state spends more than half, and usually around two-thirds or more, of its total budget on services.

If one introduces general elementary education in a country, then between 2 and 4 per cent of the gross national product will move into the public sector. When the governor of the Belgian Congo, Pierre Ryckmans, was asked in 1949 when the Belgians intended to introduce general elementary education, he looked horrified and answered that, if this was done, the Congo would no longer be a profitable colony for Belgium.[21] Private entrepreneurs will not make the masses of villagers literate in any country. Similarly, if one wants to improve health, the public section soon will include another 1 per cent of the GNP or more, depending upon the quality of the service. If one wants to build up a national road and transport system and maintain it, here again goes 1 or 2 per cent. Each of these things necessary for a progressive rural structure involves a higher responsibility of and greater burden on the government.

20 *Ibid.;* John Kenneth Galbraith, *The Affluent Society* (Boston: Houghton, Mifflin, 1957); John Kenneth Galbraith, *The New Industrial State* (Boston; Houghton, Mifflin, 1967).

21 For a more formal statement by P. Ryckmans, see John E. Burchard, ed., *Mid-Century: Social Implications of Technological Progress* (Cambridge and New York: M.I.T. Press and Wiley, 1950).

In this case, one of two things may happen. The government may not do the job at all, and there will be structural stagnation. Or it will try to do what is needed, thus encouraging the people to demand increasing services, but, in fact, it will not increase the government in size and quality to meet the demands. Then the government soon will become overburdened. It will break down in part and alienate the people. It may follow that, as part of planning for agricultural development in an emerging country, we might also have to plan for the increase and development, qualitative and quantitative, of its government sector.

Basis of Government: Popular Compliance

Regardless of the size of the public sector of a country, no government can govern effectively unless the people comply with most of its commands. And let us ask first, are they *capable* of complying? People cannot comply with a policy, or any other political command, if they lack the resources, knowledge, strength, or skill for doing so. As a country's population becomes more capable over a wider range of activities, the potential power of the government increases. Secondly, we must ask, are the people *motivated* to comply? There are four possibilities of interplay; between capabilities and motivations for compliance.

Capabilities can be high or low, and the motivation of the people to comply similarly can be high or low. The United States still can safely be classified as high in motivation for compliance. We have a population with a very wide range of capabilities and a strong willingness to comply with what the government wants. On the other hand, many an underdeveloped or highly traditional country, such as Afghanistan, Nigeria, or the Congo, probably has low compliance capabilities and habits. Some countries have low capabilities but high motivations, as for instance, pre-1868 Japan. Finally, there might be high capabilities but low compliance willingness in countries on the eve of revolution. For instance, the United States in 1775 had a population with a very high range of capabilities for its time, but with a very low willingness to comply with King George III and his ministers.

Considering both these factors, we can then ask where would we place the country with whose agricultural development we are concerned, and where is that country moving? How is that country to arrive at a high level of both capability and motivation for civic and economic compliance with the imperatives of modern technology? With a one-party system or an authoritarian pathway of development, the government would be first of all concerned with motivation. It would seek first to make men loyal, and then try to make the loyal also competent. But in a country that is constitutionally and democratically ruled, or that is not efficiently centralized, a larger percentage of the population increase their capabilities faster and earlier than they increase their willingness to comply with the government, and thus faster or earlier than they achieve their civic and political assimilation. In such cases, the central government might first have to count on growing competence, and then it might expect the competent to become increasingly loyal. There can be, of course, mixed patterns of development, but often one path or the other will prevail.

It might be interesting to ask which path is most probable at a particular time in a particular country. Arthur Mosher's emphasis on autonomous probability and processes warns us not to think that we can easily manipulate large populations. But we could ask what is likely to happen autonomously in a country, and then ask in what ways it would be possible and perhaps desirable to modify these paths to development.

A Matrix of Changes in Political Behavior

Another question-generating scheme of concepts can be drawn up regarding the degree of popular support which the government is likely to get from different groups or regions. This scheme suggests an eleven-step scale for support or opposition toward the government or toward its current policies as listed below. (This scale could apply to expressed attitudes toward the types of behavior listed, or to the behavior itself.)

Level of Support or Opposition
1. Active armed support
2. Active political and operational support
3. Active political support larger than partial operational opposition
4. Active operational support larger than political opposition
5. Passive compliance
6. Indifference or neutrality

7. Passive opposition
8. Active political opposition larger than operational support
9. Active operational opposition larger than political support
10. Active noncompliance, political and operational
11. Active armed opposition

This scheme begins with those who give their government active armed support, the people who will volunteer to fight if the government seems to need them. The next level consists of those who give active political as well as operational support. Political support means using influence in behalf of a government and its policies. Operational support consists of paying taxes, producing income, abiding by the law, and therefore, indirectly but significantly increasing the capabilities of the government.

The third level of support, not irrelevant even in the United States, consists of those people who produce a substantial amount of active political support, but at the same time a significant but smaller amount of operational opposition. These people are the half-hearted or inconsistent allies of the government. There were French businessmen in the 1950's who warmly supported their government's effort to keep Algeria French, while at the same time opposed the taxes for the Algerian war, and even falsified their income tax returns. They were operationally opposing the same government they were supporting politically.

The fourth level consists of the loyal opposition. It includes people in active political opposition, people who write letters to the papers, vote for opposition parties, and perhaps try to get another government elected—but it is an opposition which, in its net effect, is of less consequence than the operational support for the government that its members continue to provide.

The fifth level shows the lowest political support, namely, mere passive compliance. Here we find people who do little in regard to political opinions or operations, but who at least do not oppose the government, and who, when directly ordered to do something, and when adequately supervised, will perform more or less as ordered. In the sixth row, at the midpoint of our scale, are the indifferents, or the neutral population, who can still be compelled, but who certainly will not do anything voluntarily.

The weakest form of opposition is shown in level seven, corresponding to the weakest form of political support. It is the passive opposition which may be directed against the policy of the government, or the personality of the incumbent leader, or the whole constitutional regime, or even against the whole state or political community. (These people may feel, for example, that the Ewe tribe ought to have a state of its own and ought not to be included in Ghana, or that Ireland ought to be independent from Britain.)

The somewhat higher degree of opposition in level eight, corresponding to somewhat stronger support in level four, is active political opposition. It is assumed that these people are so active that their political opposition is much more important than the taxes they pay and the other operational support they provide. They are opponents of the government, and so are, to a still higher degree, the people shown in level nine, the active operational opposition.

The tenth level shows consistent opposition at the level of active noncompliance. Here we find nonviolent resistance of various kinds—people who boycott, who stay at home, who act out their opposition in many ways, both political and operational. In the last level, finally, there is active armed opposition, ranging from guerrilla operations to full-scale civil war and the summoning of foreign intervention.

With the help of this eleven-point scale, we could construct a transition matrix to analyze changes over time in political support and opposition. The eleven rows in such a matrix would then correspond to the levels of support or opposition in, say, 1958; and each of the eleven columns, to the state of affairs in 1968. From such a matrix, we could see from each row and column total what percentage of the total population was at each level in 1958, and then in 1968. We could also see what percentage of the population had not changed its attitudes, and what percentage had moved from what old position to what new one.

A Choice of Balances and Pathways

A last question would then be—is this government integrated within itself? Is it socially divided by extreme class differences? Is it nationally divided among different ethnic groups? Or is there any conspicuously visible presence of a foreign power which puts a partially foreign tinge upon the government? And from these questions, we may then ask what paths are most likely to make the government capable of dealing with its tasks.

This approach leads us to a two-pronged analysis for each developing country. One set of questions will ask what demands agricultural development will make upon governments within the next twenty or thirty years. And the second set of questions will ask, what are the paths of political development most likely to increase or decrease the capability of governments, and what will be the balance between the burdens and capabilities of governments at different levels? Depending upon what the imbalances are, and where we expect them to be most acute, we can then try to estimate in which sectors there will be success, and in which sectors we may expect setbacks, stagnation, or failure.

We may repeat the same differential analysis for regions, and we may then ask whether it is best to treat this country as a single unit, or are the differences in regions or tribes or ethnic groups so great that the unit should be broken up? At what price should what degree of unity or integration of the political unit be kept up?

Finally, what progress can be gained, and what are, from these different viewpoints, the interests of the local populations, as these interests appear to us, and as they are likely to appear to the people who live there? And what is the relation of their real and perceived interests, to the real and perceived interests of the United States?

As we pursue these questions, we can begin to get a basis for making some prognoses about the limits and the prospects of intranational and cross-national political collaboration for any major project of basic economic or social improvement.

Response

SOLON L. BARRACLOUGH

The concept of agricultural development discussed by Arthur Mosher and that of developmental change put forth by Karl Deutsch are not neatly separable. They necessarily deal with the same general development process.

It is not a simple task to identify concepts relevant to optimizing behavioral change and to making clear their implications for educational strategy for agricultural development. A number of fundamental questions arise immediately from this formulation of the development problem. What are desired changes in behavior? Who desires them? Who decides what are optimal behavioral changes? It is not enough to clarify our concepts of agricultural development and of developmental change. We must ask with Karl Mannheim, "Who plans the planners?"

A concept of agricultural development makes sense only if it is understood as part of a concept of national development. We live in a world organized into nation-states. Development is conceived and measured in national terms. Any strategy to affect its rate must work through national power structures or at least be tolerated by them. The nation-state may rapidly be becoming obsolete (It already has become so in many ways with the rise of the "super powers" and the mammoth international neoimperialistic economic conglomerates). But until the nation is replaced by something else, such as an effective world government, it is unrealistic to discuss development in other terms. Nationalism, the aspiration for national self-realization, is dominant in the underdeveloped world. Development is essentially a concept of social and economic change.

51

But obviously it cannot be just any change, rather it must be interpreted as change in some specified or desired direction. Development implies a historical process of social, economic, and political transformation in which countries become less like Ethiopia, Burma, or Guatemala and more like the present day United States, Sweden, the Soviet Union, or Japan.

There can be no single neutral and unambiguous concept to measure such a complex historical process. Even the most commonly accepted approximation of national growth, the change in domestic per capita gross product, conceals a number of serious and practically unsolvable problems of valuation and weighting. Any attempt to define development concretely inevitably introduces numerous value judgments. It can be attested that all concepts of development are basically ideological. I have participated in numerous university graduate classes and seminars on development problems, especially at the University of Chile but also at many other Latin American universities and at the American University of Beirut. I have tried to get the students to accept as simple a concept of development as possible. I asked them, each year with less conviction, to think of national economic development as a sustained increase in a country's capacity to produce which can be approximately measured, save in exceptional cases such as Kuwait, by changes in gross national product per capita. Invariably the students rejected this concept of development. They told me that development for them is much more. Usually they insisted on including all of Karl Deutsch's correlates of social mobilization. In no case would they accept a development concept that in addition to industrialization, higher incomes, and technology, did not include diminution of dependence on foreign countries and foreign economic power and a much wider distribution of income, social privilege, and political power.

I am afraid that not one of Arthur Mosher's list of six agricultural development concepts would be accepted as adequate by most groups in the underdeveloped countries. There is nothing intrinsically wrong in defining agricultural development as greater output per acre of cropland or per head of livestock; nor is there reason why any one of the other agricultural development concepts he mentions could not serve just as well, providing everyone agrees that this is what the term means. The difficulty with Mosher's list is that none of his six concepts, except possibly those of national agricultural growth per capita and of rising incomes per person employed in agriculture, would be considered by intellectuals and "developers" in the developing countries to be even partially adequate to characterize the process of agricultural development. And if a concept is not accepted as adequate by a country's professionals, one may be very sure it will encounter serious political resistance sooner or later.

I fail to understand why Mosher did not give more prominence in his list to the concept of agricultural growth per capita. This is, after all, the most widely used single index of agricultural development. It is the object of annual studies and publications by both FAO and the USDA. The statistical problem which he mentions of converting an index of the value of agricultural production to one of real agricultural output is, of course, troublesome. But its solution is no more arbitrary than the procedures used to adjust a large number of other statistical series commonly used in national income accounting. No single measure can possibly be adequate to describe agricultural development, but the concept of growth of real agricultural output per capita is most analogous to the widely used index of economic development—growth of real per capita gross national product. It has the advantage of combining effects of the most important elements of all six of the concepts in Mosher's list. Adjustments and expansions on the extensive and intensive agricultural margins are taken into account as are changing technologies and improvements in the agricultural infrastructure. Moreover, as output is related to a country's total population and not merely to the labor force working directly on farms, this index recognizes that agricultural development is an integral part of a national process of economic transformation and growth. On the contrary, an index of increased production per acre of cropland may in some situations indicate nothing more than an increasing population pressure on the land accompanied by ever diminishing returns, both average and marginal, per capita and per worker. Food intake of the population might be declining while yields are increasing. For example, output per acre of cropland undoubtedly increased far more in parts of Europe and Asia during the last century than in the United States. But it would be contrary to common sense to maintain that for this reason the United States was falling behind in its agricultural development.

I am most impressed by the small amount of correspondence or overlapping between Mosher's list of agricultural development concepts and Deutsch's indicators of social mobilization. Are we to conclude that social mobilization plays practically no part in agricultural development? Or is it simply that Mosher's list has a technocratic bias? I suspect the latter. Deutsch defines social mobilization as "the process in which major clusters of old social, economic, and psychological commitments are eroded or broken and people become available for new patterns of socialization and behavior." It involves, he says, first a stage of "uprooting or breaking away from old settings, habits, and commitments," and secondly a stage of "inducting the mobilized persons into some relatively stable new patterns of group membership, organization, and commitment." It seems to me this must be as much a part of any concept of the agricultural development process as of general development. Narrow development concepts that do not include any place for the mobilization of the participants cannot carry us very far in the analysis of our central problem: strategies for behavioral change.

Social mobilization requires rather drastic social, economic, cultural, and political changes. In fact, these changes can only be described as revolutionary.[1] We could take a big step forward in our conceptualization of the agricultural development problem if we would recognize that it is an integral part of what is an essentially revolutionary process of social change. It should be a foregone conclusion that the development process is unlikely to be peaceful and orderly. The uprooting implies not only new social, economic, and political processes; it also necessarily means new institutional structures. The relationships among social groups will inevitably change, especially those regulating the distribution and uses of wealth, power, and status. As in the American South, or even in our

[1] Robert L. Heilbroner, wrote on this brilliantly in "Counter-revolutionary America," *Commentary*, vol. 43, no. 4 (April, 1967).

northern cities, it would be folly to expect that those benefiting from the traditional social order will surrender their privileges without struggle.

There is a tendency among United States–trained economists to assume that social mobilization can be carried through without leaving any major groups worse off than they were before—that the losses of any group such as the traditional large landowners or the traditional local political chieftans, could be compensated out of the gains from over-all economic growth. This is nonsense. Even for the strictly economic sphere, it would require as a minimum a wise, powerful, and incorruptible government and, above all, a commonly accepted value system so that groups forced to sacrifice present wealth and consumption could be compensated by promises of returns to future generations. When it comes to losses in social status and political power the problem appears unsolvable, even theoretically. How does one compensate a feudal lord for loss of the *droit du seigneur,* or a traditional ruling class for its future political oblivion?

Deutsch's concept of gross power as being "the power not to have to learn" offers an invaluable insight on some of these problems. It helps to explain why traditional elites tend to be blind to the social changes that are engulfing them. His hypothesis that modernization of a country may require early accumulation of political power by an enlightened forceful government with mass support seems irrefutable. I only wish that he had spent more time in tracing the practical implications of this in developing societies instead of limiting himself mostly to a discussion of power in the abstract. Like the concept of energy in physics, the concept of power in the social sciences yields its most interesting propositions when studied in specific systems. In a developing country, political power is usually viewed by the participants in terms of their relative positions—the pecking order. It governs the relationships among persons, groups, and institutions. It is a question of who can influence whose actions, or what Deutsch calls "effective power." The various groups involved naturally see in the gain of power by one a loss by others. It is a zero sum game. If the state accumulates power, and it must to accelerate national development, other groups must lose, unless, of course, the national government reflects exactly the traditional power structure; hence, the bitter resistance.

It is possible that many conflicts in developing countries do not arise directly from the incapacity of governments to meet the actual demands of marginal groups affected by the development process. Frequently they appear to have their immediate origins in the efforts of a national popularly based government to wrest sufficient power from traditionally powerful groups in order to be able to cope effectively with the potential demands of the newly politically conscious masses.

Changing power relationships and the conflicts accompanying them explain more than anything else why development is such a tumultuous process. But much of reality is lost if one views the problem as simply one of relationships between the government and its subjects. It is the whole social structure that is in flux. The national government is a reflection of this unstable structure, and hence is generally also unstable until new patterns are finally established.

An adequate concept of agricultural development requires explicit consideration of the agrarian structure—of the changing power relationships among persons and groups in what is commonly called the "agricultural sector," both among themselves and also with other sectors of the society.[2] In fact, I question whether the very concept of the "agricultural sector" as commonly used by the economists is particularly useful for analyzing development problems of the type we face.[3] We are interested in devising strategies for influencing the behavior of various groups and classes of people who are engaged in farming. The fact that we lump them all together as "agricultural" probably conceals the most crucial differences among them that must be recognized in any successful strategy.

[2] For an extremely interesting analysis of the interrelationships among developmental change, agrarian structure, and political power see Barrington Moore, Jr., *Social Origins of Dictatorship and Democracy* (Boston: Beacon Press, 1966).

[3] Solon L. Barraclough, "Rural Development and Employment Prospects," in *City and Country in The Third World: Issues in the Modernization of Latin America*, Arthur J. Field, ed. (Cambridge, Mass.: Schenkham, 1970).

Why is it that in many so-called underdeveloped countries "extension education," "extension service," and "extension agent" are bad words to many intellectuals, public officials, peasant leaders, and politicians of nearly all philosophical persuasions? The United States concept of "extension work" is widely rejected by highly influential groups in many countries. During a decade of working in the agricultural development field in Latin America and the Middle East, with both multilateral and bilateral foreign aid programs, I have heard little said in praise of agricultural extension. I have helped recently arrived colleagues, full of enthusiasm for extension work, to be accepted locally by cautioning them against use of the term —they should call it technical assistance, agricultural promotion, adult education, anything other than extension. Interestingly enough, I had encountered some of the same attitudes when working with Negroes and poor whites in western Tennessee.

A common charge by local agricultural professionals is that extension programs fail because the foreign advisors are incompetent. It is said that they cannot communicate well, they never learn the native language, they do not understand local problems and technology, and they go abroad for a vacation or early retirement. This explanation must be rejected, however. Incompetence, sloth, corruption, and senility are not unknown among foreign experts, but this is certainly not the rule. The great majority of United States extension specialists abroad are highly competent and hard-working. They are often personally very well accepted.

The extension specialists abroad who sense the frustrations of working in a little appreciated field are often inclined to blame the natives. The less sophisticated of them talk of cultural, climatic, and even biological factors that make the peasants unreceptive. The more idealistic are likely to find fault with their professional counterparts who frequently show a sense of superiority over the peasants, an appalling lack of practical experience, and an uncanny ability to avoid getting their hands dirty. This, however, is also a superficial criticism. Under the right circumstances peasants everywhere show themselves as cooperative, intelligent, anxious to learn, and hardworking. National counterparts are frequently dedicated and capable technicians who work long hours and are inspired by altruistic and democratic ideals.

A third explanation commonly offered for this widespread hostility to extension education is that the critics have been influenced by anti-United States propaganda. They are captives of agitators and ideologies. But the difficulty is much more fundamental. It has to do primarily with differing perceptions of what the development problem is, of what development is all about and how one gets it moving. It also has to do with conflicting images of extension and its role in the development process. These differences can only be understood within their social contexts.

The United States Extension Service, created by the Smith-Lever Act in 1914, came relatively late in the development process. It arose in response to a need felt by many farmers, especially those who were politically relevant. The process of social mobilization had already proceeded very far. Exposure to modernity and mass media was widespread as were active political participation and literacy. The population was geographically and socially mobile. The occupational shift out of agriculture already had proceeded so far that the farm population was practically stabilized and on the verge of decline. The availability of alternative urban jobs for surplus farm people was beginning to be accepted as the natural order. Except for relatively small minority groups of Negroes, Indians, and immigrants there was no linguistic and cultural assimilation problem. Per capita incomes were already among the highest in the world.

The United States Extension Service evolved to meet the needs for technical assistance of a farm population which had already been mobilized socially—it was not created in order to mobilize them for development. President Roosevelt and Secretary Wallace apparently recognized this in the 1930's when they insisted on forming the New Farm Security Administration to develop and rehabilitate our more backward and depressed farm people instead of relying only on the established extension service.

Karl Deutsch tells us that "the popular acceptance of a government in a period of social mobilization is most of all a matter of its capabilities and the manner in which they are used—that is, essentially a matter of its responsiveness to the felt needs of its population." In most of today's developing countries, politically relevant groups feel no need for United States–type extension services. Who feels the need for extension help in the poor underdeveloped countries? Certainly not the mass of the rural people. These are mostly wage laborers and small subsistence-level farmers. They are caught up in an intricate web of institutional arrangements and resource limitations that would make the best extension service in the world ineffective. Exploitation by landowners, moneylenders, tradesmen, and government officials is generally a far more pressing problem to them than that of improving their technology. Improved farming practices would be almost useless to most, without access to more land, capital, markets, and alternative job opportunities. In any event, this majority group usually is politically inarticulate.

For very different reasons, the large landowners do not feel any compulsion to encourage a popularly based extension program. They find it convenient to have publicly paid extension agents on call, but they seldom believe it is really necessary, since those who wish to do so could generally hire their own technical help.

My observations suggest that where there is a public extension service the extension agents generally spend most of their efforts with the large farmers. Rationally, they can hope to affect more acres and cows per day in this way. Socially they are more comfortable with large farmers. In several Latin American countries, for example, only 1 or 2 per cent of the farm families control over two-thirds of the good farm land. These probably receive an even higher proportion of the extension services' efforts. The family-sized commercial owner-cultivators who are the mainstay of the United States extension effort hardly exist in many developing countries. Even where they are relatively numerous, as in some parts of Brazil, Costa Rica, and Lebanon, there is little need felt for extension help. Other bottlenecks in the development process such as credit, markets, and prices are likely to seem far more immediate and pressing.

In my opinion the traditional United States extension approach will usually fail in the underdeveloped countries as a strategy to promote behavioral change. It does not take into account the realities of the development process. It has a conservative bias, except for matters of technology, when what is required for rapid development are revolutionary values and changes in the entire society. Mosher's "system" to accelerate agricultural development is undoubtedly an improvement over the simple extension approach. It recognizes that a successful strategy must include more than bringing to farmers new practices and techniques. But it is still far short of what is required; it too is based on an overly limited concept of the agricultural development problem. Moreover, the eight elements in his system appear to be of two very different orders of things. Four of them, activities to upgrade the quality of the land, better research on farm technology, continuous studies of development potential, and the training of agricultural technicians are rather simple measures that any reasonably competent government could undertake. The other four, however, either presuppose a process of development and social mobilization is already underway or else they are trivial. The criterion of a progressive rural social structure, for example, if we take this seriously, means nothing less than a social revolution in many countries. Efficient public administration in itself is meaningless unless the government is dedicated to promoting accelerated development instead of to traditional particularistic ends, serving limited clienteles and classes. In any case, his "system" tells little about what strategy to follow in order to achieve either behavioral change or agricultural development.

A strategy is a general plan of how to use power and resources to attain specified objectives. It implies a sequence of coordinated decisions and actions. The strategies appropriate for very poor agrarian countries, such as Guatemala, are likely to be very different from those that are relatively more advanced, such as Chile. Furthermore, the strategy followed is inseparable from the conception of the "promised land" of development posed as the goal, and this sought-after Utopia is more of an ideological matter than a technical one.

Assuming that we know what behavioral changes we want to achieve, how do we accelerate them? Mannheim concluded that there are two general ways to change behavior and values in fundamental lasting ways. One is to change society. The other is to change personalities.[4] In practice it is necessary to do both. The idealist supposedly puts his emphasis on the personality of man as the determinant of society, while a materialist would argue that the social structure created that personality. Recent papal encyclicals, however, emphasize the necessity of structural changes, such as agrarian reform, in the developing countries. Meanwhile, many communists and socialists are eschewing revolution for education, at least for the time being, in Latin America. It would be presumptuous for us, in this Alice in Wonderland state of affairs, to recommend a strategy that did not combine both approaches. We must modify social structure and we must educate new men, or at least retread old men for new tasks and new roles in a changing world.

For a rural educational program (an extension program) to be effective, it will have to be in step with the historical changes taking place under the name of development in each country. These will be different in each place. They depend not only on where one wants to go, but on where one is, where one came from, and on one's interrelationships with everyone else. There are, however, many common elements in the development of mass-based industrial societies that give us guidelines concerning what to expect in various steps of the process. Deutsch's chapter indicates several of these.

In Chile, the traditional extension service approach had little impact. At present, however, a small agrarian reform is in process. The land distribution agency (CORA) is working with 8,000 beneficiary families and hopes to increase this number to 100,000 in the next few years. The agricultural development agency (INDAP) is working with 90,000 small farmers and expects soon to reach 150,000. These agencies do not have the primary objective of introducing new technology, but of promoting structural changes. CORA aims at creating new land tenure arrangements together with new marketing and credit institutions. INDAP aids the peasants in forming committees and cooperatives, provides credit, and aids with marketing. Both emphasize increasing the bargaining power of the peas-

[4] Karl Mannheim, *Man and Society in an Age of Reconstruction* (London: Kegan Paul, Trench, Trubner, 1940). (See especially chapter 9.)

ants in their dealings with landlords, sellers, buyers, and other institutions and agencies. These kinds of activities create conflicts. The technicians of CORA and INDAP have to take part in these conflicts on the side of the *campesinos* if they are to carry out their work effectively. Many of them do so. Interestingly enough, the peasants and technicians are now beginning to demand technical help. They see the possibility of a future. The technicians are demanding more technical content and more extension information in training courses.

There is a lesson in this. Extension education has a place in strategies for behavioral change. But it has a better chance of being effective when development is really underway. Extension education becomes a felt need when the process of social mobilization begins to reach the peasantry and the traditional rural social structure begins to break up, offering them hope and opportunity. As a hypothesis, I would suggest that "extension help" will be accepted most eagerly in a conflict situation in which the "extensionist" is aiding the farmers with their other more pressing problems.

Response

LINWOOD L. HODGDON [1]

Two facts stand out in our understanding of development and how it may be accelerated in scores of countries with diverse social, economic, and political backgrounds.

First, the United States, as a nation, has not established an education and research base adequate to ensure a reasonable degree of success in assisting scores of developing societies around the world. Second, the process of development is vastly more complex than most observers heretofore have either recognized or acknowledged. We shall need far more knowledge and skill than we now possess if we are to identify with and help fulfill the legitimate aspirations of the developing societies.

The lack of an adequate education and research base to support this nation's expanded commitments overseas has been brilliantly documented by Milton J. Esman.[2] "In what other field of endeavor," says Donald Stone in the forward to Esman's book, "has the United States engaged in so difficult and complex a task as that of assisting . . . [developing] nations in their economic, social, and governmental development without creating a research and education foundation to guide intelligent action!" He goes on to remind us that whenever, as a nation, we have sought great achievement, we have proceeded empirically to develop knowledge, scientific theory, and pro-

[1] Several of the concepts presented in this paper were developed in an earlier paper titled "The American Technician and the Development Process" presented at the Conference on Engineering in International Development, Estes Park, Colorado, Aug. 27–Sept. 1, 1967.

[2] *Needed: An Education and Research Base to Support America's Expanded Commitments Overseas* (Graduate School of Public and International Affairs, University of Pittsburgh, 1961).

fessional skill adequate to cope with the problem. We have created and concerted the essential education and research resources. Testimony to the value of this policy is found in the great network of research and educational efforts undergirding our substantial achievements in industry, agriculture, health, space science, and defense.

The fact remains, however, that in this most complex and delicate of all undertakings—the rapid development of responsible and progressive societies in diverse cultural environments —we have not done so. The consequences are familiar to all of us. Each year we send thousands of Americans overseas without adequate preparation beyond technical knowledge uniquely related to the democratic, pluralistic, and affluent technological society of the United States. We have not, as a nation, approached the problems of the developing nations on a systematic basis, nor have we recognized fully the unique societal conditions from which their problems have sprung. Consequently, U.S. assistance, which has been requested by scores of nations throughout the developing world, has been much less effective than it might have been had we developed an education and research base commensurate with the needs of the developing world.[3]

We also tend to over-simplify the development process and all that it entails. Historically, American efforts to aid her sister nations in development may be divided into two periods —the earlier Marshall Plan experience following World War II and the more recent efforts to assist the far more numerous societies emerging into nationhood since the end of the war.

The success of the Marshall Plan experience is confirmed by the rapid recovery of the nations thereby assisted, whereas only a few of the developing nations have achieved rates of economic growth or of social progress commensurate with self-imposed national goals, or even adequate to meet current needs in such vital areas as food production, population control, basic education, health and sanitation, manpower training, and unemployment. History will show that in the case

---

[3] I do not imply that external assistance alone can do the job. In the last analysis a poor country must develop its own institutions to perform the functions essential to development. But we have often lacked the insight and skill to guide intelligent action when requested to do so.

of the Marshall Plan countries the social institutions essential
to development—or, more accurately to reconstruction—were
already in existence; in the latter case they are not.

One of the most significant statements in Arthur Mosher's
paper is that the behavioral changes essential to agricultural
development are not confined to farmers or even to rural
people as a whole. This shows a clear awareness that we must
take into consideration the total *Gestalt* or pattern of the
society. We must take into account the indigenous social institutions (or social systems) and the networks of social interaction which exist in a society and guide and direct human
behavior in all spheres of life. We are not likely to make much
headway, either in developing the basic concepts essential to
understanding development or in devising strategies for societal and behavioral change, if we do not recognize this
fundamental fact.

The essential validity of this approach, presented more than
thirty years ago by Ruth Benedict [4] has never been challenged.
In it, among other things, she documents with brilliant clarity
the diversity of cultures, the powerful impact of custom, and
the essential integration of cultures on the basis of indigenous
beliefs, values, norms, and other cultural elements.

Theodore Schultz [5] advances essentially the same hypothesis
—namely, that the agricultural sector in a large class of underdeveloped countries is relatively efficient in using the factors
of production at its disposal. He recognizes the essential equilibrium of developing societies. The difficulty is that it is a
static equilibrium which can only be broken by the infusion
of new inputs, by changing the locus of the persons and agencies making production decisions, by revising absentee arrangements which are generally inefficient, by creating greater
incentives to guide and reward farmers, by creating effective
channels for the infusion of new inputs—in short, by altering
existing institutional arrangements which presently restrict
agricultural activity.

Mosher's three-fold classification of the types of activities

4 *Patterns of Culture* (New York: Penguin Books, 1934).
5 *Transforming Traditional Agriculture* (New Haven: Yale University
Press, 1964), p. 16.

and influences essential to development—namely, those relating to farming itself, those involving agri-support activities, and the agri-climate—are certainly useful tools of analysis. They represent facets of the broader institutional context with which Schultz is concerned. The two lists of concepts which Mosher has presented—one relating to those concepts which help to answer the question, "What do we mean by agricultural development?" and the other to those which are addressed to the question, "How can agricultural development be accelerated?"—are equally helpful. They correspond to the two tasks which confront Western technicians working in developing countries and, in fact, technicians within the developing societies: to understand as fully as possible the nature of indigenous societies themselves, and armed with this understanding, to devise strategies through which behavioral and institutional change can be effected.

A variety of problems confront us, however. How do we overcome our own cultural biases, derived from vastly different social environments and divergent economic and political climates? How can we reconcile and collate the useful but (by themselves) inadequate concepts deriving from the disciplines of anthropology, sociology, economics, political science, social psychology, and others into more wholistic approaches of greater validity and broader utility? How can we distinguish between those aspects of human behavior that are merely different, or even abhorrent (as reflected in our own cultural looking glass) from those which are really essential to the development process? And finally, how can we distill from the approaches of the various disciplines those common denominators characterizing all social and institutional behavior from which we can then construct conceptual approaches adequate to cope with the complex phenomena of development? These are difficult questions, but it is precisely for this reason that they need to be asked.

Virtually all of the concepts Mosher presents relate to aspects of the institutional arrangements which characterize (and circumscribe) human behavior in all spheres of life, and which must be altered and transformed in order for the relatively static condition of life characterizing this type of society to proceed along the road to development and modernization.

Subsistence agriculture is sufficient unto itself. It does not require expensive new inputs, complex agri-support activities, or an agri-climate favorable to commercial production of food and fiber. However, as a society moves from a traditional subsistence agriculture to a more commercial market-oriented economy, old indigenous institutional arrangements must be modified or new ones created to serve new functions and to meet new demands. The story of development is to be found in the types of institutional arrangements societies institute to meet new societal needs.

Karl Deutsch's comments deserve careful consideration for the following reasons. In many, perhaps most, developing societies the role of central government is all powerful in controlling the affairs of men, in establishing through legislation or other means the basic agricultural policies and conditions favorable to the agricultural sector (the agri-climate), and in creating and sustaining a network of supportive services (agri-support activities) without which agriculture cannot emerge from the generally static situation in which it may have been for decades or even centuries prior to the emergence of so many national states. (More than forty new nations have emerged since the end of the Second World War.) The institutional loyalties of rural peoples in most developing societies are severely circumscribed, thus making it difficult or impossible for existing indigenous institutions to bind the people together and to re-orient them toward the attainment of new social goals, higher levels of material well-being, or new patterns of behavior and standards of social justice. In India, for example, individual loyalties have traditionally been restricted to the extended family, the subcaste, and the local village—the three pillars of Indian society. Historically such tightly structured rural villages resisted political, economic, and social change and in the process acquired considerable survival value. Today, however, they act to India's disadvantage as she strives for modernity and a virtual transformation of social and economic life. Many examples of this could be cited, of course. It is a common observation, for example, that when a member of an extended family secures an influential government post, his loyalties and obligations to the extended family govern his behavior far more than do the mores of the larger social system in which he finds himself. Under such conditions, the role of public administration and the efficiency with which their administrations and their entire political systems perform the functions essential to nation-building is indeed, as Karl Deutsch has suggested, an awesome one.

I am often reminded of a comment by the late Prime Minister Nehru: India, he declared, does not suffer from lack of economic planning, but rather from a gross inability to implement plans. It was clear that he had reference to many characteristics of the "establishment," and the inability of its members to carry out in practice the steps or actions the planners had perceived as essential for economic progress. Many of the institutional characteristics and rigidities derived from institutional norms established in preindependence days when development was not a major societal goal.

In the two years during which I conducted research on factors associated with the adoption of new agricultural practices by Indian farmers, it became painfully clear why Indian farmers did not and could not adopt potentially profitable new practices more readily. Virtually all new inputs—from information about new practices and how to use them, to production credit and final marketing arrangements—originate with and remain under the control of government. The authoritarian behavior of extension officials and the generally unfavorable conditions under which these inputs were made available to farmers acted as major disincentives. Even though farmers may have accepted in principle the desirability of using new practices and new inputs, they could not in fact adopt them.[6]

I do not accept the doctrine that farmers do not respond to normal economic and social incentives that provide genuine opportunities for improving substantially their levels of living and their life chances. This is what the rising tide of expectations is all about. The main deterrents to achieving these goals are to be found in inadequate social institutions. Erven Long

[6] Linwood L. Hodgdon and Harpal Singh, *Adoption of Agricultural Practices in Madhya Pradesh* (National Institute of Community Development, Government of India, Rajendranagar, Hyderabad-30, Andhra Pradesh, 1964).

recognizes this crucial relationship when he states that "by far the most far-reaching institutional changes will be those which define the fundamental relations among men—specifically, those essential to realizing the potential capabilities latent in human beings at all economic and social levels." [7] He also recognizes that in the process of transformation "these changes will bite deeply into prevailing systems of social and political organization, and into strongly held values and beliefs."

I was fascinated by the theoretical approach presented by Deutsch, by the several concepts of power elaborated, and particularly by his discussion of the implications of this theoretical model for developing countries. I was continually reminded of many of the observations of the great anthropologist Malinowski who regarded the study of social change (diffusion) in process as one of the most important tasks of anthropology. [8] He viewed it as a process of reorganization on entirely new and specific lines, and considered knowledge of the social and economic conditions, and of the cultural characteristics of colonial peoples as essential in the formulation of all schemes of development whether medical, agricultural, or educational.

My own experience supports the basic hypothesis that modernization is politicalization, and that its progress depends in substantial measure on political inputs and services, as agricultural development depends upon the infusion of the new factors of production. In developing societies, for reasons already stated, the importance of government in initiating and sustaining these essential services is paramount.

We must recognize that there are fundamental differences between the industrial societies and the newly emerging societies struggling to eliminate mass poverty and malnutrition, to

[7] Erven Long, "The World Agricultural Situation as Related to Political and Social Trends," in *World Food Forum Proceedings*, The Inaugural Event Commemorating the 100th Anniversary of the United States Department of Agriculture, May 15–17, 1962, Washington, D.C. (issued January, 1963), p. 99.

[8] Bronislaw Malinowski, *The Dynamics of Culture Change* (New Haven: Yale University Press, 1945).

control the ravages of disease, to assimilate modern technology, achieve political integration and to accomplish rapid economic growth and social modernization. A major part of our task is to understand the fundamental differences between these two types of society, and how these differences affect economic, social, and institutional development.

A good place to begin, perhaps, is to recognize that nearly all developing nations are on the three great continents or land masses—Asia, Africa, South America—which have been until fairly recent times effectively isolated from that great economic and cultural revolution we have come to know as Western civilization. More important, however, from the standpoint of understanding these societies and the nature of their problems, is the fact that the great ideas, traditions, and social institutions that have molded the relatively mature economies and complex industrialized societies of the Western world have not had any significant impact upon the newly emerging nations of the non-Western world.

This is not to assert, of course, that developing societies are qualitatively inferior to our own, that they lack a degree of cultural cohesion, or that their customs and ways of life are devoid of meaning, dignity, and charm. The issue is the relation between the fundamental nature of these traditional societies as they exist today, the critical problems they now face, and their ability to attain new social, economic, and political goals as nation-states. These new goals and objectives constitute the "rising tide of expectations" of which we have so often heard.

The new societal goals to which developing nations aspire are impossible of attainment without a basic transformation of the social institutions as they now exist in developing societies. For indigenous (traditional) social institutions evolved and crystallized out of the characteristics and needs of premodern civilization. They are not addressed to progress but to survival. They are incapable of solving new problems, and are basically incompatible with the new social and economic objectives normally subsumed under the concepts of economic development and modernization.

If most modern agricultural factors of production are specific to the biological and other circumstances of the country or region in which they have developed, so too are the social systems and institutional arrangements through which agricultural and other forms of human activities are channeled and directed. A mere "transplanting" of either is likely to prove ineffective, or even disastrous. Many developing countries, for example, have experienced great difficulty in developing an effective extension system because they lack one or more of the basic societal conditions (high literacy and education, effective supportive services, trained personnel, strong demand from farmers, etc.) essential for success.

Two fundamental theses emerge: (1) Underdevelopment is primarily a consequence of institutional underdevelopment, and (2) the new social and economic goals to which emerging societies aspire cannot take place under indigenous institutional arrangements. I am in full agreement with Erven Long on the importance of institutional arrangements, and with his conclusion that "the fundamental social and political character which will emerge in the countries now about to leap into the stream of economic progress will be determined by the types of institutions they develop for the purpose." [9] The question of the future is not solely whether economic development and social transformation will take place, but what forms they will take, and whether the institutional arrangements that emerge will provide greater degrees of social justice and conditions more conducive to the optimal development of human capabilities or whether they merely replace restrictive forms of social organization which now deter development.

If we accept these basic hypotheses, economic underdevelopment is thus not primarily an economic phenomenon, but is rather a broader institutional phenomenon—a result of social institutions either inadequate or improperly oriented to meet new economic and social needs. Resources are not developed because the scientific, technological, and organizational institutions which call forth and literally "create" resources are nonexistent or inadequate. Human capabilities are underdeveloped for precisely the same reason; institutions have not evolved which would develop them. It is a matter of record that many of the developing nations are rich in natural re-

9 Erven Long, p. 98.

sources, but remain poor because the institutional arrangements (scientific, technological, and organizational) from which new forms of resources and new sources of strength emerge, are either inadequate or nonexistent.

In spite of apparent lack of agreement on a number of concepts and approaches I feel that Arthur Mosher, Karl Deutsch, and I are actually very close to agreement on virtually all major points. What is missing, perhaps, is a broader perspective on the whole picture. Perhaps then we can see how these observations and approaches, valid and useful in themselves, relate to each other and to the scores of traditional societies struggling to emerge into the modern world, and the processes and strategies by which this transformation can be accelerated.

Virtually all of the concepts presented in both papers describe *aspects* of the broad institutional patterns we are trying to understand. I was intrigued by Mosher's suggestion that we employ the "systems" approach, because this is precisely the approach I had intended to suggest. However, we are using it in quite different contexts. I have reference to the social systems approach developed principally by Talcott Parsons and Charles Loomis for analyzing the structure, functions, and interrelationships of all forms of human interaction.[10] Basically its methodology includes an analysis or cognitive mapping of the specific *elements* (beliefs, sentiments, norms, status roles, sanctions) and *processes* (communication, evaluation, boundary maintenance) which characterize all forms and levels of human activity, including those in developing societies. It combines into a unified conceptual framework more of the basic concepts in social science than any other approach. It represents the most comprehensive, versatile and useful conceptual approach available for the difficult tasks we are facing here. The following examples illustrate the com-

[10] For a definitive analysis of the social systems approach see Charles P. Loomis, "Toward a Theory of Systematic Social Change," in *Interprofessional Training Goals for Technical Assistance Personnel Abroad,* Report of an Interprofessional Conference on Training of Personnel for Overseas Service, Ithaca, New York (June, 1959), Council on Social Work Education; or Loomis, *Social Systems* (New York: D. Van Nostrand, 1960).

plex interrelation of cultural elements and social institutions.

Let us take a *single* belief (one of the basic elements of all social systems) in a *single* culture, and explore the ramifications of this belief. The Hindu belief in the sacredness of the cow, for example, has ramifications far beyond the religious realm. It reflects not only a relatively fatalistic Hindu world view in which worldly existence and its entrappings are relatively unimportant in the soul's journey to its ultimate goals, but directly affects the economic life of India and greatly compounds the agricultural problems, as any Western agriculturist who has worked in India will attest. It has obvious implications for environmental sanitation and, since the cattle are allowed to roam relatively freely, is an important factor in overgrazing, soil erosion, and competition with the human population for land use and resource utilization. Its dietary implications are obvious, not to mention its relation to the fuel supply, the power supply, and even to education, where lower caste children are frequently deprived of the opportunity to attend school because they are required to keep the village cattle out of the growing crops during the two cropping seasons from July through March. Although this analysis is far from complete, it does demonstrate the principle of the interrelationships of cultural elements and social institutions.

Margaret Mead in her classic study of the Manus, whose primitive culture she reported in *Growing up in New Guinea* and described a generation later in *New Lives for Old*,[11] documents with clarity how a people only recently correctly called "savages" have traveled in the short time of twenty-five years a line of development which it took much of mankind many centuries to cover.

The following example, a much more modest one indeed, demonstrates how an institutional arrangement that had been for centuries a barrier to agricultural development was altered to become a partner in progress rather than a deterrent.

The money lender tradition is a major impediment to progress in many nations of the developing world. Low rates of capital formation combined with the high risks of subsistence farming result in usurious rates of interest difficult for most Westerners to believe. In a study of the income/expenditure

11 New York: William Morrow and Company, 1956.

patterns of 1,500 Korean farmers which I conducted for the U.S. Operations Mission in Korea,[12] it was found that Korean farmers on the average paid 100 per cent interest for production credit to produce their crops in 1962. However, joint action by the United States and Korean governments later in the same year greatly reduced the power of moneylenders and decreased the influence of this tradition as a deterrent to development. For its part, the U.S. provided counterpart funds sufficient to provide Korean farmers with production credit requirements for a full crop season. These funds were channeled into cooperative credit structures, while simultaneously strengthening and upgrading the managerial capabilities of coop personnel. Simultaneously, the Korean government enacted legislation making it illegal for moneylenders to loan at rates higher than the 20 per cent available from cooperatives. The government, in effect, purchased existing farmer obligations to moneylenders, and repaid them from coop profits. It is highly significant that today the Korean economy is experiencing an annual growth rate of more than 8 per cent.

Much progress is being made in spite of our failure as a nation to establish an adequate education and research base to support our world-wide commitments, however, let us have no illusions about the difficult tasks that remain—those of seeking more useful tools of understanding, and of devising more effective techniques and strategies for accelerating behavioral change in developing societies with diverse economic, social, and political backgrounds.

[12] Linwood L. Hodgdon, "The Income/Expenditure Patterns of 1,500 Korean Rice Farmers," U.S.O.M., Korea, 1962.

PART II

TECHNOLOGY AND
ITS UTILIZATION

EDITORS' INTRODUCTION

In their discussions of social change some writers distinguish between strategy and tactics. If strategy is designated as the theory and practice by which large and comprehensive endeavors such as winning wars is achieved and tactics as the methods and organizational procedure whereby smaller endeavors such as battles are won, Part II focuses on strategy. In this context, the essential components of our model of change, namely the change agent–change target system model, is a form of the "means-ends schema." When the agricultural extension service as transferred from the United States to Latin America was challenged by Solon Barraclough, he raised the question, "For whom is it achieving ends?" Although this question is important for Part I, the strategy problem before us in Part II is somewhat different. In oversimplified terms: Which is more important, developing new knowledge by which to modernize traditional societies or extending existing knowledge?

University and government administrators are continually faced with the necessity of deciding how much time and money to allocate to research and investigational activities which are supposed to produce knowledge, and how much to teaching and extension by which available knowledge is made useful. The solution to this dilemma, of course, lies in optimum attention to the dual problems of creating new knowledge and making it useful. This process requires decision-making about activities relevant to the change agent–change target model at two levels: farmers and agencies in the localities and leaders in the economic, scientific, and political centers.

Although the emphasis differs, the authors of chapters 4 and 5 and the respondents support the proposition that agricultural development requires a constant supply not only of viable technology but of conducive related conditions and an extension system to promote proper application of recommended innovations. For example, Leagans advocates a strategy which requires the implementation of certain concepts at both the macro and micro levels, and specifies that agricultural modernization depends on effective integration of essential physical, technological, economic, social, political, and related elements throughout the hierarchy of the system in order to attain needed commitment to common purposes and the means to achieve them. In this context, he analyzes and emphasizes the process of extension education as the most promising instrument for bringing together new knowledge, "packaging" it, and connecting it with farmers' problems in ways that encourage and modify behavior patterns in progressive directions. To him, the task of achieving optimum complementarity of the required range of dependent, independent, and intervening variables transcends the resources of any single discipline, basic or applied, to provide the required technological inputs or the conditions optimum to their utilization.

Cummings, without discouraging the importance of getting knowledge to the people who use it through effective linkage, makes a case for creating useable knowledge on a regional basis. He challenges the commonly held belief that there already exists a backlog capable of modernizing traditional agriculture in a given region. Bunting supports him in this contention and in his synthesis of the agricultural sciences (Chapter 11), points out that: (1) the available science and technology is at present insufficient and poorly adapted to the situations of the so-called underdeveloped countries and, (2) it is insufficiently "packaged" or synthesized for use. Presumably these shortcomings are to be overcome by research in knowledge centers which will be linked to the people through education in classrooms and extension education outside the class-

room. Although agreeing with Leagans that extension education is necessary, Cummings maintains that extension would
be improved through having those change agents who carry
on the extension process also engage in research. Competent
personnel who are dedicated, production-oriented scientists
and who can facilitate successful application of all essential
elements of agricultural development, he suggests, are of first
importance in stimulating innovations.

With reference to the strategy of change in the context of
the change agent–change target model, it is Leagans' premise
that extension education offers one of the primary inputs
which has yet to be utilized to its potential in most of the
developing countries. The emerging need to achieve wide use
in the shortest possible time of the highly significant new technological breakthroughs by agricultural scientists presents a
new imperative to which a viable extension education system
may, in fact, hold the key. He suggests that the lack of success of newly established extension systems in many countries
stems not from the nature of the extension education process
itself, but from default on such requisites as proper conceptualization of its role, administrative organization, staffing,
adequate supplies of viable technology, and other conditions
required for effectiveness. Recognizing a complex set of conditions essential to a viable extension system, Leagans stresses
the importance of systemic linkage between the knowledge
centers and change targets, such as farmers and a multitude of
agencies which compose the infrastructure required for agricultural modernization, and suggests that we are entering a
new age, one which is programmed for both discovery and
extension. And, in this context, as the quality and quantity of
inputs increase, so will the need for insight into the pattern
of their use.

Discussants Marlin Cline and Joseph Matthews do not disagree essentially with the views of Cummings or Leagans.
Matthews stresses timing and location as important in launch-
ing programs. Sometimes due to unfavorable conditions, the
change agent should delay action or not start it. By the same
token, however, under favorable conditions, strategy might require that action be pushed very rapidly and energetically.

He suggests wider use of intensive "campaign" and "package" approaches to implementing the adoption of crucial innovations.

Woods Thomas emphasizes the convergence of the Leagans and Cummings chapters rather than their contrasting elements. He suggests, however, that neither gives sufficient attention to the need for more effective understanding of an implementing strategy of complementarity of items being advanced and organization used. He points out the inadequacy of existing knowledge on how to do this. The change agent, according to Thomas, has few guides for identification of change targets crucial in the decision-making process and strategy formation. Farm-level education techniques and linkage procedures are not specifically transferable from culture to culture.

Marlin Cline notes and we as editors also want to stress the fact that the deficiency in agricultural science and knowledge is not limited to the natural and physical sciences and their technology. Perhaps the greatest deficiency is now, or soon will be, in the knowledge for improving the efficiency of the agencies, the responsibilities of which are to bring knowledge into use. This, of course, in our terms, means improving the effectiveness of change agent systems and their linkages. It is our hope that leading agricultural scientists, such as Cummings and Bunting, will increasingly recognize that as fields of basic research are considered, the processes whereby available knowledge is put into use should get more attention. This means designing research to improve systemic linkage between the knowledge centers and the users of knowledge, including researches to enhance the specific application dimension of technology, the systems of extension education, and the effectiveness of change agents. This research is what Leagans calls "applied science."

4. Agricultural Research and Technology

RALPH W. CUMMINGS

Mankind is engaged in a desperate race between population and food supply, and the next quarter century will be absolutely critical in determining the outcome. This will be one of the overriding factors shaping the destiny of nations, of mankind, and of the conditions of life on earth. The most optimistic estimates project an increase in world population of at least 40 per cent by 1985 and concede the possibility of an increase of over 50 per cent (3.3 to 5.0 billion). Estimates of total population by the end of this century range between 6.0 and 7.15 billion. By that time, unless we have found effective ways of stabilizing population, the problems faced may be so formidable as to make our present ones appear simple indeed.

The inevitable prospect of substantial population growth in the immediate future before stabilization can be achieved, along with continuing rising expectations of the people, will absolutely require the annual production of greatly increased quantities of food. By the last decade of the century, food requirements can be expected to reach at least twice the present levels of production and consumption. Production at these levels as a minimum will be essential if we are to gain the time necessary to activate orderly methods of population stabilization. The achievement of such levels will require change in agricultural practices throughout the world on a scale never before witnessed.

What kind of changes are required and how can they be brought about? Traditional primitive agriculture has tended to rely heavily on land and labor, within the existing natural environment in which plants and animals were placed. The level of production required for the period ahead will necessitate widespread application of new technology, made possible by applications of modern science to production problems. This should result in more precise modifications of the environment toward the requirements of the plants and animals for high production, increases in the levels of physical inputs having their origin off the farm, changes in the genetic constitution of the plants and animals so as to make them more responsive to fertilizers and other physical inputs, and greater protection from natural hazards.

There is a growing recognition and realization that certain basic conditions must be met if changes resulting in accelerating the improvement in productivity of agriculture in a given locale are to be brought about. Within the prevailing social, cultural, economic, and physical environment, there must be:

1. The availability of technical information which will provide the basis for a change in agricultural practices resulting in substantial increases in production. These practices must have a high degree of dependability and the risk of applying them should be of a predictable order. This comes out of programs of production-oriented research. Sustained progress requires the development of a viable institutional structure which continues to turn out new and more effective innovations which can contribute to increased productivity and produce new generations of well-trained, dedicated, production-oriented scientists with a determination to advance the basis for higher and more efficient production.

2. There must be a group of trained people who have a good understanding of the elements of this technology and the basis thereof and who are in a position to demonstrate the practices and their applicability to a reasonable sample of the farmers involved. It should be emphasized that the quality of the individual demonstration involving the successful application of all essential features is much more important initially in stimulating innovation than is a large number of demonstrations.

3. The economic climate must be such that the changed practices are profitable. This implies a favorable relation be-

tween costs and returns (price structure), and the availability of a dependable market outlet.

4. Physical inputs necessary to put the practices into effect must be obtainable and readily available (seeds, fertilizers, crop protection chemicals, implements, power sources, pump sets, etc.).

5. There must be incentives to the producer in terms of availability of products and/or services in the market which the producer wants and which become available to him in return for the increased income generated by the changed practices and inputs. This, in certain situations, may necessitate the generation of aspirations and development of the realization that there are possibilities of attaining them.

6. The program must be structured so as to be acceptable and desirable to the people concerned within their social, cultural, and political situation.

7. In order to develop the above conditions, the direction of change one attempts to accelerate should be in the national and local interest of the area concerned.

There are no doubt many situations in which, even if the first five conditions are met, development or change does not take place. The knowledge available may not be suitably adapted to the needs and possibilities of the farmers. It may be difficult to communicate because the farmers lack literacy and education, or are otherwise unable to receive and apply the information. Even if they do receive and understand it, the social or economic circumstances, including marketing and trade arrangements, systems of land tenure, credit availability, or other factors, may make them unwilling or unable to accept the information or put it into effect. The success of a given program obviously requires an analysis of the local situation and the creation of conditions that not only make the changes feasible, but also cause the people concerned to desire the proposed changes and identify them with their own personal and social goals.

A careful and thorough check to make sure that all of the above considerations have been fulfilled in a workable manner within the particular context of the society concerned will greatly enhance the probability of successful innovation. It is very easy to be misled into the belief that one has met the necessary conditions when in fact one or more of the assumptions may not be valid.

In setting forth some concepts of agricultural technology and their implications, I will concentrate my attention on the first two points above. Deficiencies in technology or misconceptions and insufficient understanding in its implications have frequently frustrated developmental programs. One should be certain that a firm technological base for innovation is established before a high probability of success can be expected.

In a classification of farm yields in some of the intensive agricultural districts in India, F. F. Hill reported a three- to fourfold variation between the yields of the lowest 10 per cent and the highest 10 per cent of the farmers. It would be easy to conclude from this that the necessary technology for substantial progress was available and only awaited demonstration and adoption. If this were true, one would expect that a parallel analysis of wheat yields by farmers in a progressive state in the U.S.A. (where average yields were substantially higher; where literacy rates approached 100 per cent; radio, television, and press communication were good; ample seed, fertilizer supplies, and plant protection chemicals were available commercially; and where a well-developed agricultural extension service had been operating for many years) would not show such a spread. However, wheat yields obtained by New York farmers showed a similar pattern. It became evident that, in both societies, there are substantial variations in soils, managerial skills of farmers, availability of credit, motivation, etc., and that one makes only limited progress through attempts to bring the yield levels of the poor farmers up to that of the more productive ones. Many case studies have shown that substantial changes in productivity level of a given commodity have been preceded by introduction of a new technological innovation which enabled the whole spectrum of farmers to change their practices and raise yields, even the best. Innovation is most likely to begin with the more progressive farmers but can spread from this group across the entire spectrum if the conditions listed above can be met. There has always been a time lag between the development of technological information and the evidence of any substantial impact on average yields. Hopefully, today we should be able to shorten this lag substantially.

The Backlog

A very common assumption is that there exists an extensive backlog of accumulated research information waiting to be put to use and, if demonstrated and applied, it will increase yields. It is perhaps true that considerably more is known than is being used. In many cases, however, the increases above the very low prevailing yields forthcoming from the application of such knowledge may give insufficiently attractive economic returns. In terms of providing the increases required to meet future needs—two to three times the present yields—application of such research information may be completely inadequate.

Rice is the leading cereal crop of South Asia, yet in 1960–1962 the average yield of unhulled paddy rice per hectare was 1.5 tons in India, 1.6 in Pakistan, 1.65 tons in Burma, 1.4 tons in Thailand, 1.9 tons in Indonesia, and 1.1 tons in the Philippines. Up to that time, fertilizer use in South Asia was very low. In most of these nations, no substantial quantities of fertilizer were available prior to the end of World War II and the assumption had been made by agricultural research workers of the region that fertilizers would not be used in rice production. Consequently, experimentation with rice including variety trials had been carried out without chemical fertilizers and at very low yield levels. Varietal improvement programs were aimed at the development of varieties which were able to compete with weeds and perform dependably at low fertility levels. When fertilizers become available, these varieties gave dependable yield increases from the use of only very small quantities. Larger applications of nitrogen would increase vegetative growth in the early stages and cause the plants to lodge and might even decrease rather than increase yields. In order to achieve large increases in yield, it became necessary to develop new varieties which had a shorter stem, greater stiffness of straw, and a leaf which would stand erect even when given higher rates of fertilization and would thus be capable of using the sunlight and water fully. The results of fertilizer experiments carried out with the older prevailing varieties did not apply to the shorter, more erect varieties. These new varieties, in turn, might prove poor competitors with weeds and disappointing yielders when grown at low fertility levels and in sparse plant populations. Thus, achieving a break-through in yields required the development of a completely new package of technology—new varieties capable of responding to more intensive cultural practices, and greater physical inputs which would take advantage of the enhanced potential of the new varieties in a dependable and profitable manner. When these were put together at the International Rice Research Institute, more than 10 tons per hectare have been produced in a single irrigated crop in the dry (high sunlight) season, and using early maturing, short, fertilizer-responsive, and nonphotoperiod-sensitive varieties in succession, more than 20 tons have been produced as a total for three successive crops within a twelve-month period on the same land.

The increased yields and increased density of plant population, made possible with these varieties when heavily fertilized, bring on additional problems in plant protection. The greater density of foliage and shading within the plant changes the environment for plant pathogens and insects and may, if plant resistance is not adequately considered, increase severity of attack. Thus, resistance to pathogens and pests becomes a more important consideration in variety selection. Also, control measures for stem borer which would give yield increases of 10 to 20 per cent on a crop yielding 1.5 tons or less per hectare might be unprofitable and economically unattractive but could be highly profitable when yields of 6 to 8 tons are obtained.

Long season, low yielding, and photoperiod-sensitive varieties which mature after the end of a monsoon in certain areas can be dried readily by being spread out in the sun and stirred periodically. Higher yielding varieties which require a shorter period for maturation, however, and which mature before the end of the rainy season may require special facilities for drying to prevent spoilage.

This is only one example which illustrates the inadequacy of our backlog of technology to meet the new and greater demands of the future. Similar problems could be cited with wheat or any other crop. The experimental work of the past has not, as a rule, anticipated substantial off-farm physical inputs such as fertilizers, has not achieved the yield levels required for the future, and frequently is simply not applicable to present day needs.

Export of U.S. Technology

With average yields of approximately 1.5 tons unhulled rice per hectare prevailing in the tropical regions of South Asia, the average yields in the United States, Japan, and Australia, were 3.9, 4.8, and 6.3 tons respectively for the same 1960–1962 period—three to four times those of most of the South Asian countries. A similar situation applies with other cereal crops. The suggestion has sometimes been made that the way to increase production in the South Asian countries is to send out extension agents who would introduce the technology of these countries. Some have suggested sending teams of farmers to demonstrate the practices they have used. This has been done to some extent. However, such technology is found to have only limited applicability. Japan, the United States, and Australia grow rice principally at temperate latitudes. The South Asian rice-growing area is largely in tropical and subtropical latitudes in a monsoon climate. Adapted varieties are not comparable; photoperiod differs; pests and disease problems are not the same. For example, in the United States, the rice stem borer, tungro virus, bacterial blight, and blast are not problems. Climatic patterns, implement availability, power sources, labor costs, and farm size differ. Experience at the International Rice Research Institute has revealed that even scientists who specialized in rice research in the United States had not encountered and were not familiar with a large number of the major problems limiting rice production in the Philippines until exposed to them on location. The scientists are capable of applying the tools of science to the solution of problems limiting production on location; they are not able to apply American technological practices directly with success to a different set of rice production problems encountered in the South Asian countries. There is no substitute for experimentation on location and the development and thorough testing of technological practices and their adaptation to the local environment concerned. It is true that as we learn more about the principles involved and characterize the different environments more precisely, we are able to speed up the process of adaptation of tchnology and to predict with greater precision the applicability of a given technology in a given location, and to develop technology with a greatly increased range of usefulness. Any nation, however, wishing to establish a firm base for sustained agricultural progress, must assure a sustained input of advancing production technology.

Technology and Innovation

The present "Green Revolution" developing across Asia began to make noticeable inpact only since 1965. The relevance of technological innovation as a prerequisite or stimulant for change has been dramatized therein by the experience with rice in South Asia, and with wheat in Mexico, India, Pakistan, and the Near East. In fact, it is difficult to find examples anywhere or at any time in recent history in which substantial and rapid changes in agricultural practice and productivity have been achieved without a base of new or newly introduced technology, and, in recent years, this has usually been a product of application of modern science.

The introduction and spread of the rice variety IR 8, together with a package of cultural practices including plant spacing, fertilization, weed control, and insect control is causing rapid incrcases in rice yields in many countries. Earlier work had shown that response to high rates of fertilizer application and full use of the sunlight and other features of the environment required a plant shorter in height than those commonly grown, the ability to stand upright even with heavy grain formation proceeding soon after vegetative stature is attained, a leaf structure and habit favoring rapid photosynthesis on through to grain maturity, elimination of weed competition, and resistance to, or control of, important disease and insect pests. The basic growth habit was encountered in the variety Taichung Native I, developed in Taiwan. This had shown excellent performance in many experimental tests as well as in farmer use but had some serious defects such as susceptibility to bacterial blight and tungro virus and lack of seed dormancy. The latter resulted in premature sprouting of seed when it matured during wet periods. The strain IR

8-288-3 was developed by the International Rice Research Institute and by late 1965 was beginning to look very promising. In the first months of 1966, a few kilograms of seed were available and the Institute decided that this strain should be increased for possible release and at the same time tested more widely for its performance in other environments.

The small amount reserved as a basis for seed increase at the Institute in the spring of 1966 was space planted and heavily fertilized and was increased about eight-hundredfold during this season, providing enough nucleus seed to share with seed producers and experimenters in the Philippines and other countries in the summer of 1966. Its performance on a broad scale was sufficiently outstanding that it was officially released as IR 8 in the fall of 1966. It is now being grown in many countries and is also known as Miracle Rice and Rizal No. 1 in the Philippines, and Ria in Malaysia.

The cultural practices necessary for maximum returns include good seedbed preparation, timely transplanting, heavy fertilization, full weed control, and control of stem borers and leaf hoppers with insecticides. Using IR 8 and similar varieties, the Institute has maintained a series of demonstration maximum yield plots in continuous rice culture, growing three successive crops on the same land within a year, and using the best production technology known to the Institute scientists. The Institute has produced in excess of 10 tons of unhulled rice per hectare in a single crop grown during the dry (high sunlight) season and more than 20 tons per hectare in a given tract as a total for three successive crops grown within a continuous twelve-month period. Tests conducted over a wide geographic range in South Asian countries have been similarly spectacular, with yields of between 6 and 10 tons at a single harvest being quite common.

With such a technological advance successfully demonstrated, the response of farmers has been, if anything, more spectacular. Beginning with a few kilograms of seed early in 1966, surveys in Central Luzon during August and September, 1967, showed 52 per cent of the rice grown under controlled irrigation was planted to IR 8, utilizing the cultural methods which it requires.

In India, a half ton of seed was imported in July, 1966, with

20 tons more being obtained in September of the same year. It is estimated that Indian farmers planted 250,000 acres to this one variety in the Kharif season (July to October), 1967. The use of Taichung Native I and other lodging-resistant varieties brought the total to the figures shown below. Pakistan and Malaysia likewise imported and began increasing seed of this variety in 1966.

The dramatic spread of the high-yielding, lodging-resistant IRRI type rice varieties is illustrated by the following data:

Country	Years	Acreage of IRRI Type Rice
Burma	1966–67	19
	1967–68	8,500
	1968–69	412,400
	1969–70	355,900
India	1964–65	200
	1965–66	17,650
	1966–67	2,195,000
	1967–68	4,408,000
	1968–69	6,625,000
	1969–70	9,600,000
East Pakistan	1966–67	500
	1967–68	166,000
	1968–69	381,500
	1969–70	650,000
	1970–71	1,216,000
West Pakistan	1966–67	200
	1967–68	10,000
	1968–69	761,000
	1969–70	1,500,000
Vietnam	1967–68	1,200
	1968–69	100,000
	1969–70	498,000
	1970–71	1,300,000

This variety and this package of cultural practices do not fit all situations. They seem to work best at tropical latitudes in fields in which water levels can be well controlled. There are weaknesses in the variety which need to be overcome. IR 20, IR 22, and other new varieties developed in national programs in the Philippines, Thailand, and other countries give promise of meeting these needs. There is always the hazard of a new and devastating disease appearing, and this danger is even greater when a single variety is used so extensively. These problems are recognized and only serve to point up the need for continued research and vigilance. The example is cited, however, as an illustration of the role of dependable, profitable, yield-increasing technology as a base on which behavioral change of cultivators can be based.

A parallel story could be cited for wheat. This crop, likewise, has been limited in its response to fertilizers by its tendency to grow too tall and lodge. Moreover, a complex and shifting series of races of rusts have periodically attacked and devastated the wheat crop in the United States and other wheat-growing countries. Genes for dwarfing were introduced and incorporated into otherwise potentially high-yielding and rust resistant lines of spring-type wheats developed and grown in irrigated regions in northwestern Mexico. This lifted the ceiling on response to fertilizer and has been the spark which has made possible a 3.5-fold increase in average wheat yields in Mexico. These same wheats found a place in California and other nearby states.

The success in Mexico excited interest in the testing and utilization of these materials and methods in wheat improvement programs in other nations. Scientists from the Near East and South Asia came to Mexico for in-service training in its wheat improvement program and, in cooperation with FAO, initiated tests in their own regions with wheats originating in the Mexican program. Tests in India in 1964 and 1965 indicated that Sonora 64 and Lerma Rojo 64 appeared highly promising selections being made from unreleased genetic stocks showed promise of even better performance.

In 1965, India imported 250 tons of the above two Mexican varieties for increase as seed stocks and Pakistan imported 350 tons of selected Mexican varieties. In 1966, India purchased and imported 18,000 tons of wheat seed from Mexico and this, together with seed already produced, permitted the planting of over a million acres to the so-called "high-yielding varieties" under irrigation in 1966. It is estimated that over 7 million acres were planted to these varieties in 1967.

Pakistan decided that certain other varieties needed to be included and, in 1967, arranged for the purchase and import of more than 40,000 tons of the new varieties from Mexico. Thus, during that year, a very substantial portion of Pakistan's irrigated wheat acreage went into these new varieties. The varieties serve as the vehicle for introducing innovations in improved cultural practices, including higher rates of fertilization. And the results obtained from the new technology bring on increased demands from the farmers for new technology in other fields and improved receptivity to innovations.

In 1965, one farmer in Turkey planted about 30 kilograms of two varieties of dwarf Mexican wheat obtained unofficially from a friend. His yields were reported as 5,000 and 5,500 kilograms per hectare, about three times what he would have expected from his local varieties. In 1966, he and his neighbors arranged for import and planting of 60 tons of these varieties on 102 farms in the same area. In 1967, Turkey purchased and imported about 22,000 tons of the same wheats from Mexico for planting throughout the coastal wheat-growing areas of the country. Thus, from a beginning of 30 kilograms of seed on less than an acre, that country had moved in two years to the point where it was planting perhaps one-third of its coastal acreage to these new varieties, and at the same time was introducing the use of fertilizer on wheat on a scale never before practiced.

The following data show the rate of spread of the high-yielding, lodging-resistant, Mexican type wheats in a few selected countries:

Country	Years	Acreage of Mexican Type Wheats
Afghanistan	1965–66	4,500
	1966–67	54,400
	1967–68	301,500
	1968–69	360,800
India	1965–66	7,400
	1966–67	1,270,000
	1967–68	7,270,000
	1968–69	11,844,000
	1969–70	12,600,000
Morocco	1967–68	500
	1968–69	12,100
	1969–70	98,800
Pakistan (West)	1965–66	12,000
	1966–67	250,000
	1967–68	2,365,000
	1968–69	5,900,000

Country	Years	Acreage of Mexican Type Wheats
	1969–70	8,000,000
Tunisia	1967–68	2,000
	1968–69	32,000
	1969–70	131,000
Turkey	1966–67	1,500
	1967–68	420,000
	1968–69	1,430,000
	1969–70	1,540,000

When the then Minister of Food and Agriculture for India, C. Subramaniam, announced early in 1966 his strategy for achieving self-sufficiency in food production, based on what was referred to as the "High-Yielding Varieties Program," there was considerable discussion. Some thought it bold and ambitious. Some suggested that a more conservative approach based on smaller inputs over a larger area would be more acceptable. In summary, his plan called for introduction of the newly developed high-yielding varieties or hybrids of the major cereal crops on a selected 32.5 million acres, where water supplies were assured and the probability of success best, assuring that requisite supplies of high quality seeds, fertilizers, crop protection chemicals, and credit were made available to these same farmers. The targets by crops, together with the expected increases over past production were predicted as indicated in the accompanying list.

The impact of this program in the selected target areas was expected to spill over to some extent to other farmers. An assessment in 1970 showed that this program was substantially on target. The target acreages of high-yielding varieties of wheat and rice have been exceeded, balancing some under-achievements with the other food grains.

Crop	Acreage in High-Yielding Varieties Program by 1970–71 (million acres)	Expected Additional Grain Production (million tons)
Rice	12.5	12.5
Wheat	8.0	8.0
Corn	4.0	2.0
Soybean	4.0	2.0
Millet	4.0	1.0
Totals	**32.5**	**25.5**

This program was launched at a time when food was critically short as a result of serious drought. Prices were increasing and market demands brisk. Demonstrations had shown spectacular results in increased yields and profits. A community development and extension organization had been developed for the entire country and special organizational attention had been given to selected intensive agricultural districts and areas. The fact that other factors were favorable in no way diminishes the crucial fact that new and profitable yield-increasing technology was available at this time.

Subsequent experience in 1966 and 1967 showed the wisdom of this course and clearly demonstrated the fact that farmers will change if they can be convinced that dependable and profitable yield-increasing technology is available and they can learn how to put it to use.

Important as the other factors are, this revolution in agricultural production which has been and is now taking place in India, Pakistan, and several other countries would not have been possible if the scientific and technological base had not been available.

Changing the Change Agents

What are the implications of the above with respect to the character of the extension services, the extension agents, the other agencies, governmental and private, serving agriculture and provided by the society to support its growth and development?

These public servants must also undergo a change to meet the needs and demands of the future. They must know, understand, and be prepared to demonstrate the elements of the new technology. They need to be competent in the arts of educational technique but, at the same time, must have a good working understanding of the technology which they are to teach and demonstrate. This will, no doubt, call for an increase in specialization and the formation of teams of people with particular knowledge and competence. I would foresee a replacement of the individual multipurpose worker in contact with the farmer with a team of people each having more specialized knowledge and understanding and the personal ability to demonstrate this knowledge effectively.

These agents in contact with farmers need to be backed up

with a group of subject matter extension specialists who have a still higher level of scientific training and competence, still oriented toward production and the factors important thereto. The village extension worker will inevitably encounter situatons and problems with which he is not competent to deal and needs to have a place to which he can carry such problems and obtain help.

Further, the extension specialists need to be backed up with a group of well-trained research scientists, fully competent with the tools of modern science, but again with their orientation toward the objective of service to the farmer in helping to overcome limitations in his production and marketing problems. And in order to assure a flow of such people into the system, there should be a close link up and cooperation between the extension, research, and resident teaching functions and personnel. Each should be considered mutually supporting and interdependent and if they are to serve their constituency, none can do so effectively in isolation from another.

This will not be accomplished fully overnight but will have to be an evolutionary process. The Rockerfeller Foundation has tended to direct its attention to the development and encouragement of production-oriented research programs, to the training and education of agricultural scientists and specialists with an outward look toward service to the farmers in their attempts and desires to improve their lot, and to the development of the indigenous institutions we think are so necessary if sustained progress is to be achieved. I think that we have accumulated some relevant experience in our operating programs in such countries as Mexico, Colombia, Chile, India, and Thailand and in our participation in international projects and institutes such as the International Rice Research Institute and the International Center for Corn and Wheat Improvement. A number of techniques have been used, including organized in-service training courses in which the participants as a part of their course actually go through all the operations of growing, harvesting, and marketing a crop throughout one or more crop seasons. A scientist or specialist who has gone through such a program successfully using the best modern scientific practices and becoming familiar with the research upon which they are based can demonstrate such technology with confidence and can teach effectively.

Response

MARLIN G. CLINE

It is important to note that Ralph Cummings' experience in places where food supply is an overwhelming problem has led to conclusions which parallel a number of those of the President's Science Advisory Committee Panel on World Food Supply. He has made the point that technological innovation in agriculture of developing regions is only one of several essentials for improvement of their agricultural production, but that it is normally essential. He has emphasized that technology developed for another environment is not usually effective and that there is no substitute for local adaptive research and testing of combinations of production practices. He has projected the need for innovation in the strategies for obtaining application of proven technology.

A fundamental strategy for behavioral change concerns the breadth of understanding of those who deal in strategy. Cummings has listed seven conditions necessary for marked improvement in agricultural production. Two of these are concerned with production technology and the organization and training for its extension; the other five involve a complex of economic, social, and cultural factors which commonly limit or prevent its application. Although one still encounters some fruitless discussion about which area is more important, it is generally conceded that neither can be acceptably effective without simultaneous development of the other. If, indeed, these two broad fields are indispensible to each other for attainment of common goals, some degree of common understanding would appear essential for meaningful dialogue leading to informed strategy and action for behavioral change.

It is pertinent to ask, therefore, whether institutions of

higher learning have consciously designed strategy of training adequate for development of interdisciplinary understanding in those who will be responsible for programs of behavioral change in the years ahead. The problem is not a simple one. In this age of specialization, competence in a discipline implies understanding in depth of a specialty, and our educational procedures are geared to such training. The student cannot afford to sacrifice specialization if he is to become a competent and respected professional in his discipline. Yet there is great need for breadth of perpective in those who are parties to strategy for change.

At least one limiting factor in institutions of higher learning appears to be a lack of faculty whose business is a specialty dedicated to behavioral change. Most of us who advise and teach students are specialists first. Seldom do we pause in the feverish pursuit of our chosen disciplines to think about the significance of the ideas and principles of another field to the ultimate missions of our own. I have noticed a marked increase in cross-disciplinary activities at Cornell since we have had a few specialists in the agricultural sciences who are totally dedicated to the International Agricultural Development Program. For the first time, we have an interdisciplinary faculty seminar on world food problems, with a corps of faculty who are interacting with specialists of divergent interests but a common mission. This cannot help but have an impact on their work with students. The Graduate School quite properly insisted upon a required seminar embracing both the agricultural and the social sciences as a common denominator for a minor in international agricultural development. We now have courses in the agricultural sciences which include a joint study trip to a tropical area for on-the-spot interaction among disciplines. These innovations came only after we had faculty whose prime purpose was training for behavioral change. It would appear that faculty dedicated wholly to such a mission may contribute to breadth of perspective in training, but I would suggest that the universities need to plan deliberately for a strategy of training for the agents of behavioral change in developing regions. At the present time our training programs are largely those developed for other objectives.

In reference to Cummings' discussion of the relevance of

technology to innovation, I am not sure what different people understand by the word "technology." The dictionary definition implies the application of science to the practicing arts and the involvement of theoretical considerations. I judge that this is the sense in which Cummings has used the term. From proposals such as the "farmer-to-farmer" program for agricultural development, however, one may conclude that to some people in high places technology means simply empirical know-how.

If empirical production practices proven by empirical experience were technology, the practice of shifting cultivation in its many modifications would be included. For conditions that exist over a very large part of the world, it represents a kind of adaptation to circumstances through trial and error and, in certain forms, reveals remarkable ingenuity. It has, moreover, very substantial theoretical basis for use under some circumstances when analyzed in the light of science. Still, it is hardly an example of Cummings' technology and, unmodified, is scarcely a system for improvement of the world food supply.

We are more likely to equate the production systems of the corn belt with modern technology. They too, however, have not only theoretical bases in science but also a very significant input of empirical trial and error by thousands of farmers whose concern is not theory but how the system works. The comparison with shifting cultivation is an exaggeration, of course, but there are elements of similarity. Nevertheless, the misconception that technology can be treated as a rule-of-thumb set of procedures has led to the fallacy that we can export know-how successfully to another environment without adaptation. It is the antithesis of this which Cummings describes in his examples of successes with rice and wheat. The knowledge which can be exported consists first of the basic principles of science and, second, of the techniques and methodology for developing practice based on them.

One must ask what is the "firm technological base for innovation" which Cummings has indicated is needed for high probability of success. Technology has many elements, including the various practices derived from plant breeding, soil science, plant protection, and other disciplines. Too often, we assume that the elements of technology are independent and additive in their effects. As an example, an article which has attracted much attention contends that the only practical solution to the world food problem in view of its urgency is a massive program to dramatically increase the use of commercial fertilizers in a very short period of time.[1] The article presents data from an independent source to substantiate estimates of expected increase of production. I was particularly interested in the yield increases projected for Africa, because they were greatly at variance with British experimental data on response of food crops to fertilization in the same area under cultural conditions somewhat better than indigenous practice but geared to possible capabilities of the local people.[2] Instead of major increases of the kind required, the British responses in many trials over significant periods of time were nominal. To be sure, some were of the order of 50 per cent, but on a very low base, equivalent to perhaps 10 bushels of corn. Most of the experiments showed fertilizer alone could decrease the rate of yield decline under continued cropping. In some cases, it maintained yield levels. Few showed promise of major yield increases. The experimental data are sound; the British scientists were thorough, competent workers. They proved conclusively that use of fertilizer, by itself, was not a "firm technological base" in that environment.

The British experience in Africa is not unlike that of earlier days in the United States. During the 1930's, R. M. Salter summarized the impact of all the effort on crop breeding, fertilizers, rotations, and other elements of technology to that time in Ohio.[3] He concluded that agricultural science plus abandonment of the poorest crop land had barely made it possible for Ohio farmers to maintain state average yields. A similar ex-

[1] Raymond Ewell, "Famine and Fertilizer," *Chemical and Engineering News*, 42 (Dec. 14, 1964), 106–117.

[2] H. L. Manning and G. Griffith, "Fertilizer Studies on Uganda Soils," *East African Agricultural Journal*, 15 (1949), 87–97; E. Pawson, "The Composition and Fertility of Maize Soils in Northern Rhodesia," *Empire Journal of Experimental Agriculture*, 25 (1957), 79–94; and D. Stephens, "Two Experiments on Effects of Heavy Applications of Triple Superphosphate on Maize and Cotton in Buganda Clay Loam Soil," *East African Agricultural and Forestry Journal*, 31, no. 3 (1966), 283–290.

[3] R. M. Salter, R. D. Lewis, and J. A. Slipher, "Our Heritage, the Soil," Ohio Agricultural Extension Service Bulletin 175, April, 1936.

perience was reported for the "European" farms of Rhodesia up to 1950.[4]

Beginning with the mid-thirties, average crop yields of Ohio and adjacent states have increased consistently from year to year to the present almost unbelievable state averages. Rice yields have increased similarly in Japan since the 1880's. Corn yields have more than doubled on "European" farms in Rhodesia since the 1950's. The same phenomenon has occurred for cereals in Australia and, more dramatically, for wheat in Mexico.

As one studies these examples and the changing technology of the regions, it is obvious that yields have increased as more and more farmers have put many practices together into systems of technology which they have tried and proven for the local environment. One sees a similar relationship between technology and yield if he studies individual operations using different combinations of practices at a given time. Over the period from 1938 to 1940, I had occasion to study technological inputs and crop yields of several thousand fields in western New York. In no case was there a significant relationship between the level of input of any single practice and crop yields. If three practices were at high levels, however, average yields were significantly greater than those obtained at lower inputs of the same factors. Even with three factors at high levels, however, the deviation of yields was high. It is likely that the higher averages found were due more to the probability that a farmer who does three things well is likely to do many things well than to the impact of the three practices alone.

A firm technological base, therefore, is a package of the technologies of several disciplines. Cummings has described such packages in his examples. They are not packages of empirical practices but an amalgamation of the logical consequences of scientific principle. The formula requires testing and modification as necessary to fit the special requirements of broad but specific physical and biological environments. Success of such a system in one environment is no assurance of success in another.

Such a concept of effective agricultural technology has far-reaching implications for the strategy for behavioral change. It obviously requires specialized, competent scientists for the adap-

[4] K. W. Von Burkesroda, "Fertilizing Maize in Rhodesia," *Potash Review*, Dec., 1964, p. 12.

tive research. The challenge of finding solutions to problems in uncharted environments demands the competence in depth which we have come to associate with modern specialization. It also demands perspective of the pertinence of scientific principle to practical problems as well as perspective of the interaction among disciplines in what must be a team effort. Those of us in institutions of higher learning must ask ourselves whether our strategy of training instills that kind of perspective in our students.

If perspective as well as specialized competence is significant for the research component of the technological strategy, it is doubly so for personnel of advisory services. These are teachers of lay people. Traditionally in the United States, we have come to think of three elements of such teaching: (1) teaching of basic content of technology—the "why" as well as the "how" of practice; (2) providing a flow of information from research and experience to the farmer—by word of mouth, by the printed word, and by radio and television; (3) consulting— direct on-the-spot advice on alternative courses of action and their relative merits in the local situation.

In this country, our extension services are moving rapidly to teams of specialists. Our former generalized extension agents are no longer able to cope with technology at the level farmers demand. Farmers themselves are the integrators of technological packages, and they demand a level of specialized information which will give them sound bases for designing the highest levels of efficiency their managerial skills can accomodate.

One must ask whether specialization in the advisory services is as acceptable in a predominantly peasant agriculture as it is in the United States. Cummings implies that it is, for he suggests teams of advisory specialists. If this is valid, what is the strategy for achieving the integration of specialized technologies necessary for major change? What is the strategy of training for the advisory function? The strategy for research is clear, in my judgment, but I feel much less sure of that for obtaining practical application of the technology that results. Is the peasant farmer capable of the integration of practices which his American counterpart achieves? If he is not, what is the strategy for teaching him?

I would raise one final question. What is the role of private industry in the strategy for behavioral change? We seem, sometimes, to assume that somehow public agencies can develop a grand design which will be a solution and millions of people will accept. Granted a system other than authoritarian regimes, such as those of the communist world, it would seem that ultimate decisions must be made by the individual farmer or his landlord. Public servants can, hopefully, influence those decisions, and public policy can make certain options more attractive than others. If strategy assumes dependence upon influencing the individual's choice, what role can be played by representatives of industry? They have been extremely potent factors in our own agricultural revolution. The programs of certain companies for technological innovation by their customers in developing nations are impressive and are in no sense altruistic. Is this an undeveloped resource which public strategy should deliberately cultivate and include in its design?

5. Extension Education and Modernization

J. PAUL LEAGANS

This chapter is directed to a purpose similar to that Shelley gave the artist: "To absorb the new knowledge of the sciences and assimilate it to human needs, color it with human passions, transform it into the blood and bone of human nature." [1] A comparable task was infused as a new aim of the land-grant college system in the United States in the early 1900's when a national extension education system was established to disseminate knowledge about its technological discoveries. That action, together with Germanic models of scholarship and research already established, broadened the aims of these unique institutions of higher education to encompass the socialization of knowledge itself and the transformation and utilization of education as a force for social and economic development in out-of-school environments. The expanded aim was to put newly discovered knowledge to work.

A strikingly similar need exists today in most of the countries seeking to improve their tradition-oriented agricultural enterprises. Indeed, if the exciting new break-throughs in science and technology related to problems of agricultural modernization in low production areas of the world are to achieve quickly their potential contribution to needed repatterning of peoples' behavior, an assignment in principle much like Shelly gave the artist must be accepted and successfully performed by specialists in agricultural modernization and government leaders who influence the process.

[1] Hutson Smith *et al.*, *Dialogue on Science* (Indianapolis, Ind.: Bobbs-Merrill, 1967), p. 4.

The problem of effecting the transition of a traditional subsistence type of farming to a modern, scientific, market-oriented agriculture is one of the most crucial and complex issues facing leaders in most of the developing countries and those in more developed countries who wish to assist with the task. Promoting planned change in traditional farming patterns is a timeless process of skillfully combining the effects of many critical elements including custom and tradition, ideology and technology, physical resources and opportunity, education and a sense of purpose. A major dimension of the problem is the conflict between the forces of tradition and modernity. The human element functioning at both the macro and micro levels is central in this conflict, for it is man who must synthesize the two in systems of change. And in this process, it is not man's technology alone, but what he does with it that is of transcendent importance to his progress.

Crucial in the task of proper utilization of modern technology is education of the ultimate utilizers (farmers and leaders at the micro level) and of those who can provide environmental interventions (professional agricultural leaders and macro-level policy makers) which results in environmental variances contributory to modernization goals. In this role, education is a catalytic ingredient that modifies, relates, and activates the other elements essential for agricultural development.

As new break-throughs occur in agricultural science and technology, profitable agricultural practice becomes more achievable and, at the same time, more sophisticated and complex. Likewise, influencing desirable behavioral change (in relation to the new technology) becomes more essential and complex because as technology becomes more scientific its proper use requires greater precision. It is comparatively simple to design a technical package, but far more difficult to design and implement a scheme which implants it in the minds and actions of people. This fact suggests, universally, that as greater knowledge and precision are required in the use of technology, a comparable educational input is essential. Not to provide it is to invite less than optimum use of science and, indeed, to risk failure. The simple fact is that, for the new technologies to be effective in increasing agricultural production, they must be used by the farmers, and this requires extension of them to the farmers.

Hence, to expect, without an effective educational input, an uneducated, tradition-bound farmer to identify and clarify the most technically sound, economically feasible, politically compatible, and socially desirable goals to pursue; to expect him to assemble and effectively utilize new production technology and related inputs required to achieve modernization; and to expect him to self-generate the motivation necessary to achieve new and complex (to him) behavioral innovations in his long-practiced farming pattern, approaches sheer romanticism.

It is probably universally recognized that behavioral change among farmers—and those in the hierarchy of systems for promoting it—is one of the requisite components of the agricultural modernization process. But concepts of the nature and critical elements of strategy that promise optimum behavioral change in the time, effectiveness, and cost dimensions are often both fuzzy and diverse. In part, this condition stems from the fact that the required range of dependent, independent, and intervening variables transcends the capacity of any single discipline, basic or applied, to supply the required technological inputs or the conditions optimum for their utilization.

The process of agricultural modernization is dynamic and must change with advances in science and technology. Clearly, there are no utopian solutions to the quantitative or qualitative dimensions of the process, but three routes appear promising: (1) creating a macroenvironment that makes possible and encourages the ultimate decision makers (farmers) to modify farming patterns; (2) building a body of useful technology and available requisite production inputs that fill the modernization requirment; and (3) optimizing an extension education system that effectively relates these conditions and resources to each other, and matches them with current behavior in ways that stimulate innovations which progressively overcome achievement disparties common to traditional agriculture.

It is on point three that this chapter is primarily focused. This orientation is based on the principle that interaction of the farmer with environmental forces patterns his behavior, and that variances in behavior can be accounted for, in part, by individual differences in the characteristics of farmers; in part, by the stimulus characteristics of the environmental situation (physical, economic, political, and social); and, in part, by the

quality of interaction between the aspects of each. Full exploitation of this principle has yet to be achieved, especially in countries practicing traditional agriculture. This is largely because
the methodological implications have not yet been fully recognized and systematically exploited.

A Note about People

Because the central focus of this chapter is on the human
element in agricultural change, a note about people appears
useful, even if oversimplified and generalized, as it certainly is
here. Studies designed to characterize the nature of human
beings who have attained behavioral patterns viewed as "civilized" indicate that they possess basic traits which tend to be
common. Physically, they want to live a long life, to be healthy,
to be comfortable; socially, they want recognition, achievement,
education; economically, they want to support themselves and
their families so as to be a societal asset, not a liability. In short,
people desire improvement in their knowledge, skills, food,
clothing, home, family, health, income, creativeness, friendship,
independence, leadership, usefulness and a wide range of other
conditions. Thus regardless of their culture, people tend, on
balance, to be more alike than different in primary concerns and
aspirations.

Achievements people make toward their desired goals tend
to be in direct ratio to the effort—economic, social, physical, or
mental—which they can or are willing to make to attain needed
changes. Progressive behavioral change is purposeful whether
stimulated by internal desire or by external forces. In striving
for goals, behavioral patterns are largely determined by what
people believe is true and useful to them, not merely by their
knowledge alone. What people believe to be true is true and
real to them as they see it.

Modernization, however, requires intervention into established systems of beliefs and a rearrangement that creates patterns of beliefs conducive to progressive behavioral change.
The system of core values in human society which constitutes
the object of concern tends to be most pronounced at the biological level, and to become more diversive as human development progresses to higher levels. In this connection, empirical
observations appear to support the proposition that in the pro-

cess of development, people tend to be concerned with their biological, economic, social, and aesthetic needs, in that order, with moral and ideological values pervading and influencing both the form and content of the process.

Wherever people's behavior has been studied, it has been found possible to change it in at least the following major dimensions: *what people know*—their knowledge of themselves, of their society, and of their environment from both the standpoint of opportunities the culture offers and restrictions it imposes; *what people can do*—their skills, mental and physical; *what people feel*—their attitudes and values held about themselves: *what people think they ought to do*—the result of their evaluation of alternatives; *what people actually do*—their behaviors related to their own welfare. In this context, man's need may be generally viewed as the need to enhance his individual adequacy. This quest is complex in any society because it requires a wide range of behavior changes through which one continuously seeks to improve his ability to deal with life as it is and to utilize opportunities to improve it.

General Education

Studies of the agricultural development process increasingly recognize the contribution of general education as one of the essential elements. These studies indicate that economic growth, for example, cannot be explained in terms of capital accumulation and growth of the labor force alone, but rather, the explanation for a large and possibly the major part of economic growth lies in investments in the development of human resources through education. Adam Smith viewed increases in the quality of human behavioral patterns resulting from educational advances as a part of "fixed capital."[2] John Kenneth Galbraith suggests that "when we think of education as a consumer service, it becomes something on which we should save. . . . But when we think of education as an investment, it becomes something we should emphasize."[3] T. W. Schultz has given much attention to the relative importance of the educational

[2] Adam Smith, *The Wealth of Nations*, Everyman's Library ed. (New York: E. P. Dutton, 1933), I, 247.

[3] John Kenneth Galbraith, *Economic Development in Perspective* (Cambridge, Mass.: Harvard University Press, 1962), pp. 47–48.

input and feels that "the failure to treat human resources explicitly as a form of capital, as a produced means of production, as the product of investment, has fostered the classical notion of labor as a capacity to do manual work requiring little knowledge and skill." [4]

In support of the position that desirable changes in the agricultural enterprise can be achieved only through behavioral changes in the ultimate decision makers (the farmers), F. Harbison and C. A. Myers conclude that "human resource development, therefore, may be a more realistic and reliable indicator of modernization or development than any other single measure." [5]

Extension Education

The foregoing relates to patterns of human behavior that may accrue from all forms of educational inputs in a society—primary, secondary, college, basic, vocational, extension, professional—each with varying objectives, content, quantity, and quality. The primary focus of this discussion is on only one of the wide range of educational inputs: that which is designed primarily for adults and which aims to help them in their life setting to improve its physical, biological, economic, and social qualities. This type of institutionalized education increasingly is referred to by the term "extension education." [6] It is viewed as a specialized form of the broader concept "adult education," more recently called "continuing education."

Extension education may be functionally defined as an applied science consisting of relevant content derived from re-

---

[4] T. W. Schultz, "Investment in Human Capital," *American Economic Review,* 51 (March, 1961) 1–17.

[5] Frederick Harbison and Charles A. Myers, *Education, Manpower, and Economic Growth: Strategies of Human Resources Development* (New York: McGraw-Hill, 1964), p. 14.

[6] The term "extension education" was first used officially as an academic term at Cornell University in 1948 to designate a newly established graduate program of study leading to the Master of Science and Doctor of Philosophy degrees. The term was also used in the titles of certain courses and seminars in the curriculum of this new area of graduate specialization. Conceptually, the term is used to designate the process of synthesizing the products of knowledge centers and people's problems through structured noncredit education procedures.

searches in the physical, biological, and social sciences, and in its own process, synthesized into a body of concepts, principles, and procedures oriented to providing noncredit, out-of-school education largely for adults. In this general connection, a phrase used by Clifton Wharton is thought-provoking. He suggests that what is needed is "development knowledge," and that the process of promoting the use of this knowledge is "developmental education." [7] This idea is closely related to the suggestion that: "It [extension] is not solely concerned with teaching and securing the adoption of a particular improved practice, but with changing the outlook of the farmer and encouragaing his initiative in improving his farm and home. The effectiveness of extension . . . is measured by its ability to change the static situation . . . into a dynamic one." [8] Programs of extension education can have substantial positive effect on the production incentives of farmers once essentials such as markets for farm products, local outlets for farm supplies and equipment, and favorable price relationships exist. Extension programs not only can "take research results to farmers" and "impart knowledge and skill," but also can substitute new procedures for old traditions and values, overcome reservations about the risk and uncertainties involved in innovation, speed the transition of farmers from a subsistence to a market orientation, stimulate the development of auxiliary services, and generally make agricultural planning more realistic and practical. [9]

One basic resource for agricultural modernization in traditional societies is the unrealized potential of farmers to change their behavioral patterns when given the proper knowledge, required inputs, and other needed incentives to do so. How to effectively transmit useful information from the centers of creative thought to those who can use it, and influence them to make proper application, is a question that continues to attract the attention of scientists and educators alike. It seems likely

[7] Clifton H. Wharton, Jr., *The Role of Farmer Education in Agricultural Growth* (New York: Agricultural Development Council, 1963), p. 2.

[8] *Science and Technology for Development: Report on the United Nations Conference on the Application of Science and Technology for the Benefit of the Less Developed Areas* (New York: United Nations, 1963), vol. 6, *Education and Training*, p. 119.

[9] *The World Food Problem: A Report of the President's Advisory Committee* (The White House, 1967), II, 505.

that the advancement of skill necessary to create useful science and technology and to enhance the value of their products may be outstripping, if it has not already done so, the ability to interpret and synthesize means and ends in the ways of achieving developmental change in people's behavior.

A prelude to the process of putting modern technology into effect is the provision of a positive instrument through which knowledge may be disseminated. The primary and stable dependent variable in the extension educational process is its potential ability to continuously bring together new knowledge and to help people in their natural setting learn how to apply that knowledge in solutions to their problems. Having this basic trait, any useful content or subject matter can be fed into an extension agency, if the organizational form is of such nature as to accommodate the content. In this context, the effective change agent is neither an abstract thinker nor a user of "tricks." He is both.

Planned development of any type requires new knowledge, skills to use it, and attitudes that place value on innovation. To know about a recommended practice is not enough; to gain the skill necessary to apply it is not enough; to believe that it is valuable is essential, but still not enough. A farmer's education must encompass these qualities, but intelligent action in modern agriculture requires that he understand the relationship of each practice to other related ones. The proper use of fertilizer, for example, is related to variety of crop, type of soil, amount of rainfall or available irrigation water, and other factors. Modern agriculture then must be viewed as a system involving many complex interactions between numerous essential components which require managerial knowledge and skill.

Extension education can be the primary process through which farmers can learn the reasons for change, the value of change, results that can be achieved, the process through which change is achieved, and uncertainties inherent in change. It can be the primary source of a farmer's ability to analyze alternative actions and choose from among them the most desirable. In short, the extension educational process, effectively administered, reduces delays in translating research findings into action.

One may argue that since an extension system was one of the major contributors to the development of an immense agricultural production capacity of United States farmers, it may be viewed, with proper adaptation, as a prime candidate for a major role in helping farmers and leaders in other countries develop the same type of expertise. Education for action—the kind in which an effective extension system has no peer—is at least high on the priority list of challenges. In view of the pressing need to utilize the highly significant new technological break-throughs by agricultural and other scientists, such as those focusing on population control, an effective extension system may, in fact, hold the key to the prognostications of world food authorities whose analyses show that the population is growing considerably faster than the food and fiber supply necessary to support it. Hence, the importance of understanding the role of an extension system; developing and utilizing it at optimum levels of potential may no longer be viewed realistically as optional among the requirements for agricultural modernization in low production areas of the world.

Failure-Success Variables

National organized extension systems have been operating on a continuing basis in Western Europe, Canada, and the United States for more than half a century. Their continuity and expansion as publicly supported adult education institutions, focused specifically on agricultural development, and generally on rural development, provide some evidence of their usefulness. During the last two decades, more than a hundred other countries that have attained political independence and with it found themselves faced with the related problems of achieving biological and economic independence have established national extension systems as one of their new nation-building institutions. The organizational forms, objectives, quality of staff, financial support, administrative leadership, available technology, requisite production inputs, and other related elements in the new agencies vary widely in both scope and quality. Likewise, the extent and quality of contributions to agricultural modernization made by these extension systems have varied widely. Some of them have proven to be essentially useless when evaluated in the light of expectations. But to brand the idea of extension education as impractical, too slow, too costly, and unnecessary when useful technology is available may be a serious error.

Useful researches of the problems inherent in establishing and operating effective extension systems in newly developing countries are highly inadequate in number and scope. But a synthesis of the work done (much of which had other primary objectives, such as problems of communication, practice adoption, and issues of organization) combined with primary observations and direct experience by numerous professionals, contribute the basis for some promising empirical conclusions.

A wide range of factors is related to the lack of success including cultural and educational barriers, knowledge about promising innovations and economic benefits, weaknesses in farming systems, and failure by extension and research leaders to identify alternatives for improvement. Stated somewhat more specifically, the following conditions are among those which have imposed drastic limitations on contributions by extension systems in these developing countries.

1. Extension systems have been put into operation without significant agricultural technology and available supplies of production inputs related to the level of technology to be applied.

2. The extension process, being largely a United States invention, has been carried abroad in form and in pattern, and adopted without adequate modification to accommodate cultural norms or physical and manpower resources.

3. Extension systems have been put into operation to perform roles other than promoting agricultural production (political or ideological propagandizing, distribution of requisites, regulatory functions, and multipurpose work), with the result that focus on the central task of agricultural development has been diverted.

4. Extension systems have been established with a staff at the local level unable, by training, to establish credibility in the minds of farmers at levels necessary to influence changed behavior related to modern agricultural practices, and without adequate administrative and technical support at state and national levels.

5. Extension systems have been instituted without adequate functional coordination with research and training centers.

6. Extension systems have been established somewhat as a "fad" or a "prestigious step" without full recognition of the

highly complex, sophisticated, and costly nature of such systems, and the time and persistence required to develop requisite logistic support essential to success.

These propositions suggest much misconception, misuse, and general default in providing essential requisites to the extension system. They suggest that the problems encountered are not inherent in an extension education system per se, but stem from lack of such requisites as proper conceptualization of role, adequate staffing, effective coordination with research centers and training institutions, provision of useful technology and requisite physical inputs, adequate financing, proper organization, and effective administration. In short, the ineffectiveness of extension systems, like the slow development of agriculture itself, has resulted from inadequate availability and commitment of inputs and environmental conditions essential to successful performance. The point was well made by Pope in his *Essay on Man* when he said: "If vain our toil, we ought to blame the culture, not the soil."

Like the variables associated with failure, success variables related to extension systems in traditional cultures are not yet adequately identified. But a synthesis of researches into the problem, and recorded professional observations, augmented by implications of success factors in Western cultures, provide a basis for stating some promising hypotheses, which may, in fact, be somewhat acceptable as operational assumptions.

1. Recognition and philosophical acceptance by government leaders of agriculture as a primary industry in a nation's physical, biological, economic, social, and, to an increasing degree, political development.

2. Established macro policies favorable to increased production on such matters as price levels for agricultural products and purchasable production inputs, production credit, marketing facilities, availability of production inputs (seed, fertilizer, pesticides, and irrigation facilities), and related requisites.

3. Provision of a body of science and technology that is technically sound, economically feasible, and socially compatible, sufficient to meet modernization requirements.

4. Recognition that an extension system does not, as sometimes appears mistakenly to be the case, offer a utopian solution to agricultural modernization; that it is only one of the numer-

ous, needed inputs, and that its effect is in the nature of a cata-lytic ingredient of the modernization mix.

5. Realization that an effective extension system is a highly complex, costly, and time-consuming enterprise. It is complex because the human mind (the object of its focus) is complex; it is complex because a relatively large staff is required for wide coverage, and a professionally trained staff is required to achieve effective credibility; it is time-consuming because the repattern-ing of human behavior requires a cumulative effect to reach the high level of mental conviction that results in belief substitu-tion—a precondition for behavior modification.

6. A professionally competent field staff adequately supported by technical specialists, supervisors, and administrators at all essential levels in the organizational hierarchy.

7. A continuing source of staff training—pre-service, in-ser-vice, and advanced—for all categories of personnel, and oppor-tunities for staff development at increasingly higher levels of professional competency.

8. Financing at an effective level of all essential elements of the system, especially staff salaries and necessary amenities, needed equipment, supplies and facilities, transportation and communication channels.

9. Coordination of the extension system with research centers and colleges of agriculture in such a way that each benefits from the resources, problems, feedbacks, and achievements of the others.

10. Continuous, systematic evaluation of the objectives of the extension system—the achievements and effectiveness of re-sources utilized by the system.

The foregoing is not intended as an exhaustive list of condi-tions requisite to the success of extension systems, nor are the items equally important. In fact and by implication, however, they contribute to a viable conceptualization of situational and operational variables conducive to a success pattern.

Behavioral Determiners

The suggestion was made earlier that the repatterning of people's behavior which leads to agricultural modernization brings into direct confrontation two kinds of knowledge, skills, and values: traditional and modern.

Traditional

Masses of farmers in developing countries are trying to survive in a rapidly advancing technological parade on the frayed ends of custom and tradition. Agricultural operations in much of the world are still done by methods antedating the industrial revolution. And these methods are still trusted. Much of the problem in efforts to promote agricultural modernization stems from the fact that the masses—and some of their leaders—who have to make the needed innovations ultimately, do not understand the theories of science and technology. Most have not yet been exposed to them. Hence, conformity under the rules of counsel from above and/or long experience have been the way of life for centuries. The tried and tested, they believe, is the safe way; to venture is to risk; to experiment is to challenge the unknown, needlessly. These convictions tend to have a backward look, suggesting that the golden age was in a distant past, that the promise of tomorrow is a repetition of today. Traditional social orders tend to teach men to think deductively—from absolute principles to particulars; from tradition to current application. Traditional thinkers use the past as a fixed model, rather than a stimulus to new model building. They view the status quo as equivalent to the ideal, and this view perpetuates the static nature of a society.

Modern

Progressive cultures do not wholly trust the old ways and people tend to reason from particulars to scientific law. Knowledge is viewed as tentative, experimental, changing. As more penetrating questions are asked and answered, man's understanding of the fringes of the unknown enlarges and he moves ahead on the knowledge that he is in control of his destiny—at least, in part. His future, he believes, is measured by his own capacity to explore, achieve, and remodel the social, economic, and political world in which he lives. His golden age is in the future, not in the past. To him, the research laboratory is the great modern institution for questioning the sacred, challenging the unknown, prying into nature's secrets, and trying the untried. Modernity argues that innovation based on science is not only safe, but the only means to a better life.

In contrast to the traditional, modern thinkers use the past as a stimulus to model building rather than as a fixed model. Agricultural modernization requires that talent be placed above caste, ability and training above ancestry, science above custom; and recognition by agriculturists that scientific methods hold the promise that living conditions are improvable.

A requirement of agricultural modernization, therefore, is a set of forces sufficiently powerful to establish patterns of behavior that reflect useful modern, and refute useless traditional, practice. Kenneth E. Boulding stresses the urgency of developing an almost new form of learning and suggests, "We have to learn from rapidly changing systems. . . . Learning from changing systems is perhaps another step in the acceleration of evolution that we have to take." [10]

Progressive change, therefore, requires that the predominating influence of these two behavioral determinants be shifted from the traditional to the modern. A central role of modern agricultural science and education in this process is to clarify ambiguities within, and between, these two patterns of behavior and replace them with more understanding and certainty. In this venture, the role of the scientist is to challenge ambiguity at every encounter, and the extension educator must do likewise in his efforts to match technology with needed changes in human behavior.

Behavior and Environment

One of the assumptions made in science is that the world of man and things is inherently systematic and predictable, and that man is not a slave of the forces in his environment, but has the ability to shape them to serve his own ends. "To the extent that relevant conditions can be altered or otherwise controlled, the future can be controlled. If we are to use the methods of science in the field of human affairs, we must assume that behavior is lawful and determinate. We must expect to discover that what a man does is the result of specifiable conditions, and

[10] Kenneth E. Boulding, "After Civilization, What?" *Bulletin of the Atomic Scientists* (Chicago: Educational Foundation for Nuclear Science), 18, no. 8 (1962), 6.

that once the conditions have been discovered, we can anticipate, and to some extent, determine his actions." [11]

What is known about why people behave as they do suggests
that man is an independent living system surrounded by an
environment with which he constantly interrelates: other human beings, physical objects, social and cutural norms, and
economic, technological, and political conditions. Studies indicate that cultures tend to institutionalize at least seven primary elements (Figure 1).

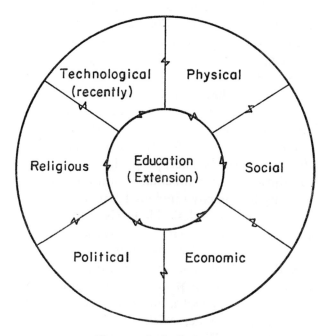

Figure 1. Societal elements

Analysis of the role and functional relationships of these elements indicates that in the present context, education tends to be
central among societal subsystems, influencing other elements
and, in turn, being influenced by them. Empirical evidence
suggests that development requires that major societal institutions have quality and continuity, function with inseparable in-

[11] B. F. Skinner, *Science and Human Behavior* (New York: Macmillan,
1953), p. 6.

terrelatedness, and operate in reasonable balance. In this context, the central role of an extension education system is to focus on the transaction between man and his environment in ways that improve the quality of the transaction. In this task, its specific role is to "orchestrate" physical, biological, technological, economic, social, and political resources so as to reduce dissonance between the status quo and desirable new economic and social conditions of living and ways of making a living.

These institutionalized forces exert constant influence over people's behavior in varying degrees of favorableness to qualities of living. The variations stem in part from the past and present culture and from natural physical endowments. Regardless of one's economic and social conditions, or of his ability to cope with them, there are usually environmental forces with which he must learn to deal if he is to survive and progress. Consequently, people have concern for the elements in their environment because physical, economic, and social needs emerge largely from maladjustments between things they want and need and environmental forces which affect achievements. In efforts to improve the balance, people have two primary alternatives: to adjust to environmental conditions, or to seek to favorably modify hostile environmental forces.

Closing the gap between desirable levels of living and the influence of negative environmental forces is the essence of man's struggle for existence and for improvements in his quality of life. Hence, the goal of modern agriculture is likely to be reached more rapidly when policy makers, agricultural scientists, extension educators, and farmers gain further understanding of the physical, economic, social, technical, educational, and political institutions which influence the provision and effective utilization that modernization requires. An effective extension system is not only dependent on this understanding but can, in turn, contribute to it.

Modern Factors of Production

Traditionally, the primary factors of agricultural production are grouped under three headings: land, labor, and capital. In this scheme, education and its effects are treated as a consumption item. Beginning roughly in the mid-1940's, however, the expansion and quality of serious study of the modernization process began to reveal the need for adding several additional elements to the production mix. For example, analyses of requirements for achieving a modern, scientific, market-oriented agricultural enterprise by A. T. Mosher, John W. Mellor, T. W. Schultz, and numerous other social and biological scientists suggest that modern technology, available supplies of purchasable production requisites, a favorable macroenvironment, and an effective extension education system are factors required in a modern production formula.

With full recognition of some questionable implicit and explicit assumptions on which rests the validity of the elements and their ordering in Figure 2, this theoretical paradigm is designed to suggest a set of dependent and independent variables which currently appear to be essential to successful programs for agricultural modernization.

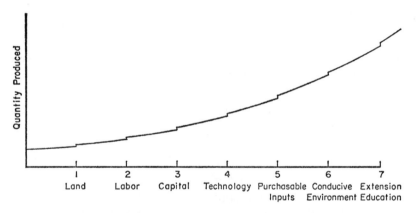

Figure 2. Theoretical paradigm for production elements

Even though Figure 2 is presented as a hypothetical construct, current knowledge of the requisite components in the agricultural development phenomenon—whether or not they are viewed in economic terms as factors of production—appears to support inclusion of the seven items. In line with the modern notion of "packages of practices," the elements listed may be viewed as "an agricultural modernization package." The order in which the elements are listed on the continuum, however, is open to discussion. Land, for example, may be viewed as a dependent variable and each of the others as independent variables. However, since land, labor, capital, technology, and purchasable inputs are internal to the production phenomenon they may each be considered dependent variables, while a conducive environment and extension education are factors external to production and may be viewed as independent variables. Still another perception suggests that extension education is not realistically equatable with the other elements because, by nature, it is a pervasively functional variable dependent for its growth and effectiveness on the presence and development of some of the others while, in turn, having the capability to integrate (package), activate and, thus, accelerate the development and effective utilization of the other variables (see Figure 3). Consequently an extension system to focus primarily on agriculture may be usefully established at, or soon after, the time major thrusts are begun to create new bodies of technically sound and economically feasible technology and related production requisites.

Although the elements are highly interdependent and, hence, derive singular and collective strength from their state of development and optimum functional interrelatedness at a given time and place, they cannot be perceived realistically as a true lineage progression. Thus, the question of how to order emphasis on the elements so as to achieve maximum complementarity and utilization can be effectively answered only by careful analysis of priorities assigned to the objectives of a country's nation-building program; for example, is a rapid gross increase in food production the top priority objective, or are some other goals perceived to be simultaneously equal in importance such as improved nutrition, sanitation, housing, family planning, and empathic feelings among rural people toward newly perceived government action related to the people's welfare? Manpower resources, and the particular status of physical, biological, economic, social, technological, political, and related variables within a given country at a given time must also be carefully examined. Nevertheless, a brief rationale for the inclusion of each of the elements in the order given (Figure 2) is as follows.

Land is the first factor of production listed on the continuum. There are currently identifiable situations in Africa, Asia, and possibly in other sections of the world, where people obtain their basic food supply from what nature alone has done to the land. In these situations, man's intervention into his physical and biological environment for purposes of modifying it in his favor is essentially nonexistent. He has not removed natural growth from the land for cultivation, a first step in substituting man's production practices for those provided by nature; instead, he takes animals from the forests, harvests fruits from the jungle, and catches fish from the streams. (It is recognized that these efforts require labor, skill, and technology, but these are of different order than efforts focused on modernization.) Hence, from land alone, with no man-designed inputs, a minimum livelihood is possible. When effective labor is added to the land, however, additional production useful to man results. Likewise, when in one or more of its many forms capital is added to land and labor, further production increases may be expected.

At this point, the production formula moves rapidly from traditional to modern, from passive to dynamic, or from laissez-faire to planned external intervention. One of the assumptions giving rise to the development of agricultural technology, beginning about a hundred years ago in Western Europe and the United States, was the notion that much could be learned about the physical and biological elements in man's environment on which he depends for a livelihood.[12] Particularly since World War II, and even more dynamically during the last two or three years, exciting break-throughs have been made by agricultural scientists, particularly on cereal grains used for human consumption. It would be redundant to undertake here an argument for the usefulness of modern technology (factor 4, Figure 2) as an element in a modern agricultural production formula. Effective use of sophisticated production technology, however, requires a parallel availability and proper use of numerous purchasable production inputs (factor 5, Figure 2), including fertilizers, insecticides, fungicides, and new methods of planting seed with germ plasma superior to indigenous varieties. These must all be applied, of course, according to their technical requirements.

Traditional, subsistence, non-market-oriented agricultural production systems have characterized for centuries the agri-

[12] For an elaboration of this point see J. Paul Leagans, "Agricultural Education," *Encyclopedia Americana* (1966), I, 244–249.

cultural enterprise in many countries which are now concerned with modernization. These patterns can, and have, operated with little concern for the nature of the macro environment (factor 6, Figure 2) and , in fact, without its concerted influence. The attitude of government toward agriculture has been laissez-faire in nature, but the attainment of new political independence, and later recognition of the essential and parallel need for biological and economic independence for the country, have resulted in new concerns for modernizing the agricultural sector. It was pointed out in the beginning of this chapter that environmental intervention is essential for increasing agricultural production to a point where it becomes adequate for providing a nation's needed food and fiber and, in addition, contributes to economic growth.

To achieve such goals on a national scale, analyses of the agricultural development process increasingly make clear the necessity for a favorable macro environment, and awareness that creating such an environment lies beyond the capacity of local cultivators and their leaders and, therefore, is dependent on both the public and private sectors. The elements of favorable macro environments are extensive, complex, and costly—financially, and often politically. They include recognition by key government policy makers of agriculture as a primary enterprise, and a firm long-term commitment of government resources necessary to achieve nation-building objectives. Political and financial commitments are required for establishing an infrastructure that includes such essential items as agricultural research institutions as well as those necessary to train the manpower needed to lead and manage the agricultural industry, and to provide the needed education of farmers that enables them to move from traditional to modern agricultural practices. Policies that establish and maintain price levels and price stability of agricultural products and purchasable inputs are also essential, as are favorable conditions related to production credit, market outlets, and production and distribution of such requisite inputs as seed, fertilizer, and pesticides, all of which make it possible for agricultural producers to maximize their capacities.

In most societies, there is an identifiable group of agriculturists referred to by social scientists as "innovators" who will take advantage of promising available inputs and utilize them to modernize their farming operations largely on their own incentive. Unfortunately, however, this group includes only a very small number of producers—usually about 5 per cent, even in highly educated and technically advanced societies in Western Europe, Canada, and the United States. Some technologists suggest that adequate conditions for rapid increase in agricultural production exist when the six elements or factors of production just enumerated are present. But this argument rests largely on mechanical grounds and overlooks a critical dependent variable in the formula, namely, the farmer who must ultimately obtain, interpret, organize, and apply effectively the production inputs in his personal situation. He has essential control over this action in free-choice societies. The great increase in wheat production achieved in Mexico is frequently used as an example of extremely rapid adoption by farmers of promising new varieties. In this instance, it is suggested that farmers changed in only a few years a wheat-importing situation to an exporting one without the influence of a national extension system, although Mexico had one in operation. But two important facts are usually overlooked: the researchers engaged in the program, both American and Mexican, played effectively the role both of researcher and of extension educator, and limited their contacts to large entrepreneurs—farmers with sizable holdings, available capital, managerial ability, and high levels of education, all factors conducive to quick and extensive innovation when sound and economically feasible technology became available. The masses of farmers, therefore, are yet to be influenced by such technology. Whether this pattern is transferable and acceptable economically, socially, and politically by large numbers of the newly developing countries is apparently yet to be proven. It may be that the same "fit" will not be achieved because of wide variations in nation-building objectives, political ideologies, and related factors such as social stratification and available resources. Furthermore, "those left behind" in many countries have increasing political power and could create some highly complex national problems if bypassed continuously.

Extension education, therefore, the last item indicated on the continuum in Figure 2, appears to be a necessary component of an agriculture modernization package capable of maximizing effective utilization of the other factors of production. Skilled researchers with appropriate equipment, physical facilities, and necessary financing can create technology, but these same resources may not be able to assure its effective and wide application by masses of farmers who need its benefits. This is because another powerful variable intervenes that can alone determine ultimate progress, namely, that the masses of farmers tend to be conservative, slow to modify their behavioral pattern, and, hence, require more powerful influences than the more elite group. The influencers lie in the realm of education. The appropriate question then, is not the inclusion of one or another but how to develop, combine, and manage all of these elements apparently essential to successful programs of agricultural modernization.

Extension Education and Change

Synonymous with agricultural modernization is change in production and marketing patterns from the traditional to those that incorporate modern science and technology. Achievements in this direction are ultimately dependent on behavioral innovations by cultivators and leaders in the hierarchy who influence them. Purposeful extension education is the variable in the suggested modernization package which focuses specifically on repatterning human behavior utilizing the power of education as its activating force. It proceeds on the assumption that the status quo can and should be changed. Consequently, an understanding of the change phenomenon is useful in conceptualizing the role of an extension education system in the agricultural modernization process.

Numerous theories are advanced which purport to explain the process of social, economic, and technical change. W. E. Moore suggests that a sense of time and perception of change are inexplicably linked in human experience.[13] The link works both ways; neither time nor change is a dependent variable. Although they do not completely agree on definitions, psychologists generally suggest that behavioral change results from an imbalance between man and his environment. This produces

13 W. E. Moore, *Social Change* (Englewood Cliffs, N.J.: Prentice-Hall, 1963), pp. 22–23.

tension, and change results from a need for tension reduction. The process has three phases: disequilibrium (uneven tension or need), a goal, and action directed at achieving the goal. This implies that there are always forces acting upon man which create needs or disequilibrium between him and his environment. Based on the tension or need which, according to the individual's perception, is most urgent, a suitable goal is chosen and action taken to achieve the desired goal. This action involves new behavior and therefore brings about change.

Sociologists suggest that change occurs by the alteration of goals, structures, or processes in a social system—group goals, norms, values, and structures.[14] Anthropologists view change as a product of the cultural diffusion process, and suggest that change is inevitable as long as there is contact and there are things (culture, facts, materials, social structures) to be diffused. Many economists suggest a theory of economic determinism which regards man's economic need as a motivating basis for change. "The mode of production in material life determines the general character of the social, political and spiritual processes of life. With change of the economic foundation, the entire immense superstructure is more or less rapidly transformed." [15]

Interaction among human beings, according to social psychologists, is the basis for change. Interaction is dynamic—change is its product. Interaction is viewed as "the process by which people influence one another through mutual interchange of thoughts, feelings and reactions." [16] For example, "Behavior X on the part of one person is likely to be followed by behavior Y on the part of another," [17] and this results in change. Ronald Lippitt recognizes three types of such forces: "(1) *change forces,* that motivate people to change by creating dis-satisfaction with the status quo, and favorable judgment of

[14] Matthew B. Miles, ed., *Innovation in Education* (New York: Bureau of Publications, Teachers College, Columbia University, 1964), p. 13.

[15] Amitai and Eva Etzioni, eds., *Social Change: Sources, Patterns, and Consequences* (New York: Basic Books, 1966), p. 7.

[16] W. W. and W. E. Lambert, *Social Psychology* (Englewood Cliffs, N.J.: Prentice-Hall, 1966), p. 84.

[17] Theodore M. Newcombe *et al, Social Psychology: The Study of Human Interaction* (New York: Holt, Rinehart, and Winston, 1965), p. 1.

potential future situations; (2) *resistance forces,* which motivate people not to change, that rise from uncertainty of the unknown and inability to change; and (3) *interference forces,* which obstruct change without being directly related to it." [18]

Dealing with the methods of change, Warren Bennis mentions "the law of non-intervention" and "the law of radical intervention." He argues that planned change is "the only feasible alternative to these methods" and defines planned change as "a conscious, deliberate and collaborative effort to improve the operations of a system . . . through the utilization of scientific knowledge." [19] "Human beings are naturally endowed with power to change themselves educationally and their environment physically and are constantly attempting to create and maintain a satisfying adjustment between internal forces created by inherited human traits, and external forces imposed by environment." [20] This adjustment is achieved through structured action between internal and external change forces that results in progressive innovation.

George Foster contends that "each society can be thought of as a host of two kinds of forces: those which seek to promote change, and those that strive to maintain the status quo. These forces are locked in perpetual combat. The former, trying to throw the latter off balance to gain the ascendency, and the latter, trying to prevent this from happening." He goes on to suggest that "the most successful, guided technological development occurs when program planners and technical specialists are aware of the struggle between the forces for change and the forces for stability found in all cultures. Not only must the presence of the forces be recognized, but in a specific situation, they must be identified and related to one another. The strategy of promoting change is then relatively simple—in theory." [21]

[18] Ronald Lippit *et al., Dynamics of Planned Change* (New York: Brace, 1958), p. 6.

[19] Warren J. Bennis *et al., The Planning of Change* (New York: Holt, Rinehart, and Winston, 1961), p. 2.

[20] J. Paul Leagans, *The Role of Extensive Education in Rural Development,* Cornell International Agricultural Development Bulletin No. 3 (Ithaca: New York State College of Agriculture, 1963), p. 4 (also in Spanish translation).

[21] George M. Foster, *Traditional Cultures and the Impact on Technological Change* (New York: Harper and Row, 1962), pp. 58–59.

The foregoing theoretical formulations of the change process are projected from a wide range of disciplinary vantage points and on the basis of differing assumptions. Identifiable in them, however, is an almost pervasive proposition, expressed or implied, that the essence of behavioral change results from the interaction of two sets of opposing forces: change incentives and change inhibitors, which create tensions that motivate action and result in change. Each set at a given time and in a given situation may consist of certain manifestations of physical, cultural, economic, psychological, biological, technological, political, aesthetic, religious, or educational forces. The interaction influence of these two sets of opposing forces shapes and controls the nature of change, which may be broadly classified as passive, dynamic, or semi-dynamic.

Figure 3 is an interpretation and synthesis of the several behavioral theories just enumerated in the form of a conceptually functional model. The items included as change inhibitors and change incentives in the three phases are selections from researches designed to identify the physical, economic, social, technological, political, and educational forces which comprise "pushes" and "pulls" on people's behavior. The kind, number, and valence of these items included in the paradigm are intended only as illustrations, since they vary by situation.

It will be noted in the construct that people's behavior is represented by a central curve continuing through each of the three phases and that this curve is horizontal in phase 1, noticeably inclined in phase 2, and is inclined in phase 3, but less so than in phase 2. The group of change inhibitors is the same in each phase. Likewise, the group of change incentives in phase 1 is found also in phases 2 and 3. It is assumed that basic economic, social, and other conditions constituting change inhibitors and change incentives exist in most, if not all, situations and exert some degree of influence for relatively long periods of time. It is further assumed, however, that the extent of force they exert on patterning people's behavior can be changed in desirable ways; that is, change inhibitors can be weakened and change incentives can be strengthened by planned programs of intervention.

This analysis provides the framework in which some suggestions can be made about the change process. Phase 1 indicates that a static situation exists. Such an equilibrium is

Figure 3. Paradigm of change and role of extension education

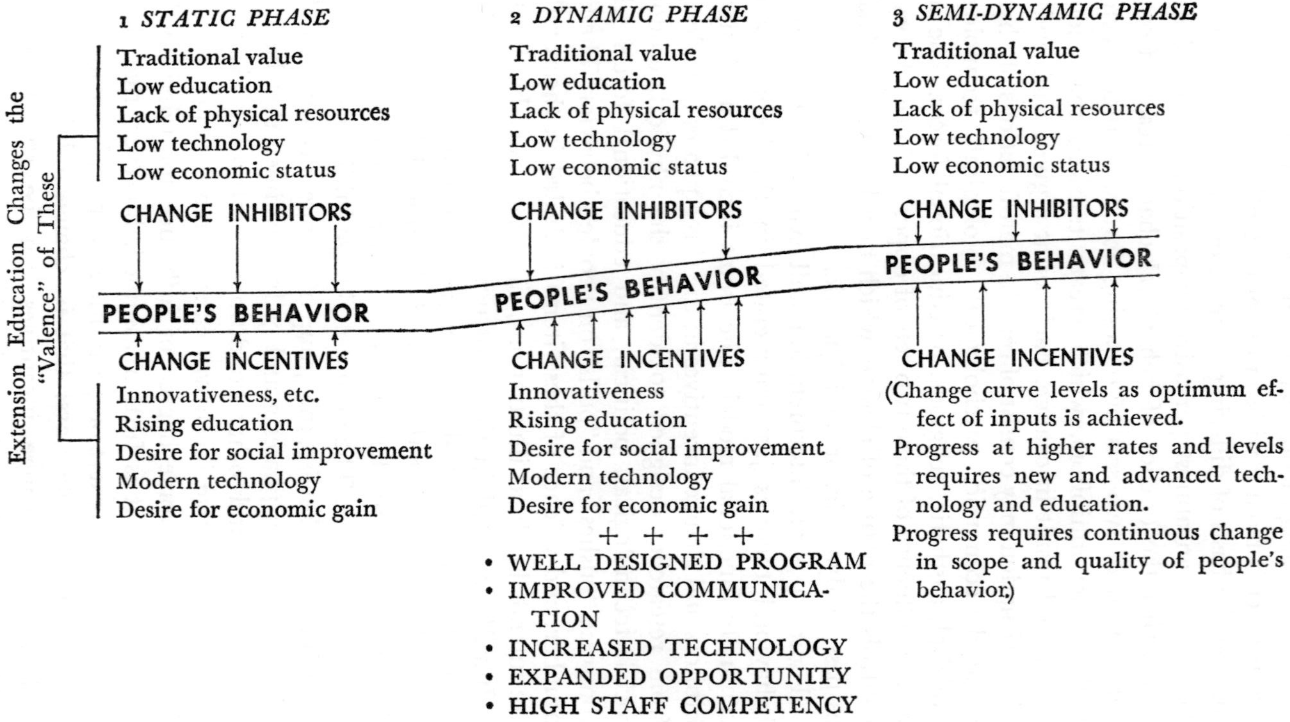

1 STATIC PHASE

Traditional value
Low education
Lack of physical resources
Low technology
Low economic status

CHANGE INHIBITORS

PEOPLE'S BEHAVIOR

CHANGE INCENTIVES

Innovativeness, etc.
Rising education
Desire for social improvement
Modern technology
Desire for economic gain

2 DYNAMIC PHASE

Traditional value
Low education
Lack of physical resources
Low technology
Low economic status

CHANGE INHIBITORS

PEOPLE'S BEHAVIOR

CHANGE INCENTIVES

Innovativeness
Rising education
Desire for social improvement
Modern technology
Desire for economic gain

+ + + +

- WELL DESIGNED PROGRAM
- IMPROVED COMMUNICA-
  TION
- INCREASED TECHNOLOGY
- EXPANDED OPPORTUNITY
- HIGH STAFF COMPETENCY

3 SEMI-DYNAMIC PHASE

Traditional value
Low education
Lack of physical resources
Low technology
Low economic status

CHANGE INHIBITORS

PEOPLE'S BEHAVIOR

CHANGE INCENTIVES

(Change curve levels as optimum effect of inputs is achieved.
Progress at higher rates and levels requires new and advanced technology and education.
Progress requires continuous change in scope and quality of people's behavior.)

Extension Education Changes the "Valence" of These

created when the cumulative behavioral tendencies of people influenced by the cluster of change incentives in their environment are equalized and, consequently, offset by an equal force exerted by an existing cluster of change inhibitors. When these forces for, or against, behavioral change offset each other, a static or status-quo situation prevails.

This situation gives rise to the central question with which promoters of change leading to modernization are concerned: What must be done to introduce and sustain desirable change? To create a dynamic situation (phase 2 in Figure 3) requires the introduction of change incentives sufficient to create an imbalance, or a greater force for change than is exerted by the existing change inhibitors. To create such an imbalance, at least four major steps are necessary: (1) introduce forceful new incentives (note the additional ones in phase 2), (2) strengthen change incentives already present, (3) improve the complementarity of the change incentives, and (4) weaken or remove the change inhibitors present in the situation. The processes are educational in nature and hence constitute the central roles of extension education systems.

Rates of change are largely determined by the number and kinds of change incentives introduced, the valence of each as measured by the extent of their contribution to attaining change objectives, the complementarity of the inputs, the speed with which they are introduced, and the effectiveness with which they are internalized by the people in a position to utilize them.

Phase 3, the semi-dynamic phase, suggests that the upward trend tends to revert to a static situation, but it remains at a higher level of desirable behaviorable change, and the upward trend continues with a slight incline resulting from accumulation or multiplied effect. This situation results when physical, technological, educational, and other inputs reach optimum levels of effect. To redynamize the situation requires the introduction of advanced technological inputs and other change incentives with greater "push power" than those present in the situation. To increase the incline of the behavior curve also requires introduction of other production incentives needed to further minimize the valence of change inhibitors. In this process, the role of an extension system is to change the static situation into a continuously dynamic one through the influence of an educational input that changes the total valence of incentives and reduces the valence of inhibitors. This paradigm is intended to illustrate a theoretical concept of the agricultural modernization process and to indicate the pervasive role of an effective extension system as a catalytic agent which, through its educational force, activates and synthesizes the modernizing elements into a system with maximum developmental force.

Institutionalization of Extension Process

The roles assigned to an extension education system in the foregoing sections are posed as essential to the agricultural modernization process. They may conceivably be utilized in many forms ranging from no locally organized extension agency, public or private, as in the wheat propagation program in Mexico; to a national extension system which, in large measure, contracts units of the system to business and industrial groups, as in Colombia; to a national system involving co-operation and responsibility at state and local levels as in Canada, some western European countries, and the United States.

But it has been long recognized that organized forms of educational efforts are most effective. A rationale for institutionalization is as follows: Institutions are instruments created by a society to help "fix the confines and impose form upon the activities of human beings" [22] in achieving their objectives. An organized extension education system is an institution; and, like other institutions, the adequacy of its development, technological resources, administrative support, and utilization determines the quality and quantity of its impact on the change process.

Nothing survives in modern human society without some degree of institutionalization. The significance of institutionalization stems largely from the fact that human beings are social and like to associate with others. This association leads to interaction—of a sensory, emotional, or intellectual type—focused on physical, social, economic, political, or other areas of concern to particular groups. Changes in behavior which emerge

[22] W. H. Hamilton, "Institutions," in *Encyclopedia of Social Sciences* (New York: Macmillan, 1937), VIII, 84.

from this interaction need to be ordered and regulated for harmonious and cooperative living. It becomes necessary, therefore, to order the new relationships through some type of organization and control so that individual behavior is "in the form of an accepted, standardized, expected, predictable and enforceable pattern. . . . Without conformity to such established universal and known patterns of behavior there can be no harmony, coordination and not even the minimal efficiency of operation that is essential to satisfactory progress and living and working together." [23]

Farmers, like others, view themselves as parts of the system in which they live. Hence, attempts to change their patterns of behavior without creating, modifying, and developing an institutional system conducive to progressive change may not only be difficult, but perhaps impossible. Planned agricultural development, therefore, not only requires plans and statistics, targets and budgets, technology and method, material aid and professional staff, but effective institutionalization of these educational means for changing the minds and actions of cultivators.[24] The central question, then, is not whether institutions —including agricultural colleges, research centers, supply agencies, and extension systems—for modernizing agriculture should be created and maintained, but whether these will be developed to required levels of quality, and their impact channeled in directions which maximize their potential contributions to agricultural development, and social and economic growth.

From Macro to Micro Concepts

The foregoing conceptual structures comprise bases for strategies with primary relevance at the macro level, but they are not confined to this level. The purpose of the analysis is to help clarify the nature and role of an extension system as one of the requisite components of a viable infrastructure needed to modernize agriculture, especially in traditional societies. The cen-

[23] J. O. Hertzler, *Society in Action* (New York: Dryden Press, 1954), p. 91.

[24] J. Paul Leagans, "Extension Education in Community Development," *Extension Education in Community Development* (New Delhi: Ministry of Food and Agriculture, 1961), pp. 1–15.

tral role of an extension education system is in the nature of a catalytic ingredient of the modernization mix which serves to activate and "orchestrate" other essential elements. At this point a useful question is: What concepts give rise to effective strategies for promoting behavioral innovation at the micro level?

An exhaustive compilation of concepts involved at the micro level lies far beyond the limits of this chapter; the attempt here is to identify only a relatively small number of concepts viewed as central in the extension process. Those presented emphasize the role of extension as a mechanism for linking the knowledge centers and the farmer's needs by a change agent using education as the activating force.[25]

The concepts that follow assume that the change agent's effectiveness stems from his technical knowledge, skill in programming, communicating, and evaluating both means and achievements. It is further assumed that the process of synthesizing useful technology from physical and biological sciences with that from the behavioral sciences, and applying it to the problems of planned agricultural modernization, is the essence and role of extension education, and that the relationship of change agents with their respondents is central in the process.

In examining these concepts, one should be aware of a trend at the present time in organized education, analytical writing, and purposeful learning toward the use of "concepts" as the focal point in the logical analysis of what is to be learned, and in the psychological analysis of concept formation in the learning process. It is this phenomenon that, in large measure, gave rise to recent team research efforts, interdisciplinary teaching, and the idea of "package programs" for agricultural development. The concepts presented here constitute some of the "mental anchors" in the form of conceptualized clusters of content related to behavioral change that are useful to change agents in designing educational strategy.

[25] The term "change agent" is used interchangeably with the term "extension educator" to mean any individual (usually professional) who performs purposeful activity designed to influence change in a particular situation. For an elaboration of the change agent concept, see Ronald Lippit *et al.*

Needs

Efforts to promote planned change in conditions of "free-choice participation" are successful only to the extent that they focus on the important needs of people and are effective in helping people meet these needs. Under voluntary conditions of participation, people concern themselves with programs of change only when they think the program offers help in meeting personal, family, group, or community needs which they themselves recognize. The element of needs, therefore, should be a central concern of change agents.

The term "need," in essence, signifies the lack of something that, if present, would in his or another's view further the welfare of an individual or a family. Anything that is requisite to the maintenance of a desired state of affairs is a need. Hence, needs represent an imbalance or lack of adjustment between the present situation or status quo and a new or changed set of conditions assumed to be more desirable. More specifically, needs may be defined as the differences between *what is,* and *what ought to be* and, hence, always imply a gap between these two conditions.[26]

What is can be determined by a study of the situation including facts about the people—their attitudes, knowledge, what they think their needs are; facts about physical factors—soils, crops, livestock, home conditions, farm implements, production resources, community services; and facts about public problems—programs, policies, and trends.

What ought to be can be determined by examining both research findings and the value judgments of people and their leaders. For example, the results of research may show that the use of recommended practices in rice production will result in per hectare yields one-third larger than those obtained with present practices. A farmer, however, may not place great value on reaching a higher level of production. He may place greater value on spending available resources to reach another goal

[26] For a more extensive, theoretical treatment of the concept of "needs" see J. Paul Leagans, "A Concept of Needs," *Journal of Cooperative Extension,* 2, no. 2 (Summer, 1964), 89–96. Also see A. H. Maslow, ed., *New Knowledge in Human Values* (New York: Harper and Bros., 1959).

such as better education for his children. Deciding what ought to be is the process of selecting program targets, goals, or objectives—the essence of programming.

Final decisions about the selection, or rejection, of needs on which to focus programs are crucial not only because the future of a people and their conditions will be influenced, but because extensive physical, monetary, and human resources will be committed to meeting the needs.

Motivation

Motivation explains how men are moved without being pushed. Robert Burns says motivation is "essentially made of two aspects, (a) basic needs that an individual has, and (b) a conscious effort to gratify or satisfy those needs." [27] According to R. H. Ewing, motivation is the "process by which individuals are encouraged or impelled to think, behave or act in a favorable manner." [28] It is, thus, a subtle and more indirect system of influencing people than strict orders, direct commands, or mere exhortation. J. W. Atkinson, in trying to summarize the definitions of motivation given by various authors, concludes that motivation is "direction, vigor, and persistence of behavior or action." [29] In essence, motivation seems to be the goal-directed, initiating stage which leads to increased activity and persists till the ends are achieved. The arousal of the initiating stage may be effected by internal forces, or by external stimuli.

Various authors emphasize the importance of human needs as the basic source of motivation. There appears to be almost unanimous agreement that the prior satisfaction of so-called "basic needs" is a necessary condition if human beings are to be concerned with, and active in, performing higher level functions. Understanding of the motivation variable by change agents in their efforts to repattern farmer behavior is essential

[27] Robert K. Burns, "Management and Employee Motivation" (Chicago: Research Reprint Service of the University of Chicago Industrial Relations Center, 1959), no. 91, p. 1.

[28] R. H. Ewing, "Principles of Motivation," unpublished paper, National Institute of Leadership, Beverly Hills, Cal., 1960, p. 11.

[29] J. W. Atkinson, *An Introduction to Motivation* (Princeton, N.J.: D. Van Nostrand, 1965), p. 276.

to designing strategy with performance expectation significantly beyond chance. To utilize the potential impact of farmer motivation on agricultural development, extension educators must identify and relate forces stemming both from the farmer as a human being and from his environment that serve to structure his behavior. These forces should be taken into account in all major phases of a change agent's efforts—programming, communication, and evaluation.

Learning Experience

The teaching-learning component of the educative process is one of the most delicate, significant, and complex of all social processes because it changes the way people think and act, and these behaviors determine the nature of a society. The crucial factor in the teaching-learning process is providing an effective learning experience. This is the criterion by which all teaching and learning must ultimately be judged. An effective learning experience is one that results in a maximum of desirable change in behavior on the part of learners.

The term "learning experience" is a highly meaningful label for a concept lying at the core of the educational process. In essence, it is the mental and/or physical reaction one has through seeing, hearing, or doing the things to be learned, and through which one gains meanings and understandings of the material presented. In this sense, a learning experience is "a series of activities and appraisals from which one gains meanings that can be used in facing new problems and planning new experiences. Action tends to accompany conviction; doing and knowing are interactive components of all learning pertaining to beliefs, attitudes, skills and understandings." [30]

Learning is something that takes place within the learner, and is personal to him; it is an essential part of his development, for it is always the whole person who is learning. Learning takes place when an individual feels a need, puts forth an effort to meet that need, and experiences satisfaction with the result of his effort. The thing learned then modifies his view of it and related phenomena, and thus affects the mental and/or overt behavioral tendencies of the learner. The products of

[30] Paul Eissert, *Creative Leadership of Adult Education* (New York: Prentice-Hall, 1951), p. 14.

learning are of several principal types: "Integrated behavior patterns, values or ideals, meanings, facts, achieved abilities, and skill." [31] These products of learning are all achieved by the learner through his own activity. R. E. Hilgard suggests that three simultaneous processes are involved when learning is being experienced: (1) acquisition of new information, (2) transformation (the process of manipulating new knowledge to make it fit the new task), and (3) evaluating (checking whether the way the information has been manipulated is adequate to the task).[32] Similar to these processes are the five stages generally identified as components of the farm practice adoption process: awareness, interest, evaluation, trial, and adoption. These stages comprise a learning experience through which a person is changed in his behavior.

But the fact that all genuine education comes about through experience does not mean that all experiences are genuinely or equally educative. Effective learning experiences involve more than simply placing one's self in a position to learn. Activities such as attending a meeting, listening to a radio, or observing a demonstration, constitute situations that offer opportunity for learning, but these actions are usually not enough by themselves. It is what a participant *does* while in a learning situation that is the all-important factor. Theodore Harris suggests that seven conditions must be present for a worthwhile learning experience to take place: (1) the goal of the learner, (2) the learner's readiness, (3) the learning situation, (4) the interpretation, (5) the response or action, (6) the consequence (confirmation or contradiction), and (7) the reaction (others consider it as adoption).[33]

William Burton divides learning experience into two parts: direct experience and vicarious experience.[34] Vicarious experience supplements direct experience. In a direct learning experience, learners actually participate, do the work, and

---

[31] William H. Burton, *The Guidance of Learning Activities* (New York: Appleton-Century-Crofts, 1952), p. 28.

[32] R. E. Hilgard, *Theories of Learning and Instruction* (Chicago: University of Chicago Press, 1964), p. 100.

[33] Theodore L. Harris and Wilson E. Schwahn, *Selected Readings on the Learning Process* (New York: Oxford University Press, 1961), p. 9.

[34] Burton, pp. 42–44.

undergo change, but people learn also by vicariously experiencing the direct experience of others. In many instances, the long and laborious processes of discovery can be short-circuited. Learners can appropriate ideas, understandings, and attitudes by reading, listening, observing, pondering, and analyzing the experiences of others. The function of a learning experience is to evoke desirable responses, to strengthen these responses, and to hasten the weakening of undesirable responses.

It is the responsibility of the extension educator to provide professional and sympathetic guidance to learners in their efforts to modernize their patterns of behavior through new learning. His success at this central aspect of the extension educational process will largely determine his professional usefulness.

Learning Situations

An effective learning experience can be had only in a well-structured and skillfully executed learning situation. A primary role of the change agent, therefore, is to create learning situations that stimulate and guide effective learning activity. A good extension educator is one with deep faith in people, a broad and forward vision of the extension educational process, a thorough and current knowledge of useful technology, a willingness to serve people beyond minimum requirements and the ability to bring together people, technology, and educational methods in ways which produce optimum learning. Here the total range of extension methodology enters the picture.

An effective learning situation consists of five essential elements of which the change agent is one.[35] His role as instructor is to conduct himself and manipulate the other four elements effectively. Figure 4 shows learners as the central element in the learning situation. The other four elements become means for achieving the end product.

There is a continuous reaction by learners to one or more of the other four major elements. A learner may at one time be reacting to the instructor, to his mannerisms, or to his voice;

[35] J. Paul Leagans, *Guides to Extension Teaching in Developing Countries,* Cornell International Agricultural Development Bulletin No. 5 (Ithaca: New York State College of Agriculture, 1964), p. 17 (also in Spanish translation).

at another time to his teaching equipment or the manner in which he handles it; or to some aspect of the physical facilities, such as a hard chair, poor lighting, or excessive heat; and, at some point, to the subject matter. The effectiveness of a learning experience is related directly to the manner and extent of the learner's mental concentration on the subject matter to be learned. To become proficient at creating learning situations requires that the change agent work hard at the tasks of analyzing teaching problems, knowing the audience, gaining new technology to extend, developing further understanding of the teaching-learning process, and achieving greater skill in selecting, combining, and using the methods of extension education.

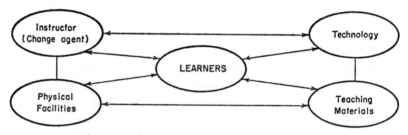

Figure 4. Major elements of a learning situation

Decision-Making

The word "decision" implies conscious choice or judgment, and is related to action. The farmer who sees a new practice, gets more information about it, weighs its desirable and undesirable points, compares it with the practice he uses, and finally chooses either to try it or reject it, is acting according to the decision-making process.

An analysis of this process indicates a systematic sequence of steps or stages varying in number depending on the detail of analysis. Irma Gross suggests three steps: Seeking alternatives, thinking through the consequences of these alternatives, and selecting one of the alternatives.[36] A more detailed way of perceiving the process is given by Preston LeBrenton who considers six stages: (1) analysis of objectives of the plan, (2) listing of alternative solutions, (3) listing of significant variables, (4)

[36] Irma H. Gross and E. W. Crandall, *Management for Modern Farm Families* (New York: Appleton-Century-Crofts, 1954), p. 21.

assigning values to each variable, (5) the probability assigned to each variable, and (6) selection of solution.[37] In any event, a particular act of decision-making starts with the identification of a problem and ends in selection of the alternative considered most relevant to attainment of the goal.

Some decision-making activities are done individually while others are performed by a group. The adage that "two heads are better than one" implies that group-made decisions are superior to individually made decisions. When the decision maker is faced with no operable means for evaluating a decision and with limited data, he has no recourse other than to utilize a group, both as a security operation and as a validity tester. "This is not to say that this method is the most effective; quite the opposite. It may be the most expensive, invalid, and tedious. Nevertheless, psychologically, it is functional." [38]

Understanding the attributes of good decisions logically appears to be prerequisite to making good decisions and to guiding others in doing likewise. Change agents should take upon themselves the task of making available feasible alternatives and information on problems that confront farmers. For example, when a farmer decides against a new practice, it may be that he thinks the risk is too great, that he cannot afford to lose a year's crop and consequently, a year's subsistence. Decisions by farmers are not always made on a purely technical basis. Usually their decisions are affected by the individuals and groups around them, and by physical, cultural, economic, and political conditions. One of the results of effective extension educational inputs should be reflected in the quality of decision-making.

Diffusion of Innovation

Physical and biological scientists define diffusion as the process by which the particles (molecules or ions) of a substance dissolved in a solvent constitute a state of continuous random movement. They tend to spread from areas of high to low concentration until the concentration is uniform throughout

[37] Preston P. LeBreton, *Planning Theory* (Englewood Cliffs, N.J.: Prentice-Hall, 1961), p. 9.

[38] Warren Bennis *et al., The Planning of Change* (New York: Holt, Rinehart, and Winston, 1961), p. 440.

the solution. Social scientists define diffusion as the process by which cultural innovation—a new idea or practice—spreads from its source of origin, invention, or creation to its ultimate user. Interaction takes place when a person or group communicates ideas to another person or group. Elihu Katz defines diffusion as the process of being concerned with acceptance, over time, of some specific item—an idea or practice, by individuals, groups, or other adopting units, linked to specific channels of communication, to a social structure, and to a given system of values, or culture.[39] Everett Rogers feels that the essence of the diffusion process is the human interaction in which one person communicates a new idea to another. Thus, at its most elemental level, the diffusion process consists of (1) a new idea, (2) individual A who knows about the innovation, and (3) individual B who does not yet know about the innovation. "A major difference between the diffusion process and the adoption process is that diffusion occurs among persons, while adoption is an individual matter." [40]

Adoption of Practices

In contrast to the diffusion process, adoption requires individuals to exert energy, seek information about new ideas, try them out, and start using them. Adoption requires a perception of the potential rewards of a new practice at a higher level than the anticipated efforts required for adoption. Five stages are generally accepted as essential in the adoption process:

1. *Awareness.* A person first learns about a new idea or practice. He has only general information about it.

2. *Interest.* The farmer develops an interest in the new thing he has learned about and wants more detailed information.

3. *Evaluation.* Here, a person weighs the information and evidence accumulated in the previous stages in order to decide whether the idea or practice is basically good for him.

4. *Trial.* The individual is now confronted directly with utilization of the practice on a trial basis. He tries to learn how,

[39] Elihu Katz, "The Social Itinerary of Technological Change: Two Studies on the Diffusion of Innovation," *Human Organization,* 20 (Spring, 1961), 70.

[40] Everett M. Rogers, *Diffusion of Innovation* (New York: Free Press of Glencoe, 1962), pp. 13–14 and 76.

when, where, how much, etc. The usual pattern of trial acceptance is to try a little at first.

5. *Adoption.* Finally, a person decides that the new idea or practice is good enough for full-scale and continued use.[41]

These stages represent a useful way of describing a relatively continuous sequence of actions, events, and influences that intervene between initial knowledge about an idea or practice, and actual application.

Communication [42]

Of all the influences to which people are subjected, the influence of ideas is probably the most important. Man's greatest enslaver has always been ignorance; his greatest emancipator has always been truth, well understood, and wisely acted upon. Hence, the overriding challenge to change agents is to have ideas useful to an audience, to make their meaning clear, to get the ideas accepted, and to motivate people to adopt and practice them.

Successful communication is the process by which two or more people exchange ideas, facts, feelings, or impressions so that each gains a common understanding of the meaning, intent, and use of the messages. In essence, it is the act of getting a sender and a receiver tuned to each other for a particular message or series of messages. Hence, communication is a conscious attempt to share information, ideas, and attitudes with others. For two or more people to engage in a cooperative effort, they must be able to communicate.

Powerful forces tend to slow changes in people's behavior. To overcome these forces, a powerful communication effort must be constantly exerted. The pay-off in agricultural development comes only when people act on new knowledge, not when they merely have been exposed to it. Diffusing technology is a relatively easy task; getting people to understand, accept, and apply it is the difficult one. At this point, skillful communicators are separated from the ineffective ones.

[41] Herbert F. Lionberger, *Adoption of New Ideas and Practices* (Ames: Iowa State University Press, 1964), pp. 22–23.

[42] For a more extensive treatment of the communication process see J. Paul Leagans, "The Communication Process," in *Extension Education in Community Development*, chap. 19, pp. 362–397.

Central to each episode of communication are three basic elements: *expression, interpretation,* and *response.* The quality of these elements is critical in communication. If the expression is unclear, the interpretation inaccurate, and the response inappropriate, one's effort to communicate will not succeed. It is comparatively easy to control the expression or transmission of messages, but difficult to control how an audience interprets and responds to them. Success at this task requires a thorough understanding of five key elements,

1. *Communicator.* A key factor influencing the effectiveness of communication is the person who originates and sends the message. Who is he? What are his motives? What does he know? What are his attitudes and skills? The credibility of a communicator, as perceived by his audience, is a powerful determinant in communication. "His prestige is a major factor in judging credibility, and audience confidence the determinant." [43] The content of a message is made more believable when it is linked with a credible source. A communicator's credibility depends upon two major factors: (1) the extent to which he is perceived to be a source of valid assertions—his technical expertise; and (2) the degree of confidence in the communicator's intent to transmit the assertions which he considers most valid—his trustworthiness.[44] The resultant value is referred to as communicator credibility.

Audience perception of the expertness exhibited by a communicator is influenced by numerous factors. Among these are technical training, experience, age, values, interest, group affiliation, and perception of recipient needs. David Berlo suggests that "there are at least four kinds of factors within the source which can increase fidelity. They are, (a) communication skills, (b) attitudes, (c) knowledge level, and (d) position within a social-cultural system." [45]

[43] J. Paul Leagans, *The Communication Process in Rural Development,* Cornell International Agricultural Development Bulletin No. 1 (Ithaca: New York State College of Agriculture, 1963), p. 10.

[44] Carl I. Havland, Irving L. Janis, and Harold A. Kelley, *Communication and Persuasion* (New Haven: Yale University Press, 1954), p. 21.

[45] David K. Berlo, *The Process of Communication* (New York: Holt, Rinehart, and Winston, 1960), pp. 40–50.

In addition to technical competency, the effects of a message are modified by the attitudes an audience holds toward the communicator, such as feelings of affection, admiration, awe, and fear—based on perception of his power to reward or punish, or on trust and confidence in his knowledge, intelligence, and sincerity. J. H. Campbell and H. W. Hepler found that "the individual is motivated to accept conclusions and recommendations which he anticipates will be substantiated by further experiences, or will lead to reward, social approval and avoidance of punishment. These anticipations are increased when a recommendation is presented by a person who is believed to be informed, insightful, and willing to express his true beliefs and knowledge, and are decreased when cues of low credibility are present." [46] Hence, to develop and maintain an effective level of credibility, change agents need adequate technical knowledge, skill in dealing with people, and proficiency in the educational process. They must demonstrate confidence, humility, persistence, empathy, integrity, and flexibility. The level of the communicators' credibility depends ultimately on their ability to recognize and eliminate behaviors which lower their credibility, and strengthen the behaviors that enhance it.

2. *Message (content)*. A message is the information a communicator wishes his audience to receive, understand, accept, and act upon. Messages may consist of statements of scientific facts, descriptions of actions being taken, reasons why certain actions should be taken, or steps necessary in taking action. Potential messages range as widely as the content of programs. Messages are not, however, the same as the subject matter or technology involved. They are generalized ideas based on the subject matter; for example, "Fertilizer must be used properly to attain maximum results," or "Food combinations are closely related to the quality of nutrition." Subject matter that supports such messages consists of facts and other material assumed by the change agent to justify his propositions. Messages must be clear, significant to the needs and interests of the audience, specific, accurate, timely, and manageable by the communicator and his audience. Messages constitute the relevant cargo to be

46 James H. Campbell and H. W. Hepler, eds., *Dimensions in Communication: Readings* (Belmond, Cal.: Wadsworth, 1965), p. 114.

carried to an audience through the channels of communication.

3. *Channels.* Senders and receivers of messages must be "tuned" to each other. Channels provide the physical bridges between the sender and the receiver of messages—the avenues or media used to transmit messages to and from an audience. A channel may be anything used by a sender of messages to connect him with intended receivers—radio, books, bulletins, letters, newspapers, group meetings, and personal contacts of many kinds are commonly used channels.

4. *Message treatment.* Treatment has to do with the way a message is handled to get the information across to an audience. It relates to the technique—details of procedure or manner of performance essential to expert presentation. It includes the appeals which are used, and the various techniques of writing, speaking, visualizing, or acting. The purpose of good treatment is to make the message clear, understandable, and realistic to the audience. Designing treatment requires knowledge of subject matter, insight into the principles of human behavior, and skill in creating and using refined techniques of presentation. Fuzziness in treatment is sure death to a message. People respond best to messages that are reliable, realistic, relevant, and understandable.

5. *Audience.* An audience is the intended receiver of messages, and also the intended respondent to message-sending. It may consist of one or many people. A communicator must accept an audience as he finds it; he then attempts to move people toward his objective. Audience response to a message usually varies widely in understanding, acceptance, and action. Influencing the desired response through communication is a complicated phenomenon, because success in programs of planned change comes only when people move in desirable directions. Preparing the messages involved in modernizing agriculture and distributing them to millions of farmers in developing countries pose a paramount challenge to change agents and all others included in the process.

Persuasion

Extension education may be viewed as the process of persuading people to repattern their behavior in ways assumed to be advantageous to them. In essence, persuasion is a matter of convincing someone that your point of view is "right" for them. Persuasion requires useful content or subject matter and effective communication. J. H. Worsham believes the essence of persuasion can be stated quite simply: "Individuals (or masses of people) are persuaded through the influence of the things they want. In actual operation this means: Find out what people want (not just need); be in a position to convince them that what you offer will satisfy the want, and place your proposition within their reach." [47] The simplicity of the suggestion disguises the work involved in satisfying the criteria implied.

History suggests that there are two major forms in which persuasion has been applied: Force—administered usually through autocratic means by limiting the number of acceptable behaviors and punishing deviant ones; and education—administered through institutions that promote an understanding of useful knowledge. Numerous factors play a part in determining how successfully persuasion operates. Completeness and flexibility help, as does specificity. Frequency of use lessens the amount of persuasion required. Support from higher authorities usually helps to persuade an audience. It is important that change agents be aware that definite steps can be taken to increase the effectiveness of persuasion, and that many of these factors lie within the range of their control.

Empathy

Empathy is the tendency of a perceiver to assume that another person's feelings, thoughts, and behavior are similar to his own.[48] The theory of empathy rests on the assumption that one's similarity to others forms the foundation of an understanding between them. When a person experiences empathy, he feels as if he were experiencing somebody else's feelings as his own. He sees, feels, responds, and understands, as if he were, in fact, the other person.

The relevance of the empathy concept to change agents lies

[47] J. H. Worsham, *The Art of Persuading People* (New York: Harper and Bros., 1938), p. 8.

[48] H. C. Smith, *Sensitivity to People* (New York: McGraw-Hill, 1966), p. 93.

primarily in the area of understanding their clientele. Change agents having empathy are better able to see needs beyond their clientele's "felt" needs and goals, create settings which enable clients to evaluate the reality of their perceptions of themselves, and give clients help in discovering new ways of acting based on the need for new skills. A change agent with a high degree of empathy is in good position to understand dissonant elements in a program. Similarly, he tends to be realistic in choosing devices for evaluating and modifying the methods he uses to lead his clients in the direction of rejecting the status quo in favor of desired or purposive change.

Even though the empathizing change agent enjoys a superior position because he is a resource whom his clients consult, he must be a humble man to resist the temptations of a position with built-in authority. Both the dimensions and significance of the empathic problem tend to be greater in traditional than in affluent societies. The problem stems largely from physical, social, and psychic propinquity. The empathic gap between farmers and government officials is often of such magnitude that essential program content is not transferred through education from "paper plans" to the minds and actions of farmers.

Satisfaction

To extension educators, the significance of the emotional feeling called "satisfaction" is derived from the fact that individuals tend to persist in a task, no matter how difficult, if they get enough satisfaction from doing so. The first requirement of learning is that the learner be interested in the subject; the last is that the changed behavior be accompanied by a feeling of satisfaction—an emotional response, generally of pleasure, zest, or enjoyment. It is one thing to encourage, induce, persuade, or otherwise cause a farmer to go through the necessary motions of learning about and adopting a new farm practice, but quite another to ensure that he derives satisfaction from his actions and their consequences. An implication of the law of effect is that a neutral tie between the stimulus and the organism is strengthened through a satisfying response. If a farmer's response to a recommendation in a certain situation is satisfactory, then, in a subsequent, similar situation, that same response is likely to be elicited in hopes of further, or greater satisfac-

tion. Continued learning, therefore, depends on the achievement of satisfaction. This fact explains, in part, why adoption
of new farm practices is not always permanent.

Evaluation [49]

In this scientific age, it is considered a mark of professional
indolence to make important decisions on the basis of opinions
when facts are available. Throughout recorded history, man, in
his search for "truth" on which to base his actions, has turned
in general to six primary sources of help: custom and tradition,
religious beliefs, authority, personal experience, reasoning from
apparently self-evident facts, and scientific inquiry. Evidence to
support human behavior, derived from one or more of these six
sources, constitutes man's current basis for decisions about what
to do and how to do it. But the forces of science today have influenced a universal trend toward placing greater emphasis on
the last mentioned source—scientific inquiry. This is because
the others do not seem adequate to cope with today's complex
problems. Acceptance of scientific inquiry as a source of truth
on which to base important actions, and a consequent tendency
to reject the other five, or at least place them in a secondary
position, constitutes one of the most significant current trends
in human thought.

Evaluation is a form of scientific inquiry. It is an effort to
place a true value on the "goodness" or "badness" of educational decisions, and their outcome. Evaluation involves six
major considerations:

1. Objectives of the program or activity.
2. Action taken to reach the objectives and the methods
used.
3. Collection, analysis, and interpretation of valid and reliable evidence (data) showing what happened as the result of
action taken.
4. Comparison of actual and anticipated results.
5. Drawing conclusions from this comparison.
6. Using the findings to guide and improve future action.

Hence, evaluation is an orderly and scientific way of pro-

[49] For an extensive treatment of the evaluation process applied to
extension education see *Evaluation in Extension,* Darcie Byrn, ed.
(Topeka, Kansas: H. M. Ives and Sons, 1959), pp. 1–106.

ceeding, in order to find out the kind of changes that result from extension programs, and to identify ways to strengthen both the content and the methods. An educational activity can be strengthened only through a process of discovering its weak points, and executing procedures to correct them. Consequently, it becomes necessary to evaluate the means used to promote educational change as well as the results obtained. To improve the ends requires modification of the means in any process of change. Evaluation, therefore, should be viewed by change agents as a integral part of the extension education process.

Concluding Statement

One of the basic premises of this chapter is that an effective extension education system is one of the requisites—but only one—of agricultural modernization. The central role of an extension system is to focus on the transactions between man and his environment in ways that improve the quality of these transactions. In this task, its specific role is to "orchestrate" physical, biological, technological, economic, social, and political resources so as to reduce dissonance between the status quo and desirable new economic and social conditions. A significant gap always tends to exist between what is already known and its widespread use in actual practice. For this gap as related to agricultural modernization to be narrowed by this generation of farmers, the educational input must focus on adults, for it is they who now are, and for some time will be, the final decision makers.

Effective extension education enhances development of the capacities of component human systems including farmers, agricultural specialists, and administrators by interpreting essential, relevant information which makes possible the growth and development of the agricultural system. Consequently, persistent attempts to promote change resulting in modernization will be the agriculturists' highest task during the next decade in the countries of the world concerned with modernizing their agricultural systems. In these attempts, effective extension education can be one of their important tools. Scientists and educators alike, therefore, need increasingly to work at the art of breaking agricultural production bottlenecks, because this is requisite to improving human welfare for two-thirds of the

world's people. Overall, developments in the agricultural enterprise will increase as useful technology, production requisites,
and extension educational forces are made effective in reducing
defenders of the status quo and increasing active advocates of
progressive change.

Response

JOSEPH L. MATTHEWS

J. Paul Leagans in Chapter 5 has advanced the theme that extension education is basic to any successful national effort of agricultural and rural growth in developing nations. Every country needs a viable and effective extension service as an integral part of its agricultural and rural development system,[1] an institution with the function of disseminating technology and seeing that it is applied for the improvement of the life of the cultivator of the land and his family. The emphasis is on the function of obtaining the desired changes in agricultural production and rural living, regardless of the name.

Since the early 1950's there has been a general lack of appreciation for and a neglect of the extension role and its potential contributions by the United States and foreign governments.[2] To a lesser degree the same may be said of the U.S. educational institutions involved in agricultural and educational development overseas.

An AID–land-grant university report indicated that extension achieved less in developing nations than was accomplished by research or academic teaching.[3] It was found that in too many cases attempts were made to impose the U.S. form of

[1] *The World Food Problem: A Report of the President's Science Advisory Committee,* Volume II, *Report of the Panel on World Food Supply* (The White House: May, 1967), p. 600.

[2] Albert H. Moseman, *Building Agricultural Research Systems in the Developing Nations* (New York: The Agricultural Development Council), p. 71.

[3] *Building Institutions to Serve Agriculture: A Summary Report of the Committee on Institutional Cooperation* (Lafayette, Indiana: Agency for International Development, Rural Development Research Project, Purdue University, 1968), pp. 57–58.

extension upon the foreign university for which a U.S. institution had a contract with AID. Sometimes a new institution was established in competition with an existing one.[4]

Six important generalizations are stated in the report regarding ways in which attempts to develop extension service overseas have been inadequate. All are relevant and could be detailed further by naming specific defects. Others could be added, for example, the support and assistance to the developing country extension services themselves have been at times inappropriate and intermittent. Usually assistance has been provided at the national level only, when it was needed at the farmer level and also at intermediate levels.

The United States extension system was slow to develop even in an environment that has more of the needed inputs than are usually available in developing countries. Yet, assistance from the United States has been broken by frequent staff changes and time periods during which assistance was unavailable. The "continuity" concept is significant here. Possibly a limited-role concept for the United States advisory staff held by our own country and by recipient country governments has affected their performance.

It should be recognized that success in agricultural development may be practically impossible at certain times in a particular developing country because of cultural, economic, political, or other prevailing situations. It may be the strength of the forces opposing change, the unavailability of the resources needed for the extension effort, or it may be lack of other inputs that are required for success.

Generally nations function with limited resources and competition for priority by many national needs and goals. Consequently, agriculture in a country, regardless of its priority, because of limited national resources and the magnitude of the need cannot reasonably be expected to have enough money, professional manpower, and other needed inputs. The situation calls for decisions regarding the allocation of available resources. For the extension service, a major decision should be the scale of organization and operation. The first choice is likely to be a nation-wide extension organization and programs with resources too limited for competent staff and other requisites to

[4] *Ibid.,* p. 58.

be effective. An alternative may be to reduce the size of area to one that insures success with the available resources.

Few, if any, developing countries can adequately support more than one effective nation-wide field organization. When there is more than one field organization with extension functions, it may be advisable to consolidate all field staff into a single organization for all field programs. Effective in-service training and adequate support for the single field staff should make it possible for the organization to provide most of the field programs usually found in developing countries. For example, the organization could perform extension services for crops, livestock, food and crop production, health education, family planning, home improvement, youth programs, and agricultural credit, if it were given the needed technical support, staff training, and cooperation of the appropriate national ministries. Combining educational and regulatory functions should be avoided.

When it is found that the necessary inputs other than extension are not present and not in prospect, the wise course may be not to attempt an extension program for a whole country. It may be better to have an area agricultural development effort, even a small one with the needed resources and inputs, rather than an unsuccessful national one.

The current emphasis on agricultural modernization and increased production in the developing countries may suggest to uninformed persons that the major or only role of an extension service in a developing country is to increase agricultural production. Yet historically, both here and abroad, the scope of extension programs has known no such limitations. Typically it has included programs for the homemaker and youth and dealt with many facets of rural living. Leadership development and helping people organize for self-help programs has had a prominent place. In view of the magnitude of the problem, family planning education could complement the usual child rearing and family feeding programs.

The role of extension in adaptive research is not listed among the variables. The term "adaptive research" is used here in the sense that Mosher uses "local verification trials" in writing about the farming district.[5] Routinely in the United States and in

5 A. T. Mosher, *Creating a Progressive Rural Structure to Serve Modern Agriculture* (New York: Agricultural Development Council), pp. 6–7.

many foreign extension programs, field demonstrations have been a basic extension teaching method supplemented by other means of reaching the farmer and his family. The label "test demonstration" is used for practical field demonstrations to show the potential of improved varieties and new crops along with new cultural practices. It is not only an effective teaching method, but also an important way of supplementing in-country research to quickly prove the local adaptability and worth of imported crop and methods. Methods and result demonstrations have been proven the most effective in motivating and teaching farmers how to use new crops, and have proven useful as tools for diffusion, communication, and gaining adoption of new ideas among farmers.

The Report of the President's Science Advisory Committee in regard to the world food problem gives two major reasons for the disappointing results of extension programs in this area: insufficient numbers of well-trained extension personnel and ineffective means of communicating with and motivating the people.[6]

When an extension service is examined or evaluated out of the context of the setting in which it operates and the results expected of it, there is danger that the judgments about it will be invalid and unfair.[7] Clearly some of the negative judgments expressed about extension service overseas are of this character and not infrequently are made by persons who are ill-informed about the country or the local situation. In addition, they may be poorly informed about the basic extension role, functions, and requirements for success. The true test of an extension service is not in terms of the American or some other country's model, but rather how well its organization and processes are geared to obtain the desired results over a period of time.

Writing for foreign readers who may be in a position to influence their own extension service can be hazardous. The writer cannot anticipate every eventuality in terms of the practical in-country conditions, nor can he guard against the misinterpretations that stem from the foreign, social, political, and economic orientation. The problem of accurately conveying a proper understanding that can be implemented in extension organization and processes is not unique to extension written

[6] *World Food Problem,* p. 621.
[7] *Building Institutions,* pp. 144–145.

materials. There is ample evidence of widespread failure to communicate to key offiicials the fundamental ideas and essential requirements for successful extension teaching. Reading all that is written about the extension service does not necessarily result in fully understanding it. This in part is because understanding extension is more of a maturing than a communicating process. The key is gaining insight that comes from observing and experiencing, particularly with respect to what must happen at the level where the extension worker is in contact with the farmer or members of his family.

Understanding the extension service must include the concept of program: its processes, its significance, and its functions. An effective program is the essence of extension; without it, the rest becomes unimportant. This concept without involvement and experience with it is difficult to communicate, to observe, and to evaluate, because it consists of planned and organized action over years to achieve certain predetermined ends. A program progresses through a sequence of stages from initiation to achievement of the desired results. At any given stage of a program, there is little to observe that will help with assessing its worth. Continual observations made through several of the stages can convey a sense of the rate of progress. However, fully dependable and accurate assessment likely will require collection of information for the full program cycle.

Termination of projects after a few years, before the institution-building task is finished, has been a factor in lack of success of some foreign assistance efforts. Projects were often initiated without adequate planning for the role of the host institution. A minimum of eight to ten years of sustained assistance may be required for a host institution to achieve a level of maturity that will enable it to have a major role in increasing agricultural production.[8]

Leagans has covered a great deal of material about extension education, and what he has written is useful. However, it will likely raise more questions for many readers than it will answer. The reader with little background and experience with extension conditions may be impressed with the complexity of the subject. Writing a comprehensive piece on a complex subject under severe space limitations makes it difficult to clarify ideas

[8] *Ibid.*, p. 53.

without specific examples to convey practical meanings for the reader.

Assessing the performance of the extension service from written reports of programs and staff activities is not very fruitful. Likewise, occasional visitations to the field staff and field locations for brief periods and talking with local extension workers, except on a continuing basis and by experienced and understanding persons, can be misleading. Often in places overseas where extension service performance is poorest, it is common for staff members to speak glibly with apparent familiarity and understanding of all aspects of extension work.

It may have been a mistake to translate into foreign languages the materials about the extension service written for U.S. consumption. However, there is no question that materials prepared from the basic ideas and principles of extension, adapted and written especially for use in the developing nations, have been helpful to government officials and extension personnel alike. The ideal way of instruction is showing and providing successful supervised experience in their own land under practical conditions.

Some persons, Americans included, do not understand that special professional preparation is required for an individual to succeed in extension work. To assume that all agriculturally trained persons can be successful extension workers in this country or overseas is incorrect. Meeting the stated criteria of personal characteristics and professional preparation does not guarantee success—the proof is in demonstrated ability to lead others to improve.

As agriculture has become more scientific and complex, and as the complexity of rural life has increased in the United States, extension services and staff members have to use more sophisticated ways of thinking about the extension service as an institution, its functions, and about the job of the extension worker. Today the extension professional with only technical preparation in agriculture is severely limited in trying to meet the demands of his work with farmers. The same is true of the person with only preparation in extension education and related subjects.

Before World War II, the land-grant institutions began offering summer school and graduate courses in extension education and the behavioral sciences to supplement the technical education that most extension staff members brought to the job. Now about twenty-five universities offer graduate courses or a degree program for extension personnel. The problem of limited time for advanced study conflicts with increasing numbers of courses in both technical subjects and the social sciences. Both are considered appropriate areas of study in the education and training of extension service professional staff, but the decision must be made how much of one or the other is needed in the preparation of a particular individual.

This situation led the professors of extension education to seek a new way of getting at the essential knowledge and reducing duplication and nonessentials in existing graduate courses and curriculums for extension workers. It was decided that concepts offered a practical way of identifying what is relevant. At the same time, they could provide a means of organizing and integrating knowledge from the variety of disciplines and fields of study that could contribute to the preparation of an adequately educated and trained extension professional. The professors concluded that concepts can serve as the basic content and organizing elements of extension education for much of the technology and for the behavioral sciences subject matter.

In the beginning, agricultural colleges were oriented primarily toward preparation for farming. Practical farming experience was then considered an essential part of the agricultural graduate's background. Later, a vocational emphasis was retained while the employment objective became more professional and scientific, leading to a career in a broad range of occupational areas.[9] Practical farming experience or a farm background came to be valued less with time until today it is not considered a necessary part of the equipment of the agricultural graduate.

In many jobs overseas, practical farming experience is about as important as it ever was in this country. In fact, the more primitive the agriculture, the more important it is to have first-hand practical farming experience. The agricultural staff in the developing nations tends to come from the towns and cities where the educational facilities and resources are superior to the

[9] "Trends and Issues in Education in the Agricultural Services," *Bio. Science,* vol. 15, no. 11 (November, 1965).

rural areas. As a result, relatively small numbers have any practical farming experience or understanding of rural life. And furthermore, the agricultural schools and colleges seem to do little to remedy this deficiency.

The concept of change is basic to the whole realm of extension and agricultural development. Yet we know that in many parts of the world the belief that man can control his own destiny has little acceptance. Promoting the idea that man can influence his environment may necessarily be a part of early extension efforts in motivating people to move toward agricultural development.

Leagans writes of the difficult process of converting new agricultural technology in behavioral change. Today the demand is for men and women who can bridge the gap between the source of the appropriate technical knowledge and its application in the field of the farmers. This talent is relatively more scarce than technical competence.

The time requirement for accomplishing changes in production practices among leaders is properly included as part of the extension service function. In this role, the extension worker functions as thinker and planner and as teacher and motivator, combining these roles in whatever way the situation requires.

Mosher, in writing about the role of the agricultural extension agent, comments on misunderstandings of the agent's role by research workers and by teachers of academic extension education courses.[10] He points out that the functions of taking "research results to the farmer" and "teaching" are both only partially correct. He goes on to enumerate some of the organizing and expediting functions that are legitimate tasks as they historically have been in this country when there are not other technicians or agencies to perform them.

A basic assumption is that successful agricultural development involves behavioral changes by many different kinds of people in a given country. In accepting this idea, we are saying that achieving behavioral change is a basic function of agricultural development. Changing behavior is certainly the business of agricultural extension.

Institutional development is an assumed objective of agricultural development. This is important because the indigenous institutions that persist and function effectively after the devel-

[10] Mosher, pp. 8–9.

opment efforts from the outside are terminated must become the forces to guide future agricultural development. Thus, developing viable and effective extension services is an important part of agricultural development.

The macro concepts discussed by Leagans are useful in planning and studying the strategies and processes of international agricultural development. Just as they are basic to development, they are no less relevant to agricultural extension when it is considered alone. Clearly, these must be understood by those responsible for development efforts in a country, and attention must be paid to the organization and implementation of development programs.

Modern education borrows from a variety of disciplines for its content and processes. Extension education does the same, drawing more heavily on the behavioral science than many formal education programs. In addition, in practicing the profession, extension persons draw heavily on the biological sciences and basic agricultural research. The range of highly relevant concepts from the various disciplines and the relevant fields of study are many, and Leagans has performed a useful service in identifying and discussing the concepts that are relevant to extension in a total agricultural development effort.

The interdisciplinary character of extension education poses problems for the teacher of courses in agricultural development, for the agencies and institutions involved in agricultural development, and for the field workers actually engaged in agricultural development overseas. The question is: What knowledge and skills are of the most use under practical agricultural development situations? It would be desirable to synthesize the required knowledge and skills into a package that could be made available in useful form to both students in the classroom and practical operators in international agricultural development.

Among the failure and success factors, trained staff is listed as an essential requisite for successful extension education. Meeting this need requires basic preparation in agriculture and extension plus continual in-service training to keep the staff up-to-date in subject matter and to prepare them to work effectively with new programs.

Staff training is second only to good program planning in preparing for effective extension work. Even the best basic education and preservice training does not reduce the importance of receiving the new subject matter and methods instruction in preparation for working with the farmer. For example, introduction of the new high-yielding crop varieties of rice, corn, and wheat calls for the extension worker to learn some new cultural practices and techniques for demonstrating and teaching the farmers how to grow them. The higher the yield potential of the crop, the greater the risk of loss through neglect of a single important production practice.

There are insufficient numbers of well-trained extension personnel and lack of effective means of communicating with and motivating the producers. This could be at least partially corrected by appropriate in-service types of training for conducting specific food production programs. This problem can be generalized to other crop and livestock programs. Training of the supervisory and local staff members for an entire country or a sizeable area within the country can be a major part of the solution. Part of the solution is to teach staff members practical skills that can be imparted to the producers of the crop. Personal observations indicate that often this need is not appreciated and met by a national extension service.

Leagans writes of the farmer and of the family—the audience. Presumably, the farmer is the individual who can put to practical use what extension brings to him in his roles as a cultivator of the land, a manager of a farming enterprise, a landowner or tenant, or the head of a rural family. Depending on the family role, each individual must be reached in a different way with particular technology adapted to his situation. Family includes the wife, the mother, the homemaker, a female member of the family labor force and usually a decision-maker—sometimes the most important individual in the particular family. Children and extended family members are part of the labor force, a noncontributing consumer, or both. An extension service goal is to have every capable member an effective contributor to the family welfare.

Criteria for evaluation of extension education are included in the rural development research project of the Committee on Institutional Cooperation.[11] Five general criteria are stated:

[11] *Building Institutions,* pp. 124–125.

(1) the concept of role and function of extension; (2) identification of priority activities with the country's needs; (3) coordination of activities with other public and private agencies; (4) efforts to accommodate the system to local environment; and (5) use of modern methods of communication and motivation. These criteria are intended to measure institutional progress and maturity.

To the above should be added the degree to which extension goals are consistent with identified priorities and changes by the people reflect extension efforts to achieve predetermined goals. This is the ultimate test of extension service effectiveness.

Synthesis Response to
Cummings and Leagans

D. WOODS THOMAS

J. Paul Leagans undertook the rather monumental task of presenting the fundamental concepts of extension education and the strategy implications of these concepts for behavioral change in the context of international agricultural development. He has done a remarkable job of laying out the basic concepts of extension education ranging from those of a philosophical nature to those of a pragmatic and operational nature. He has condensed into one chapter much of what is known or believed about extension education as an art and a science.

Ralph Cummings treated the concepts of agricultural technology and their strategy implications for behavioral change in international agricultural development. He has effectively and emphatically utilized the most outstanding examples of the role of science and technology in increasing agricultural output.

Leagans and Cummings start from widely differing points on the spectrum of developmental change. It is interesting and comforting to note that they arrive at essentially the same destination and appear to be in complete accord. On the one hand, Leagans builds his case around the general thesis that an effective system of adult or extension education for farm decision makers is a prime input to the modernization of agriculture and that useful technical information provided by agricultural science is the essential grist of this specialized educational input. Dr. Cummings, on the other hand, builds his case on the premise that a prime input for the modernization of agriculture is useful technical information provided by an adequate scientific base and implies a specialized educational system directed at farm decision makers as the essential vehicle for the utilization of the scientific input. Both admit, explicitly, that there are other sets of variables important to agricultural development which they understandably assume away for purposes of their analyses and presentations.

There are several additional points relevant to the relationships among international agricultural development, extension education, and agricultural science worthy and deserving of consideration. Equally, there are several additional strategy implications for behavioral change, which follow, in corollary fashion, these points.

Both authors concentrated their attention on behavioral change at the primary production level. Behavior on the part of farm decision makers as it might affect the level of agricultural output was emphasized, explicitly or implicitly, in both cases. To avoid too narrow a range of discussion, let us recognize at this point that agricultural development and increased agricultural production are *not* synonymous. Let us also recognize that change in the behavior of farmers alone will not guarantee agricultural development.

In the first instance, agricultural development is concerned with the evolvement of the economic sector which will be viable through time and *responsibly responsive* to the demands of the ever-changing economic and social system of which it is a part. To be sure, the efficient production of food for domestic consumption is an important part of the total contribution of agriculture to the improved welfare of a nation. It is, however, only a part. Consideration must also be given to the ability of the agricultural sector to provide capital to the industrial and public sectors, to contribute to a nation's foreign exchange earnings, to contribute to the expansion of domestic demand for the goods and services of the industrial sector and to provide human resources to the industrial, commercial, and public sectors as demanded and required.

In the second instance, it is clear that farmer decision-making and behavior relative to the most desirable set of production and consumption alternatives is relevant and important. It is equally clear that the range of choice available to the farmer is restricted by decisions and behavior of individuals and institutions in both the public and the private, nonfarm sector. This tends to be of critical importance in situations where agricultural development is to be stimulated by overt actions on the part of indigenous public institutions and by outside agencies and organizations.

From the first of the above points follow considerations of import to the conceptualization of the contributions of science, in general, and agricultural science, in particular, to agricultural development. First, it is doubtful if research directed solely or primarily toward the technical production problems of primary producers can provide the "mix" of useful scientific knowledge required for rational and "right" decisions in the broad complex of development. In the simplest of cases, conceptual and empirical analyses of production problems require not only technical production information but also appropriate information on prices of products, prices of factors, the behavior of relevant institutions and people, and about such things as the vagaries of the weather. In the most complex of cases involving the whole range of problems inherent in the broadly and properly conceived process of agricultural development, these same kinds of information tend to be required about all aspects of this process where either private or public decision and action are called for. This, coupled with the facts that (a) little is known about any of these sets of variables, and (b) such information can be produced only through systematic, scientific inquiry, suggests that the necessary role of science in agricultural development and sustained growth is far broader than one of concentration on farm-level, technical production problems.

Second, under this broader conceptualization, there are three fundamental issues that must be resolved if science is to contribute the maximum to international agricultural development. In question form, these issues become:

1. What constitutes the optimum *rate* and *form* of investment in such scientific inquiry?

2. What constitutes the "least-cost" system of *organizing* these research resources?

3. What *set of strategies* will maximize the chances of attaining the optimum rate, form, and organization of research investment?

None of the above questions is associated with a simple answer; it is probable that highly accurate quantitative answers are neither attainable nor necessary. It does appear essential, however, that this set of questions be considered as systematically and objectively as possible by all in position to influence the course of future scientific events. This includes national, international, public, and private entities. The point is that investment funds, both public and private, are scarce. These scarce resources have alternative uses. There are numerous possible patterns of investment in research—in quantity, form, and organization. Each such pattern will have a different impact on the rate of agricultural development. The objective is to have a society choose the particular pattern that will most nearly maximize the impact of science on agricultural development. In a development context, the operational question is one of devising a set of strategies which will assure the attainment of this objective.

At this point, let us return to my earlier contention that concentration of attention on farm-level decisions and behavior unduly restricts the range of relevant discussion. Here, it might be argued that such concentration tends to assume that all other factors affecting agricultural development are in place and nonlimiting. Reality in the less developed world, of course, rejects this assumption. Rather, societies in which agriculture has failed to contribute in optimum fashion to the development of the society tend to be characterized by multiple, nonfarm imperfections which constitute significant restraints to agricultural progress. I refer to such things as political instability and irrationality, imperfections in the agricultural infrastructure including the research and educational systems, imperfections in the product markets and in the factor markets, negative or neutral public policies and programs. Where such impediments exist, the question becomes one of identifying the means by which they might be removed as barriers to progress in the rural sector.

Here, I would argue, the most promising avenue to "right" decisions and appropriate behavior turns out to be the same as in the case of farm-level decisions and behavior. This is the *educational process* directed at this particular order of problems and at the responsible sets of individuals within the society. One might hypothesize, with some degree of logic, that pay-offs from this type of extension education in the developing societies would be greater over a significant range than would be the pay-offs from similar efforts directed at the farm decision maker.

In approaching such issues, however, extension education appears to encounter, both at home and abroad, a series of difficulties that it does not encounter when operating at the micro, farm, decision-making level. There are multiple reasons for this. Among these reasons is the fact that relevant and important problems at the micro, nonfarm level as well as at the macro, private, quasi-public and public levels tend to be far more complex than at the primary production level. Information about "what is" may not exist or may be highly controversial. Concepts of "what ought to be" may vary in the extreme. Consequently, problem identification and conceptualization become most difficult. Equally, the body of theory explaining much of this type of behavior tends to be less well developed than at the farm level; hence, there are fewer guides to educators in providing decision makers with a relevant analytical model, with data of the kind and form to make the model operational and with appropriate criteria for decision-making and subsequent action. Further, identification of the individual decision maker of the decision-making body in these situations is not always easy. Finally, strategies appropriate and useful to the promotion of improved behavior at the farm production and consumption level may be neither appropriate nor useful in this realm.

It is my impression that the theory and practice of extension education, having evolved largely out of the United States agricultural experience, is not particularly well equipped to handle this order of problem. If I am correct in this assertion and in my observation that nonfarm individual and institutional behavioral change are important to international agricultural development, then a fertile area for systematic investigation by the behavioral sciences, including extension education, is identified.

The field of inquiry embracing the phenomenon of strategic human behavior is an evolving one. Equally, it is one that many of us involved in agricultural development have failed to give as much attention as might be useful. For the sake of clarity, then, permit me to specify the context in which the term *strategy* is used in what follows. Here, strategy is conceived as an objective pattern of action and/or nonaction on the part of one entity designed to bring about some predetermined pattern of behavior on the part of another. For our purposes, the entities may be individuals or they may be organized groups of individuals functioning as a decision-making and action-taking unit.

In this context, there are several types of strategy situations of relevance to international agricultural development. The following classification suggests itself:

1. Interpersonal strategies
2. Individual to institution strategies
3. Institution to institution strategies

The first of these, interpersonal strategies, is of the one-to-one type in which an individual follows a behavior pattern designed to produce a specific, changed behavior pattern of another. In the present context, this is exemplified by the extension agent/farm decision maker relationship. In the agricultural development milieu, however, it is not limited to this classical pair. It may pertain at all levels where change in individual behavior is essential to removal of barriers to agricultural progress.

The individual to institution strategy situation is one in which an individual follows a behavior pattern with the objective of bringing about specific changes in the "behavior" of some institutional entity. This might be exemplified by the individual faced with the proposition of bringing about essential change in the structure, organization, philosophy, and program of, say, a school of agriculture, a ministry of agriculture, or an agricultural planning agency. Agricultural development activity is replete with such situations.

The institution to institution type of strategic situation is that in which one organization develops and follows a course of action or pattern of behavior designed to bring about a desired, and hopefully desirable, change in the behavior of another. International agricultural development experience provides a wealth of examples: government to government aspects of technical assistance, institutional development through university to university relationships, foundation to university programs.

The point of all this, coupled with my earlier contention that change of both individual and aggregate character "beyond the farm gate" is essential to the development and sustained growth of agriculture, is that interpersonal strategies alone do not constitute a set of operational tools adequate to the task of modernizing the agricultural world. We must, I think, pay specific attention to this matter.

It is difficult but not impossible to diagnose the ills of an ailing agriculture. It is possible to specify a set of treatments that will materially improve the situation. The really difficult, time-consuming and frustrating problems tend to arise in attaining implementation of the treatments. I submit that one important source of this difficulty rests in the paucity of theory and principle applicable to the three types of strategy situations identified above.

PART III

THE ECONOMY AND THE POLITY

EDITORS' INTRODUCTION

If the change agent–change target system model for directed change were to be cast in rigorous terms developed in the fields of economics and administrative science, it would come to its own in Part III. Actually, the model may be used with computers to simulate action as it transpires in games or in bargaining, in marketing, in terms of cost-benefit analysis, and in other ways. Both Kenneth Parsons and Frederick Frey think in system terms.

In terms of our change agent–change target system model Parsons' most insightful and historically based message runs somewhat as follows: In accordance with principles acceptable to nontotalitarian societies, nothing is so important for agricultural development as freedom of choice for farmers and others. "The basic and central problem . . . [is that] of system creation and . . . making operative the powers of the state in the release of energy in the economy." Of course, this means that if the government is considered the change agent and the economy the change target, certain norms and goals must be laid out. The actors of the change agent system must endeavor to establish means whereby the actors in the target system conduct their own behavior in terms of their needs and wishes. This is harmonious with making "the primary objective of agricultural development policy . . . the achievement of a system of agricultural economy which has the capacity to carry the burdens of development." Parsons notes that "traditional systems of agriculture . . . lack the capacity for growth."

Crucial to Parsons' approach is the assumption that farmers and others act "rationally." "The term rationality is therefore a 'personification' of acts of choice"—in a free-choice system. Parsons and most of his economist colleagues maintain that even within the institutional framework of traditional agriculture the farmer and peasant are, in general, rational and make choices in such a manner that scarce resources are "economized." Central to his argument is the belief that "great mischief has been done" by those change agents who maintain that neoclassical advanced economics is pertinent only to the commercial segment of traditional societies and not to the peasants and farmers engaged in subsistence agriculture. He would maintain that the effective linkage of commercial as well as subsistence farmers to the economy and to the polity must be activated and may be analyzed in terms of inputs and outputs whereby even the marginal product of labor in the overpopulated areas is "efficient but poor." Parsons has mentioned elsewhere the supervised loan procedure discussed earlier; this he would favor as supporting freedom of choice. By the same token he would condemn the military government or any other totalitarian model for achieving agricultural development.

The discussant of Parsons' chapter, Chandler Morse, and a later discussant and summarizer, James Heaphey, raised problems pertinent to the reasoning presented by Parsons and his desire for "order without restraint" so that free choice and free markets would prevail. Morse sees disorder and violence preceding the establishment of order in developing countries. Heaphey sees control as necessarily a part of order. Reminiscent of the arguments of Talcott Parsons and others, he maintains that decentralization to get freedom of choice and free markets requires value consensus on the part of the citizens. Somehow, the balance of relation between the polity and the economy must take care of this so-called "Hobbsean problem." If powerholders are interested only in personal gain and function as traders, how do you control the gangsters in terms of our model? For either the change agent system or the change target system, there must be agreement on some norms or many policemen will be needed to make freedom of choice possible.

The second major author of Part III, Frederick Frey, although he does not use the terms of the change agent–change target system, presents his materials and develops his research out of a tradition especially congenial to this model. As a social scientist specializing in the study of power and administration, Frey's focus is upon what we have called systemic linkage. He feels that most administration problems can ultimately be traced to a breakdown in one of the fundamental linkages which come into being when intermediaries play important roles between the rulers and the ruled. Frey's whole presentation so well fits the model as we have tried to develop it that it is not necessary to proceed further in emphasizing this relationship. The reader interested in the linkage of government to the people or of governmental change agents to the people will profit from his chapter. Such relationships as those between the government of traditional India and the people are typed by Frey as exploitative. When exploitation is overcome and agricultural development is being attempted by governmental change agents, feedback administration may result. He, like Deutsch, stresses the importance of an excellent communication system between field and center, and further notes that one of the problems of developing societies is simply that the necessary linkages "aren't there to accomplish the task which they have set themselves." He has elsewhere made short shrift of those who make an end of what they call "democracy." "I don't want the airplane on which I am flying to be run in a democratic way. . . . I do want . . . the political science department . . . [in which I work] to be run in a democratic way."

In broad system terms as he considers the effectiveness of change agents in getting through their messages and efforts to transform the change targets, Frey tentatively concludes that, in general, interaction (and/or empathy) between change agent and change target, as emphasized by Daniel Lerner in *The Passing of Traditional Society,* is of crucial importance. It is more important, he believes, than special mental components such as achievement orientation emphasized by Harry Triandis in Part V and David McClelland in *The Achieving Society.* Placing this thinking in our context, it would read as follows: The more actors in the change target system are exposed to the potentials of change through "diversity of experience," the greater the change. A change agent should get members of the target system "exposed" to such potentials. A somewhat parallel situation is the casino owner hoping the gambler gets "hooked" on a number of wins before the losses start occurring.

Speaking in terms appropriate to our change agent–change target model, John Montgomery said he would like to discuss "the social scientist as change agent." He noted that Americans, as they become change agents abroad, frequently fail to realize that the actors in the change targets abroad are not American; their values and infrastructure are different. However, it is not only American change agents abroad who fail in this. He notes, "Some governments hear the voice of the peasant in the paddy and others don't." Agreeing with Frey that contact and availability of change is important, he observes that the influence of the rural free delivery on the innovational attitudes of farmers in America may have been as great as that of the agricultural extension agents. Siding with Parsons, he notes that "the essential problem in development administration . . . is finding ways of releasing social and individual energies without excessive application of the government." In terms of the change agent–change target model, Montgomery seems to be advocating that a change agent in governmental service should work himself out of a job.

Jayant Lele agreed with John Montgomery that in many instances functions of development should be moved from old-line civil services to development ministries to avoid the reputation of past exploitation prevalent in the traditional civil service mentality in traditional society. Lele stresses the fact that very often administrative agencies were burdened with various regulatory duties. The change agent who must check up on and punish actors in the change target for violating agency or societal norms may find it difficult to perform the educative function. Thus, Lele notes that change agents who are civil servants imbued with the tradition whereby rules are enforced by applying sanctions and collecting taxes may make poor development officials.

6. Agricultural Economics

KENNETH H. PARSONS

An attempt to identify key concepts in agricultural economics and to consider their relevance for a strategy of behavioral change in less developed countries requires a selective consideration of the ideational structure and orientation of the discipline of agricultural economics as it has developed in the Western world.

General Terms of Reference

Economics as a professional discipline comes to a focus upon what we call the provision of the material and service bases of civilization, or the task of making a living. Although the definitional base may be more rigorous, as the science of economizing of scarce resources, we will accept more general terms of reference for our purposes. One of the stark facts about the agriculture of truly underdeveloped areas is the nearness of the people to hunger and the hazards of nature. What we call subsistence economies are also brute survival systems.

In developed countries agricultural economics is everywhere considered to be an integral part of the more comprehensive "general" economics. This is as true in the Marxian-communist–oriented systems as in the market economies of the Western world.

As agricultural economists move out from this modern base, either intellectually or physically, and consider the problems of agricultural economics in the truly underdeveloped areas, we find the proportions between the agricultural part of the economy and the rest of the economy to be quite different and even reversed. In effect, agricultural economics becomes the general economics in the initial stages of truly underdeveloped areas.

Economics, from the early days of political economy down to the present, has had a basic policy orientation. In a free-choice society this means that economics as related to policy analysis is basically a volitional science, attempting to understand and improve the choices or decisions of key participants in the economic system. Since policies are by their very nature attempts to create, sustain, or modify a functioning system or concern of some sort, economics in the general formulations always honors some kind of a part-whole concept, whether we call it proportionality, allocation of resources, stabilization, or growth.

We have noted above that economic analysis always runs in terms of a system. This practice has at least two interrelated explanations: (1) Any modern economy, any economy which takes advantage of, or exploits the potentials of specialization, division of labor, investment, etc., is a highly interdependent system of human association; and (2) to understand any part, we must have a fairly clear idea of the whole. As Alfred North Whitehead observed thirty years ago: "Our progress in clarity of knowledge is primarily from the composition to the ingredients. The very meaning of the notion of definition is the use of composition for the purpose of indication." [1] This is a root explanation of the intellectual productivity of economic theory.

Over the two centuries of professional specialization in economics, the economists of the western world (i.e., the non-Marxian economists) have gradually achieved an interpretation of the nature of an economic system in terms of functions and interrelations. Thus when economists visualize a system of economy, they see a system in which participants function as entrepreneurs, investors, laborers, managers, producers, and consumers, through households, firms, and markets. So formulated, many of the sets of interrelationships became amenable to mathematical formulation and manipulation, in terms of coefficients of elasticity, maxima, minima, and, in recent years, input-output matrices, linear programming, and operational research. It is to be noted, however, that this emphasis is selective, in that the economy as a system of human relations is usually at the periphery of the analysis, essentially treated as a datum, or if recognized to be problematical, as being the concern of political science, sociology, or law.

[1] "Harvard: The Future," *Atlantic Monthly*, 158 (Sept., 1936), 260, 263.

We are here trying only to suggest something of the intellectual climate and professional matrix within which agricultural economists in the United States are now working. In terms of the analytical emphases within this general framework of economics, we need note only that agricultural economists who are working at the frontier of the modernization process in commercial agriculture are concentrating on such aspects as the impact of a dynamic technology, of capital intensification, of large-scale integrations—both vertical and horizontal, and even computerized farm accounting systems.

Underdeveloped Agricultural Economies

Agricultural economics as a field of professional specialization is a product of modern economies. There was little emphasis on agricultural economics in the United States prior to this century. By this time, many of the issues which are now confronted in agricultural development of the less developed world were behind us. By 1900, we had a nation-state of continental dimensions, crisscrossed by thousands of miles of railroads. The public domain of agricultural potential was mostly settled, held under clearly defined property relations; our agriculture was tied into systems of national and international markets; the farmers had used their power as citizens to bring about regulations of railroads and warehouses as aspects of the general drive to make the marketing processes more equitable; steel-based manufacturing industries were well established, facilitating greatly the mechanization of agriculture in an economy in which labor was scarce. Our vast system of public education was already well established.

By the end of World War II, after which American agricultural economists were drawn in increasing numbers into the consideration of the agricultural development problems of underdeveloped areas, the modernization process in American agriculture was proceeding at an unprecedented rate. In sum, American economists of all sorts, including agricultural economists, approach the problems of the underdeveloped world with views articulated by interpretations of a complex, modern economic system.

Almost all of the economies of the underdeveloped world are mainly agricultural (the major exception being those in which mineral extraction has become dominant). Futhermore, the agriculture is mostly of a traditional subsistence type, that is, the agricultural system is mostly of the ecological sort, reflecting adaptations to nature. These traditional subsistence economies are basically the kind of survival economies which a people have worked out without benefit of modern science and technology, using homemade tools, guided by conventional wisdom with a minimum of market contact, and with only minimal degrees of public order.

But the agriculture of virtually all of the so-called underdeveloped areas had by the end of World War II also undergone some degree of modernization, mostly through the production of export crops. To this degree, therefore, the agricultural economies of the underdeveloped countries were caught up in a comprehensive network or system of monetary transactions, markets, credits, and debts. Correlatively, the export agriculture centers in the cities. In fact, the comfort and luxuries of the cities of the less developed countries rest upon the agricultural export economy; it is through agricultural exports that automobiles, gasoline, modern household fixtures, and even modern clothes are purchased.

Prior to this United Nations age, with the proliferation of new nation-states, it was possible to measure economic progress in the underdeveloped world by rates of growth in national product, most of which originated in the agricultural export sector. In fact this is almost by definition the key character of a colonial economy. But in the new political order, in which virtually all people live in independent nation-states, development policy must become truly national; that is, in principle, everyone counts. This means that agricultural economists must now consider agricultural development policies from national perspectives. In effect this means that the modernization of agriculture must be viewed as an integral part of an interdependent national economy, even though export agriculture continues to be of major importance.

Confronted by a dualism in the types of agricultural economy —the traditional subsistence agricultural economies and the more modern export sectors—national development policy must deal with a dilemma. Should agricultural development concentrate initially upon expanding the modern agriculture, with the hope and intention of gradually assimilating all of agriculture to the established modern modes of production, or should agricultural development policy concentrate initially on transforming the traditional subsistence agriculture. Through assimilation the traditional system is simply displaced, in contrast to the transformation. However, the two emphases are not contradictory or mutually exclusive in principle.

The assimiliation of the subsistence economy to the already established modern agriculture is more congenial to the thinking of contemporary economists than is the transformation of the traditional subsistence agriculture. By working out from the established base, the whole apparatus of theory and analysis is available for application and use. No one, to our knowledge, has stated this position more cogently than Earl Heady.

The knowledge is already at hand, theoretically and practically, in explaining the development of agriculture. . . . The economic development of agriculture is nothing more than the use of more capital resources, in substituting one form of capital for another or for land or labor, and in increasing output. These changes in resource demand and product supply are encouraged only if the prices of resources and products are favorable, the supply quantity of resources (usually reflected through supply prices) is conducive, the revenue and cost structure (the economic expression of tenure conditions) of its farm firms is appropriate and the degree of certainty or the planning horizon promises a sufficient payoff of durable investment. . . . The mysteries of agricultural development are small indeed. More mysterious and complex are the "outside" policy, planning, political and cultural processes which provide restraints to appropriate changes in the "growth variables" or policies which relate to agriculture.[2]

Thus, Heady recognizes that the analysis of agricultural development requires much in addition to economic analysis. The real mysteries are not a part of the quest for the economic requirements of an efficient and productive agriculture but rather in the "outside" policy, planning, political, and cultural processes. That is, in this view, the unresolved problems of agricultural development are in other disciplines—the other social

[2] From the opening paragraphs of "Process and Priorities in Agricultural Development," paper presented to a seminar, University of Florida, 1966.

sciences. An alternative view, and the one accepted in this chapter is that the conception of the nature (or definition) of economics be broadened to include both the substantive operations of the economic system and the procedural or organizational structure of the economic system in ways in which property relations, opportunities, corporations, and tenure relations, for example, are viewed as economic problems.

One of the issues that has been of most concern to agricultural economists in considering the relevance of the contemporary United States formulation of agricultural economics to agricultural development is the question of whether peasant people honor the principle of economic rationality in their behavior. This issue was argued in the classic exchange between Frank Knight and Melville Herskovitz.[3] With few major exceptions economists are in substantial agreement with Knight and accept the rationality postulate.

The issue is faced frankly by John Mellor in an essay on the theory of agricultural development: "The controversy concerning the extent to which peasant farmers in low-income countries make economically rational decisions is important. If they do, their actions may be changed in a predictable manner by manipulation of the economic environment; if they do not, then more direct action is necessary to achieve public ends. Empirical evidence largely confirms the hypothesis that peasant farmers do act in an economically rational manner. . . . Much of the contrary evidence appears to rise from misconceptions about the objectives of peasant farmers and about the environment within which their decisions are made." [4]

Possibly economists see a quite different meaning in such a position than do other social scientists. Economists do not mean that human beings are rational calculators about which Veblen once chided them. They mean essentially that peasant farmers (in this context) are sensitive to the dimensions of their alternatives, and do make sensible choices therefrom. The term

[3] "Economics and Anthropology: A Rejoinder," *Journal of Political Economy*, 49 (April, 1941), 269–278.

[4] In "Toward A Theory of Agricultural Development," chap. 2 of *Agricultural Development and Economic Growth*, Herman M. Southworth and Bruce F. Johnston, eds. (Ithaca: Cornell University Press, 1967), p. 37.

rationality is therefore a "personification" of acts of choice. The function of this characterization is to permit economists to concentrate upon policies which "manipulate the economic environment" in conformity to our liberal conception of freedom and dignity of the individual, rather than to resort to "direct action to achieve public ends."

This concentration upon the characteristics and interrelations of the economic environment becomes generalized in contemporary economics in what Kenneth Boulding calls the "universe of commodities."

The basis of the economist's system is the notion of a commodity. The economist sees the world not as men and things, but as commodities, and it is precisely in this abstraction that his peculiar skill resides. A commodity is anything scarce, that is, in order to get more of it a quantity of some other commodity must be relinquished. . . . Once it is understood that the economist's interest is not human behavior, but the behavior of commodities then his development of something as psychologically peculiar as the marginal analysis takes on more meaning. The core of the economist's interest is not human behavior as such but the *behavior functions* which relate his economic quantities, his prices, and his quantities of commodity produced, consumed or exchanged.[5]

From such analytical bases, price theory has come to serve as the core of formal economic analysis in the consideration of the problems of commercial agriculture, which is the major focus of agricultural economics in the United States. As has been suggested above, we consider this formulation to be too narrow and restricted to serve as the terms of reference for analyzing agricultural development in sufficiently comprehensive terms to embrace the problems of behavioral change.

Before turning to the problem of interpreting and supplementing these views of economists in terms of the strategy implications for behavioral change in agricultural development, it is essential to recognize something of the role which two-sector models play in the consideration of economic development.

The most influential presentation of a two sector model of economic development is that of Arthur Lewis in his "Economic

[5] *The Skills of the Economist* (Cleveland: Allen, Howard, 1958), pp. 9, 29.

Development with Unlimited Supplies of Labor" [6] in which he distinguishes a subsistence sector and a capitalistic sector. In terms of theory, or concept, Lewis addresses himself to the question as to whether, why, and under what conditions the approach of the earlier classical school of economists was more relevant to the analysis of the problems of underdeveloped areas than is the more recent neoclassical and Keynesian analysis. The essence of his argument was that once the supply of labor becomes limited, neoclassical economics become relevant.

Much of the writing and theoretical analysis of economic development have moved out from Lewis' formulation. In one aspect of this movement, Lewis' two-sector distinction between subsistence and capitalistic sectors has become identified as a distinction between agriculture and industry, in which agriculture is the subsistence and industry (or nonagriculture) is the modern or capitalistic sector. Great mischief has been done to the formulation of the problems of agricultural development by this identification of agriculture with the subsistence sector, for the subsistence sector disappears in the process of modernization—in the formulation.[7]

This model, which admittedly we have only pointed to, has stimulated much discussion about whether the marginal productivity of labor in traditional subsistence agriculture was positive. The general judgment of investigators is that the marginal product is positive, with the seasonality of cultivation and peak-load labor requirements explaining both why labor in the agricultural villages might be both underemployed during much of the year but be needed and positively productive during a few crucial weeks of the crop season.

One outcome of this judgment has been an enhancement of the economists' confidence in the relevances of the current theoretical formulation of economists for the analysis of all of agriculture of underdeveloped countries. This is the central thrust of Theodore Schultz's analysis of the transformation of tradi-

[6] *Manchester Studies in Economics and Social Studies,* vol. 22, no. 2 (May, 1954), pp. 139–191.

[7] Lewis is no doubt largely responsible for this identification, through some remarks at page 173 of the original article observing that in practice the agricultural and subsistence sectors might be identified. But this confused the deeper issues.

tional agriculture with his brilliant characterization of traditional agriculture being "efficient but poor." [8] One of the key policy implications is that the way to develop agriculture is to make available to cultivators, at remunerative prices, the inputs of both conventional (machinery, fertilizer, etc.) and the unconventional sorts (especially mentioned is education).

We should recognize however that among analysts who are most adept in precise theoretical formulations along the lines noted, there is general recognition that there is very much in the process of agricultural development that escapes the terms of reference of accepted theory. Especially there is recognition of institutional factors, of the need for major reforms, along with the correlative shifts in power, of the role of education, of public administration, of the strategic influence of transport facilities and social overhead capital. There is also recognition that the very conception of agricultural economics has changed distinctly during recent decades. As agricultural economists have become more consciously "economists," the approach to all analytical problems has become more influenced by rigorous model formulations. "Agricultural economists had an early tradition of eclectic approaches to problems. Much of this they have lost with increasing specialization. In learning to comprehend the problems of transforming traditional agricultures they are finding renewed need for interdisciplinary perspectives." [9]

Unnoticed also is the whole problem of the adoption of the thinking about fiscal and monetary policy in the United States to the problems of underdeveloped countries, with the problems of incipient inflation and the concern about the possibilities of deficit financing.

We have tried thus far to identify the concepts in contemporary formulations of economics and agricultural economics which set the tone of contemporary graduate studies in agricultural economics in America; necessarily the emphasis has been most selective. But perhaps it is sufficient to enable us to at least pose some of the issues concerned with agricultural development, particularly as we attempt to consider the issues of the strategy for behavioral change in agricultural develop-

[8] *Transforming Traditional Agriculture* (New Haven: Yale University Press, 1964).

[9] Southworth and Johnston, p. 4.

ment. We now turn from an attempt to identify the basis of consensus among agricultural economists to the more hazardous task of trying to find the bridges over which other social scientists and economists might travel to find common ground in the formulation of agricultural development policies.

Behavioral Change: An Economic Perspective

The establishment in an underdeveloped country of an "environment conducive to achieving behavioral patterns required by modern agriculture" is, as the terms of reference suggest, the central issue in agricultural development policy, at least from the perspective of economics. The environment in this aspect is a national economic system, for development, and particularly the development of the agricultural sector of a country, is a national undertaking. Thus the primary objective of agricultural development policy is the achievement of a system of agricultural economy which has the capacity to support development. By primary, it is not intended that such a system must be achieved as a temporal precondition of development, but rather that the achievement of such a system needs to be pursued as a high priority objective in the transformation of a traditional agriculture. The traditional systems of agriculture, by whatever name, lack the capacity for growth.

As an economist considers the tasks of development, he thinks in terms of functions within a system; consequently the conceptualization of the nature of the system is the matrix for the whole scheme of analysis. In most general terms the modernization of the agriculture of a truly underdeveloped area is basically the transformation of an antecedent, traditional, largely subsistence, ecologically based agriculture into an economy in which investment, specialization, and exchange are major characteristics. In short, a common-sense agriculture hitherto based upon the exploitation of natural fertility is transformed into one in which the potentialities of science, technology, division of labor, exchange, and investment are exploited. When such development functions are converted to behavioral functions, we have investors, entrepreneurs, laborers, marketing agents, consumers, and public officials and civil servants. Such functions can be performed in many different ways, with the result that the behavioral functions as actualized through human actors form significantly different systems of agricultural economy. For example, the state has quite different roles in agricultural development according to the political philosophy which articulates development planning. The role of public officials (and the state is what public officials do with the powers of the state) is quite different in an agricultural development plan which is based upon direct public administration of agriculture including the state ownership of land, from what officials do in a state in which agricultural development is based upon private ownership of agricultural land. Furthermore, the role of that state or of any other particular behavioral function changes as a nation develops.

The "central tendency" of agricultural economics as practiced in the United States is that of improving the efficiency of the given *system* of agricultural economy. Although the structure of the agricultural economy is changing, through increases in size of farm, capital intensification, integration, etc., yet the possibilities and procedures for such changes are essentially institutionalized as a part of the established system of economy. But when one looks to the underdeveloped areas, it seems obvious that the modern social framework or system of economy, which we can take as a given in American agriculture, is not to be found in most of the underdeveloped areas. If so, agricultural development policy for dealing with the problem of behavioral change in the underdeveloped areas must be cast in more comprehensive terms than in the United States.

Any national system of economy, of course, has its own unique characteristics, since it must have deep roots in the culture and experience of a people; that is, the system is necessarily "naturalized" to the situation, which requires in effect that a substantial part of such a system must be drawn, though shaped and modified, from the experience of a people. It is therefore not possible to discuss with much precision the issues of agricultural development and system achievement in global terms of underdeveloped areas. Although we shall attempt to approach these policy issues from the perspective of behavioral change in the developing, or underdeveloped countries, we shall, for some purposes, need to distinguish type situations. In one situation, and this type presents the most comprehensive tasks of development, the present system of agriculture is predominantly traditional and the nation-state is not yet secure; this is the case in equatorial Africa. In a second situation population pressure is heavy and the countries are confronted by rates of growth in population which exceed the present or prospective growth rates in nonfarm employments. We may call this the Asian case. In this kind of situation, the task which falls upon the agricultural sector is not only to produce the needed food and fiber, but there is also the task of providing opportunities for sheer subsistence survival for people who are not really needed anywhere. In a third situation agricultural development policies must be pursued in situations where there are great disparities of power and poverty; this is the case in Latin American countries with large peasant populations.

The agricultural development problems are different in such diverse situations, particularly the task of creating or modifying the economy as a system of human relations.

Freedom of Choice through Secure Opportunities

We shall attempt to formulate the issues of agricultural development policies by initial consideration of the systems requirements for significant degrees of freedom of choice by farmers as participants in an integrated economy. Through such a selective focus on a few aspects we may be able to state the issues more precisely, and thereby suggest more accurately the nature of the measures which are ingredient to agricultural development policies which would optimize behavioral change through free choice, starting from the present situations of underdeveloped countries.

The argument developed first emphasizes the achievement of, the nature of, and the necessity for secure and objective opportunities. For occupations are realized essentially by occupying and exploiting opportunities, which occupying can be done only by persons who have the appropriate "matching" abilities. There is always a question in individual cases regarding the ability to succeed in the occupation but that is a different problem, considered later. The meaning of this conjunction of abilities and opportunities for the progress of peasant farmers was noted precisely by John Stuart Mill more than a century ago in a remark on the poverty of the Irish cottiers: "Almost alone amongst mankind the cottier is in this condition, that he can scarcely be either any better or any worse off by any act of his own." [10] The question of behavioral change from the perspective of peasant cultivators thus becomes a problem of creating and sustaining a system whereby the peasant cultivators of a country, or some significant proportion of them, are in a position by which they can improve their condition of life by acts of their own.

Since we are attempting to articulate some aspects of a theory of development policy, and since our American experience in agricultural development is considered to have been at least moderately successful, we shall first consider how economic opportunities were made reasonably secure, even objectively secure, in our tradition. We can then turn to the consideration of opportunities in agricultural situations in less developed countries. A theory of the design of opportunities is essential if we are to have effective policies for creating economic opportunities and making them secure. Even if such a formulation lacks universality, it should still be suggestive of the nature of the issues.

The great procedural fact in Anglo-American history regarding the establishment of secure opportunities on the land is the reduction of the power of (absolute) prerogative once exercised by the British crown to the exercise of power within the constraints of constitutional government. By this restriction on the exercise of arbitrary power by the king to command services and payments at will, modern private ownership of land in England came into being in a continuing struggle from 1066 to 1700. As John Commons wrote more than forty years ago, interpreting the way in which property in land was achieved out of feudalism: "It was not necessary, of course, to change the nominal title of ownership which, in England, remained in the king. But the real owners, nevertheless, are the tenants because the rent charges are definite taxes in terms of money, but the indefinite residuum which marks the real ownership, because it marks the orbit where the will is free, is transferred to the nominal tenants." [11]

The great achievement here, out of struggles and civil wars

[10] *Principles of Political Economy,* Book II, chap. 9, p. 3.
[11] *Legal Foundations of Capitalism* (Madison: University of Wisconsin Press, 1924), p. 221.

lasting many centuries, was the creation of an indefinite residuum, an orbit where the will of private persons was free, through restrictions on the exercise of arbitrary power by the crown. For this indefinite residuum, which initially was quite small, was the source and beginning for individuals (at first only a few) of both liberty and opportunity.

From this base of opportunities on the land there has developed the whole structure of property rights, by that complex set of working rules which we call the law of real property. In this way both sovereignty and property were differentiated from prerogative. Sovereignty over land use is exercised by what we may call the retained powers of the state: eminent domain, police power, and taxation. Thus, while taxes represent the retained rights of the state in land, the rent of land reports the value of the achieved rights of the owners to the use of the land, the indefinite residuum. Thus are land taxes and rents interrelated, as every farm owner understands.

Similarly from this same base in the indefinite residuum (beyond the arbitrary power of the crown) the liberties of persons have matured into citizenship, as persons have come to share in the exercise of the sovereign powers of the state.[12] There is thus an intimate reciprocal involvement in our tradition between and among representative constitutional government responding to the needs and wills of the people as citizens, the stabilized exercise of public power through the state, the interpretation and enforcement of the rules of the game, and security of expectations and opportunities for the occupancy and use of land. Something of the significance of the vast complex set of relations is evident in the property relations within which land is used. The rules of property in a modern economy by which individuals are assured of the rights to use land are enforced by the state; the same is true for creditor-debtor relationships, contractual obligations, and many more.

[12] It is not possible here to do more than suggest the nature of the issues. For a brief but more adequate exposition of these ideas see my "Agrarian Reform Policy as a Field of Research," in *Agrarian Reform and Economic Growth in Developing Countries,* papers from a seminar on Research Perspectives and Problems, Farm Economics Division, Economic Research Service, U.S. Department of Agriculture (Washington, March, 1962).

Within this complex system of state and economy in which sovereignty and property are clearly differentiated, the owner of land, or by his consent persons with lesser interests, may make improvement on, or mortgage, or alienate the land at will. It is through such procedures that agricultural land becomes part of the capital structure of a modern market-oriented agricultural economy.

From this basis of (very meager) interpretations, it may be possible to suggest something of the general character of the problem of the exercise of the powers of government in the design and operation of an economic system. The elementary parts of such a system are the working rules by which people deal with each other, the most powerful of which were those sanctioned by governments, and the sanctions by which they are enforced. Within this basic system, the other functions of government are carried out, notably in economic development the provision of the social overhead of services and facilities.

Since the traditional systems of economy, whether they be called feudalism, communalism, tribalism, or familism, lack the capacity for modern development, some kind of modern system is necessary as a part of the development process. Systems of economy, essentially systems of political economy, which honor freedom and opportunity are constructed by the institution and operation of working rules which create and honor zones of discretion by participants in the economy. Basically such rules are procedural rules which define limits within which choices and decisions are made; insofar as they focus upon specific acts, they characteristically define specific avoidances, not performances. In such a system, opportunities have an objective security, and it is therefore possible in planning for agricultural development, to the degree in which opportunities and liberties are shared, to depend upon and to assist cultivators of the soil to participate in such a system as responsible self-propelled persons. This is the central behavioral problem in agricultural development for farmers, as self-willed entrepreneurs.

However, not only do such integrated economic systems not exist in most of the underdeveloped world, but it seems also that more authoritarian systems of economy are much easier to design and institute during earlier stages of development. Where the powers of the state are controlled by authoritarian groups, of which the military and Marxist-oriented communists are the more sophisticated, we have essentially government by prerogative. This mentality is congenial to duty-states. Consequently the working rules which give structure to the economy as a system of human association tend to place primary reliance upon working rules which stipulate specific performance for everyone in the system. The will of the military or bureaucracy is supreme. In such systems, opportunities as we know them in our tradition simply do not exist; neither do the working rules operate to create a system of property relations rooted in opportunities. Also, in such a system the problem of the behavior of the cultivator is a matter of command and obedience. In principle his will counts for little.

In sum what we have been trying to say is that the issue of behavioral change in agricultural development centers in the nature of the system within which performance occurs. For the system is not the sum of the individuals, but an organized set of relationships. Furthermore, one of the hallmarks of our times is the competition between and among systems. In its most generalized form, we have the cold war.

The major point to be made, however, is that agricultural development policy in underdeveloped countries can neither escape the necessity for modifying the antecedent system of economy, nor escape the consequences of the choices made regarding the nature of the system. Such issues may be made clearer by brief comments on different situations in underdeveloped countries.

The problems of agricultural development are most inclusive or comprehensive in the newly independent countries, such as are found in equatorial Africa, for here development not only must take hold of an agriculture which is mostly traditional and subsistence-oriented, but the nation-state itself is in the formative stage. Since the services and functions of the state are so crucial in national economic development, agriculture cannot be developed very far until the state becomes a stable and serviceable institution.

If one views agricultural development from the perspective of a peasant cultivator in a largely traditional and subsistence agriculture, it is evident that the modernization process requires both capital intensification and an increased involvement in an exchange economy; that is, in a modern agriculture the farmer becomes, in varying degrees, the proprietor of a firm in which investment, business, and managerial decisions become of strategic importance. Actually a substantial proportion of village cultivators in equatorial Africa, for example, have already made some progress along this pathway to modernization. As a general rule, modernization has been concentrated in export agriculture, sometimes by the development of a peasant-export economy as in Nigeria,[13] but more usually by an enclave type of export agriculture. That is, a considerable degree of market orientation and the correlative modernization of the farm as a firm can be achieved without profoundly altering the traditional subsistence practices in the agriculture upon which people rely for their food supply. Thus, it is the integration of the domestic food-producing agriculture into an investment-oriented, exchange economy which is the basic problem of agricultural modernization.

Accepting market involvement and capital intensification as a shorthand characterization of development, it is clear that the achievement of the capital investment function presents the more difficult behavioral adaptation. Thus, it is the role of investor that is the limiting factor.

But investment and growth change the interpretations of the time horizon. Not only does investment entail the choice between present and future goods, but investment requires some modicum of security of expectations regarding the future. The future must be sufficiently secure so that the investors can be assured of a reasonable prospect for reward. Such a creation of security of expectation is an institutional achievement. This requirement must be met in an exchange economy honoring freedom of choice through security of expectations regarding buying and selling, borrowing and lending.

Generalizing somewhat loosely, it may be noted that the land which a cultivator uses is "owned" according to customary rules. In this part of the world the land is likely allotted to family groups within a tribal territory. Within family shares, the right to use the land is allotted to individual members

[13] Carl Eicher, "The Dynamics of Long-Term Agricultural Development in Nigeria," *American Journal of Agricultural Economics,* 49 (Dec., 1967), 1158–1170.

through the inheritance process, as a matter of right. Thus cultivators inherit usufructuary rights in particular plots of land according to the size of the family patrimony in land and the division of land among heirs.[14]

The customary rules under which land is so allotted and held have the implicit public purpose of security and group survival. Although agricultural land is in principle neither bought and sold nor mortgaged, there is a widespread practice of borrowing or loaning land, for a consideration. Such arrangements, as we understand them, are essentially of the bailor-bailee type (in which the identical object is taken and returned) rather than of a less personal creditor-debtor, or buyer and seller type of transaction. Since ownership rests with the family (or more inclusive group), relatives of the person "loaning" a particular tract of land have the right, by customary law, to redeem the land by repayment to the one who "borrows" land of the original consideration in such a bailor-bailee transaction. Obviously the more the "borrowed" land is improved through planting of trees or other physical improvements, the greater the value of the privilege of redemption. In terms of land use of particular plots borrowed, such a right of redemption must surely forestall any major permanent investment in improvements on "borrowed" land.

Such a right of redemption would also operate to prevent consolidation of scattered plots into a unified holding through exchange of land. In order to give security of ownership to the consolidated holdings of land (assembled through exchange of ownership of plots) in the highland areas of Kenya, a statute of limitations on the right of redemption was invoked.[15]

From such considerations it seems clear that if agricultural development is to be achieved in situations where the right to land use and occupancy is defined by customary rules and the privilege-status within families, then the only persons who can engage in the product of a market surplus for sale on an appreciable scale are those persons who by virtue of family status have

[14] Charles K. Meek, *Land Law and Custom in the Colonies,* is a pioneer work in this aspect of development (London: Oxford University Press, 1949).

[15] For a nontechnical discussion of this program, see Elspeth Huxley, *A New Earth* (New York: William Morrow, 1960).

claims to relatively large areas of land. One may hypothesize, from this premise, that much of the peasant-export surplus produced, as well as the cashcropping for domestic markets in a traditional society operating under customary rules of land ownership, comes from the holdings of those people who have claims through family connections to land not essential for the production of self-subsistence food crops. That is to say, if agricultural change agents are to stimulate modernizing changes in the behavior of peasants in such situations, their prospective clientele is to be found among the higher ranks of the social hierarchy in the villages. In some villages there may be considerable "elbow room" for such developments, in others, not.

For many reasons, it is impossible to make much headway in agricultural development within a wholly customary set of working rules regarding land use and occupancy. Basically, both investment in land and a considerable degree of "mobility" of land resources are essential conditions for effective use of agricultural land. A modest degree of modernization brings pressure for land transfers, even as the necessity for investment brings pressure for a generalized security of title. It is commonplace that the urban areas in underdeveloped countries are islands of legally sanctioned land ownership even in a vast sea of customarily owned agricultural and wasteland. In short the development so far achieved in less developed areas, as well as the history of agricultural development in the western world, testifies to the necessity for a shift from customary ownership rules for land to legally sanctioned rules of property as an integral part of a shift from a traditional exploitative agriculture to an investment-oriented agriculture. Such a shift is required both to increase production sufficiently to cope with the growth in population and to facilitate the economic transformation integral to development. Similar necessities push an agricultural economy toward a deep involvement of the participants in creditor-debtor, and buyer-seller relationships, if an economy develops under a philosophy honoring "free choices."

Such words as property, debts, and contract are meaningful only in the context of a system of state and economy in which the powers of the nation-state operate in specific ways. It is necessary, therefore, if we are to visualize the nature of the problem of behavioral change in development to consider the role of the state as being in effect what public officials do with the powers which they exercise. The basic and central problem is actually that of system creation and making operative the powers of the state in the release of energy in the economy.[16] We turn therefore to the problem of creating a modern system in which the sovereign powers of the state are used in conjunction with and in support of the energy, initiative, and participation of citizens in an economy.

The problem of creating an integrated system of state and economy is the achievement of the strategically essential security of expectation, or, more formally, of achieving order, particularly public order and economic order. The achievement and maintenance of order is generally recognized as being the major "precondition" to all the other functions which a state is required to perform if national economic development is to be achieved, including the provision of the social overhead of public facilities and services, development planning, and a host of others. Order, in turn, provides the matrix for, defines the procedures by which, and the limits within which agricultural development occurs.

This general issue is stated succinctly for the new nations by Robert Heilbroner: "To begin with, there are areas of the world where the immediate tasks are so far reaching that little more can be expected for some decades than the primary missions of national identification and unification. Most of the new African states fall into this category." [17] We propose here to interpret how the "primary mission" of national identification and unification relates to the preceding discussion of the institutional basis of investment processes in agricultural development. Hopefully, this will indicate something of the strategy required of public officials in promoting behavioral change related to scientific agriculture.

Although the achievement of independence from colonial rule is usually greeted by great enthusiasm for national independence, and rightly so, the system of state and economy

[16] See Williard Hurst, *Law and the Conditions of Freedom in the Nineteenth-Century United States* (Madison: University of Wisconsin Press, 1956), especially chap. 1, "The Release of Energy."

[17] "Counter-revolutionary America," *Commentary*, 43, no. 4 (April, 1967), 34.

virtually always receives deep shocks by the transfer of power from external to national authority, basically from government by authority of external prerogative to government by authority of national sovereignty. Although many countries in Asia and the Middle East, including the Philippines, have achieved national independence in recent decades in ways in which this shift in the locus of authority created difficulties, the situations in the new states of Africa provide the most dramatic instances in our times of the search for national identification and unification.

Again to generalize somewhat loosely, the situation in colonial Africa prior to national independence was characteristically one in which commerce and trade were carried on according to the business rules of the occupying power, while subsistence agriculture, inheritance, and family relations were left to customary, tribal law. One of the more dramatic contrasts under such distinctions came between the institutional basis of the foreign-owned enclave export agriculture and the traditional subsistence agriculture. The land for such enclave agriculture was usually owned under modern rules of property, the sanctions for such rules were derived from external authority. With the coming of independence, these enclaves are mostly being nationalized. In notable instances, as in Indonesia, the plantations were invaded and occupied by peasants, the "ownership" reverted to the customary kind, and formal, legally sanctioned property relations disappeared.

A central problem in much of Africa is that of creating a state out of traditional tribalism, for with the withdrawal of the sanction of external prerogative, the contest over the exercise of sovereign powers is then between the emerging national government and the heads of tribes. In extreme cases as in the Congo and more recently in Nigeria this contest leads to civil wars.[18] Rightful citizenship and rightful ownership of land are realized only where government by prerogative is reduced to constitutionally exercised powers in which the officials of government are required to follow some sort of due process.

An operative system of modern state and economy may not be possible for decades, with the consequence that the agricultural development process may be forced to operate within customary

18 This is, of course, a basic problem in Vietnam.

rules of property at the village level (i.e., without alienation or hypothecation of land). Correlatively this also means in effect the economy will operate through family, village, or tribal units of social action, rather than center on individual entrepreneurs.

One may guess, and even suppose, judging from the history of the West, that as and when national governments become representative governments responsive to the demands of citizens, that something like objective rules of legally sanctioned property will eventually encompass agriculture, as subsistence agriculture is transformed into a more productive investment- and exchange-oriented system of agriculture. But both citizenship and the property rights which emerge might very well come to a focus upon people in terms of village units of both economy and political action.[19] Also, it is difficult to see how economic development even through increased market orientation can lead to a pervasive individualism unless the ownership of land is alienable so that land can be assimilated to the capital structure.

The task of agricultural development in a nation which is overpopulated presents peculiar difficulties. Although there are pockets or local areas of population pressure in most underdeveloped countries, the more severe and chronic instances usually cited include most of India, East Pakistan, and Java in Indonesia. In these countries of southern Asia the problem of nation building, the mission of national identification and unification, to use Heilbroner's phrase, is quite similar to and only a little less urgent than in equatorial Africa. But in these Asian areas there is virtually no space left into which a subsistence agriculture can expand, except in the outer regions such as the islands of Indonesia. Agricultural development particularly in India and Pakistan must therefore concentrate on intensification, on investment and modernization of existing agriculture.

All this is well understood. However, the rural population is growing so fast, not only in India and Pakistan, but over almost all of the underdeveloped world that the prospects are very slim for creating economic opportunities through investment processes sufficient to match the growth in population. Although this is commonplace, one aspect of the problem has not re-

[19] This seems to have been the case in Mexico, where the Ejidos served as units of both economic and political action.

ceived sufficient analytical consideration. Subsistence agriculture, which has become traditional in all parts of the world, has not only served over centuries as the basic array of opportunities for survival for all persons who could not survive by other means, it has, in the process, acquired its own set of public purposes.

We may see something of the significance of this by asking what is the public function of agriculture? The answer in the United States and other modernized countries is simple: The function of agriculture is to provide the basic food and fiber needed by the nonagricultural parts of the economy (national or international). The question of how many farmers is subsidiary. We need only as many as there is room for, account being taken of the modernizing potentialities of science, technology, and investment.

However, if one looks at the traditional subsistence economy in which most of the rural people of the world still live, it is evident that the private purposes of individuals and families are security and survival. Such private purposes become accepted as public purposes by the larger community. In tribal Africa today, the social practices by which survival-security is honored as a major public purpose can be observed in the tenure, marriage, and inheritance practices which are sanctioned by groups, through the authority of chieftainship. Similar purposes and practices operate in the peasant cultures of Asia.

Escape into subsistence agriculture at the frontier (of bush or jungle) has been the means whereby the "surplus" population could survive; this alternative has actually provided the reservation wage in occupational choices regarding wage employment in the modern sectors of the economy. As the areas open for "squatting" become less and less, or become so poor in physical potential that survival is not possible by traditional agriculture, or this way of life simply becomes unacceptable (to the young man especially), there then comes a wave of migration to the cities. This flight from a traditional subsistence survival system is simply swamping the cities of the underdeveloped world, with much more to come.

The situation in the United States is not now so very different; the subsistence economy (which only a generation ago was honored in public policy by a national Subsistence Homesteads Administration) has simply withered away. The poverty, unrest, and riots of recent migrants from rural areas to the central city ghettos are forcing a reappraisal of our own public purposes for national agricultural policy. The situation seems to be that national agricultural policy for commercial agriculture has been solved at least as a problem in commodity economies, so that we may look forward in this country to an increasing output of agricultural products on fewer but larger farms exploiting new technologies, provided incentives are maintained through adequate price stabilization, educational, marketing, and credit policies. Thus, for the U.S. Department of Agriculture the flight from rural areas to the cities is becoming a most urgent matter; this is now considered to be the strategic unsolved problem for national policy for rural areas.

As we look to optimizing desirable behavioral changes in agriculture, we are again confronted with the need to visualize the crucial characteristics and public purposes of the system within which behavioral changes will occur. Confronted with the stark facts of population growth and the likely rates of migration, we seem driven to honor as a major public purpose the provision of the possibility of opportunities for decent survival careers in a predominantly subsistence agriculture over most of the underdeveloped world. There must be, and in fact are, better and worse ways to organize a subsistence agriculture—but the educational, political, scientific, and investment dimensions are quite different from those of a modern market-oriented, investment-based agriculture.

The use of the powers of government for public purposes is so crucial in optimizing both the rates of growth in agricultural development and the behavioral changes essential thereto, that consideration needs to be given to this aspect of the agricultural development problem.

Although one might characterize the control of the government exercised by small bureaucratic elite groups in countries which have experienced major communist revolutions (as in the U.S.S.R. and China) as private ownership of government [20] by the bureaucracy, there are other and more appropriate examples in the noncommunist world. The type of problem we are think-

[20] The phrase is from Henry A. Wallace, *New Frontiers* (New York: Reynal and Hitchcock, 1934).

ing about occurs in situations where there is economic power based upon private property in land, in which the economic power of an elite group is augmented by both political and social power. This is the situation in a number of Middle Eastern and Latin American countries, and is not completely unknown in modern Western nations, including the United States. The seriousness of the problem is a matter of degree. But in general it is somewhat correct to say that the use of the powers of government for private purposes is endemic to Latin America.

These countries have long since passed through the stage of achieving national identities; furthermore, the continuity of government has become stabilized over more than a century through procedures by which power is shared and passed around among elite groups.[21] What seems to be lacking in the procedures followed for the stabilized continuity of the exercise of power is the reduction of the powers of government to constitutionally limited sovereignty through procedures which include a meaningful citizenship for all the people.

It is not that elections are lacking, rather that historically the people who really count in such elections are the members of the establishment. The historic transition of European institutions to Latin America, by which the preferential position of the descendants of the European elite was established, has led to a dualism both of institutions and power. This has been particularly acute in countries in which a substantial proportion of the total population has descended from indigenous or slave people. Not only do most of the descendants of the indigenous people live in subsistence type of agriculture, they have had so little voice in the use of the powers of government, that those powers have been concentrated on the services to the modern sector, the cashcrop, property-based, modern agriculture of the elite.

Consequently the use of the powers of government in the service of agricultural development, even in such elementary service as access highways, market facilities, land registration,

[21] Charles W. Anderson, *Toward A Theory of Latin American Politics,* Occasional Paper No. 2, Graduate Center for Latin American Studies, Vanderbilt University, February, 1964; Reprint No. 10, Land Tenure Center, University of Wisconsin.

and titles which permit the inclusion of agricultural land in the capital structure of the country, has been restricted largely to the cashcrop, and largely export crop, sectors of agriculture. Although there are in principle ways in which "homesteaders" may go onto unutilized land to occupy and use it, thereby establishing a preemptory claim to ownership, in actual fact this has not been an accessible alternative to most "settlers."

It is this historic institutional dualism, this polarization of agriculture between a modern market sector and the great sea of traditional subsistence agriculture, this lack of effective citizenship among the peasant cultivators, which is basic to the *latifundista* vs. *minifundista* problem in these countries. This is, in consequence, the seedbed out of which come the invasion by *campesinos* of the hacienda and much of the revolutionary ferment.

To the problems of population growth and eventual pressure, we need to add for Latin America and most of the Middle East the problem of directing the use of the creative developmental powers of government to truly public purposes. Although this aspect of the development problem is largely political, the means by which it can be resolved must surely include the development of a class of people who have sufficient independence economically to exercise political power independently—the historic function of a middle class.

Although a reform which redistributes opportunities is perhaps the most obvious short-run remedy in such circumstances, the problem needs to be seen in deeper terms. The basic problem we have suggested is to achieve the use of the powers of government for public purposes. Should enlightened political groups see the possibilities for growth and advancement inherent in the focus of the use of the powers of government upon the problems and situations of the "excluded" poor, amazing growth rates might occur.

Some Interpretations

If behavior is, in its very potentialities, a function of systems of human association, then the key to behavioral change is through the changing character of the system. We have accepted the necessity for the modification of antecedent systems, the achieved traditional subsistence system of economy of the agriculture of the less developed world. The old forms are simply inadequate.

The modification of the earlier economic systems of agriculture requires, and is even the high priority task of, creative statesmanship, in the new countries particularly. So intimately are state and economy interrelated in the deeply integrated way which makes property relations possible that it seems both accurate conceptually and reasonable from the perspective of policy to speak of a national system of state and economy. In large measure this viewing together of state and economy as an integrated complex of human association reflects the emphasis here on policy, rather than economics only; we are dealing with development policy issues. But both economics and policy deal with part-whole relationships; in both the basic referrent is one of system.

Are the concepts, systematized as bodies of theory, which now shape the intellectual climate and the modes of professional thought in agricultural economics relevant to the analysis of the agricultural development policy issues in the underdeveloped countries? There can be no simple and conclusive answer to this question. But if systematic economic analysis and policy analysis both function within systems of human association, basically national systems, there is at least a formal common ground both between economic and policy analysis and the analysis of national economic and policy issues, wherever the national locus. The possibility of fruitful comparative analysis is further strengthened if we accept the proposition that the behavior or performance of individuals in an economic system can be considered as a function of the alternatives which are confronted at moments of creative choice or decisions.

We may now restate the original question and inquire whether common ground is afforded to systematic thought through the conception of alternatives or opportunities in the evaluation of the relevance of the concepts of contemporary agricultural economies in the United States for the problems of agricultural development in the less developed areas of the world. Again, the answer is affirmative; there is something of objective opportunities in any system which honors freedom of choice. But an understanding of the grounds of comparison requires resort to both history and political philosophy.

In U.S. agriculture, the opportunities of concern to agricultural economists, in the main, are market opportunities for commodities or labor. In our agriculture the processes of commercialization have run so deeply for so many decades, that the opportunities have come to have price dimensions. Thus the major aspects of agricultural policy for some two decades have been "price policy" and the operative integrating economic theory of a market economy is price theory. In the underdeveloped world the economic opportunities, particularly in traditional subsistence agriculture do not have such predominantly "price" dimensions. This means, in effect, that the viewing of the scope of economics as the analysis of the universe of commodities is inadequate for the analysis of the problems of the early stages of agricultural development. Yet this recognition may also suggest the means of reconciliation of the divergent formulations. The price dimensions of economic opportunities in agriculture become inclusive at the conceptual limit of the full integration of agriculture into the systems of monetized market relations. But at the early, less integrated stages of economic development the structure of opportunities must be considered as a problem. Whether or not the objective characteristics of opportunities in agriculture move toward a nearly complete price dimension depends both on the political philosophy which articulates agricultural development policy and the stage of development.

In subsistence agriculture, survival is the outcome of man matching his wits and skills against physical nature. The key acts are therefore actions and reactions with nature. This aspect of behavior persists in all types of farming. The modern version of it is in physical science and technology which evidence modern man's control over physical nature. We use production-functions to analyze the way in which such actions and reactions with physical nature are integrated into our farms as modern firms. The changes in the relationships of man to nature are thus a continuum from the most primitive to the most modern forms of agriculture, and provide one pathway to modernization.

But man's relation to man is also a dimension of man's behavior in even the most underdeveloped agriculture—for man neither lives nor works alone. The group ways in a subsistence economy are essentially ways of group survival. Thus the ways of human association which a cultivator can count upon as dependable, become built into his alternatives for making a living from the soil. In societies and economies which are pre-state, the rules of the game, the working rules of human association, are customary and enforced by whatever sanctions are at the disposal of those who exercise authority. In the modernization process the types of association become differentiated basically no doubt because of efficiency of the means of survival and the enrichment of human association, but ideology also exercises great influence because man always makes decisions in terms of the *meanings* of things—not things. The result is the formation of states, which enforce the rules by the legal sanctions of physical violence, which rules we call laws. But economic concerns also get differentiated out of these once conglomerate forms of associations, with their own working rules and forms of human association. The strategic rules here are accorded the sanction of the state in modern economic organization, including those which relate in a "choice" economy to buying and selling, borrowing and lending. It is these rules of property and contract in our system, to use a simplified statement, that make the relationships of state and economy integral one to the other.

This dimension of opportunity is not one of action and reaction but one of transaction with other persons. The expectations regarding the likely outcome of both kinds of actions (action and reaction, and transactions) get built into the behavior patterns of farmers as dimensions of the alternatives which require judgments and which elicit performance. This transactional dimension of opportunities and alternatives is therefore of strategic importance in the study of behavioral change. Here is the central problem of economic institutions.

Arthur Lewis builds his theory of economic growth upon two behavioral interpretations.[22] First, given a situation with development potential, economic development is basically an act of will. No group, no nation ever develops without the will to do so, which must include enough willful developmental behavior to make an economic system go and grow. This will

[22] *Theory of Economic Growth* (Homewood, Ill.: Irwin, 1955), developed in chap. 2, "The Will to Economize."

to effectuate development must somehow be a national will. We can see this now shaping up in Mexico as a truly great developmental phenomenon. In several of the Latin American countries such a collective or national will seems to be lacking. And in most of Africa today this task of achieving such a general will does not yet have a national identity and unity to give it a habitation.

This will to economize, to develop, is activated and channeled by institutions, by the working rules which define the terms of access to opportunities and reward for effort. In Lewis' phrasing: "Institutions promote or restrict growth according to the protection they accord to effort, according to the opportunities they provide for specialization, and according to the freedom of maneuver they permit. . . . Men will not make effort unless the fruit of that effort is assured to themselves or to those whose claims they recognize." [23]

These behavioral dimensions of development become crucial as farmers get caught up into the network of interedependent associations and transactions which we call an exchange economy. Since a truly productive exchange economy requires both specialization and capital intensification, one must think of a modern economy as an investment-exchange economy. The two are inseparable.[24] The two functions, investment and (market) exchange, impinge upon traditional economic behavior in different ways.

An investment-based agricultural economy has a different time horizon than a traditional subsistence agricultural economy, based upon the exploitation of nature with homemade tools and conventional wisdom. The contrast may be noted most clearly in terms of the contrast between a very civilized view from African tribal culture and our own situation. C. K. Meek quotes a Nigerian chieftain to say: "I conceive that land belongs to a vast family of which many are dead, few are living, and countless numbers are still unborn." [25]

In this view, time is flat, by implication future time is as

[23] *Ibid.*, p. 57.

[24] In totalitarian systems the "exchange" is more a function of direct rational allocation and less a function of markets than in our own system.

[25] Charles K. Meek, p. 178.

real and meaningful as present time. Time is a repetitive continuum; the present occupants of land are trustees. This view is no doubt appropriate for the use by the human family of a great trust, and we need to honor this insight. But an economy of negotiable property with calculated rates of interest on investment places a high premium on the proximate future.

This leads to the second basic change in attitudes or behavior which development requires of people who move (perhaps through their children) from a subsistence to a market economy of agriculture. Economic survival and personal progress become more dependent upon participation in an "exchange" economy; economic relations become depersonalized. As Arthur Lewis sums it up: Trade and specialization will be facilitated by treating "strangers fairly." [26]

John Commons deals with the issues in terms of institutional innovation in his discussion of the price-bargain—capitalism and exchange value.[27] Here he analyzes the way in which "negotiability" becomes an accepted practice in an economic system. The essence of his argument is that whereas "modern capitalism begins with the assignment and negotiability of contracts," the primitive common law was prevented from acceptance and enforcement of "the assignment or negotiability of contracts" by the "concept of property as tangible objects and the concept of contract as a personal relation." [28]

The central points can be sensed, perhaps, by recognizing that originally the basic character of all promises and contracts was personal, very much like promises to marry today. They were too personal to be salable. Similarly the holding of land was more like our conception of holding public office than of a commercial relation. To us, also, the buying and selling of "public office" is offensive.

The viewing of economic relations as personal is evidenced today in Africa by the nature of the family ownership of lands with descent of lands by inheritance and the prohibition of the alienation of land, reflecting deep commitments to practices which honor group survival. Similarly may not the persistence of money lending as the principal way in which peasant people borrow money and incur debts be explained in large part by

[26] *Ibid.*, p. 103.   [27] *Legal Foundations of Capitalism*, chap. 7.
[28] *Ibid.*, pp. 253 and 246–247.

the deeply personal character of their credit and debt transactions?

The vast field of institutional innovation must somehow be understood so that institutions can be used to "liberate and expand" individual action, as well as "restrain" or "control" it.[29] Must be, that is, if economic development is to honor and exploit the potential productivity of freedom and willing participation.

The point we would emphasize here is that economic opportunities in a pristine subsistence economy are natural opportunities to wrest a living from the soil, man against nature. But a developed or modernized economy is an economy of pervasive interdependence, "one with another." This interdependence makes any individual dependent upon the behavior of vast numbers of people in a economic system, so much that the dimensions of opportunity of farmers become dependent on the functioning of the whole system of economy, on the behavior of consumers, marketing agents, processors, public officials, and bureaucrats.

If this is the fate of man in the underdeveloped world, either to survive with increasing precariousness in subsistence economies or to learn how to live in an interdependent economy, such a transformation becomes the overriding consideration of agricultural development policy. The strategic key to the transformation is in the design of the system, particularly in the nature, dimensions, and terms of access to economic opportunities; if market opportunities are accessible they will be seized upon. In terms of performance it is essential also that there be both the will and the ability to qualify for and occupy such opportunities.

The problem of system creation and continuity is the primary task; it is for this reason and at this point that the ideological conflicts come to a focus in our time.

[29] John Commons, *Institutional Economics: Its Place in Political Economy* (Madison: University of Wisconson Press, 1959), I, 73.

Response

CHANDLER MORSE

My feelings in relation to Kenneth Parsons' chapter are illustrated by a story concerning Oscar Wilde. Overhearing one of Wilde's witticisms at a dinner party, a guest remarked, "I wish I had said that." To which Wilde replied, "You will."

The application is that I found the issues discussed, the points raised, and the arguments presented by Parsons so congenial to my own way of thinking, my own conceptions of priorities and tasks, that I found myself saying, "I wish I had written that," and fearing that anything I might say by way of comment would echo the original so closely that readers might justly observe, "You did." Still, because I shall be employing a different mode of discourse, I may perhaps escape the charge of mere reiteration.

One of the things I liked about the chapter was a quality which, at the risk of being misunderstood, I can only call polemical. It presents and defends a point of view (several related points of view, in fact) that have clear ideological overtones, that call for making value judgments. And while it adheres firmly to the canons of high scholarship, it does not shrink from confronting the need to make such judgments. Parsons has shown that, notwithstanding a discouraging weight of evidence to the contrary, it is possible for a Western scholar to avoid both the Scylla of cultural bias and the Charybdis of bland and noncommittal neutrality implicitly supportive of the status quo.

Three themes, skillfully interwoven, seem to me to provide the basic framework of the chapter. The first main theme is that development policy in general and agricultural development policy in particular must be truly national, and that this requires concentration on modernization of the subsistence sector. More specifically, the modernization of agriculture must be viewed as essential to the development of a domestic exchange economy, though export agriculture may continue to be vitally important. The implication of this judgment for subsistence agriculture is derived by asking whether agricultural development should initially concentrate on expanding modern export agriculture in the expectation that this will lead eventually to the modernization of all agriculture, or should concentrate initially on transforming the traditional subsistence agriculture. Parsons' answer is that transformation of the subsistence sector is the preferred target, an objective which should be pursued as a matter of high priority. The need to adopt this approach arises because a considerable degree of market orientation, together with modernization of the farm as a firm, can be achieved in export agriculture while leaving virtually unaltered the traditional practices in subsistence agriculture upon which a people rely for food supply. Integration of the domestic food-producing subsistence sector into the investment-oriented, exchange economy is thus the basic task in any program of agricultural modernization. In short, a truly national development policy must recognize the need to take explicit account of the fact that, without a conscious effort to modernize the production of food, which occupies most of the energies of the bulk of the population in the less developed portions of the world, the chances of escape from the dominant struggle for mere survival are small indeed.

The second main theme is that institutional innovation is basic to the modernization of subsistence agriculture, and that this calls for a different sort of analytical approach, a different set of concepts, than those "systematized as bodies of theory" in both general economics and agricultural economics. The central analytical issue, says Parsons, involves a double task. On the one hand, the theoretical formulation must incorporate an analysis of the functioning (and modification) of an established system of agricultural economy as a universe of commodities. On the other hand, it must take account of a modern agricultural economy as a system of human relations, or institutions, properly integrated into the national state and economy. He notes further that focusing upon altering the

behavior patterns of peasant farmers requires that this behavior, and therefore the determining institutional context, be
analyzed in terms of the need for significant freedom of choice
by farmers as manager-entrepreneurs. This, in turn, implies a
need to couple reliable opportunities to succeed in modern
agriculture with ways of assuring competence in the managerial-
entrepreneurial role. To change the behavior of peasant cultivators thus requires the establishment of an economic system
in which the peasant cultivators of a country—or some significant proportion of them—can improve their condition of life
by their own acts. What is needed to guide the process of creating such a system is "a theory of the design of opportunities."

Finally, the third main theme stresses the inseparable conjunction of changes in political and in economic institutions, in
the mutuality of private and public purposes, and the consequent importance of the power structure in defining, pursuing,
or aiding the pursuit of these purposes. The British transition
from a system of royal prerogative and monopoly to one of
private property and freedom of choice protected by the state
is sketched to illustrate the "reciprocal involvement" of polity
and economy and to suggest the ways in which governmental
powers influence the design and operation of an economic system. It is noted that the "design and operation" of an economy
are embodied in working rules, and that in systems that honor
freedom and opportunity these rules "define specific avoidances,
not performances." The relevance of this for agricultural development is, first, that economic systems in most of the underdeveloped world do not provide much freedom of choice and,
second, "that more authoritarian systems of economy are much
easier to design and institute during earlier stages of development."

Of particular importance in this connection is Parsons' emphasis on the concept of an economy as a *system,* specifically a
"system of human relations," which also is "an integrated organization of state and economy." There is a vast difference
between a system in which the working rules operate to facilitate free choice among ever-changing opportunities and one that
places "primary reliance upon working rules which stipulate
specific performance." The latter type of system, which pre-
dominates in the underdeveloped world, lacks the capacity for

modern development. Hence, the system must be changed. But a free-choice framework cannot simply be laid over the existing system and expected to function well. The problem thus appears to be one of designing a transitional system that, while not itself "modern" (this would be too big a jump), is capable of modernizing the subsistence sector.

To sum up, the essence of Parsons' three-pronged argument, as I understand it, is first, that a development policy should be truly national (a value judgment), and that such a policy must of necessity focus on modernizing the subsistence sectors of the underdeveloped world (an analytical judgment). Second, that this is a matter of changing political and economic institutions, for which economic analysis—concerned primarily with providing policy guidance for the *operation* of a free-choice, price-oriented type of economy, not with guiding the processes of institutional *innovation*—is only partially relevant. And, third, that, as in the past, the superior power of the state must play a crucial part in creating a modern economy, no matter whether the economy so to be created is intended to be based on a free-choice or a command design, or a mixture of the two.

Having argued this, the author emphasizes that from such general principles it is difficult to derive specific policy guidance. To underscore his point he discusses the implications of his argument for three types of underdeveloped situations, represented broadly by Africa, where except in a few areas, land is abundant but systems of land tenure create developmental difficulties; Asia, where land is scarce relative to people, and increasing urban overcrowding is a major consequential problem; and Latin America, where the narrowly based structure of power, and the consequent limited conception of public purposes, prevents the achievement of what, with broader perspectives, might be "amazing growth rates."

That I regard the foregoing conceptualization and treatment of the issues favorably has already been indicated; let me therefore proceed to introduce a few quibbles and then to add some interpretations and elaborations of my own.

My first quibble relates to the discussion of "the achievement and maintenance of order as a major 'precondition'" for national economic development and agricultural development. I am not quarreling with the importance of order, which is inherent in the notion of a system. Rather, it is with the failure to mention that *disorder* is often, indeed usually, a precondition for changing from one type of ordered system to another. To remain silent on this issue in a discussion that stresses the need for fundamental institutional change is to suggest, by implication, that there can be a smooth, orderly, evolutionary transition to a modern system from either an "integrated organization of state and economy" or from the imperfectly integrated systems found in most of the newly independent countries today. I do not believe that this is possible and I doubt that Parsons does. Certainly his references to the "struggles and civil wars lasting many centuries" that accompanied the creation of a private enterprise system in Great Britain suggest an awareness of the historical record. Similarly, an awareness of current political realities in Latin America, the Middle East, and elsewhere can be seen in his suggestion that, although the problem of agricultural development calls for "reform which redistributes opportunities," it "needs to be seen in deeper terms" involving "the use of the powers of the government for public purposes." Parsons suggests, moreover, that solution of the problem requires "development of a class of people who have sufficient independence economically to exercise political power independently," but he must recognize that this is not likely to be consummated without a power struggle. If Western social scientists are to escape the trammeling effects of the smugly bland assumption that all social change can and should occur in an orderly evolutionary manner, it is necessary for those who reject the assumption to say so in no uncertain terms.

My second quibble relates to the interpretation and use of W. A. Lewis' views concerning the developmental importance of a "will to economize." It has always seemed to me that, by implication at least, Lewis was questioning the economic rationality of subsistence farmers as a psychological phenomenon. It is true that he discusses the relevance of the institutional context, but the use of the term "will" inevitably gives the discussion a psychological slant. While this may be right and proper, Parsons (citing Mellor) lines up with those who believe that subsistence farmers, given the opportunity to respond rationally to price cues, will do so. If this is correct, the problem is not at all the psychological one of "will" but entirely the

institutional one of opportunities and (trained) abilities, as
emphasized earlier by Parsons. A second difficulty with the use
of Lewis' views is that Parsons casually equates "will to economize" with "will to develop." I have already indicated that
Parsons sees a fundamental and important difference between
"economizing" behavior and "developmental," or institutionally innovative behavior. To equate them is therefore inappropriate and, I think, inconsistent. Moreover, the notion of a
"will" to develop, which "must somehow be a national will,"
seems to imply the existence of a "group mind," to apply a
psychological concept at the social level. I doubt that this was
Parsons' intention. If it wasn't, it would be less misleading to
discuss the problem as one of consensus concerning "public
purposes," thus centering attention on the locus of power in
the society, the interests of those who dominate the power
structure, and the consequent ways in which power is likely
to be used. This would have the added virtue of employing concepts presented and developed in the body of the chapter, and
would explicitly tie back to the discussion of political realities
in Latin America and the Middle East.

My final quibble concerns the use of terms like "modern"
and "modernization" without undertaking to define them.
Definition of these terms has always seemed to me to be fundamental to any discussion of modernization, whether narrowly
conceived as agricultural development, more broadly as economic development, or inclusively as cultural, social, and political development. The reason is that, unless we specify our
meaning, our implicit theorizing and our explicit policy recommendations will always be wrong, or deficient, in at least two
respects. On the one hand, we shall tend to think of modernism
solely in terms of its tangible and highly visible *substantive
attributes*—technological know-how, occupational skills, sophisticated machines, complex organizational forms—instead of in
terms of the intangible, less visible, institutional framework—
the "system of human relations" that shapes the acquisition
and determines the use of these modern attributes. On the
other hand, by failing to think analytically about the essential
characteristics of a "modern" institutional framework, we fall
into the trap of implicitly assuming that modern institutional
forms, equally with the tangible substantive attributes of mod-

ernism, must be identical to those with which we are familiar. In fact, the essential characteristics of modern institutions can be embodied in a wide variety of different structural forms.

The possible coexistence of essential commonalities and inessential differences among societies that are entitled to be called modern seems to be the meaning of Parsons' comparison of man's relations to nature with man's relations to man. The former, epitomized by the concept of production-functions, constitute "a continuum" and provide one pathway to modernization. The latter, focusing on transactions and expectations, constitute "the central problem of economic institutions."

While I agree with this, as far as it goes, it seems to me to stop short of enlightening us concerning the essence of modern institutions and the nature of the solution to the postulated "central problem." Diffidently, therefore, but in the hope of provoking critical responses that will clarify all our thinking, let me try to amend the alleged deficiency.[1] In the process I shall try to show that my formulation can cover the analysis of an economy both as a "universe of commodities" and as a "system of human relations."

That modern societies are characterized by built-in institutional change, especially technological change, is by now a commonplace idea. What has been lacking, however, is an analysis of the structures and processes that assure this result. As I see it, the societies we call modern, regardless of their ideologies and their political and economic systems, are those that have succeeded in creating a set of *problem-handling mechanisms* that facilitate and regulate *innovative behavior.* These mechanisms take over when—but *not* whenever—*equilibrative behavior* produces unsatisfactory results. Equilibrative behavior, it should be noted, is behavior of the kind implied by the postulation of behavioral functions—demand and supply schedules, and the like—in economic analysis. The important characteristic of all such behavioral functions (which play a role in all social disciplines) is that they embody *institutionalized* responses to cues of various kinds, such as quantity responses to

[1] For a fuller (and later) statement of the ideas to follow see my chapter, "Becoming versus Being Modern," in C. Morse *et al., Modernization by Design: Social Change in the Twentieth Century* (Ithaca: Cornell University Press, 1969), pp. 238–382.

price cues, and vice versa, in commodity markets. There is no "problem" of what to do, no question of bringing about any kind of institutional change. There is only an adjustment, an equilibration, so that uncomfortable, inappropriate, or inefficient relationships are rendered comfortable, proper, or efficient.

It may happen, however, that an attained state of equilibrium is unsatisfactory—equilibrium prices are "too low," for example, or slum rents "too high." Alternatively, equilibrium may be unattainable; there may be a chronic state of disequilibrium owing to certain built-in or adventitious constraints on equilibrative behavior, as in the case of persisting involuntary unemployment, traffic jams, urban overcrowding, or atmospheric pollution. In either case there is a need for institutional change, innovative behavior, to replace the inadequate or blocked equilibrative behavior. If I may define a *social problem*—or, more accurately, for reasons to be explained in a moment, a *potential* social problem—as a situation of one of the foregoing kinds, calling for innovative behavior as defined above and rigorously distinguished from equilibrative behavior, I can justify a contention that innovative behavior, in order to be successful, requires the existence of what I have called problem-handling mechanisms. As I conceive these mechanisms they perform an analytical function that is analogous to but different from that played by behavioral functions in economic theory. That is, they render certain forms of behavior predictable, the difference being that neither the kinds of cues, nor the kinds of responses are precisely definable in advance. This accords with the fact that both the occurrence and the outcome of innovative behavior are largely indeterminate (at least in terms of readily obtainable data). It should be noted, however, that innovative behavior can be just as rational, in its way, as equilibrative behavior.

The advantage of formulating the essential characteristics of modernism in this way is that it permits the complex processes of institutional innovation to be analyzed, to be broken down into separately evaluatable component parts. I see these processes as consisting minimally of three problem-handling steps. The first step is the *formation*, that is, the articulation, specification, and recognition of a social problem. This does not occur automatically, either at the level of society or within one of its component organizations. Dissatisfaction may persist for long periods without being recognized—that is, institutionalized—as a social problem. This was the case with unemployment and old age in the United States before the New Deal, and we have not yet institutionalized the problems of racial discrimination and chronic poverty. In order for social problems to be formed there must be effective, unhampered mechanisms for expressing dissatisfaction and for getting someone with adequate power to recognize the existence of a situation requiring remedial action of a kind that is beyond the scope of equilibrative behavior. Our so-called plural society, with its multiplicity of news media, voluntary associations, and political channels does pretty well in providing problem-forming mechanisms, but we would do well to recognize that it is less than perfect. Even in a modern society, therefore, some kinds of institutional change may be blocked before they can get off the ground. In premodern societies the processes by which sources of dissatisfaction become institutionalized as recognized social problems scarcely exist or are effectively blocked.

A major function of leadership in modern societies, and especially of scholars as specialists in perceiving the nonobvious, is to articulate sources of (present and future) dissatisfaction, to specify and define, and even to press for recognition of social problems. Parsons does this in his chapter, where the word "problem" occurs over and over again. As the result of an initial process of problem forming, in whatever way it is carried out, the solution of a social problem may become, in Parsons' phrase, a "public purpose." But also it may not. To articulate and specify is only a necessary, not a sufficient, condition for getting problems recognized. When Parsons says, for example, that "we seem driven to honor as a major public purpose the provision of the possibility of opportunities for decent survival careers in a predominantly subsistence agriculture over most of the underdeveloped world" the "we" refers to the community of scholars, not to the holders of command posts, who are by no means so easily "driven to honor" the stated public purpose, to recognize the transformation of subsistence agriculture as a social problem. Problem forming is successful only when it culminates in effective social recognition of the problem.

The second step in problem handling is to *operationalize* the newly recognized problem. By this I mean that responsibility for doing something about the problem must be assigned to some new or existing organizational structure, along with access to the resources and powers needed to discharge this responsibility. To outline in full the structural characteristics of organizations that facilitate successful attack on problems is impossible in this short commentary, but we may call attention to the special operational importance of what Commons and Parsons have referred to as the creation of an "indefinite residuum," "an orbit where the will of private persons was free." In Western economic theory the significance of this phenomenon is seen in the incentive that maximization of the indefinite residuum provides for running an economically efficient business enterprise, but for present purposes the significance resides in the availability of an economic surplus, of what Cyert and March call "organizational slack," to be manipulated at the discretion of its claimants to solve the social problem for which they are responsible.[2] The fact, noted by Cyert and March, that the firms which spend the most on research are not those in the most serious difficulties but those with the greatest slack, illustrates the importance of a discretionary access to resources, and also suggests why it is that progress, once started, tends to feed on itself. Moreover, the ability to generate and use internal surpluses effectively facilitates access, through credit, to the unutilized surpluses of others. The relation of economic surpluses to innovation is illustrated, too, by the fact that few firms grow by simple replication, and those that do soon run out of opportunities. It is the innovators that grow fastest, and so with societies, too. But one of the requirements of innovation is that the innovators be free, within limits, to introduce change, to behave "deviantly." This, too, is part of the orbit in which "the will is free." Paradoxically, therefore, the institutionalization of institutional innovation requires a certain freedom to engage in quasi-institutionalized change. The rigidities of traditional societies, no matter how successful they may be in generating and channeling an economic surplus, militate against its innovative use

[2] *A Behavioral Theory of the Firm* (Englewood Cliffs, N.J.: Prentice-Hall, 1963).

and, perhaps in consequence, conduce to its consumptive use.

Finally, the organization of political and economic capacity to solve a given problem or set of problems, which is what we mean by operationalization, must be supplemented by the intellectual and social capacity to work out and effect a *solution*. That is, there must be a process of continuing social interaction by which the ends implied in the broad definition of the problem are specified in operational terms, and in which the legitimized access to means provided by step two above is translated into the specifically required and available resources that are to be mobilized and used in solving the problem. Those branches of economic theory concerned with the business firm in particular and with economic efficiency in general take little or no account of these needs. Ends and means, and functional relationships connecting them to each other, are assumed to be given, embodied in behavioral and transformation functions and constraints, leaving as the only "problem" the mechanical selection of the "optimal" combination. Problem solving in the present context, however, is not so cut and dried. It is a social interaction process in which the general objectives, directives, constraints, and opportunities of the problem solver's environment are translated into the specific terms required for innovative action. Stated otherwise, neither production functions nor behavioral functions can be fully specified for modes of transformation and action that have never been tried before, which is the essence of innovation. Hence there is an often lengthy and always somewhat indeterminate process of selective specification, proceeding by trial, feedback, and the evaluation of marginal benefits and costs toward an ever closer approximation to what seems to be a workable and appropriate set of transformation and behavioral functions, together with a set of constraints that are accepted as preferable to incurring the costs of removing them. Then and only then does cut and dried optimizing behavior of the kind treated in efficiency economics become relevant. And this, it seems to me, is wholly consistent—I hesitate to suggest more than this—with the views expressed by Parsons. He asks: "Are the concepts, systematized as bodies of theory, which now shape the intellectual climate and the modes of professional thought in agricultural economics, relevant to the analysis of

the agricultural development policy issues in the underdeveloped countries?" And he answers: "There can be no simple and conclusive answer to this question." But I think that
he has given an answer. He suggests that "price policy" economics has a universal relevance for the relations of man to
nature but not for the relations of man to man. In my terms
one could say that insofar as social interaction processes are
concerned with the technical dimensions of problems there is
a certain objective tendency for solutions to come out one way
rather than another, but that this is less true of the human
dimensions of problems. Is this not at least partly the meaning
of Parsons' statement that, "in the modernization process the
types of association become differentiated basically no doubt
because of efficiency of the means of survival and the enrichment of human association, but ideology also exercises great
influence because man always makes decisions in terms of the
meanings of things—not things?" And is it not an implication
of both our analyses that different organizational forms, alternative types of institutional innovation, are available to solve
any given problem or type of problem. The different methods
would necessarily lead to different results, and a man from
Mars might be able to rank them according to some ordered
scale of quality, but if so it would be his ordering and not
necessarily acceptable to those concerned. But he might then
be able to show, in terms of the earthlings' own avowed set of
values, or a mutually agreed set, that his quality ordering was
superior to theirs. In other words, while we must be careful not
to impose our own value judgments on the solutions worked
out by others, we must also recognize that an objective application of the criterion of what is good and bad for mankind in
general may permit us eventually to escape the *ignoratio
elenchi* buried in the doctrine of cultural relativism.

A feature of the foregoing analysis of institutionalized institutional change is that there are limits to the kinds and degrees
of innovation that can and will be carried out legitimately. A
corollary of this is that there are some kinds of change that can
only be effected by noninstitutionalized processes. According
to institutionalized canons of behavior, such processes are
always immoral by definition. Almost by definition, as well,
they are usually disorderly, and when they are disorderly they
often lead to violence. But the behavioral canons of the status

quo cannot be used to judge behavior designed to change the status quo. Some higher ethical standards must be applied. I shall not attempt to say what they are. In a real sense, they do not "exist," but must be sought. Of only one thing am I confident: that the search is difficult, and one can never know whether he has been successful. Humility in judging noninstitutionalized behavior must therefore be the order of the day.

Now let me turn to what seem to me to be the practical implications of the Parsons analyis as supplemented by that above. I shall relate my observations to my problem-handling model.

First, let us consider the definition of the problem of agricultural development. I agree with Parsons' contention that modernization of the traditional subsistence sector is the central problem of agricultural development but I arrive at this conclusion at least partly by a different route. While he seems to depend exclusively on a value judgment (which I share) that development should be of national scope, I would add that the alternative, dependence on export agriculture, is incapable of leading a country along the path to modernity as I have defined the term. This is because (1) my definition requires that a modern country develop and operate its own set of problem-handling institutions, and because (2) an empirically supportable argument can be made that dependence on agricultural or other exports makes a country so dependent on external decisions and problem-handling processes, so subject to externally oriented innovative behavior, that it never succeeds in developing its own problem-handling capacity. While not conclusive, the many cases of boom, bust, and mass impoverishment that have occurred in the so-called export economies are certainly suggestive. Alternatively, there are cases of countries that have followed more inward-looking policies—Mexico, the U.S.S.R., or South Africa, to take widely contrasting examples —which have done considerably better than the export economies in combining economic growth with diversification. Therefore, if we regard "modernization" as the goal, we are led, in my view, to give priority to modernization of subsistence agriculture rather than to encouragement of export agriculture (though Mexico has taken the other course, perhaps mistakenly).

Supposing this is accepted, the question arises concerning

the way to operationalize the modernization of subsistence agriculture. Bearing in mind the need to couple responsibility with access to the requisite resources and powers, our Western inclination is to suggest some form of private enterprise. On the other hand, there is much to be said in support of Parsons' view that authoritarian systems are easier to institute and operate in the early stages of agricultural development. Small family farms, even if one acknowledges a presumption of economically rational behavior, will be faced with a multitude of potential problems related to input supply, technological choice, and product demand that lie beyond both their innovative capacities and their ability to initiate effective problem-handling processes in the larger social system. Under these conditions it seems clear that innovative behavior will be required at two levels, inside each productive enterprise and in the institutional environment of all the enterprises taken together. This suggests that organizational forms which combine private incentives with public powers and decision making would offer the best chances of success. The Gezira scheme, where decisions concerning what and how to produce were made centrally, and where responsibility for providing inputs and disposing of product were handled by the over-all organization, but where actual production was individualized and rewards depended on results, is the prototype of what I have in mind. But the possible variations on the theme are, I am sure, infinite. What is needed is an open mind and a wealth of experimentation if we are to have any hope of developing a "theory of the design of opportunities."

To be sought for each enterprise are the economies of large scale in decision making, information flow, command over the environment, and ability to initiate effective problem-handling processes that are enjoyed by a well-run agricultural factory such as the private plantation or state farm, while achieving the economies of execution on a small scale together with the incentive effect derived from distributing the fruits of effort in ways that, being visibly and securely related to the quantity and quality of performance, induce responsible attention to detail. Productive expectations need to be stabilized through centralized decision and control over external hazards while assuring the stability of distributive expectations based on effort removed from the threat of superior intervention.

For a group of enterprises, however the group may be defined, an overarching organizational structure is needed to assure supplies of modern inputs, including extension services, and effective marketing of output. Cooperatives and marketing boards have some of the organizational attributes, but need to be assigned problem-handling responsibilities more explicitly and to be granted suitable access to internally generated or externally allocated surpluses. Since their effectiveness in promoting economic efficiency has often been criticized, and is not likely to be much improved, they should at least play a positive developmental role.

Finally, there is the question of the over-all strategy, of the broad lines of the solution to be worked out. Bearing in mind that modernization of the subsistence sector, specifically of food production for the home market, is the proposed target, that one of the objects is to reduce the migration of people from farm to city, and that capital is scarce, certain requirements must be met. One is that output of food per farm family be increased. A second is that this be done by increased inputs of modern forms of organization and technology, and by shifting to high value foods, rather than by massive inputs of capital. A third is that a market for the increased food production be assured. The first two conditions constitute the substance of the agricultural modernization process. The third is necessary to make it succeed.

The third condition, the balancing of supply and demand, is the most difficult of the three. Offhand, it seems simple. Given the recognized need for greater quantities and better qualities of per capita food consumption throughout the world there should be no lack of potential outlets for any likely rates of increase in supplies. The chief difficulties are to bring about the requisite dietary changes (provided nontraditional foods are to be produced), and where this obstacle has been avoided or circumvented, to solve the economic problem of effective demand. For individual subsistence farms, solution of the first problem brings solution of the second, but specialization in the production of marketable surpluses of one kind of food requires production of similar surpluses of other kinds having equal value at some set of mutually remunerative prices. Some of these other surpluses may consist of food production, leading to internal exchanges, but in the long run the food-producing sector as a whole should be expected to have a surplus to be exchanged in the cities for their surpluses of goods and services. It has become fashionable among economists to extend this argument by maintaining that the savings of the agricultural sector taken as a whole should exceed investment in that sector so that investment in the nonagricultural sectors taken collectively can exceed their saving. I must confess to a sneaking suspicion that this is the wrong problem to worry about. Thus, *if* the subsistence sector, as a whole, can be brought to the point of producing a marketable surplus of food, traditional or nontraditional, it would not bother me if this were exchanged for any feasible combination of producer and consumer goods and services from the cities. I suspect that the growth engendered by such dynamically potent reciprocity would, in a fairly short time, generate aggregate savings and investment somewhere in the economy that would more than make up for any conceivable savings that might have been squeezed out of the subsistence sector by any effective set of austere policies. But I *would* want to be sure that the modernization of the subsistence sector concentrated on labor-intensive, capital-saving methods of increasing output per acre and per manhour. The real strategy is to develop *the people* right where so many of them are, in the subsistence sector. Hence this is the problem for which new problem-handling mechanisms are needed. As stated in Parsons' concluding section, the "vast field of institutional innovation must somehow be understood so that institutions can be used to 'liberate and expand' individual action, as well as to 'restrain' or 'control' it." Not all innovation has a liberative and expansive effect, but most of it surely does, especially in the forms ordinarily characterized as radical.

7. Developmental Aspects of Administration

FREDERICK W. FREY

Developmental administration, I suppose, refers to administration in developing societies or for developmental goals. Delineation of the field would therefore involve careful stipulation of the characteristics of such societies, definition of the processes of administration and development, indication of whether both public and private administration were to be considered, and so on. Beside these elements and processes would be the assumption that there is some reasonably differentiated body of knowledge to which we refer under the label "developmental administration" and whose distinctive concepts are helpful for understanding behavioral change in agriculture in the emerging nations.

Viewed against my interests and experience, this is at once too broad and too limited an assignment. Administrative theory and organization theory are today such rich realms that even a rather barbaric ransacking of their offerings seems too formidable a task.[1]

The rubric of "developmental administration" seems too

[1] The reader can convince himself of this by consulting the packed and laconic summary volume by James G. March and Herbert A. Simon, *Organizations* (New York: Wiley, 1958), or the 1,200 double-columned pages of *Handbook of Organizations,* edited by March (Chicago: Rand McNally, 1965). A volume specifically devoted to *Bureaucracy and Political Development* has been edited by Joseph LaPalombara (Princeton: Princeton University Press, 1963). March and Simon dutifully numbered the major variables employed in their survey of the field and emerged with some 206. A more eclectic, less synthetic summary could easily double that number.

limited in that I feel it important to discuss several topics such as the analysis of power that are more generally political than purely administrative. I also wish to trespass a bit in the domains of the social psychologist and the rural sociologist.

Three Administrative Cultures

Let us start with a Weberian foray into the historic relations between rulers and their subjects. The most critical problems of administration occur when considerations of size (both population and area) and task complexity (requiring specialized skills) preclude direct rule. Under such circumstances, the chief decision makers of a social system are confronted with the problem of establishing a set of power intermediaries between themselves and those whom they govern. A useful, if brutal, formulation of the focal problem of public administration asks how this can be accomplished. How can the highest authorities in the state create a corps of agents whom they can effectively and predictably influence and who, in turn, will be able to influence the larger public in desired ways?

This basic formulation holds whether the chief decision makers are elected representatives or a despot and his henchmen. It says nothing, of course, about the wisdom of their rule and the legitimacy of its goals. At the most fundamental level, the problem of administration is the same regardless of the type of regime or political system.

In simplest terms, two vital links characterize the administrative process: the link between rulers and administration, and the link between administration and public. Incapacities in administration can thus be categorized into those in which either the first or second link is impaired (or both). Either the rulers do not have the ability to control the administration sufficiently to achieve regime goals or else the administration does not have the ability to influence the appropriate public sufficiently to achieve regime goals.

Examples of both types of breakdowns can easily be found in today's developing world and in the traditional realms of long ago. Contemporary discussions of problems of administration in transitional societies refer almost unanimously to the dangers of an overpowering bureaucracy which dominates those formally designated as chief decision makers and which overwhelms the institutions (legislatures, parties, etc.) that are supposed to give top formal authorities control over the administration. Earlier days witnessed the same generic phenomenon in the domination of the Egyptian state by the Mameluke slaves of the Ayyubid sultans, in the deposition of Ottoman sultans by unruly Janissaries and ulema, and in the many usurpations of power by governors, ministers, priests, and generals.

Similarly, it seems obvious that in many developing nations the administration is presently incapable of getting farmers to refrain from denuding forests or from having too many children, is incapable of inducing shopkeepers to pay specified taxes or squatters from migrating to overcrowded cities, and is incapable of preventing civil violence or extensive smuggling. Even greater debilities clearly plagued most states in past centuries.

In fact, one of the most neglected yet important problems of administration that is sharply revealed by this model is the relationship between the two basic power linkages of the administrative process. There seem to be situations in which the very mechanisms employed by rulers to control the bureaucracy act to undermine that bureaucracy's actual or potential influence with the public. An example would be the case in which elite education and isolation are used to mold a unified and dedicated higher civil service, as perhaps in Britain or China, but at the expense of the separation and alienation of that administrative echelon from the mass of the society. Conversely, an administrative unit may have to take such steps to influence its relevant public that the other nexus—the chief decision makers' power over the administration—is undermined. Regulatory agencies in many countries seem to become allies of their publics and impervious to higher political authority. As Peter Blau has illustrated, the posture and actions which an agency must sometimes adopt in order even to be partially effective vis-à-vis its public may lead it to resist or subvert directives from higher authorities.[2]

The compatibility of the ruler-administration and the administration-public linkages needs close scrutiny. Not a few of the intractable problems of developmental administration seem to lie in this area.

[2] *The Dynamics of Bureaucracy* (Chicago: University of Chicago Press, 1955).

Insight into certain additional difficulties of developmental administration is furnished by some gross historical characterizations. Consider the position of a traditional monarch—say, the emperor of Terra Incognita. His problem is essentially that of controlling his provincial governor in Miasma in order to achieve certain goals such as the collection of troops and taxes. Though apparently simple, the problem is ultimately quite complex. To analyze it one needs information regarding the goals of the emperor, the influential strategies open to him, the characteristics of the provincial governor and the influential strategies open to him, the position and nature of the critical actors in Miasma, their available influence strategies, and so on. But let us examine the situation very generally from a communication and power perspective.

One means of control which the emperor might use would be to maintain constant communication with and surveillance over the activities of his administrator in Miasma. The governor might inform the emperor of situations as soon as he encountered them, and the emperor would supply the governor with instructions for dealing with these situations (though he might not call his instructions "decisional premises"). In organizational theory this type of arrangement has been christened "feedback" control. It offers the great advantage of flexibility—the capacity to adjust decisions quite rapidly and specifically to local conditions or central changes in policy. If Terra Incognita were a modern industrialized nation such a control system might be employed by the emperor. But it was not available to him as ruler of a traditional society since it demands a kind of communication network and channel capacity which no such society possessed.

Actually, most rulers of Terra Incognita, recognizing the inadequacy of their communication facilities, followed a very different strategy. They called in the man whom they had decided to designate as governor in Miasma and, in essence, made a deal with him. The emperor would furnish him with a few soldiers and a seal (called "legitimacy") and authorize him to collect taxes and troops in the emperor's name. The governor, however, being far away and commanding more bodyguards than the emperor had troops in Miasma, would be unlikely to go to the trouble of collecting taxes and recruits for the emperor on the basis of friendship, altruism, or weakness alone.

If the emperor assembled his army and proceeded against Miasma, he could punish a disobedient governor, but he could hardly do this very quickly or often. Hence, the emperor suggested that the governor simply send to the capital a fixed sum of tax money each year and a fixed number of recruits. The governor, presumably also being interested in money and power, could keep all taxes and recruits over and above the emperor's share. Since the emperor had some potential power and considerable mystique in Miasma, this arrangement would be advantageous to the governor as well.

The emperor knew his man and the deal was concluded. We can call this type of administrative arrangement "venal control." It allowed for the deficiency of communication between Miasma and the capital (reflected in the fact that the per cent of all tax money collected which the emperor actually received from his governors was inversely proportional to their distance from the capital). But the venal control system was really quite wasteful and greatly limited the emperor's capacity to affect most behaviors of his subjects.

Some of the emperors of Terra Incognita were so frustrated by these limitations of the venal control system that they introduced various modifications, such as keeping selected members of their governors' families in the capital to ensure better administrative performance. This tactic, however, often produced ugly hostility or, worse, a large collection of mothers-in-law to feed and humor in the Imperial Palace. A few of the wisest emperors of Terra Incognita adopted a different strategy. They tried to select their prospective governors while very young. The chosen young men were then sent to a special school where they were trained, not only in tax collecting and military recruiting, but especially in dedication to the emperor and the ideology of dynasticism. They were indoctrinated, insofar as possible, with an appropriate and uniform approach to administrative problems and they developed a fervor for imperial service (for which they were also quite well rewarded, especially in terms of prestige and deference from other subjects). Had they been able to read later descriptions of what they did, these emperors would have called their system of administration one of "programmed" control.

It was, while it lasted, less wasteful and more potent than venal control. But it was difficult to maintain full programmed

control for more than a few generations of officials. The fervor
seemed usually to abate after that period, since later generations of officials were raised in a different environment from
that which produced the initial fervor. Administrative control
based primarily on ideology and socialization proved rather
ephemeral. It also created problems of rigidity when the emperor wanted to alter basic policies, since reprogramming the
administrative class was quite difficult. Again, the palace schools
seemed to function properly and with dedication for awhile,
but then, when it became recognized that they provided the
main channel of access to top positions, they frequently became
increasingly arrogant, corrupt, remote, and out of touch with
the rest of the empire and its problems.

Historically, these three types of administrative control systems (and they are neither exclusive nor exhaustive, merely
most prominent) seem to be very loosely associated with different emphases in regime goals. The system of "venal control"—
that is, taking both human motivations and the deficiencies in
communication and power for granted and attempting to make
it in the administrator's venal self-interest to behave in the
way the rulers preferred—seems mainly to have been associated
with regime goals that are not unfairly labeled *exploitative*.
The power and privilege of the dynasty and the administration
were the uppermost values of the regime.

Although exceptions were numerous, there seems also to
have been an historic association between "programmed control" and regime goals that were primarily *regulatory*, although
at times reform considerations also loomed large. Finally, the
modern state, able to use "feedback control" much more extensively, seems to place a major emphasis on *developmental
or welfare* goals.

Whether these associations are historically accurate, necessary in some sense, and revealing is a topic which requires
further research and discussion. Nevertheless, it is important
to note that the developing nations of today seem to present
us with varying combinations, frequently unreconciled, of
these three systems of administrative control and of regime
goals. Much bureaucratic practice in these nations is still (and
more than vestigially) venal control, and for the same historic
reasons. Westerners tend to deplore corruption in developmental administration without analyzing it as a manifestation of

venal control under traditional ideas of motivation and poor communication, legitimized by millenia of realistic acceptance as one way, perhaps the only way, of getting certain jobs done. Nepotism is no less deplored. But in a traditional society lacking an impersonal ethic covering obligations to strangers or novel roles, nepotism may be an extremely rational administrative practice. The decision maker is willing to trade efficiency for reduced risk (i.e., added control). His brother-in-law may be more stupid than another candidate for the branch office in Dengue, but he can appeal to well-known familial obligations to ensure that his brother-in-law does not betray him. General ethical standards which would reduce the risk of employing the more talented stranger are lacking. Actually, Western survey researchers working in developing areas frequently follow the same approach; we use honesty rather than talent as our primary criterion for recruiting interviewers, since our risks are less if we trade some of the latter for more of the former.

Historic legacies which produce very difficult and complex administrative patterns are even more demonstrable in the case of regime goals. As I have argued, most traditional regimes tended to be primarily exploitative in nature. Some more enlightened traditional societies, many colonial regimes and most nineteenth-century democracies tended to be primarily regulatory in their administrative goals, while contemporary regimes tend, at least formally, to stress welfare and developmental objectives. However, within many developing societies real unanimity regarding regime goals is as rare as uniformity in the predominant type of administrative control. Certain agencies, such as state economic enterprises or planning commissions, are deeply committed to developmental goals; other ministries such as Interior or Justice may be just as deeply committed to a regulatory outlook; and the local potentates or village head men may be no less consistently following a traditionally exploitative policy.

The reactions of the public to these variations in administrative orientations seem to depend very much on the nature of the contacts between the public and particular administrative actors. It is sometimes difficult for planning commissions or central officials to comprehend peasant suspicion of governmental programs. In the eyes of the modern and often deeply altruistic and dedicated central officials, convinced of the importance of their mission and the sincerely developmental nature of their goals, these peasant reactions are simply stupid and obstructive. But look at the same administrative picture from the peasant's perspective. Through centuries his kind had encountered the venal and exploitative forms of government. The regime came to the villages in most traditional societies generally for one of three purposes: to collect taxes, recruit troops, or arrest some villager who had violated a law or offended the elite. Peasant contacts with the government were almost entirely negative from the peasant's perspective.

"Ah, but all that is changed," objects the developmental administrator. "We now earnestly wish to improve the peasant's lot. We want to bring him schools, roads, health, and other good things which, although perhaps not as much as we, he clearly wants." Here however, is where a little empirical research is salubrious. My own studies of peasants in Turkey and Venezuela, two of the more developed less-developed societies, indicate that there is a very great lag in perceived changes in regime goals among various sectors of the society. Elites and especially top administrative echelons take for granted the developmental goals of the state. But peasants are chary about accepting such changes as bona fide—with good cause in most cases. Despite Turkey's half century of developmental struggles, our survey of the Turkish peasantry in 1962 indicated that by far the most frequent contacts between peasants and administration were still of the traditional type which the peasant would regard as negative. As Table 1 shows, the most ubiquitous contacts were still with police and gendarmes and the next most inescapable were with the tax collector. Contacts with development officials were markedly less extensive. The view of regime goals from the seventh floor of a central ministry and the view from behind the mud walls of most villages are currently rather understandably discrepant. Developmental administration courts failure when it does not recognize these perceptual discrepancies.

I am suggesting that one of the basic problems of developmental administration is produced by the fact that at least three rather different systems of administrative control and regime goals operate in most developing societies. With changes in communication capacities and political ideology, there have been successive encrustations of divergent administrative forms and orientations. Portions of the nation and its administration are employing feedback coordination and striving to reach developmental goals, other portions are essentially relying on programmed coordination and pursuing regulatory goals, while a significant residuum is still operating with venal controls and seeking exploitative objectives. These three (or more) systems are barely integrated and the over-all administrative problems thus exhibit extreme complexity. National coordination demands successful operation in at least three divergent worlds, three different administrative cultures. Integration of

Table 1. Frequency of different types of official contact with Turkish villagers: Per cent of villagers living in communities visited by officials at various intervals *

Type of official	Visited at least once per month	Visited less than once per month	Never visited
County prefect or district director	25	41	34
Military personnel	7	19	72
Police or gendarmes	91	6	2
Tax collectors	19	76	4
Educators and teachers (nonlocal)	7	60	32
Agricultural officials	22	34	42
Health officials and doctors	54	27	18
Postal workers	62	11	27

* Percentages may not add horizontally to 100 because of rounding. The base for each set of percentages is approximately 6,000 respondents. Our Turkish data do not seem to show much association between attitudes toward development and the amount of governmental contact of the peasants, probably because of the mixed nature of this contact. Further analyses will explore this distinction between positively and negatively valued contacts. Samuel Eldersveld found evidence in Delhi State in India for a rather modest but clear attitudinal "pay-off" from administrative contacts among Indian farmers. See his "Bureaucratic Contact with the Public in India," *Indian Journal of Public Administration*, 40 (1965), 216–235. Our Turkish survey is described in Frederick W. Frey, "Surveying Peasant Attitudes in Turkey," *Public Opinion Quarterly*, 27 (1963), 335–355, and in reports available from the Center for International Studies, M.I.T.

these various administrative cultures is a crucial task for developmental administration.

Although most truly modern systems of administration are distinguished in part by the capacity to employ feedback coordination, applying that label alone to them is a bit misleading. They tend even more to be characterized by an effective blending of administrative controls of venal, programmed, feedback, and other types. Thus, modern organizations take cognizance of the need for their members to be able to satisfy many of their basic values through the organization and of the need to adapt to the basic values of their relevant publics. This appeal to the existing self-interests of members and publics is analogous to venal control, save that our insight into human motivation now extends to more dimensions than those usually handled by traditional systems of venal control. Still, it is widely and explicitly accepted that the administrative system must be adapted to the human characteristics of the administrators and the public.

Modern administrative systems also have not abandoned programmed control. We now call it role socialization, training, professionalization, internalization of appropriate values, and so on, but it amounts to the same thing. The difference is that less heavy and exclusive reliance is placed upon such controls, and we are supposed to have better insight into what they can and cannot do, when they are appropriate and when not. One hallmark of a fully modern administrative system is that these and other forms of control over the administration and over the public by the administration are well integrated into a complementary system of reinforcing controls rather than existing as distinct and competitive administrative worlds.

But it is now time for us to peer more systematically at the whole problem of power and its analysis, for this is the essence not only of administration but of the relationship between administration and "politics" more generally interpreted.

Analysis of Power [3]

I should like to be able to report that students of politics had long ago elaborated a proven and diversified set of tools

[3] This analysis of power is a revised version of a discussion first presented in a paper on "Political Science, Education, and National Devel-

for power analysis. Unfortunately, such is not the case. Although political scientists have been worrying about problems of power for a long time, the attempt to construct sharp, appropriate, and empirical techniques for the analysis of power is embarrassingly recent. From various disciplines we have assembled many data on persuasion, propaganda, and certain kinds of influential communications. Numerous studies of "community power structures" have been attempted, a few with promising sophistication. A number of insightful case studies of bureaucratic decisions and of the enactment of legislation have been accomplished. Constitutions have been analyzed. Prominent formally political roles, such as legislative committee chairman, cabinet member, parliamentary backbencher, precinct committeeman, president, prime minister, and so on, have been scrutinized, particularly from a legalistic viewpoint. The power positions of the judiciary, political parties, interest groups, social classes, etc., have been examined in fundamentally *ad hoc* fashion. Case studies and histories of "political development" in various societies have been produced. And certain activities that are material components of the process of allocating power, such as voting, recruitment, etc., have been rather carefully studied in depth.

From all these efforts much can be learned. But the great bulk of the work that has been accomplished has not been conspicuously informd by any very general theoretical perspective. The political scientist's self-conscious effort to arm himself with trenchant concepts and techniques for power analysis is really quite new. Nevertheless important progress has recently been made.

In the realm of power analysis, four kinds of methodological problems seem to be most critical, or, to put it more positively, work in four major areas seems to offer most promise. These areas are: (1) explicating the concept of power, (2) developing fruitful subordinate conceptualization, (3) improving techniques for the location and measurement of power, and (4)

opment" prepared for the Conference on Comparative Education, University of California, Berkeley, California, March 25–27, 1966. This paper, and others from that conference, appear in a book edited by Dr. Joseph Fischer, *The Social Sciences and the Comparative Study of Educational Systems* (Scranton: International Textbook, 1970), pp. 349–408.

establishing methods for summarily describing and accurately comparing power structures. I shall deal briefly and selectively with each of these areas.

Concept of Power

Lasswell, Catlin, Simon, Dahl, March, Cartwright, Parsons, Deutsch, Shills, Blau, Lenski, MacIver, and many other social scientists from various disciplines have examined the fundamental conception of power or interpersonal influence. Almost all have found it profoundly promising, perhaps vital, but all have found it more or less elusive. Many would apparently agree with Robert Bierstedt who opined that, "In the entire lexicon of sociological concepts none is more troublesome than the concept of power." [4] But, like Bierstedt, they seem to feel that it is such a central notion it is very much worth worrying about.

Actually, there is a good deal of agreement among the social analysts who have appraised the concept of power. Almost all are agreed that the underlying phenomenon of reference is an interpersonal relationship. Almost all are agreed that this is a dynamic behavioral relationship in the sense that the actions of one party are related to changes in the actions or states of another party. On the whole, the psychological basis for the notion of power seems to lie in the intuitive awareness that, although human behavior is affected by many things, one critical factor is the behavior of other human beings. The analysis of power is a search for regularities surrounding those situations when a given human being does or does not affect the behavior of another specified human being. Hence, if we peruse the literature on the concept of power, it seems that one is most appropriately led to the following sort of definition: power is an interpersonal relationship such that the behavior of one actor(s) alters the behavior of another actor(s). By "behavior" is meant any change in the state of an individual from one time (t_1) to a later time (t_2).

Attention even to this basic formulation of the concept would seem to be useful for would-be power analysts. For instance, it indicates that adequate description of a power relationship

[4] "An Analysis of Social Power," *American Sociological Review*, 15 (1950), 730.

minimally requires a *quadripartite* statement. One must identify the influencer, the influencee, the relevant behavior engaged in by the influencer (influential behavior), and the affected behavior of the influencee (scope). Strangely, most field studies have not been guided by an understanding of the essentials of the power relationship, and so they have failed to make critical observations of all four aspects of important power relations even when such observations were clearly possible.

Another way of expressing these ideas is to say that: since no one influences all other people, one must designate the *influencee;* since no one is influenced by all other people, one must designate the *influencer;* since no one affects all behaviors of any other person (except perhaps by killing him), one must specify the behaviors affected *(scope)*; and since just anything an influencer does is not likely to produce a given effect, one must specify the specific effect-producing behavior *(influential behavior)*. Thus, the power relation can be represented schematically as in Figure 1, where R refers to the influencer (designated by idiosyncratic naming, role occupied, or some other characteristic, e.g., sex), where E refers to the influencee (similarly designated), where α refers to the influential behavior (e.g., bribery, speech making, threat of expulsion), and where β refers to the scope (e.g., voting for a certain candidate, running an errand, doing homework). The arrow indicates the direction of the influence. Power is defined as an irreflexive and antisymmetric concept.

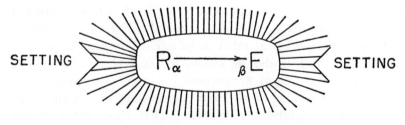

SETTING   SETTING

Figure 1. Schematic representation of power relation

Actually, since virtually all power relationships hold in some settings and not in others, one must also designate the relevant setting or context for the relation.

The most conspicuous problem suggested with regard to such a conception of power revolves about its causal character.

That causal nature becomes clear if we examine the notion of "alteration" built into the definition. R has power over E if R's behavior alters E's behavior. That is to say, if some observable action of R is at least a partial or contributory cause of E's behavior being different from what it otherwise would have been, R is said to have power or interpersonal influence over E.

Two or three prominent problems are engendered by this formulation. First of all, how does one know what the behavior of E would otherwise have been? Is not a formidably complete social and psychological theory necessary to enable us even to assert that a power relation exists? Are we not in a position of needing a more profound theory in order to develop a less profound one?

One answer to this objection is best illustrated by specification of the ideal experiment that underlies the concept of power. To assert that R has power over E, we should ideally like to hold everything else constant, let R's behavior vary in a prescribed fashion, and then ascertain whether E's behavior changed subsequently, regularly, correspondingly, and predictably with R's engaging in or not engaging in the designated influential behavior. Of course, one cannot be satisfied that one ever has held all crucial factors constant unless one is armed with theories describing the relationship of these factors to the dependent variable (E's behavior). But this problem is the vicious circle that all experimentation confronts and that makes the development of science such a cumulative and corrective process. The problem is simply more acute in budding sciences, such as the social sciences. The analysis of power as defined no more demands an impossible general social and psychological theory than does any other social science inquiry. It no more demands a more elaborate theory to get a less elaborate one than does any natural experimental science. The problem of ensuring the control of all factors other than the hypothesized independent variable—or knowing what those other factors are—pervades all experimental inquiry. There is, of course, a problem of measurement that is severe, because under most circumstances we cannot create or well approximate this experiment. It is essentially conceivable, but unfeasible. I shall return to measurement problems later.

A second objection to the concept of power as a causal notion is simply the contention that causation is a discredited approach in modern empirical science. Hume demolished it, and non-causal bodies of scientific thought, such as quantum mechanics, finally interred it. My convictions are well stated by Ernest Nagel, when he says,

It would be a mistake to suppose that, because in one meaning of the word the notion of cause plays an important role in some field of inquiry, the notion is indispensable in all other fields—just as it would be an error to maintain that, because this notion is useless in certain parts of science, it cannot have a legitimate role in other divisions of scientific study . . . however inadequate this notion of cause may be for the purposes of theoretical physics, it continues to play a role in many other branches of inquiry. It is a notion that is firmly embodied in the language we employ, even when abstract physical theories are used in the laboratory as well as in practical affairs for obtaining various results through the manipulation of appropriate instrumentalities. Indeed, it is because some things can be manipulated so as to yield other things, but not conversely, that causal language is a legitimate and convenient way of describing the relations of many events.[5]

There are several basic notions of causality, including a general principle of causality as well as special causal laws or theories (e.g., classical mechanics). Any theory of power relations would be a special theory, not a general one. Moreover, one can seemingly "modernize" the notion of cause so as to eliminate objections to certain older formulations. Thus, one can say that a given event (*R*'s behavior) can be labeled a "cause" of another event (*E*'s behavior) if that first event must be included in the premises of a valid scientific explanation of the second event. A power relationship exists if one must adduce *R*'s behavior in order validly to explain *E*'s behavior. Thus, the task for the power analyst is first to locate those instances in which one individual's behavior is essential to the explanation of another individual's behavior, and second to ascertain what similarities or patterns, if any, can be perceived among such instances.

A third objection to the causal character of the power concept is based upon the following type of argument. A theory of power, is by definition, a theory of causality. But a truly

[5] *The Structure of Science* (New York: Harcourt, Brace and World, 1961), pp. 73, 75.

general theory of causality would explain everything and, hence, clearly be either impossible or uninteresting. The study of power is therefore a step in the wrong direction. We should not define a causal relationship and make that the focus of our investigative efforts. We should rather concentrate on other kinds of phenomena.

This argument seems to me to be a *non sequitur*. It fails to make the distinction that Nagel urges between a general principle of causality (which is probably devoid of empirical content) and special, limited empirical theories of certain kinds of causal relations. That a general theory of all causal relations is impossible or trivial does not mean that limited theories of certain specific kinds of causal relationships are not both possible and rewarding.

Another problem regarding the concept of power is worth mentioning. Some writers choose to define power as an ability or potentiality, thereby conforming more closely to the most common lay usage of the term. Other writers find it more satisfactory to adopt a conception of power as an exercise of ability, that is, as an actual, rather than potential, behavioral interrelationship. My preference is to define power as an actual relationship, largely because establishment of potential relationships is a much more difficult task and is generally some kind of inference from actual conditions. Regardless of which conception is adopted, power as ability or power as actuality, both conceptions are required. If power is defined as an ability, then the notion of its exercise is essential. If power is defined as actuality, then the notion of a corresponding potentiality is clearly fruitful if we are to use power analysis as an important tool for helping to understand and predict social system performance.[6]

6 This point is very well made in James March's article, "The Power of Power," in *Varieties of Political Theory*, David Easton, ed. (Englewood Cliffs, N.J.: Prentice-Hall, 1966), pp. 39–70, especially in the discussion of the "basic force" and "force activation" models. March, unfortunately in my view, concludes with a rather negative judgment regarding the utility of power as a social scientific concept. I cannot debate the issue here, nor can he, but my opinion is that his conclusion is not justified by his preceding discussion. For a similarly negative judgment see Otto A. Davis, M. A. H. Dempster, and Aaron Wildawsky, "A Theory of the Budgetary Process," *American Political Science Review*, 60 (1966), 544.

Finally, a few writers, of whom Robert Dahl is probably the best known, define power is probabilistic terms. I do not think that this is a particularly burning issue, and, even though I do not choose at present to employ a probabilistic definition, it is quite fruitful to speak of the probability that a given power relationship does or does not exist. Probabilistic approaches will have a significant part to play in future power analysis, especially in the analysis and simulation of large-scale power structures.

Subordinate Conceptualization

Although careful attention to the basic conception of power is vital to the effective analysis of political systems, it is plainly true that one does not get far with the concept of power alone. It will be a long, long time—if ever—before anything resembling a general theory of power is developed. Our efforts will have to focus on power in manageable subsystems, perhaps even much smaller than the agricultural sector or even rural administration, probably at the level of the specific village-type and agency-type. We must investigate specific kinds of power and specific aspects of power relations. For all this, one of our most urgent requirements is appropriate subordinate conceptualization elaborating the basic concept of power. Through such subordinate conceptualization one can become as detailed as the most traditional scholar should like, while at the same time maintaining an awareness of how the immediate phenomena of interest relate to other power phenomena. Put another way, through such integrated subordinated conceptualization the door to fruitful comparison is fully opened and we are led to look beyond the walls of our immediate interests.

Space precludes a full treatment here of subordinate conceptualization for power analysis. I can outline certain main directions which such efforts can take and furnish some useful

---

The critical point is that power is but one factor affecting the performance of a social system and must not be taken as totally determinative of that performance. However, it is difficult to be satisfied with some recent predictive models of system performance whose variables seem to be very *ad hoc* and of limited applicability. I obviously find it difficult to conceive how the performance of a social system can be at all profoundly understood without coming to grips with the analysis of power.

examples of distinctions that have been made. A start already exists in the sense that four fundamental distinctions flow directly from the concept of power itself: influencer, influencee, scope, and influential behavior. I argued earlier that any minimally complete description of a power relationship must provide information along these four dimensions.

One of the most fruitful organizations of this subordinate conceptualization seems to be in terms of aspects of power and types of power. In other words, it seems useful to divide the set of all power relationships into more manageable subsets that, ideally, would be mutually exclusive and exhaustive. This is what I have in mind when I refer to types of power. One can also think of aspects of any power relationship, that is, features which can characterize all kinds of power relationships regardless of type. However, if one pushes this distinction between types and aspects very hard, it breaks down. I continue to employ it in order to distinguish two different and specific ways of categorizing power relations, though admittedly many other schemes are both possible and useful.

Aspects of Power

Some of the more salient aspects of power relations that have been distinguished are as follows:

1. *Domain:* Domain refers to the set of actors over whom a given influencer has power. Three further subordinate distinctions are minimally required.

a. Domain (*ib*): The set of persons, regardless of scope, whose behaviors are altered by a given influential behavior of a given actor (*R*). For example, this notion refers to all persons influenced in whatever way by an extension agent's demonstration, though some might be influenced favorably, some unfavorably, and some irrelevantly from the agent's viewpoint.

b. Domain (*s*): The set of persons, regardless of influential behavior, whose behaviors are altered with the same specified scope by some collection of behaviors of a given actor (*R*). For example, this notion refers to the set of farmers whom a given extension agent somehow induced to use fertilizer, although the agent's influential behavior might have been different in each case.

c. Domain (*ib/s*): the set of persons whose behaviors are

altered with the same specified scope by a specified influential behavior of a given actor (R). For example, all farmers induced to use fertilizer by an extension agent's demonstration.

2. *Power Field:* Power field refers to the set of actors having power over a given influencee (E). Again, three further subordinate distinctions are minimally required.

a. Power Field (ib): The set of persons who, with the same influential behavior, have power over a given influencee (E), regardless of scope. For example, all persons who can influence a designated farmer by threatening his credit, regardless of what they influence him to do.

b. Power Field (s): the set of persons who, regardless of influential behavior, have power over a given influencee (E) with the same specified scope. For example, the set of persons who can do something, whatever it is, that will induce a given farmer to adopt fertilizer.

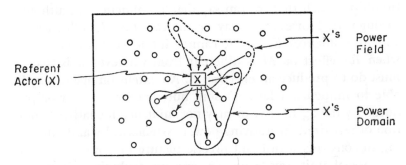

Figure 2. Schematic representation of power field and domain

c. Power Field (ib/s): The set of persons who, with the same specified influential behavior, have power over a given influencee (E) with the same specified scope. For example, all persons who can successfully induce a given farmer to adopt fertilizer by threatening his credit.

A schematic (directed graph or digraph) representation of the notions of power field and domain is presented in Figure 2. The concepts of power field and domain are analogous to the concepts of "inbundle" and "outbundle" in the theory of directed graphs (or row and column totals in power matrices). Like some of the other aspects of power, they may seem rather obvious or trivial to some readers, but they are critical building blocks for rigorous structural analysis along sociometric lines and even for more sophisticated impressionistic analysis.

Actually, the diagram presented is highly oversimplified and unrealistic when contrasted with observable power structures. This is brought out by another essential subordinate concept:

3. *Directness (or Transitivity)*: Directness refers to whether there are actor intermediaries between the influencer and influencee. For a power relation to be indirect (or transitive), the scope for the influencee in the first part of a linking relationship must be the same as his influential behavior in the second part of the link. Thus,

(transitive) $\quad R_{\alpha} \longrightarrow_{\sigma} M_{\sigma} \longrightarrow_{\beta} E$

(intransitive) $\ R_{\alpha} \longrightarrow_{\sigma} M, \ M_{\gamma} \longrightarrow_{\beta} E$

(direct) $\qquad R_{\alpha} \longrightarrow_{\beta} E$

In other words, in a direct power relation, R influences E and that is all there is to it. In a transitive (indirect) power relation, R influences M who in turn influences E, and the relationship is such that we can say that R influences E, although through M. However, it may be the case that R influences M and M influences E, but R cannot influence E. That occurs when R's effect on M is different from whatever it is that M must do to produce an effect on E. An extension agent may be able to influence a farmer's son, but that son's behavior produced by the agent may or may not influence his father's adoption of fertilizer. In studying power systematically and attempting to construct a full and precise picture of power structures in a social unit, say, a village, one must obtain information about the scope and influential behavior of each power relationship. Otherwise, one cannot locate the indirect chains of influence in the unit. In fact, the problem runs even deeper than this, but it would take me too far afield to pursue it here. In some of our earlier studies of the power structures of small organizations we neglected to obtain information about the influential behaviors employed in each relationship and found that we could analyze only direct power relations, thus securing an unrealistic picture. Incidentally, a critical problem in all this is fruitful specification of influential behaviors and scopes. Directness and many other aspects of power relations are badly blurred if influential behaviors and scopes are too broadly, too narrowly, or too unrealistically defined. Unfortunately, there is no algorithm for obtaining appropriate definitions. This is very much a matter of "feel" and intuition—of understanding garnered from deep experience in the substantive matters being investigated.

4. *Dyadic and Polyadic Power Relations:* A dyadic power relation involves only two actors, R and E. A polyadic power relation involves more than two actors. It may be R-polyadic in the sense of involving more than one influencer, but only one influencee. It may be E-polyadic in the sense of involving more than one influencee, but only one influencer. Or, it may be mutually or generally polyadic, involving more than one actor on both sides of the relationship.

5. *Conjunctivity (or Sufficiency):* A conjunctive power relation is one in which the influential behavior or scope *necessarily*

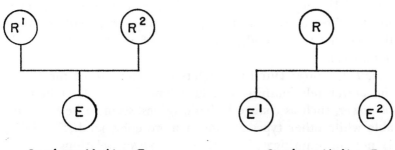

Conjunctivity <u>R</u>   Conjunctivity <u>E</u>

Figure 3. Conjunctive power relations

involves more than one actor as R or E, but not simply as an indirect power relationship. For example, if neither the extension agent nor a farmer's best friend alone can persuade a farmer to adopt fertilizer, but if *both* talk to him (intentionally or accidentally, alone or together), they can persuade him to do so, then the power relation is said to be conjunctive. Or, if the scope of influence exerted by a given influencer is such that it demands more than one influencee, such as inducing the formation of an eight-oared crew, then it can be said to be a conjunctive power relation. In depicting power field or domain, such conjunctions of R's and E's are sometimes best represented as single actors. Conjunctive power relations may be illustrated as in Figure 3.

6. *Rapidity:* The rapidity of the power relation refers to the length of time that elapses between the influential behavior and the influencee's scope (response). Some power exercises produce instantaneous results while others seem to have delayed reactions. If one expects the former while the relation is of the latter type, he can be seriously misled. In the broadest of terms, this is what seems to have happened regarding foreign aid. The initial expectations of leading developmental economists seemed to be that aid would work its effects in five or ten years, whereas it now seems that double that time or more is required for the critical influences to take place. The same consideration applies in the area of education (along with the notion of conjunctivity E). Here, some writers have argued, literacy seems in certain respects to be a threshold phenomenon. Until certain critical proportions of the population have attained literacy (possibly around 40 per cent, or elite literacy, for the first major effect and around 90 per cent, or mass literacy, for the second), some kinds of reactions (scopes) do not appear.

7. *Durability:* Durability refers to a measure of the life of the power relationship—i.e., how long it lasts. Certain types of power, such as change in basic values, seem to be very durable while other types are much more ephemeral. Durability is not an unmitigated asset. Some power relations are unfortunately long lasting. This can be awkward if the influencer, such as the change agent, wishes to terminate them and replace them with others. It is like the parent teaching independence to his child. The parent works hard to establish influence over the child and then must sometimes work no less hard to terminate that influence in certain scopes. Programmed control or ideological conditioning is especially prone to this type of difficulty because of excessive durability. Thus, for example, I should predict that if Mao wins in China and his strategy of very strong reliance on ideological conditioning is followed, China may have grave problems of rigidity in her developmental efforts.

8. *Reciprocity:* Reciprocity refers to any power relation in which there is a form of feedback or role reversal in the relationship, that is, in which R influences E and E, in turn, though subsequently, influences R. When we specify influential be-

havior and scope, as we must, four main sub-types of reciprocity appear.

a. $R_\alpha \longrightarrow_\beta E, \ E_\beta \longrightarrow_\alpha R$
b. $R_\alpha \longrightarrow_\beta E, \ E_\delta \longrightarrow_\alpha R$
c. $R_\alpha \longrightarrow_\beta E, \ E_\beta \longrightarrow_\gamma R$
d. $R_\alpha \longrightarrow_\beta E, \ E_\delta \longrightarrow_\gamma R$

The first type is the case of a spiralling, vicious circle relationship such as a feud or arms race. One nation raises its arms level, which induces another to raise its arms level, which induces the first to raise its level again, etc. The second type is the essential relationship of democracy. It can be exemplified by the situation where the rulers influence the ruled, but the ruled, in turn, can influence the original type of influential behavior of the rulers. Congressional legislation alters the tax-paying behavior of the electorate. But the electorate, through voting, can in turn alter the legislation regarding taxes of the congress. I should define a democracy as a political system in which the relative incidence of such reciprocal power relationships is very high. Obviously, one danger of such relationships is that they can, in the absence of considerable consensus or compatibility of views regarding how the power game is to be played, lead to mutual frustration, stultification, and inaction. Each of the actors can stymie the other, over time. Such an observation—indeed, a much deeper general understanding of reciprocal power relations of this type—is critical to a knowing operation of a democratic system, be it at the national level or at the local level of extension agents and village worker.

The third type indicates that the reaction produced in the influencee (E) feeds back upon the influencer (R), but to produce a different type of behavior. For example, an extension agent conducts a demonstration which leads several farmers to use more pesticides, which in turn leads the agent to concern himself with increasing the available supply of pesticides in the community, etc. The fourth type of reciprocal power relationship is in most ways not really different from two separate power relations, save that the same actors are involved and their influencer-influencee roles switch in the two relations. That switch, however, is quite significant in some cases when it is recognized by one or both parties, since it often affects their future power relations.

Finally, I should point out that again with these reciprocal power relations the specific substantive definitions of the influential behaviors and scopes selected are vitally important. Definitions that are too broad, for instance, lead one to inaccurate perception of the type of reciprocal relationship involved, just as they may lead one to think that certain indirect power relations are transitive when they are actually intransitive. For instance, whether an observed reciprocal power relationship is of the first or the third type depends critically on the definitions of alpha (α) and gamma (γ).

Most of the aspects of power so far adumbrated refer to the pattern of relations across the influencer and influencee. A number of other aspects refer primarily to a single actor, although these concepts naturally come in symmetric pairs, one referring to the influencee and its counterpart to the influencer.

9. *Recognition:* The basic concept of recognition refers to the awareness of the existence of a given power relationship by any or all of the participants or by designated outsiders. The relationship is either recognized or unrecognized by R, E, both R and E, or relevant outsiders. Other refinements of the concept of recognition refer to the awareness of various aspects of the power relation apart from its mere existence. For example, the type of power involved, its directness or indirectness, and so on, can all be recognized or not by the actors described.

Recognition seems to be a very important aspect of power relations. I shall examine it a little more fully, largely to illustrate the kind of treatment that could easily be afforded all the other aspects of power sketched herein.

The perception of existing power relations which is held by members of the social unit seems to affect the power that such members actually have as individuals. It is not only that the more powerful members usually are in a position to make better power assessments, but also that they are aided in becoming more powerful by the relative accuracy of these assessments. Moreover, recognition implies only perception, not truth. A man widely recognized (i.e., perceived or believed) to have power usually *ipso facto* does have power. Certainly the behaviors of the other members are greatly affected by their conceptions of their own power and that of others in the system.

Part of the equipment of the effective leader, be he extension agent or tsar, may be an especially good insight into the distribution of power in the system and to his own person. We even find ourselves involved with the recognition of recognition of power, if that is not too tortuous a topic.

The connection between the recognition of power and the scope and durability of power relations might be summarized, hypothetically in the following fashion. Recognition of the power relationship by the influencee tends (1) to reduce the scope of the relationship, (2) to terminate it altogether, or (3) to lead to a dissonance-reducing and power-enhancing reperception of the influencer by the influencee. But these effects hold only to a certain point. If the power of the influencer is perceived as being extremely great, virtually inescapable, then there may be an acceptance of the inevitability of the relationship and a possible increase in its scope. Such a reaction is obviously related to so-called "bandwagon effects" and would seem to lie behind the efforts of political movements to create an aura of inevitability about themselves. It is reflected in the TV advertisements which argue, "Sooner or later you'll change to Lethal, why not sooner?" The wisdom of producing increased recognition of one's power would therefore depend greatly upon the perceived degree of that power. Below the inevitability threshold, recognition is usually weakening; above that threshold it is usually strengthening. On the other hand, failure in a power attempt is generally unfortunate from the viewpoint of the future power of the influencer, and he should attempt to minimize its recognition.

Certain power relations are durable only on condition of nonrecognition by various actors. Illegal activities and bribery, for example, frequently are terminated by recognition on the part of outsiders. Power exerted by a status inferior over a status superior tends also to be destroyed when the status superior perceives that the status inferior or relevant outsiders recognize the relationship. This is manifested in the difficulty of transferring from one area to another innovations developed at very low levels of developmental administration. For this transfer to occur, a status superior in the bureaucracy must ordinarily have been influenced by status inferior. Usually, this is possible only if outsiders and perhaps even the status inferior himself are perceived by the status-superior-turned-influencee as not recognizing the existence of the power relationship. One way of overcoming this barrier to development would be deliberately to create situations where status superiors could be influenced by the innovative ideas of status inferiors without anyone but the status superior being aware of this fact. For example, local level administrators from one area could discuss their problems and suggestions before superior officers from a similar area, but superiors who were not their own. These superiors could then select ideas that seemed useful to them, carry them back to their own districts, and adopt them without fear of anyone's perceiving their source in inferior levels. Many more hypotheses and suggestions utilizing the concept of recognition of power could be suggested, but space precludes more than this illustration.

10. *Intention:* Intention refers to a desire for the existence of the power relation on the part of the influencer, the influencee, both, or outside parties. Like recognition, however, it can also be extended to cover intending various other aspects of the relationship, including, in fact, that it be recognized or unrecognized by various actors. Any given power relation may be intended, nonintended, or anti-intended, according to whether the actor desires the relationship, has no feeling about it one way or the other, or desires that it not exist. Intention permits of degrees, so that an associated concept is that of the strength of the intention.

Basic subordinate concepts such as these permit more precise definition of other well-known power concepts of a higher order. For example, recognition and intention together permit a more precise definition of the common notion of "manipulation." Manipulation refers to a power relationship that is intended and recognized by the influencer and anti-intended and unrecognized by the influencee. Since, like many other power relationships, manipulation depends on nonrecognition by the influencee, a useful strategy for an outside party who wishes to terminate or reduce the relation is to get the influencee to recognize the relationship—make him aware of the manipulation. As I have said, many power relations of various types are fragile under recognition by certain actors. One sometimes neglected aspect of extension work may be to provide the farmer-influencee with a chance to be influenced by the change agent without others—his friends and family—or perhaps even himself recognizing this fact.

Two most promising and essential concepts for power analysis, but also two of the most difficult and elusive, are the notions of resistance and cost.

11. *Resistance (or Inertia)*: Resistance refers to the "difficulty" of affecting the influencee in the designated scope. It involves the "distance" between his preinfluence and post-influence states. It is intended to provide an objective assessment of how hard it was for the influencee to make the change in his behavior that occurred in the power relationship. For instance, a given extension agent may induce two men to adopt fertilizer. Do we want therefore to say that the agent had the same power over the two men? Superficially, yes; but, in a deeper sense, not necessarily. It depends on how hard it was for each of them to make this change. If one farmer were well known as a ready innovator while the other were an equally well-known diehard, our analysis should be able to take account of this difference. Similarly, if we wish to compare the power over a specific farmer of two change agents, the extension agent and the village-level worker, how can we do so? We cannot unless we have some measure of resistance which permits us to assess how hard it was for the influencee to make the changes in his behavior which each agent has induced or failed to induce.

Of course, so defined, resistance is an extremely complex notion, dependent on further development in psychology. However, it may ultimately be measured by an index constructed from three basic types of components: (1) measurement of the physical effort involved in the behavioral change, (2) measurement of the amount of cognitive restructuring involved in the change, and (3) measurement of the influencee's evaluation of the change (its "valence" for him in all its aspects), including his evaluation of the physical effort and cognitive restructuring demanded. Obviously, I cannot pretend that this is anything but an extremely large order. But many developments in contemporary social science are hopeful. For example, the work on cognitive structuring and the attempts to elucidate the notion of cognitive centrality along with least-effort types of hypotheses seem particularly promising. In other words, the attempt to identify cognitions as being more or less central or peripheral—more or less embedded or linked with other cognitions—and to investigate the hypothesis that the more central a cognition, the harder it is to change, appear to offer important promise for developing a fruitful and measurable concept of resistance. And, as I have said, the concept of resistance is essential to any very widely applicable interpersonal comparisons of power.

12. *Cost:* The concept of power cost was first, to the best of my knowledge, specifically brought to our attention by Karl Deutsch. It is the counterpart for the influencer of the concept of resistance for the influencee. It refers to how difficult it is for the influencer to engage in a given influential behavior. I should point out that both cost and resistance are slightly misleading labels in the sense that either can be positive or negative rather than always being positive. The influencer, for example, may actually intrinsically enjoy the activities which lead to his power over the influencee. Cost, again, would seem to have to be measured according to the same very simple model suggested for resistance, that is, in terms of the physical effort, cognitive restructuring, and evaluations of the influencer. Moreover, as John Harsanyi has suggested, cost (and resistance as well) would have to include some assessment of the "opportunity cost" of engaging in the behavior involved. One of the costs to the influencer of engaging in a particular influential behavior vis-à-vis a particular influencee is that it usually precludes his doing something else with his time and resources, including sacrificing opportunities to influence someone else. This can be especially important in development administration where resources are notably scarce. The change agent usually has to select a very limited set of targets for his attention, and he incurs serious opportunity costs thereby. Some explicit attempt to ascertain these opportunity costs would be useful in many instances. Actually, better knowledge of the power structure of the unit he is dealing with, presumably obtained through the kinds of analyses and techniques under discussion, is one very conspicuous way of minimizing some of the opportunity costs of agricultural development. If one can only focus on a relatively few people in a community it becomes

critically important to know which people are most powerful and likely to be receptive.

As with the other subordinate concepts being examined, resistance and cost also are useful as building blocks for more abstract notions. Thus, Deutsch's suggestions of "gross power" and "net power" can be given precise interpretation through cost and resistance. An alternative "net power" notion that also seems promising is intention (strength and direction) minus cost—or, more crudely, the value of the power relation to the influencer less its cost to him.

This compilation by no means exhausts the aspects of power relationships which it seems fruitful to distinguish, although it may exhaust the reader. Various writers have gone on to stress such aspects as "dependence" (whether the relationship depends on the continued physical presence of the influencer or on his continuance in the influential behavior), "compliance observability" (whether the influencer can tell if the influencee has responded to the power attempt as the influencer intended), "formality" (whether the power relationship is explicitly and authoritatively prescribed), "power drive," "persuasibility", and so on.

When such aspects of power relations are distinguished, many interesting hypotheses are suggested. For example, the more indirect the relationship, the less the likelihood that the terminal influencee recognizes the influence over him of the original influencer. Many power relations would seem to be deliberately indirect for this reason.

Types of Power

A typology of power relations can be developed by focusing on any one or more of the four basic elements of the power relationship: influencer, influencee, influential behavior, or scope. Thus, one typology could be organized in terms of different kinds of influencers—say, males as opposed to females, or politicians versus administrators. Another typology could be in terms of various categories of influencees—say, sophisticated versus naive, or subsistence versus commercial farmers. A typology that would be extremely useful would be one in terms of influential behavior. What are the different kinds of acts a person can perform that influence others? How can we class them? Finally, a valuable typology can be developed in terms of scope. What are the different basic ways in which a person can be affected by the behavior of another person?

As James March has suggested, the main requirement for the last two types is really that of a model of the state of an individual at a given time. The simplest such model that has rather wide currency in the social sciences is one which distinguishes physical alterations from psychological, though, of course, a given reaction may partake of both types. The psychological alterations are frequently further broken down according to whether the alteration was in the cognitive realm or the motivational realm, and the latter is then subdivided into a drive-impulse-need-value side, on the one hand, as opposed to a norm-ethic-moral principle-super ego side, on the other. Analogous refinements can be made within the cognitive category, and even within the physical category.

As I have said, most scopes (responding behaviors) are really complex mixtures of these analytic types, which makes the typology less valuable than if its categories were mutually exclusive. But many scopes seem intuitively to be more of one type than another (physical, cognitive, cathectic, or normative). And various common combinations can also be discerned. Reflection and observation, using these categories, seems to reveal how very many power relationships are primarily cognitive in emphasis, that is, how many power relations mainly involve cognitive change on the part of the influencee. Incidentally, the empirical differences between these various types of power can be interestingly brought out by describing each, insofar as possible, in terms of the previously enumerated aspects of any power relation. Thus actual physical force tends, compared to other forms of power, to be recognized by both parties, and by outsiders; tends ordinarily to be intended by the influencer and anti-intended by the influencee; to be direct and rapid, but not very durable; to be completely dependent on continued action by the influencer, etc. Bribery, on the other hand, which is essentially a cognitive type of power (i.e., produces mainly cognitive change in the influencee) tends to be recognized by both parties but not by outsiders, to be intended by both influencer and influencee, and so on.

A fuller example may be useful at this point. Some time ago

in an interesting study, Morris Rosenberg and Leonard Pearlin questioned the nurses and attendants in a large public mental hospital.[7] They put to each respondent the hypothetical but realistic situation that a male schizophrenic patient had recently developed the habit of sleeping during part of the day and then getting up during the night, walking around and disturbing the other patients. The offending patient, however, was not especially nervous or depressed and could understand anything an attendant might tell him. The query: How would the attendant get this patient to change his habits—how would he get him back to bed at night?

Rosenberg and Pearlin coded the responses to this question into five basic categories. Moreover, they asked the respondents also to rank these five ways of handling the situation. The categories were: coercive power ("I would force him to go to bed when everybody else does"); authority ("Since a nurse or nursing assistant has the right to tell a patient what to do, I would simply tell him to change his habits"); contractual power ("I would offer him certain privileges or grant him certain benefits if he changes his sleeping habits"); persuasion ("I would try to explain to him the reason for changing his sleeping habits and try to convince him that it is for his own good or the good of the other patients"); and manipulation ("I would try to figure out some ways to keep him busy during the day so he would want to sleep at night").

It is easy to imagine a similar study of change agents in developing societies. In fact, very grossly analogous research has been done.[8] The Rosenberg and Pearlin study is instructive here in that it illustrates several concepts I have been introducing. It also illustrates the point that different kinds of influencers and influencees seem to find various influence styles or strategies differentially congenial and effective. For instance, over half the nurses said they would use persuasion as their first power strategy and over a third said they would use manipulation. Very few chose the other three strategies. Persuasion

---

[7] "Power-Orientations in the Mental Hospital," *Human Relations*, 15 (1962), 335–349.

[8] For example, see Herbert H. Hyman, Gene N. Levine, and Charles R. Wright, "Studying Expert Informants by Survey Methods: A Cross-National Inquiry," *Public Opinion Quarterly*, 31 (1967), 9–26.

and manipulation were also regarded as the two most effective methods, except that manipulation was thought to be most effective by more respondents than chose persuasion. In other words, a significant proportion of the respondents settled for an influence technique that was not regarded theoretically as maximally effective, but apparently did so because of their perceived lack of skill with the better technique, because of cost considerations, etc.

In any event, the nurses gave very insightful evaluations of the different influential behaviors considered. For instance, the objections to coercion were that the nurse might get hurt in a scuffle with the patient (cost); that such influence would be very temporary (durability); that it generated resentment on the part of the influencee (cost and resistance); that it might produce harmful publicity (recognition, cost in another domain); and that it produced guilt feelings for the nurse (cost). These reactions were summed up by the observation, "Over the long haul, then, it is easier and more effective to get someone to want to do as you like, or to be willing to do as you like, than to force him to do as you like."

The objections to contractual power, such as offering the patient a cigarette to get back to bed, lay mainly in cost considerations and in the danger of outside recognition. The patient might begin to expect a cigarette every time, or other patients might see the transaction and demand cigarettes. Authority was rejected largely on the grounds that it did not exist —it was not recognized by the patient and so would not work. In routine matters, authority was the most common form of power; but in extraordinary circumstances it tended to evaporate or be unavailable.

Persuasion was favored because it was consonant with the dominant ideology of the institution and its members, but not always preferred because of doubts as to its effectiveness. Manipulation, on the other hand, was thought to be effective but not always available since the would-be influencer lacked the necessary skills. Moreover, manipulation made rather costly demands on the time and patience of the influencer and was sometimes thought to take too much time (rapidity) during which other patients might be awakened.

This example suggests the possibilities for systematic codification of types of power relations and for a general evaluation of their characteristics in specified settings. The fundamental typology that I have been employing differs somewhat from that of Rosenberg and Pearlin. As I have said, the initial distinction of the typology used here is between physical force and other forms of power. By physical force I refer to the actual physical manipulation of the human body as a physical entity in a physical world. The category does not include the threat of the use of such force, since that is essentially cognitive change, not physical manipulation. The kinds of behavioral change that can be induced through direct physical means are very limited. It is not a strategy that is appealing to the change agent in a developing society.

On the psychological side, an initial distinction was made between cognitive influences and motivational influences, although it is well recognized that while the two can be analytically distinguished they are functionally interrelated. Under the cognitive rubric it is useful to distinguish at least four subtypes of power: threat of value denial (punishment), promise of value satisfaction (reward), provision of information, and invocation of legitimacy. Value denial and satisfaction, or punishment and reward, are perhaps the most prominent of all power techniques and there is a large literature analyzing them. Actually, it is the threat of value denial or the promise of value satisfaction which is influential, although actual punishment or reward may be necessary with varying frequency to make those threats or promises plausible. Careful study of the most effective forms and frequencies of punishment and reward is an important part of the analysis of power, but I know of little work in this area which has been concerned with administrative behavior. It may be, for example, that under careful analysis the mix of carrots and sticks which the government employs to influence the farmer in various ways would prove inefficient. My impression is that, in general, public administration leans more heavily toward the value denial (punishment) side than a learning theorist would recommend. This is particularly unfortunate in developmental administration where one usually wishes to get farmers to do certain things, in contrast to regulatory administration, where the paramount objective is usually getting farmers to refrain from doing certain things.

Although almost everything cognitive can be viewed from a reward and punishment perspective, it is useful to distinguish another subtype of cognitive power—informational power. This does not involve, except remotely, the threat of value denial or the promise of value satisfaction. It refers to a more subtle process, namely, shaping the contours of an individual's view of the world. A good example is the Pennsylvania Economy League, which furnishes municipalities in that state with free research on budgetary and personnel problems.[9] It claims to be a nonpartisan, fact-finding agency performing a public service for understaffed local administrations. The league is financed by key industrial and commercial enterprises in the state. It exerts its influence by molding the picture which local officials have of their environment and its possibilities. Although most of the changes it produces at any given time are small, the cumulative effect of this constant informational guidance seems quite significant. While one might not support the aims of the league, its tactics are really quite similar to those of successful technical assistance. Comparative study of agencies of this type (including lobbyists) might yield major rewards for developmental administration. The league, for example, makes a marked effort to avoid publicity (recognition), shows great deference to local officials, and tries hard to avoid any appearance of criticism of their activities or ideas. It operates only at the request of the locality and is quite cognizant of the need for an appearance of expertise, for privacy, and for delicacy and subtlety in exercising informational power.

The last subtype of cognitive power which I have distinguished is legitimate power. Actually, I regard legitimacy as an aspect of any power relation. It rests on the fact that people have conceptions of what constitutes proper power relations against which they compare actual power relations, noting the degree of fit between the two. An actual relationship which conforms to the internalized norm is said to be legitimate. The dimensions along which conformity is measured and how much

[9] See Edward F. Cooke, "Research: An Instrument of Political Power," *Political Science Quarterly*, 76 (1961), 69–87.

conformity is needed for "legitimacy" are two important problems which have not been very deeply studied up to now.

Two kinds of legitimate power must be distinguished: (1) the inculcation of conceptions of what constitutes proper power relations, and (2) changing an individual's perception of the role of an actor so that previously established conceptions of legitimacy can be invoked. Here I am referring solely to the second type.

Authority may be defined as the legitimate power of one role over another. Again, we need to distinguish the inculcation of authority from the exercise of authority. The latter relies on the former and is almost always cognitive. That is, if an influencer has authority he then merely has to be perceived to perform according to the requirements of his role (issue his command in a certain form) in order to secure compliance from an appropriate influencee. The tremendous advantage of authority lies in its low cost and its rapidity. However, the original costs of inculcating the belief in authority—the conception of what is proper for whom in the realm of power—are often quite high. The low maintenance costs and rapidity of authoritative power are, nevertheless, so valuable that even the most blatant dictatorships work hard at trying to establish as much legitimacy as possible.

Finally the influencee may be changed not in any physical or cognitive way, but in terms of his basic values or norms—not in his picture of what is, but in what he wants or what he thinks ought to be—in short, in his motivations. This type of power seems rather difficult to achieve except over the young and inexperienced. If one can shape the motivations and ethics of an individual, the effects are likely to be far-reaching indeed. But I believe that the opportunities for this type of influence over adults are severely limited and that much of what appears to be motivational influence over adults is essentially cognitive.[10]

---

[10] The Northcote-Trevelyan Report of 1854 which set the basic recruitment principles for British bureaucracy recommended the recruitment of young men partly on the grounds of their "superior docility." Richard Rose, "England: A Traditionally Modern Political Culture," in *Political Culture and Political Development*, Lucian W. Pye and Sidney Verba, eds. (Princeton: Princeton University Press, 1965), p. 115.

Other useful typologies can be and undoubtedly will be developed. The paramount point here is the importance of such efforts and, in general, the great significance of empirically oriented, carefully thought out subordinate conceptualization if power analysis is to be brought down out of the clouds of cosmic speculation. We are clearly going to proceed to more general hypotheses largely through the empirical establishment of quite limited findings. Effective subordinate conceptualization is essential for this purpose.

Location and Measurement of Power

Probably the most critical problem challenging our ability to analyze power relations is that of locating and measuring power—of determining who has it, over whom, of what kind, and how much. The ideal experiment described previously might be the most appropriate technique for locating and measuring power, but such experimentation is plainly impossible. Our existing techniques must all be considered crude approximations of the ideal experiment, most of them, alas, quite far from the ideal.

What would we like in a measure of power? Among other things, a completely suitable measure would (1) conform precisely to the defined concept of power, (2) yield a standardized quantitative result, (3) be applicable to all groups regardless of size, (4) furnish information about major aspects of power such as scope, influential behavior, intention, recognition, etc., and (5) indicate specific interpersonal and interrole linkages. Needless to say, no such measure is on the horizon and the expectation of full success in ever finding one is probably naive. A "shotgun" approach involving simultaneous use of several measures will undoubtedly be necessary. It is nevertheless useful to weigh the existing measurement techniques against these basic criteria in order to establish the advantages and disadvantages of each technique.

Our judgments about power usually rest on one or more of several types of measures. Implicit in many impressionistic studies, for example, is the inference of an individual's power position from his position in another structure. Thus wealth, status, and formal authority have all frequently been employed as indicators of power. The basic problem with this method is that we have reason to believe that power is imperfectly and moreover inconsistently correlated with these other attributes so the inference is tenuous at best. To justify it we need empirical demonstration of the degree of correlation existing between the power structure and the other structure. To get such a correlation we need an independent picture of the power structure, which is the very thing we do not have. In other words, inferring power from other structures will be truly possible only after we develop some independent measures of power which will then permit us convincingly to establish the association between power and those other attributes.

Again, power is often inferred from activity. Those who are most active in a social unit are frequently assumed to be most powerful. Once more we encounter a clear conceptual difference between the measured notion, activity, and the inferred notion, power. Hence, the degree of association between the two becomes an empirical question whose solution requires an independent measure of power—the very thing we are after.

A related measure is the influence attempts or influence attempts/successes type of measure. In its latter, more sophisticated form this technique involves ascertaining how often various actors attempted to influence some other actor, how often each of them was successful, and expressing their relative powers as the ratio of attempts to successes, similar to a baseball batting average. The main difficulty with this technique is that its applicability is very limited. Only in very highly structured situations is it possible to obtain much agreement on what actions constitute influence attempts or what responses are successes. The measure ordinarily neglects resistance and cost considerations so that all successes are considered equal. The implicit conception of power which underlies the measure tends to ignore nonintended influence. Moreover, the measure provides us with very little information about who actually influences whom—about the structure of power relationships in the unit, so that we can be aided in predicting unit behavior. Instead it gives us a rather abstract and uninformative comparative score of meager predictive utility.

The opinion change method has also been widely used. Essentially, it involves ascertaining attitudes on some issue. Then, after conflict-resolving interaction over that issue occurs, attitudes are again determined. It is assumed that those actors who show attitudinal change after the interaction have been influenced by those who remained stable in the attitude toward which others changed. This technique, too, demands a rather structured situation featuring a clear-cut interactional period which resolves existing conflicts. Such conditions are most likely to be found in experimental contexts, and that is where the technique has been most used. It has been very profitably employed, for example, in studying husband-wife interaction over revealed differences—situations where husbands and wives resolved explicit differences of opinion between them and came to some familial decision. In such cases it was possible to determine whether the final familial position was closer to the original position of the husband or the wife, and to infer therefrom who was more influential. This technique has obvious limitations of applicability to large groups and in less structured settings. Logically, it also runs afoul of problems created by "satellites" and "chameleons," and it usually furnishes little information about aspects and types of power.

Decisional analysis is another method for examining power structures. It consists of tracing presumably representative or critical decisions through the system, trying to perceive or reconstruct who influenced whom, how, etc. It has the advantage of indicating exact linkages, of normally furnishing information about aspects and types of power, and of being parsimonious in that one supposedly deals only with the actors actually involved. Its main drawbacks are that generally it must focus on some community or unit "issue," being less appropriate for more subtle and pervasive manifestations of power, and that it is so time-consuming for the researcher that only a few issues can be considered. Hence, there are serious problems of issue sampling—of determining how representative or revealing the issues studied really are. If the decisional analysis is based on interviewing and retrospection, then all the usual difficulties associated with selective perception and recall are encountered. On the other hand, if direct observation is employed, then it is very difficult to cover all the points in the decisional series and there is greater interference with natural processes.

Techniques of systematic direct observation, sometimes called "communication audits," have also been employed without any strict issue or decisional focus. For example, observing the power activities and communications of administrators at randomly selected time periods would be one use of this technique. The observer attempts to record and code his observations and infer structure from these samplings. Obviously, this technique depends on excellent access to the subjects, is very demanding of skilled personnel, involves many coding and recording difficulties, and courts observer-effect biases. However, it has been used to produce interesting studies of congressional subcommittees and of the socialization of school children. New electronic devices may greatly increase our capacity to exploit this approach, although without candor and safeguards the respondents are likely to feel exploited, their privacy invaded. Still, it is now feasible and I believe it would be interesting to monitor, with their consent, selected samples of the communications of various groups, such as farmers in communities that were the targets for change programs, the change agents themselves, and so on. Unfortunately, these data-gathering innovations also bring a grave risk of the researcher's foundering in data and coding problems.

Probably the most common method for studying power empirically is the "attribution" or "reputational" method. The essence of the attribution method is that it attempts to use respondents as power informants or observers. Ideally, we should like to have innumerable perfectly trained and invisible social scientists and be able to station one with every actor in the system to record all relevant behaviors of that actor. Since such an ideal situation cannot be created, a reasonable alternative is to try to use the actors themselves as observers. They are the only people who may possibly have been in a position to make the necessary observations about who influences whom in the system. Why not take advantage of that fact and obtain their observations?

Up to now, three main varieties of the attribution method have been employed: (1) the cobweb or snowball method, (2) the sampling method, and (3) the panel method. The first involves selecting some purposive or accidental starting points in the social unit and asking those persons whom they perceive as most powerful in designated kinds of activity. One then proceeds to the persons named and asks them the same question, continuing in this fashion until an arbitrarily decided amount of repetitiveness in naming is encountered. The second variant involves putting the same kinds of questions to a fractional sample of the relevant population.

A major problem with both approaches is that the respondents may not have been in a position to make useful observations of who is very powerful in that unit. Thus, one may get reputations rather than reality. The third variant attempts to circumvent this difficulty by querying a select panel of informants. These panel members are supposed to be individuals who have been in a position to ascertain who is most powerful in the unit, though the demonstration of this is very problematic. Nevertheless, there are various refinements of the panel technique which give one somewhat more confidence that he has singled out knowledgeable informants. At best, though, the end result from cobweb, sample, and panel forms of the attribution method is a collection of names of the twenty or fifty or two hundred most powerful people in the unit. Nothing like a full or detailed picture of the pattern of interrelationships in the unit as a whole is produced.

I have been working for several years on what seems a more useful variant of the attribution method, which is the only general method that is applicable to groups of widely varying size, to all kinds of scopes or issues, and which can provide detailed information about types and aspects of power. The two most conspicuous drawbacks of the other forms of the attribution method are, again, that they demand observations which the respondent has not been in a position to make and that they do not reveal the structure of the unit as a whole. They merely generate the names of a slice of the top power wielders in that unit.

Our approach is to get around these two difficulties by asking respondents not about "who is most powerful," etc., but about themselves. We ask them whom they influence in certain ways and who influences them, whom they communicate with on certain topics with designated frequency, and so on. And, we ask these questions of everyone in the unit, not merely of a sample or a panel. Thus, we gain certain advantages. We can obtain a complete sociometric picture of the power structure of the unit, not just a slice of it. This ultimately makes possible detailed analysis of the paths of influence on the issues studied, and prediction and simulation of system performance in that area. The complete enumeration enables us to check a respondent's claims by ascertaining if the person whom he says he influences also states that he is influenced by that respondent. On the other hand, a drawback of this technique is that since everyone, or almost everyone, must be interviewed (usually twice), we can apply it only to groups of up to about one thousand persons. There are also problems of tedious and formidable questioning and of establishing uniform frames of reference. Our hope is that we can develop propositions about power based on these analyses which can then be tested in larger arenas with other more indirect and inexpensive techniques. We hope to apply this technique to about a dozen social units (villages, bureaucratic offices, business firms, labor unions, urban neighborhoods, etc.) in each of several nations in the next few years. Only with data of this type does it seem possible really to come to grips with questions of how much variation there is in power structures, why such variations exist, what effects particular types of power configurations have on other system characteristics such as responsiveness to certain types of changes, and so on.

Summary Description and Comparison of Power Structures

Let us assume that we are able satisfactorily to locate who has power over whom in a political system and what are the particular influential behaviors and scopes involved in the power relations of our concern. Two related problems then arise: (1) the problem of presenting a summary picture of the power structure of that system without inflicting the full matrix of interrelations on someone, and (2) the problem of developing accurate objective means for comparing that power structure with other power structures. In fact, it is potentially misleading to speak of *the* power structure of a social unit, since there may be a different structure for each important scope. For example, the power structure of a village with regard to agricultural innovation may be quite different from the power structure in that same village with regard to partisan political matters. On the other hand, the innovative power structure might be quite similar to the power structure prevailing with regard to village finances or the choice of religious leaders. The power analyst needs refined and systematic methods for making these structural comparisons, both within a given social unit and between social units. I shall very briefly indicate the general nature of a few such structural notions and indices which we have developed.

The first two indices are descriptive of the power structure of a single unit, though they can obviously be used to compare units. They are measures of the "amount," "density," or overall level of power in the social unit and of the degree to which that amount of power tends to be concentrated or dispersed among the members of the unit. The amount of power index is essentially a measure of the total number of actual power linkages in the unit divided by the number of possible linkages in a unit of that finite size. The distribution of power index is more complicated, but it is based upon a comparison of the power fields and power domains of all members of the unit. The amount of power and the distribution of power measures must really be jointly considered for most purposes, since the amount of power measures tells one how "linked up" the system is—how much power there is in the unit regardless of its gross distribution—while the distribution measure portrays the degree of concentration or dispersion that exists with regard to the given amount of power in the unit, whatever that amount may be.

Employing large-scale sociometric measures of this type, one hopes ultimately to be able to make the amount and distribution of power in social units of various types a quantified variable to that he can then search more effectively for their associations with other important variables. Hopefully, he can then begin to explain why it is that one system is much more centralized in power than another, or why one system seems to have the capacity to mobilize its personnel through influence mechanisms while another has been unable to establish those mechanisms.

Although they were devised as summary descriptions, these two measures clearly are useful in comparing political systems and subsystems. Nevertheless, we have sought other types of comparative measures. A basic question would seem to be, "How many changes must be made in the linkages of one system to make it isomorphic with another system?" Two comparative measures have been created that pertain to this question. The first, which we call a measure of "structural isomorphism," answers the question without regard to the characteristics of the occupants of the power positions in the social unit. It simply inspects the political system of the unit as a pattern of points and connections, that is, as a directed graph (digraph), and ascertains the minimal number of changes necessary in one to match the structure of the other. Unfortunately, this means at present that the measure is applicable only to units of the same size. This index of structural isomorphism is presently most useful for measuring how the power structure of a social unit in one issue-area, say financial matters, differs from or resembles the power structure of that same unit in other issue-areas, say external relations or recruitment of personnel. Severe mathematical problems are encountered when one attempts to extend the approach to units of diverse sizes, though we have hopes of resolving those problems.

At present, the index of structural isomorphism offers us the opportunity to distinguish those systems whose structure of power is the same regardless of issue from those systems whose structure of power differs from issue to issue. The index also helps us to compare the power structures of a given social system through time, assessing more precisely the degree of structural similarity between the political system of the social unit in one period and in another.

The second comparative structural measure which we have employed is called an index of personnel isomorphism. The index of structural isomorphism compares power structures without regard to the individuals occupying various positions. In other words, if one man held all power over financial decisions in a social unit and another man held all power over promotions, there is complete structural isomorphism between the two power structures, assuming that the amounts of power are the same. In each case all of the existing power in the social unit is in the hands of one person. For certain purposes, however, it is interesting to know how much tendency there is for the specific personnel (or roles) of the social unit to maintain constant or fluctuating relative power positions across different issue-areas (scopes). Dahl, for example, found that the city of New Haven displayed what he called "dispersed inequalities of power." [11] By this he seems to mean that, for the various issue-areas he considered, there was a high degree of structural isomorphism. In each area, power was rather highly concentrated. But there was a rather low degree of personnel isomorphism, in the sense that the actual people who were at the top of the power structure in one area were unlikely to be at the top in another area. The notions of structural and personnel isomorphism are also useful in comparing the power structures of a social unit with its communication, status, friendship, and other analytic structures.

Finally, brief mention of another structural concept, power base, also appears useful. Actually, the concept refers to the same kinds of phenomena as the idea of concentration of power. But since it seems so valuable for many purposes and is logically somewhat different, it is worth mentioning at this point. The notion comes originally from graph theory, where one finds the idea of a "point basis." I say this mainly in extenuation of using a term, "power base," which Robert Dahl has already employed with a quite different meaning.

The communications application of the point basis notion perhaps gives the best initial indication of its meaning. The point basis of a directed graph, or, in this instance, the "communication base" of a graph representing a communication system, consists of the smallest set of members of the system from which a message can reach all other members of the system. Switching now to a political or administrative system, the power base of that system can be defined temporarily as the smallest set of actors in that system who can influence all other members of the system. Obviously, the size and composition of the power base may change from scope to scope and influential behavior to influential behavior. Moreover, one can readily define variations on this theme. In a legislative body one might think of the minimal set of persons who could influence a majority of that body in some respect, or who could influence a majority of the members of the majority party. In a village one might think of the smallest set of persons who could influence a

[11] Robert A. Dahl, *Who Governs?* (New Haven: Yale University Press, 1961), p. 11 and *passim*.

majority of the male household heads to adopt some innovation.

Numerous political studies have suggested an important hypothesis that is most clearly expressed using the conception of power base. It is that the larger and more heterogeneous the power base in any given system, the less the probability of organized and extensive political action. One of the most graphic depictions of this relationship is Edward Banfield's work, *Political Influence*.[12] Banfield draws a clear picture of the debility introduced into Chicago's governmental efforts at urban development by the fact of the large formal power base, consisting of more than a dozen separate agencies, all of which must agree before any major undertaking can be accomplished. An opponent of any measure merely has to prevail over one element of the power base to doom the measure. David Riesman and his associates invoke a similar notion in their discussion of "veto blocs" at the national level of U.S. politics.[13] Similarly, in many developing societies problems occasioned by the large size and heterogeneity of the power bases of the national political system are conspicuous.

In sum then, the student of developmental administration and of agricultural development who investigates power structures within and between rural communities needs to be able to pin down structural differences and similarities before he can stand a chance of explaining them. The type of thought and work in political science and developmental administration here described, even though it is very recent and still crude, would seem essential to any broad understanding of agricultural development.

Complexity and Cognitive Change

In this concluding section I shall focus briefly on two overarching problems or approaches that are often ignored. The first of these is the problem of complexity. The social changes which we readily label development or modernization are manifold and intricately interrelated. Even at the village level, the developmental administrator is trying to fathom an extremely complex system and to move it in certain directions. At present

[12] New York: The Free Press of Glencoe, 1961.

[13] David Riesman, Nathan Glazer, and Reuel Denney, *The Lonely Crowd* (New York: Doubleday Anchor Books, 1955), pp. 244 ff.

we have a plethora of suggestions regarding which aspects of the system are most critical. There are a thousand possible pressure points which seem to need attention. Various "experts" plump for the importance of roads, fertilizer, education, marketing, empathy, pesticides, national identification, credit, etc. Moreover, we are seldom altogether clear regarding the precise nature of the desirable directions for change and how change in one direction will affect other goals. Christopher Alexander's description of the designer's contemporary plight beautifully fits the developmental administrator, who is perhaps the most ambitious designer of them all:

Today more and more design problems are reaching insoluble levels of complexity. This is true not only of moon bases, factories, and radio receivers, whose complexity is internal, but even of villages and tea-kettles. In spite of their superficial simplicity, even these problems have a background of needs and activities which is becoming too complex to grasp intuitively.

To match the growing complexity of problems, there is a growing body of information and specialist experience. This information is hard to handle; it is wide-spread, diffuse, unorganized. Moreover, not only is the quality of information itself by now beyond the reach of single designers, but the various specialists who retail it are narrow and unfamiliar with the form-maker's peculiar problems, so that it is never clear quite how the designer should best consult them. As a result, although ideally a form should reflect all known facts relevant to its design, in fact the average designer scans whatever information he happens on, consults a consultant now and then when faced by extra-special difficulties, and introduces this randomly selected information into forms otherwise dreamt up in the artist's studio of his mind. The technical difficulties of grasping all the information needed for the construction of such a form are out of hand—and well beyond the fingers of a single individual.

At the same time that the problems increase in quantity, complexity, and difficulty, they also change faster than before.[14]

The entire problem of comprehensive developmental administration would, in truth, seem to be well beyond the easy intuitive grasp of any single administrator or group of admin-

[14] *Notes on the Synthesis of Form* (Cambridge, Mass.: Harvard University Press, 1967), pp. 3–4. The entire discussion in this seminal work is of great relevance for developmental administration.

istrators, although they often have a vested interest in denying this. What is needed is not a complete rejection of administrative intuition in favor of formalized and computerized systems analysis, but supportive technical aid to the overburdened administrator to help him bring his judgment and intuition to bear at appropriate and crucial phases of the administrative process. Sooner or later some computerized assistance to help organize and simplify the kaleidoscopic demands placed upon the conscientious administrator will have to be introduced. Alexander suggests an interesting technique for taking extremely complex problems and logically dividing them into a hierarchical tree of much more manageable subordinate problems. These subordinate problems are organized so as to be relatively independent of each other. Thus one maximizes the prospects for solving each without having to solve all, or without having that solution change the nature of the other problems one has worked to understand. Whether or not Alexander's answer is fully feasible in developmental administration, it seems clear that decisional aid must be furnished if developmental administration is not to be swamped in complexity.

In concluding, however, I wish merely to flag the problem of strategies for dealing with complexity itself, regardless of the substantive specifics of that complexity. The second topic on which I want to focus is an oft-mentioned but little analyzed facet of developmental administration. With specific reference to agriculture, Arthur Mosher has well christened it the problem of "agri-climate." I refer to the administrator's need to consider and use the more general and indirect social and cultural environment—the mighty advantages of creating what is often called an appropriate climate for national development. I should argue that such an approach is particularly important in agricultural development. As others have remarked, making steel is a comparatively uniform process all over the world; farming is notoriously variable. Agriculture is, and would seem likely to remain for a long time, very dependent on local information, that is, information at the level of the individual village and farm, even the individual field. Frequently, only the farmer himself has the information requisite to wise decision-making for his lands. This essential fact appears to dictate a basic strategy of making the farmer a better decision maker, more strongly motivated, better informed, and more adaptable.

The pay-off from creating an appropriate developmental climate seems especially large in the agricultural sector. Yet, developmental administrators often appear either unaware of or unconvinced by this argument. Through conviction, ignorance, or institutional incapacity, they seem generally to neglect the great opportunities they may have for indirect influence via the over-all cultural climate and to favor rather narrow direct programs, except perhaps for rural education. Thus, to take but one example, the recent five-year plans for India and for Turkey allocate less than one half of one per cent of planned public investment to the mass media—an instrument that has repeatedly been shown to be strongly associated with more "modern" orientations among the rural populace. I do not argue against highly focused and specific programs; I merely argue for increased consideration of indirect programs to affect the environing climate for development.

A communications approach to development affords one of the best introductions to this thesis. It is most instructive, for instance, to examine a series of maps portraying various kinds and levels of development in almost any transitional society. Look at a series of overlays reflecting urbanization, industrialization, literacy, roads, railways, death rates, assorted measures of productivity, cinemas, newspapers, income, education, and so on. Granted that there are variations in the hatchings and shadings, nevertheless in most developing societies there is usually an impressive similarity of pattern across all these maps. That pattern can be characterized in various ways. Initially, it strikes one that development seems to be some sort of suffusion or epidemiologic process. In grossest terms, it seems to move from coastal areas to the interior, along rivers and trade routes. It seems to be held up by natural barriers which increase isolation. Moreover, its movement seems to depend not just upon topography or climate but also upon proximity to external modernizing forces and upon the the technology of transport and communication. In short, such a geographic gestalt strongly suggests a communications theory of development, namely, that modernization suffuses primarily according to ease of communication with more modern sources. This conviction, incidentally, is reinforced if one considers not

merely currently developing nations but also the development
and spread of high civilizations such as the Greek, Roman, and
Renaissance.

Admittedly, there are anomalies in this gross geographic
pattern. The predictive power of an extremely simple theory
based on the physical aspects of communication, while surprisingly great, is less than we should like. But deeper analysis
seems to strengthen the general argument. For example, when
we descend to the personal level through survey research in
developing nations we find that the personal aspects of "modernity" also seem to be distributed in a fashion which urges a
suffusion-through-communication hypothesis. Individual modernity appears to move from urban areas to rural via the relatively well-educated and literate, male, media-exposed, well-
traveled individual whose occupation exposes him to different
experiences and who further expands his range of contacts
through voluntary associations.

Stepping back from the particular research findings for a
moment, one searches for an underlying factor. What, if anything, do these different modernity-enhancing attributes and
variables have in common? Knowledge of a common component
might aid in stimulating individual modernity. Moreover, we
shall realize a sorely needed criterion for evaluating various
developmental strategies, at least as they affect the orientation
of the individual.

Several suggestions have been made as to the psychic well-
springs of modernity. David McClelland has made a case for
achievement motivations, Daniel Lerner for empathy, others
for trust, identity, deferral of gratification, the Protestant ethic
and, even for guilt, God, or greed. My reading of the evidence is
that Lerner has come closest to an appreciation of the essentials of the process of individual modernization, but that his
formulation can and needs to be further generalized or ab-
stracted.

It seems to me that the cardinal feature of personal modernity
lies in one's attitude toward change. Of course, not all people
in modern societies are personally modern—far from it. But at
the critical stations in modern societies one tends to find persons who, relative to others in nonmodern societies, find change
congenial. Indeed, this is reflected in our universities today. The

factual training that many of our engineers and scientists receive at the university is sometimes obsolete just a few years after graduation. Rather than teaching facts, what the university does is to teach the individual how to learn, how to change himself, and how to generate change. Probably the most characteristic and revealing processes of truly modern societies are self-conscious research and design, the foundations for planned change. Neither is found in traditional cultures. Above all, a stable modern society requires individuals who psychologically can "handle" change, who, compared to others, find it acceptable, even desirable. It requires a comparatively large and strategically located contingent of individuals having a high degree of cognitive flexibility, people who are relatively good at stretching their minds to entertain new ideas, new roles, new practices, and new experiences. Its critical personnel must exhibit reduced levels of resistance to the indubitable work that is involved in what can literally be termed "changing one's mind."

All this appears fairly innocuous until we look at the other side of the coin. If cognitive flexibility—a relatively reduced level of psychic resistance to change, per se—can be accepted as a fundamentally important dependent variable for development, what of the independent variables widely found to be associated with this cognitive flexibility? What about education, travel, mass media exposure, urbanization, literacy, occupational sophistication, etc.? In terms of their psychic effects, what all these variables have in common is that they are all vehicles for exposing the individual to change; they all represent, in one fashion or another, his exposure to diversity of environment.[15]

---

[15] I do not want to imply that mass media exposure and travel, for example, necessarily conduce to cognitive flexibility, merely that they usually do so among contemporary peasant populations. That they do not always do so is fully in keeping with my basic hypothesis, which predicts *when* they will not. *Media exposure enhances cognitive flexibility only when it increases the exposure to change of the audience.* Thus, if the media content is primarily hackneyed, the media will be more narcotic than stimulant. Similarly, one would predict a greater association between media exposure and cognitive flexibility in nations where the media are new and expanding than in media-saturated societies. Again, factory work would enhance the cognitive flexibility of a peasant farmer, but not that of a man whose father and close associates had all

Hence, the basic rub in the developmental process is that we are caught in a vicious circle: for durable development we require people who find change congenial, even necessary; but the basic process for developing such people is through exposure to change. Social inertia is tremendous. A static society, left alone by the outside, will tend to remain static; a dynamic society will tend to continue to be dynamic. People in traditional societies have been so little exposed to change that they find it particularly trying, even when slightly exposed. Their cognitive flexibility or psychic capacity for handling change is under-developed because they have experienced only a static environment.

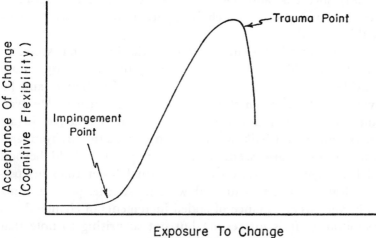

Figure 4. Cognitive flexibility

The pattern I am discussing can be represented, though oversimplified, as in Figure 4. The hypothesis is that there is a lower threshold (called the "impingement point") below which change does not impinge upon the individual often enough to produce any significant psychic reaction. This is generally the case in a traditional village, whose peasants are psychologically

been factory workers, and the impact of such work even on the peasant should clearly diminish after a few years' experience. Each dependent variable which putatively enhances cognitive flexibility will be found to do so only to the extent that it increases exposure to change.

unprepared for change and tend to find it intrinsically repugnant. When change (i.e., qualitatively different experience)
does begin to come frequently and markedly enough to produce
a psychic reaction, as in the initial stages of development, the
acceptance of change is extremely low. The developmental
dilemma encountered at this stage is that the resistance to
change is strongest just when the forces pressing for change are
likely to be weakest. As in almost any process involving acceleration, movement from a standing start demands the greatest
power. Such demands have proved too much for many systems.
Their power supplies get drained and momentum subsides.
After a hiatus for pressure again to build up, for motivational
batteries to be recharged, a new start is made; but it, too, only
partially succeeds, and one observes the halting and sporadic
developmental process which is apparent in so many parts of
the third world.

With increased exposure to change, the individual seems to
make the psychic adjustments necessary to take change more
in stride. He learns to anticipate and predict change, and he
develops a repertory of strategies for dealing with it. He even
comes to find emotional gratification and challenge in its
variety and would balk at any return to a static environment.
However, there also seems to be an upper threshold beyond
which change impinges on the individual faster than his psychological equipment can deal with it. At this point trauma
sets in and his acceptance of added increments of change drops
precipitously. It is interesting but not surprising to note that
the same relationship holds for social systems as well as for
their individual constituents. If change floods in upon a social
system too rapidly, many of its important processes are stopped
or altered and the system retreats to a much reduced level of
responsiveness to change.

Earlier I indicated that this hypothesis was slightly oversimplified. One significant qualification that needs to be introduced is the individual's evaluation of the changes he
encounters (in Lewinian terms, their "valence" for him). Theoretically, one's attitude toward change has two components:
(1) the underlying level of resistance to change per se, regardless of the specific content of the change, and (2) an evaluation
of the specific content of the change. Certainly we have every

reason to believe that negative experiences of change would lower the slope of the cognitive flexibility curve, even though they might not change its sequence of signs (basic shape).

What is the import of all this for the developmental administrator? The answer is that this hypothesis, if true (and I do not here have space for a full discussion of the relevant evidence), seems to suggest a fundamentally different approach to rural development from that now generally pursued. It is an approach which takes as its main goal producing new attitudes toward change among the rural populace, rather than producing such and such an increase in the use of fertilizer, in the area sown to new rice varieties, or even in farm productivity or income. Not that the latter types of change are unimportant, but they are to be regarded as essentially derivative. They will be products of or vehicles for the human changes which must be stimulated. All the existing kinds of extension, marketing, and mechanization projects would still be required, but they would be oriented and organized around the basic objective of cultivating the farmer, of working a change in him so that he will himself demand those programs most relevant to his situation, as is common in Iowa but rare in India. Without such change in the peasant population the specific input programs for fertilizer, pesticides, credit, and the like become one-shot injections which wear off quickly rather than devices for stimulating a self-sustaining process of rural development. The ultimate foundation for self-generating and durable agricultural development must rest on the people themselves, and it should be the final purpose of developmental administration to help create an appropriate rural populace.

More specifically, our hypothesis suggests to the developmental administrator that he realize his main problem in most traditional villages is to quicken the static condition of life, to expose the villagers to change so that they will become less resistant to future change. Yet he must do this without exceeding the "trauma point" where added change will be rejected by most of the target population. Perhaps the main goal can be expressed most economically in the jargon of some psychologists: the developmental administrator's most important job in the traditional village is to ensure that the villagers have a "successful learning experience" with change. He must select specific developmental projects whose results will be highly visible to and highly valued by the villagers. At least at first it should be a project whose probability of success is very great and whose realization time is relatively short. It must be a change, and it must be perceived to succeed. Within such general criteria as these, the specific content of the project is relatively less important. The crux of the project is its impact upon the orientations of the peasantry, not its marginal contribution to gross national product. Hopefully, there will be many situations where these two criteria coincide; but whenever there is conflict the long-run pay-off lies with pursuit of the former. All too often in developmental administration we seem to have concentrated for program evaluation on economic or technological criteria, whereas the prime focus should be upon the consequences of the program for the orientations toward change of the affected rural population.

Response

JAYANT LELE

Any discussion of the concept of power usually contributes to the already saturated confusion regarding its meaning. Frederick Frey very definitely escapes that criticism by providing a lucid discussion of the possibilities for measurement of power in its various dimensions. He takes the two basic components of a power relation, an influencer and an influencee, and builds an intricate and complex network of the various aspects of such a relationship. Though the argument is presented in terms of single individuals as actors, Frey assures us that there should be no difficulty in applying his framework to groups or organizations as actors. He suggests that once "we are able satisfactorily to locate the basic power relations such as who has power over whom in a political system and what are the particular influential behaviors and scopes involved" it is possible to present a summary picture of the power structures of a system, say a village. He also suggests some ways of comparing several power structures within and between systems.

Frey's main concern is with the ways of actually measuring power relations. He illustrates the utility of such an exercise for the study of power in small communities which dominate the world of a "change agent." Using digraph techniques he illustrates his logically consistent and comprehensive scheme for isolating various dimensions of a power relation and for emphasizing their interrelationships. He clearly suggests the danger of any simple unidimensional assumptions regarding power relations even in a small community. By specifying some universally significant units such as directness, conjunctivity, durability, reciprocity, etc., he provides a general scheme which should correct all the major weaknesses of the traditional studies of community power structures.

Rather than addressing himself to the literature on "development administration" or "development politics" he chooses to give us an elaborate exercise in theory building related to the concept of power. He modestly pleads that the rich realms of administrative theory and organization theory deserve more than a barbaric ransacking. Later on, and only indirectly, he adds that in spite of the proliferation of both theoretical and empirical writings in the field of administrative theory the literature on "development administration" fails to address itself to the most important aspects of power linkages between administrative and political units. This indirect justification for Frey's decision to pay attention to basic power linkages is, it seems to me, very crucial.

Politics of Development and Change

The level at which Frey chooses to operate is thus dictated not just by the richness of the realms of administrative theory (and one may add all theorizing in political science) but the glaring imbalance in these realms due to the neglect of important problems. The interest of the political scientists writing about developing societies has been largely concentrated on the descriptions of entire polities. They have developed new terminologies to describe the nature of polities of developing nations and to explore relations between political and economic development. Their indices for the analysis of these relationships have been aggregative and gross generalizations regarding the effectiveness and efficiency of political structures in performing some ideally prescribed functions.

Due to their preoccupation with the general theory of political development, the political scientists, including those concerned with the bureaucracies, have concentrated on isolating the essential elements of a polity or a "developmental administration" and on comparing developing nations and their polities with ideal types of political functions, inputs and outputs, democratic and oligarchic forms of government and rational administration. Political development is thus indexed in terms, mostly, of the structures. They include electoral procedures, party organizations, legislatures, bureaucracies, and interest groups. The ideal type of a developed polity is, despite protestations to the contrary, derived from a Western model of democratic organization of societies. The focus of the discussion of political development is always the adequacy of mainly formal political and social structures. Their performance is judged on the basis of their adequacy for developmental functions, mainly those of planning and implementation of development programs. The rational model, based on the Weberian logic and North American idiom, tends to dominate the discussion of political development in general but is especially rampant in the literature on administration in developing societies.

Such a model treats the political elite in the low income countries as a composite of party (political) leadership and bureaucracy. The party leadership, usually dominated by individuals with a fair amount of education and exposure to the West, is assumed to be motivated by the goals of rapid modernization and economic growth. Its major task is assumed to be the transformation of a mysteriously homogeneous and inert mass of public. Based on scanty anthropological case studies in some instances but without any empirical evidence in most, the political scientists and others writing on modernization have been successful in evoking an image of a sluggish, unmotivated, docile, apathetic society with a limited world view. The dominant theme is that of a *Gemeinschaft,* sacred, ritualistic, traditional, diffused, folk, and rural end of a continuum being pushed along towards a *Gesellschaft,* secular, active, modern, refracted, and urban end by a small highly motivated political elite blessed with Western education and aspirations. The development efforts of this elite are often described as herculean, its frustrations are blamed on the unresponsive mass wallowing in its morass of tradition and custom.

Leadership position of the politicians at the helm of affairs of the state in the low income countries is usually explained in terms of their superiority due to education, wealth, exposure to the cultures of the imperial rulers (past, present, or future), their disciplined way of thought and action as members of the armed forces, or due to Western education and their command over the mass media of communication.[1] The question of

[1] In most low income countries, mass media of communication are only in primitive stages of growth. Their influence is often exaggerated, inferred from their role in the West. The traditional media of face-to-

public support for the party elite is rarely discussed and when it is brought up, it is usually explained away either by a Weberian mystique of charisma or in terms of traditional authority or regulatory control through a system of administration inherited from the colonial past. It is not without significance that usually the mass that is assumed away as inert and apathetic is the mass of peasantry.

Some anthropological studies tend to perpetuate this image not because they portray the rural life as static, but because they treat the dynamics of rural communities in total isolation from that of the nation-society of which they are an integral part. The links between the villages and the nation-society are themselves very dynamic and particularly so in the context of power links. This is brought out quite clearly in a number of studies.[2] I myself have done a detailed study of such links in India during the national elections in 1967.[3]

Bureaucracy and Political Development

If my description of a political scientist's conception of the party elite seems slightly overdrawn, in the case of a bureaucrat it is perhaps an understatement. It is not a mere coincidence that an administrator in a low income country is usually the most accessible, the most articulate, and the most vocal informant for a political scientist.[4] It is not difficult to see why the conceptions of political scientists of the problems of behavioral change in agricultural development resemble the attitudes of the colonial and postcolonial administrators who conceived of

---

face communication are much more difficult to investigate, empirically, in the political context and are therefore ignored by the Western political scientists.

[2] P. R. Brass, *Factional Politics in an Indian State* (Berkeley: University of California Press, 1965); F. G. Bailey, *Politics and Social Change* (Berkeley: University of California Press, 1963); D. Ashford, *National Development and Local Reforms* (Princeton: Princeton University Press, 1967); G. D. Ness, *Bureaucracy and Rural Development in Malaysia* (Berkeley: University of California Press, 1967).

[3] "Local Brokers and National Leaders: A Study of Support Linkages in a Developing Polity" paper presented at American Political Science Association Meetings, Washington, September, 1968.

[4] In many situations an administrator is much more accessible to a Western political scientist than he is to a domestic researcher.

themselves as the guardians of an infantile peasantry (or of the early christian missionaries, for that matter, who claimed to be charged with the goal of "development of the soul"). One continuously runs into generalizations in the literature on political development such as "the stronger the government, the more easily it can teach, train, indoctrinate, and reorganize its subjects to comply more fully and effectively with its orders" where the government in the modernizing states is automatically assumed to have at least a minumum of "strength, enlightenment, and skill to act" for the rapid development of its subjects.[5]

I do not deny that there are frequent references in the literature to the capabilities of the politician and the administrator in planning and implementing social change. Deutsch, for example, argues that the governments are accepted on the basis of their responsiveness to the felt needs of the population. This is true, however, during the period of social mobilization, according to Deutsch, and not while the peasant is still an apathetic subject.[6] There is no doubt a great deal of concern about the capabilities of the administration. Invariably, however, it is expressed in terms of the limitations placed by traditional society on its "modernizing elite." Such efforts, therefore, lead to abstract formulations such as Riggs's model of a prismatic society, dominated by formalism, attainment orientation, and heterogeneity.[7]

One also comes across a rather neat model of a "Western" public administration characterized by differentiation, achievement criteria, and secular attitudes. Often a condescending

[5] Karl W. Deutsch, Chapter 2; "Social Mobilization and Political Development," *American Political Science Review,* 55, no. 3 (September, 1961), 502.

[6] "Social Mobilization," p. 502.

[7] F. W. Riggs, "Prismatic Society and Financial Administration," *Administrative Science Quarterly,* 5, no. 1 (June, 1960), pp. 1–46. Riggs's basic categories based on some acute observations and impressions do help in clarifying some of the problems of developmental capabilities of bureaucracies in low income countries. Though his model is much too wedded to the *Gemeinschaft-Gesellschaft* continuum it has the merit that it attempts to devise ways of looking at intermediate stages. The prismatic societies, unfortunately, tend to look like mysterious and inexplicable interplay of fusion and refraction generating more poetic than analytical delight. Riggs's categories are thus only descriptive devices for phenomena which demand a multivariate analysis and not just labels.

comment is added to say that even a minimally Westernized public administration can get on with the job of modernization and that a totally rational administration is not a prerequisite for development.[8] Like all conceptions of the ideal types as ends of a continuum, such a conception of administration is deceptive. One of the greatest contributions of the latter day administrative theory is the exploding of this myth of a rational process of decision-making in organizations, Western or Eastern, public or private, economic or religious. Even in a production-oriented unit such as a firm where technical criteria of maximization of the profit should dominate, R. Cyert and J. March find that the behavioral elements of goal-making and implementation tend to be dynamic social interaction processes.[9]

The assumptions regarding the relationship between the bureaucracy and the peasantry in the literature on "development administration" can be summed up in a quotation from S. N. Eisenstadt:

The emerging bureaucracies are also the major instruments of social change and of political socialization in their respective countries. They are initially, at least, based on universalistic and functionally specific definitions of the role of the official and the role of the client. But the majorities of the populations of these countries have a different orientation. In their social life their traditional orientations and structures, such as the extended family, are predominant. The major part of a person's role relations in these societies are set within traditional groups. Rights and duties are defined in terms of personal relationships. Previous experience with bureaucratic organization is restricted and rarely of great importance.[10]

At the empirical level of research such a conception of bureaucracy and its clients has led to the studies of training and skills of civil servants and their capacity to formulate and implement development programs. At the policy level prolifera-

[8] J. LaPalombara, "Bureaucracy and Political Development: Notes, Queries, and Dilemmas" in *Bureaucracy and Political Development*, J. LaPalombara, ed. (Princeton, N.J.: Princeton University Press, 1963), pp. 34–61.

[9] *A Behavioral Theory of the Firm* (Englewood Cliffs, N.J.: Prentice-Hall, 1963).

[10] "Bureaucracy and Political Development" in LaPalombara, ed., p. 112.

tion of community development programs manned largely by the layers of civil servants and administrators has taken place. It is assumed that an apathetic traditional community can be mobilized in a desirable direction by the intervention of the bureaucrats in all the spheres of village life. Most criticism of the development programs is based on the inability of the bureaucrats to mobilize masses in a predetermined direction. Proliferation of programs and inadequate training of the personnel are also mentioned as being responsible for the failure.

The great value of Frey's analysis of power is that it takes a major step away from the conventional jargon and presuppositions of "development-minded" political scientists. He states the three essential links of an administration: the ruler, the administrator, and the public. In elaborating on the ruler-administrator link he suggests a lucid and simple classification of types of administrations and the goals of the regime. The exploitative goal is roughly associated with venal control, the regulatory goal is associated with the programed control, and the developmental goal is associated with a feedback control of the administration. Frey hastens to add that elements of all the three goals and control mechanisms are found in all regimes and administrations and that the classification is more in terms of tendencies rather than exclusive categories. Frey goes on to add that the difference between the administrations in developing and modern countries is the degree of integration of three different administrative cultures.

Since administrative cultures seem to vary in their primacy due to regime goals one of the major tasks of a political scientist should be an exploration of the determinants of regime goals, treating them as dependent variables. Existing literature on developing polities and development administration fails to provide any clues in this direction and hence Frey is perhaps right in ignoring most of the contributions in this field. One would, however, expect, in Frey's chapter, an attempt to speculate on this crucial area of interest.

Such analysis has to be attempted within the framework of the power linkages, power structures, and bases of political support. Frey's concern for the measurement and multidimensional analysis of power is therefore fully justified. It is unfortunate that he has not had the time to elaborate more on this subject. Like most political scientists he takes for granted the developmental goals of the administration in low income countries, based on the verbalization of such goals by the articulate, vocal, administrative elite. This leads him to concentrate on only one of the crucial relationships between the three links of an administrative system. While emphasizing the link between the regime and the administrator he assumes that the relationships between the administrator and the public and between the regime and the public are unidimensional. The dimension between the administrator and the public, for him, is the same as that assumed in the existing literature on development administration. The link between the ruler and the public is, however, ignored. Perhaps there is an implicit assumption that the party elite is development-minded and legitimate and that it only operates through the administrator. It is consistent with Frey's other assumptions regarding the communications between the regime and the public. He assumes a gap between them and expects that it will be filled by the administrator.

There seems to be no logical or empirical reason to assume that the developmental goals as verbalized by the politician and the administrator in public statements and plan documents are the actual goals for implementation. Even if one can locate the stated goals which are actually attempted implementation of, there is no reason to believe that they are not transformed in the process of implementation.[11] One of the basic problems of the analysis of development administration is the problem of analyzing policy-making and implementation as a total, continuously interacting process.

Once we accept that goals are not necessarily a "given" (or stable even in the short run) element of administrative analysis, we must explore the power relationships which may lead to changes in goals or shifts in emphases on alternative goals and means in the process of implementation.

A study of such a process demands that attention be paid not only to the actions and protestations of the modernizing elite as the independent variables (with the mass or public as a dependent variable) but to these as dependent variables deeply affected by the shifts and changes in the response or demands

[11] G. D. Ness, pp. 88–89.

of the public. Frey gives one example of the response of the public to the administrator in Turkey. It is not enough, however, to assume that the rural public responds as a single undifferentiated whole as assumed in nation-wide sample surveys of peasants.

One of the main characteristics of the colonial administrations, as Eisenstadt points out, was that they were concerned almost exclusively with the regulatory goals of the colonial regimes. A fairly large number of these colonies inherited the colonial administrations almost intact with their personnel, institutions of training for civil servants, codes, and conventions of conduct within the administration and with the public. Some of the recent research indicates that the transformation following independence has not necessarily been in terms of acceptance of new developmental goals by the administration but has led to major changes in the continuously verbalized developmental goals in the process of actual implementation by a predominantly regulatory system of administration. One is inclined to accept A. Etzioni's evolutionary hypotheses regarding the eventual tendency towards congruence in kinds of power, compliance structures, goals, and effectiveness of an organization. It will be interesting to find out, for example, as to when and which goals get transformed in the process of creating congruence between goals and structures and when and which structures change to become congruent with goals in low income countries.[12]

Power Structures, Development Goals, and Administration

Whatever little empirical evidence is available on various levels of political activity in low income countries indicates that there is a close relationship among the nature of administrative control (by the regime, of the administrator), the nature of support of the political elite, and the adaptation of structures and goals of development. It is not possible to go into a detailed analysis of any of the recent studies; a brief statement about their findings may, however, be in order.

These findings suggest that though the structural differentiation of the peasant communities is low, their response to the

[12] *A Comparative Analysis of Complex Organizations* (New York: The Free Press of Glencoe, 1964).

political processes, set in motion prior to and after independence from colonial rule or after the transfer of power to the elite verbalizing developmental goals, has been varied and dynamic. In India, for example, the response has been analyzed in terms of the variables of ascriptive local factions, coalitions of these factions into brittle alliances and the dominant role played by the control of the sources of patronage by the political elite.[13] It is suggested that even apparently developmental goals and plans gain or lose salience in terms of these variables. Similar inferences can be drawn from studies of the Middle East, Pakistan, Malaysia, etc.[14] They all indicate a dynamic interaction through the medium of power among all three links of an administrative system suggested by Frey.

His own findings about the Turkish peasants seem to lead to the same conclusion. One may wish to add that perhaps the fact of greater communication with the traditional type of administrator is not enough to explain the skepticism of the peasant. It will be interesting to see how far the development administrator in Turkey relates himself to the public in the traditional idiom of a regulatory administrator while verbalizing developmental jargon. One is likely to find that the so-called development administrator is not radically different in his attitudes and in terms of structures within which he works from the regulatory administrator.

Subordinate Conceptualization of Power and Strategy of Development

At this level of analysis, however, Frey's brilliant exposition of the concept of power seems to offer few short-run conceptual scaffoldings for the understanding of administrative problems of behavioral change in development. It tends to keep us restricted to an operation at the level of a small community, say a village, where we start with a single change agent and a population of a few hundred clients. Even with such a small number of persons the web of interpersonal influence relationships becomes very complex. Almost every interaction needs to be examined for the power implications and evaluated in terms

[13] J. Lele and V. Sirsikar, "Indian Democracy: A New Perspective," unpublished manuscript.

[14] See the works of Ashford, Bailey, Brass, Lele, and Ness cited earlier.

of who is influencing whom and in what direction. If the task of plotting the power graphs is to be assigned to a village-level extension agent one must not ignore the danger that he will give up the effort in frustration even at a substantial cost to his effectiveness. Even if we were to assume that he is presented with a digraph of power links of a community the value of such a specific complex instrument may be overemphasized for him. Such a graph is more likely to emphasize a static power complex with an isolationist assumption about a community when, in fact, it may not be warranted.

In the long run, when a complex network of a wide range of specific influence relationships has been completely plotted, one may be able to present a summary description of the various power relations in a community or a society. Until then, however, one may have to operate with a crude and a less quantifiable conceptualization of power relations. Frey has rightly avoided an attempt at a comprehensive typology of power. His classification of administrative cultures does, however, provide a clue for isolating a few important types of power relations that are particularly relevant for a developmental strategy. For example, the programed administration roughly associated with regulatory goals seems to coexist with a special kind of a power linkage between the regime and the public. We will denote this power linkage as authoritarian. An authoritarian power structure is characterized by noncontingent support for the regime from the public. It tends to maintain itself through the manipulation of symbolic elements of the culture. It emphasizes basic values and expressive beliefs which legitimize the regime and place it beyond the manipulative reaches of the public. Inherent qualities such as nobility, divine right, or guardianship of the infantile masses are used as justifications and an attempt is made to inculcate these attitudes in the public. Noncontingent support may substitute or supplement the use or threat of physical coercion. The important point here is that these attitudes are sought to be inculcated not only in the administrator but also in the public and perhaps more so in the public than in the administrator.

In order for developmental goals to replace the regulatory goals it is not enough to have a few members either of the regime or of the administration verbalizing the value of moderni-

zation. A feedback administrative culture and developmental
goals are likely to coexist with that power relationship between
the public and the regime which can be characterized as responsive. Responsive power relationship is based largely on support
from the public contingent upon the fulfillment of the felt
needs of the public by the regime. Responsive regimes are open
to challenge on the grounds of efficiency and effectiveness in
problem-solving where problem formulation and solution implementation are based on a continuous feedback between
public and the regime as well as between public and the administrator and between the administrator and the regime.

For the emergence of a responsive regime and the congruent
developmental goals and feedback control in administration a
workable strategy for creating areas of contingency for regime
support becomes necessary. Such a strategy may simply lie in
creating institutional structures which will eventually create
differentiated interests and an awareness that fulfillment of
such interests can be made a contingency for political support
of the regime. This is not intended as an attempt to introduce
a Western interest articulation aggregation model by the back
door. Traditional sociocultural or new ecological interest units
may emerge in varied forms of politicization. A total societal
ideology of involvement, development, or national defense
may characterize a society, engulfing subordinate interests.
The emphasis should be on institutional avenues for generating
and maintaining support contingent at least in part on the efficacy of the regime and the administration. One may view the
creation of supervisory committees of citizens to oversee the
performance of the development administration as a significant
strategy move. In the short run, such agencies as local governments, supervisory boards, and cooperative management units or
party cells may acquire the attributes of the regulatory administration itself as seen in the democratic decentralization in
India.[15] However, one also sees a gradual change in the power
relation between the administrator and the supervisory committees where the administrator is becoming responsive to the
felt needs at least of his supervisors if not of the public.

This illustrative exercise of adding a new link to the per-

[15] J. Lele, *Local Government in India* (Ithaca, N.Y.: International
Agricultural Development Program, Cornell University, 1965), p. 27.

ceptive analysis in Frey's paper is not intended as a substitute for his brilliant formulations and plea for measurement and location of power. Frey has simply sketched an outline of the types of political power. I join him in emphasizing the hazards of hasty typologies. My main contention has been that in order to develop strategies for developmental administration we must confront the problem of power at a level qualitatively different from, if not higher than, the level of interpersonal influence.

In summary, therefore, I would like to say that an administration charged with developmental goals is not by definition a developmental administration. The problem with many administrative structures in developing societies lies with the fact that they are regulative structures charged with developmental goals. A regulatory structure of administration will attempt to use authoritarian power to implement developmental goals and will use manipulation of symbols to maintain a high level of noncontingent support. Case studies of such structures in developmental administration provide adequate evidence to suspect that this is a usual short-run tendency of congruence among the structures, the goals, and the power links. Politicians and administrators attempt to use developmental symbols to perpetuate regulatory power.

The second important conceptual implication of my argument is that the public, in the context of development administration, cannot be treated as a dormant homogeneous entity. Its responses to developmental stimuli vary in terms of its structural differentiation, political and social as well as ecological. These responses may create an institutional nexus which tends to alter the very nature of the stimuli, their scope, salience, and intensity. Frequently in the transitional stages of development, verbalization of goals and formal structures of implementation may not change while the processes underlying the goal-making and implementation are transformed. What appears as formalism, heterogeneity, and attainment orientation may be true about the structures without meaningfully applying to the basic transitional processes.

The strategy implications of our formulations of power and support relationships between the regime, the administrative structures, and the public can be stated rather simply. The problem, in many societies today, is of transforming the power linkages from an authoritarian to a responsive base. The value of responsive power relations between the regime and the public is that for developmental goals as well as for any other goals an administrative structure of implementation is open to inspection with regard to its capacity to effectively perform.

Frequently, such attempts at institutionalizing responsive power through supervisory structures fail as a result of the fact that those occupying supervisory positions themselves acquire the attributes of regulatory power. This will be particularly true where the social bases of power have traditionally been dominated by regulation goals as in feudal systems of land tenure. This hopefully is a short-run effect. There is modest evidence to suggest that creation of formal structures of responsibility tend to widen the power base, though often imperceptibly, and generate demands for contingency from enlarged classes of politically mobilized public.

I have found Frey's ideas about the administrative cultures much more useful than his analysis of power. My omission of his venal administrative culture needs little explanation. Frey makes a valid point that the idea of venal administration transforms into self-interest and actualization of this interest through institutional channels in a feedback administration. Interest actualization is basic to all exercise of power and the venal aspects of administrative culture appear in different forms in both the programed as well as the feedback administration and do certainly pertain to the contingencies on which the regime support is based.

There should be no doubt whatsoever about the enormous importance of the results of empirical investigations of power relations based on the scheme presented in Frey's paper. He has opened for a systematic inquiry one of the most abused and misunderstood variables of political and organizational analysis of development. The peasantry in developing societies has been neglected in empirical analysis of administrative and political development. Nation-wide sample surveys of peasant attitudes and motivations supported by equally scientific studies of institutional and group variables are essential prerequisites for an attempt to isolate concepts of developmental administration which have strategy implications for behavioral change.

Synthesis Response to Parsons and Frey

JOHN D. MONTGOMERY

Social scientists have always studied human behavior, among other reasons, in the hope of "improving" it. Even in their more detached moments, gatherers of social data and spinners of social theory have ventured to hope that their efforts might be of some good. Although most such efforts have addressed local or at least familiar conditions, social scientists are now beginning to make their services available abroad. Their ready availability should subject their credentials to special scrutiny.

Social scientists have been increasingly successful (and increasingly uncomfortable) in their manipulative activities in western countries. They became change agents in the first instance because the evolving complexities of organized society had so obviously begun to challenge the capacities of its traditional arrangements, and they continued to find their new role congenial because the increasing power of their theoretical and analytical tools enabled them to suggest and design the required new arrangements.

The decline in the acceptability of traditional arrangements first became apparent in commercial and industrial sectors in the West, long before the rise of social sciences in their present form. Economic and administrative instruments that were devised to meet the needs of the eighteenth and nineteenth centuries had become increasingly obsolete: the notion that pure competition provides a sufficient restraint upon its own excesses, which was highly congenial during the first successes of capitalism, is seldom encountered in the mid-twentieth century. At the same time, newer conventional solutions of Marxist origins that called for total government planning and management have come equally under challenge. Economists have found that they could not improve the modern functions of industrial production and distribution by recourse to the conventional bromides of either "capitalist" or "communist" ideologies. To a lesser extent, and for different reasons, traditional arrangements for agriculture, whether practiced in underdeveloped countries according to the time-honored ancestral customs, or in the United States following the relics of the nineteenth-century land-grant mythology, are becoming outmoded. The search for appropriate agricultural policy in the mechanized, overabundant United States economy is not less challenging to tradition than the need to increase agricultural productivity in the underdeveloped world.

Increased capabilities of the social scientists in both theory and method have caused a rising demand for their services. If business led the way by applying their statistical methods to the analysis of cyclical changes, government was to follow by calling upon them to help reduce their devastating effect upon society. And after the great American depression had legitimized economics, World War II continued the trend by exploiting anthropology and psychology. The social sciences soon rose to that state of eminence or political power conferred by recognition in the National Science Foundation, and one of them, at least, occupies a unique position of power from the vantage point of the president's council of economic advisers. Whether or not economics is scientific, it is at least useful.

Such gains for the social sciences have been most apparent in industrialized countries; what influence they have in the underdeveloped world they owe largely to foreign aid. In the low income countries economists, including agricultural economists, have risen to positions of influence because they are needed in the planning of development activities, especially where external financing was involved. Development administration has not yet achieved even that status, but the obvious deficiencies in the management of public-supported programs of modernization will produce increasing demands for the invention of new institutions for government programs of all kinds. The question both groups of social scientists must now face is not whether their aid will be sought in adjusting to the new requirements, but whether they are capable of supplying the needed guidance.

Social scientists do not find it easy to achieve much detachment in examining their capabilities for providing policy guidance in the agricultural sector. Technological innovation alone has increased productivity enough to generate a halo of overconfidence on the part of Western advisers in agricultural economics and development administration. As they become more committed to specific policies, especially those involving institutional change, it becomes all the more important to examine the sources from which their judgments spring.

The social scientist serving in a crosscultural context must be prepared to examine himself both as an actor in the new setting and as a product of his own active culture. One way of identifying these interrelationships of culture and doctrine might be to note in the two disciplines described by Parsons and Frey their common elements as products of Western society and then to consider how the perspectives of each illuminate the assumptions of the other as they approach their mutual tasks.

Some Common Elements

There is a natural symmetry in this grouping together of agricultural economics and development administration. Both are applied, and distinct, branches of an older discipline, and each presents a microview of selected elements of a larger whole. Economics works best from macrostudies of large-scale behavior, such as the gross national product, the foreign exchange balance, and concrete aggregates that can be reduced to abstract per capita estimates; while public administration also concerns itself generally (though not exclusively) with large-scale behavior, notably in organizations which are parts of a national government or its lesser political subdivisions. The agricultural economist, then, focuses upon factors in rural productivity and consumption, leaving other segments of the economy to his colleagues; and the development administrator, in turn, is increasingly concerned with means of introducing change as a distinct purpose among the total responsibilities of government, leaving to others the task of improving performance in the traditional staff and regulatory functions. And it may be only a matter of time before the specialized demands upon the development administrator call for a further subdivision of the field into agricultural development administration, educational development administration, and the like.

Both of these offshoots of the parent disciplines are recent: neither can trace its origins back much before the twentieth century, and development administration is really a product of the 1950's. Since both emerged in modern societies, their relevance to the underdeveloped countries arises primarily from their method and approach rather than from the data they have already gathered. Even so, the question of their social origins is an important one because the very methods they use incorporate assumptions derived from Western experiences. In both theory and method, these two disciplines must be prepared to review the relevance of their favorite approaches as they are applied in the underdeveloped countries.

Problems of Theory

Theory is used by these disciplines to explain observations already made, to anticipate behavior not yet observed, and to show possible interrelationships among these observations and predictions. At its highest and most abstract level, social theory rises above immediate observation by generating categories and hypotheses for the whole conceivable range of behavior. It thus postulates a giant matrix of interrelationships, including some that may not be known empirically at all: most of its cells, in fact, may be entirely empty of data. As observation proceeds, of course, many of these boxes are filled; and studying clusters of known data becomes the proper function of "middle-level" theory. "Operational" theory, to extend the metaphor still further, would be a third and lower level, presumably concerning only one or two boxes of known data.

Most social science thus concerns itself with known and observed parts of the universe, only rarely extrapolating its "middle-level" theories and data into adjacent empty cells. However complete its highest theory may be, therefore, the practice of social science is distorted by its incomplete experience—the empty cells. Economists know more about dollar-measured wealth than other forms; sociologists can describe criminality and deviation better than normality; administrators understand efficiency but have few measures of effectiveness. In societies where such truths are accepted for the sake of convenience, not much harm is done by their obvious distortions because policymakers and citizens have a general contextual consciousness of their inadequacies.[1] It is when these conveniences are arbitrarily extrapolated into the unknown cells of non-Western societies that the professional social scientist, in all his fresh innocence, is most likely to project errors he cannot himself identify.

Problems of Method

Scarcity of data and difficulty of access both limit the capacity of these two disciplines to respond to the needs of their clients in the underdeveloped world.

Even if one assumes that the categories and concepts used in the two disciplines are adequate for crosscultural operations, there remain obvious difficulties in applying them in underdeveloped societies because of the shortage of suitable and comparable data. Few prescriptions, if any, are universal: they require detailed knowledge in order to analyze and classify different situations which in turn call forth varied approaches in the planning of government programs and design of public policy. It is almost always necessary to work in underdeveloped countries without adequate data, or with extrapolated data, or even with wrong data.[2] Per capita income figures, for example, are arithmetical *means* that have little to do with real individual wealth, especially in the underdeveloped world. Until *modal* income averages are available, comparisons between rural and urban life will always be distorted in one way or another, usually making the peasant appear more prosperous than he really is. In the absence of any data at all about actual behavior, the commingling of facts may actually mislead more than ignorance would. Annual rice consumption in Thailand used to be calculated by multiplying the estimated population

[1] See Bertram M. Gross, ed., "Social Goals and Indicators of American Society," *The Annals of the American Academy of Political and Social Science* (September, 1967).

[2] See Wolfgang F. Stolpher, *Planning without Facts* (Cambridge, Mass.: Harvard University Press, 1966).

by the per capita rice consumption in a neighboring country. When the resulting figure was challenged, the ministry of health supplied a new, lower, but equally irrelevant factor: physicians' estimates of the minimum caloric requirement.[3] The data made it "unnecessary" to find out how much food, and of what quality, people actually ate.

Wherever a body of doctrine has to be applied differentially to various classes of cases, there is opportunity for gross error. The categories used may themselves be fanciful; and moreover, in applying them it may be impossible to suspend action until information is gathered that would permit classification to take place. This limitation is fairly well recognized as it applies to economic programs for the agricultural sector. But it applies as well to administrative policies that depend upon the perceptions of development and the political values of the bureaucracy. In spite of their sociological appearance of homogeneity, recent evidence suggests that, like farmers, bureaucrats do not think alike as a class, at least where development is concerned.[4]

One way social scientists seek to minimize such data problems is to classify underdeveloped countries differentially so that analogies can be drawn from like countries to create presumptions of similarity and thus fill in the gaps. In this way, different types of countries can at least be observed in their own terms instead of as mere collective deviations from the industrialized world. When Kenneth Parsons classifies underdeveloped countries according to three agricultural types (African, Asian, and Latin American), he is engaged in a legitimate form of extrapolation from better-known to less-known situations. But this process helps to simplify the differences among these societies only so long as the resemblances within each type are not overstated. It is well recognized, of course, that significant variations exist within all "regions," however grouped.[5] The social scientist cannot be sure that the elements of assumed identity in any given classification, orginally

[3] John D. Montgomery, *The Politics of Foreign Aid* (New York: Praeger, 1962), p. 29 and pp. 108–114.

[4] Glenn D. Paige and Doo Bum Shin, "Aspirations and Obstacles in Korean Development Administration: An Application of Self-Anchoring Scaling," *Public Policy*, Vol. 16 (1967), pp. 3–28.

[5] Bruce Russett, *International Regions and the International System* (Chicago: Rand McNally, 1967).

adopted in the interests of finding elements of homogeneity, may not turn out to be the crucial differentiating ones. The solution is at best an improvisation.

A related problem is that of access. It arises from the fact that these disciplines, developed in industrialized countries in response to their own internal conditions, have produced professionals whose practice is indigenous to those circumstances. "Native" professionals may be, in a sense, culturally displaced persons, with distorted perspectives of their own societies. Sometimes Westerners seek to reduce their own cultural limitations by applying in one country the experiences gained in another, hoping thereby to minimize the gap between Western conditions and those in a still unknown country.[6] This approach is helpful as a starting point, but its primary usefulness is not in providing data so much as improving intellectual access to the new situation. In gaining physical access to current data, however, the foreign scholar increasingly encounters xenophobic responses from the host society even if it accepts his discipline and expertise. Even if qualified native specialists are present to join with him in prescribing policies, the fear of academic imperialism often undermines the acceptability of his efforts.[7]

Access to data does not necessarily assure the participant social scientist of an adequate perception of the cultural context in which he is working. Differences in social values, social infrastructure, and political orientation often account for the gaps between what he thinks he is doing and what in fact he may actually do in a given situation.

The rationality and other social values of an underdeveloped society, identified in national terms, must be distinguished from those of individual citizens who happen to be its farmers or bureaucrats. Individual responses to incentives and achievement needs can be identified and predicted in most (if not all) societies because of psychological similarities among men; but the social standing of these values may differ markedly from place to place. Large-scale incentives are thus not necessarily

[6] Elsewhere I have referred to this technique as the source of the "transfer" error. "Crossing the Culture Bars," *World Politics*, 13 (June, 1961), 553.

[7] "Form and Content of International Development Research: Implications for Cooperative Ventures," *Asia*, Summer, 1968.

the same as individual incentives. Indeed, a society may punish individuals for responding to economic incentives.[8] The action capabilities of societies are limited by dissonances among the national development goals assigned by governing elites and the self-immunizing capabilities of both the bureaucratic change agents and the rural population who constitute the ulti-mate "target groups." The consultant in agricultural econom-ics or development administration cannot assume on the word of the national leadership that policies which would be feasible in his own society are acceptable in another country.

Apart from the values of those most directly involved as in-dividuals, the social infrastructure of most underdeveloped countries lacks the resources for development in the Western pattern. The absence of an entrepreneurial class, for example, may force the planner to rely more heavily on governmental action than would be considered desirable in a situation where alternative social forces exist. But the government's own ad-ministrative resources may also be inadequate. Alternatively, if the practitioner offers recommendations which favor enter-prise outside government channels, he may incidentally and unwittingly espouse something approaching political revolu-tion. In effect, he is expressing a preference for leadership by a class which is not characteristically represented in the elite structure. The risk of repudiation under these circumstances is faced as much by the economist who recommends the establish-ment of a fertilizer industry as by the administration adviser who proposes to set up an autonomous semipublic corporation.

A third question of context is the political orientation of government leaders in an underdeveloped society. In the indus-trialized world—even in communist states—politicians are in-creasingly responsive to citizen pressures, and the posture of government in its action programs tends to become typically decentralized and service-oriented;[9] but quite different con-

---

[8] George M. Foster, "International Relations in Peasant Society," *Human Organization*, 19 (Winter, 1960–61), 174–184. See also *Traditional Cultures and the Impact of Technological Change* (New York: Harper, 1962), pp. 52–54.

[9] John D. Montgomery, "Sources of Bureaucratic Reform," in Ralph Braibanti *et al.*, *Political and Administrative Development* (Durham, N.C.: Duke University Press, 1968).

ditions generally obtain in underdeveloped societies. The relevant question for the Western adviser confronting a political orientation significantly diverse from that of his own society is whether the consequences of his proposals will favor the elite structure of the society or whether they will compel the government to adopt a posture toward its rural citizens which is incompatible with its basic political system.

Questions like these, which are important to policy-oriented activities in both of these disciplines, ought to be considered by any practitioner who perceives his role as that of change agent. The analytical techniques and approaches to individual farmers and bureaucrats taken by each of these sciences can offer predictions and suggest prescriptions to deal with individual target groups, but taken in a larger context, their consequences may be socially, politically, and culturally counterproductive in their collective impact.[10]

Political implications of these approaches may border on the revolutionary. They include using government policy to balance the claims of the privileged elite off against incentives to the rural poor; finding substitutes in private or associational institutions for government action; and decentralizing or devolving decision-making from the capital city to provincial towns and villages. Changes of this magnitude cannot be expected to emerge anywhere in the absence of a powerful and widely shared national will to develop. Since so much depends upon this national will, development administration planning cannot accept it as a fixed element. The social scientist is strongly inclined to temper the judgment of practicing politicians and the accidents of national leadership with rationality.

This temptation should not be entirely rejected. A nation's

[10] For examples of economic fallibility see Albert O. Hirschman, *Development Projects Observed* (Washington, D.C.: Brookings Institution, 1967), pp. 9–34, 160–190; and Arthur Smithies, "Inflation and Development in Latin America," in *Public Policy*, 13 (1964), pp. 206–238. For an appraisal of the applicability of political science, see Ralph Braibanti, "The Relevance of Political Science to the Study of Underdeveloped Areas," in Ralph Braibanti and J. J. Spengler, eds., *Tradition, Values, and Socio-Economic Development* (Durham, N.C.: Duke University Press, 1961), pp. 138–181; and John D. Montgomery, "Public Interest and the Ideologies of National Development," in Carl J. Friedrich, ed., *Nomos V: The Public Interest* (New York: Atherton Press, 1962).

"will to develop" is probably unmeasurable, but it may be estimated in terms of effort proportionate to needs and capabilities. All three of these factors—effort, need, and capability—can be observed over time, and even to some extent quantified. Moreover, there are rational means of influencing the national will, so defined. The three groups most directly concerned in agricultural development are public servants, local leaders, and farmers, and they can be more effectively supplied with information than they now are by the use of modern communications techniques; and development programs can be so designed as to minimize the threat of change to each of them, again with the intention of fostering positive attitudes.

As development administration begins to incorporate these dimensions into agricultural programs, questions of political objectivity, professional ethics, and cultural neutrality reach their most serious levels. Recent foreign aid legislation has called for intensive study of political development with a view to using this knowledge to enhance the effects of economic and technical assistance.[11] This frank recognition of the political potentials of foreign aid is long overdue, but social scientists must now accustom themselves to bearing new burdens of self-restraint and self-knowledge.

Some Economic Considerations

Economists may not be very enthusiastic about Frederick Frey's definition of development administration as including all administration in developing countries. Some administrative activities that presently consume substantial portions of the national effort are economically unnecessary or at least unrelated to development. Some survive merely as a protected preserve for clerks trained in the colonial tradition who have been elevated to administrative eminence by the departure of their former colonizers. In other cases government programs

[11] Ralph Braibanti, "External Inducement of Politico-Administrative Development: A Design for Strategy," in Braibanti *et al.* A six-week study conference under AID sponsorship was devoted to political development and foreign aid in the summer of 1968, the results of which are summarized in David Hargood, ed., *The Role of Popular Participation in Development* (Cambridge, Mass.: MIT Press, 1969).

are a form of welfare activity providing work for the literate, the well-born, or the ethnically favored population.

If it were possible to ignore political considerations, economists would doubtless prefer to streamline and houseclean these activities along with the routines and the old-line functions of government, such as customs management, record-keeping, and a host of supports known as "general administration." But in recent years, administrative reforms designed to bring about improvements in these sectors of government activity have not really been treated as elements in development administration at all, since they are not intended to influence the forward motion of a government's development program. They may of course represent an important contribution to government efficiency, to the extent that they release funds and scarce manpower from unproductive work and improve government performance in the routines that constitute the infrastructure and necessary base of development administration. For these reasons, reforms in personnel management, accounting, finance management, and the like—the conventional tasks for the public administrator—are welcomed for their contribution to efficiency. But they are not regarded as the essential province of the development administration specialist because they are already competently discharged by the use of conventional techniques. To be sure, improvements in the staff routines and other problems of management efficiency are far from standardized. Their application to administrative reform programs requires careful examination of local circumstances and requirements, and still runs the risk of offending the existing civil service. But the tasks of development administration require the injection of technological considerations related to program goals. They touch upon the organization of nongovernmental institutions in the first instance, but they also involve the consideration of alternative systems for introducing modern technologies and distributing their benefits.

The gradual transition of development administration from concern with conventional management problems to an orientation toward the developmental aspects of government activity—especially in the "professional" fields—reflects a response to economic priorities. It parallels a new perception on the part of program planners in agriculture, public health, and other sectors that administration is an important element in the infrastructure of technological modernization.[12] For these reasons, public administration specialists are serving increasingly as staff associates to technical assistants in foreign aid missions and as members of various development ministries. They are also becoming increasingly involved in the host government's effort to relate national plans to the programs of the development ministries. And the use of the traditional public administrator as a specialist in "pure" organization and methods, or as a kind of efficiency expert working exclusively out of a central office, is gradually dwindling.

Frey's distinction between the two linkages of politics and administration (ruler-bureaucracy and bureaucracy-public, respectively) provides a useful base from which to examine the economic implications of bureaucratic reform. His classification suggests that exploitative regimes use venal mechanisms as a control over the bureaucracy, that regulative regimes maintain control through program devices, while development and welfare regimes rely on feedback controls of various types. This classification helps to explain why bureaucratic reform in the interests of efficiency involves much more of a change in the political system than appears to be the case. The difficulties of carrying out even standardized administrative reforms in underdeveloped countries has provided an additional reason for abandoning "public" administration in favor of "development" administration and for the increasing assignment of administrative specialists to development ministries. Clearly the application of simple bureaucratic reforms in the interests of efficiency is appropriate to development and welfare regimes, but it would be threatening to regulative regimes (where the local autonomy of administrative units needs to be protected) and to exploitative regimes (where the desire to protect the political spoils would be injured by standardizing administrative response). If development administrators direct their reform efforts not to the bureaucracy as such but toward the developmental requirements of the program ministries like agriculture, public health, and education, the frontal assault

[12] John D. Montgomery, "The Challenge of Change," *International Development Review*, (March, 1967), 2–8.

on traditional sources of privilege can be deflected in favor of more professionally oriented approaches. The ruler-bureaucracy linkage would become less a sociological than a technological one.

The bureaucracy-public linkage can also be strengthened by the proposed focus on technology and innovation. The economic requirement for gaining a better peasant response to government incentives and other pressures to produce certainly suggests the need for fundamental changes in bureaucratic attitudes and purposes. The peasant's typical encounters with the government have not led him to view its activities as a service to his farming effort. The kinds of demonstrations required to improve these attitudes are more likely to involve fundamental changes in bureaucratic activities and attitudes than simple changes in organization and procedure. Experimentation must take place in the design of whole programs addressed to securing farmer response.[13] Technology does not often come in ready-made forms, and attempts to prepackage new techniques into administrative units and routines, or to fit technology and administration together by formula, often weaken the impact of government programs. Administrative tidiness looks more economic than it is.

Development administration has not yet derived much practical benefit from the conventional political scientist's approach to power. Frey's analysis adds new dimensions to its possibilities, however. The range of governmental postures toward the interacting human factors in power relationships clearly transcends the legalistic and regulatory preoccupations of many politicians and bureaucrats. Leadership involves the skillful use of a variety of influences on men, including those urged upon us by economists. New ways of initiating change and of responding correctively to the resultant behavior of those affected by governmental power emerge from the model.

It is encouraging to note that this approach to power coincides with an important insight from economics: one of the critical problems of development is the release, rather than the control, of nongovernmental productive energies. When power

[13] Arthur T. Mosher, "Administrative Experimentation as a 'Way of Life' for Development Projects," *International Development Review,* 9 (June, 1967), 38–41.

includes action-liberating functions as key elements in the administrative relationships required for development, the coercive and regulatory role of government need no longer justify our conventional neglect of other sources of initiative and innovation.

Development Administration Implications

A cynical friend remarked some years ago that the science of economics had discovered only one law that really worked: that of supply and demand. I was delighted at finding that at least one truth was universal, and clung to it until a few years ago when the United States went through a cost-push price inflation during a period of high unemployment and low demand. Once more I was left without any dependable economic verities except rising taxes. In spite of this disillusioning experience, I still see the economist as a fixer of natural policies and a designer of grand strategies, and the administrator as a tactician. In the agricultural sector both are concerned with the deployment of a series of small-unit decisions.

Elsewhere I have described three governmental modes of response in executing national programs: direct action, promotion of collateral activity outside the government, and exercise of leadership in providing ideology and its institutional supports to advance national purposes.[14] The ultimate target of government agricultural policy in the underdeveloped countries is, of course, the majority of its own citizens, who must be led, aided, and motivated to make choices favorable to the national goals.

The first administrative problem for a government in this position is to find mechanisms for dealing in volitional terms with the least accessible portion of the public, the rural majority which is not fully assimilated into the national political system. As essentially "free" agents making myriads of private choices that constitute their contribution to national productivity goals, farmers are the final links in the communication chain between national leadership and national performance.

[14] "A Royal Invitation: Variations on Three Classic Themes," in John D. Montgomery and William J. Siffin, eds., *Approaches to Development: Politics, Administration, and Change* (New York: McGraw Hill, 1966), pp. 259–263.

Yet farmers as a client group of government have probably received the least attention in conventional public administration of any element of the society. Evidence in the U.S., for example, suggests that accidental social changes like the innovation of rural free delivery and the activities of commercial suppliers had more to do with productivity increases than did the work of the USDA.[15] Psychology and communications sciences, along with economics, have much to contribute to development administration. For once the economic rationale has been worked out at the farm level, the devices for linking individual choices to social capabilities require our understanding of human cognition and volition as well as organizational potential.

A second problem posed by the governmental dependence on the rural masses for improving productivity arises in the ultimate distribution of the added income, especially export earnings, when much of the wealth thus generated goes for the benefit of city dwellers. Because farmer motivation is at stake, export earnings deriving from the agricultural sector, and indeed even wealth generated from other sectors, sometimes have to be used to provide rural incentives. This redistributive need poses problems of real political consequence, since it compels the national planner to sacrifice the immediate interests of groups that have hitherto provided the strongest support to modernizing goals. The planner must therefore find policies that represent as little inconvenience to present elites as possible, while at the same time bringing rural elements into the modern sector. He might approach this goal by incorporating the private sector into the distribution system for farm supplies and equipment, especially of low cost, high volume commodities.[16] But for reasons of both administrative economy and political feasibility, he must so use this process as to provide motivations for both farmers and businessmen, while at the same time reduce the coercive role of the civil service. These requirements suggest the need for introducing administrative devices that do not rely heavily upon civil ser-

[15] Wayne E. Fuller, *RFD: The Changing Face of Rural America* (Bloomington: University of Indiana Press, 1964).

[16] Stephen A. Marglin, "Towards a Revolution in Agriculture," *Economic Weekly* (*Bombay*), 16 (15th Annual Number, February, 1964), 343–349.

vants for the interpretation of enforcement of centralized regulations. The search for supplements to the civil service is therefore one of the most important unrecognized problems in development administration.

Capable administrative manpower is among the most limited of all resources in the underdeveloped countries, especially those handicapped by heavy reliance on a professional civil service for the performance of both productive and regulatory functions. Ideological factors and class interests in such cases seem to foreclose the use of any alternative sources of managerial and administrative talent for carrying out government programs in the agricultural sector. The generation of administrative organizations outside the framework of government,[17] combined with price theory (the revisionist's version of supply and demand), probably still offer the most promising approaches to these problems of development administration. But implementation of these approaches is more a political than an economic problem. Favorable price relationships require an equal attention to farm inputs and outputs, not a favorite preoccupation of planning units; they involve enterprise as well as controls, not a favorite preoccupation of agriculture ministries. The search for such alternatives to the conventional civil service promotes a gradual weakening of authoritarian preferences found in most underdeveloped countries, but it is sometimes aided by the obvious need to offset the shortage of administrative manpower.

A third problem of mutual concern is that of land tenure. Western economists generally prefer either private, individual ownership of farms or a substantial and stable contract system for individual leasing of lands. This preference arises, of course, out of the expected use of private profit for incentive purposes. But administrators are constantly impressed with the difficulty of carrying out land reform by using conventional administrative machinery. They are only now beginning to consider new approaches to land reform, downgrading the traditional role of administrators and technicians, avoiding con-

---

[17] For an example, see John D. Montgomery, Rufus B. Hughes, and Raymond H. Davis, *Rural Improvement and Political Development: The JCRR Model* (Washington, D.C.: The American Society for Public Administration, 1966).

ventional dependence on aerial surveys and title registration, and seeking new ways to invest local authority with the necessary powers and skills to devise equitable tenure procedures.[18] In many countries real imagination will be necessary to conceive of institutional devices that will substitute for simultaneous, standardized deeds registration, minutely accurate title investment methods, and the elaborate litigation procedures of Western law.

Implications

There is, of course, an element of tension—not to say inconsistency—among the propositions argued here. I have said that social science must resist the natural tendency to extrapolate from its relatively small known universe to the much larger reaches of the unknown; and in my next breath I suggested that development administration, following economics, should concern itself somewhat less with its traditional routines as applied at the national level, and work rather with the range of activities at local levels and in the private and semiprivate sectors that can influence the pace and course of development. I have even suggested ways in which these social sciences can involve themselves in matters heretofore left in the hands of the politicians. Yet I have also acknowledged that social scientists are too ignorant to do these things very well. The reason for my ambivalence is a conviction that ignorance is no excuse for inaction; it should only make us careful about what we, in the last analysis, have to do.

To say that development administration should exploit the potentials of the private sector and various semipublic associations, and treat them as the bearers of economic policy in agriculture development, sounds almost reactionary. In a period of declining foreign aid and perhaps of increasing mercantilism as well, it is important to avoid any suggestion that seems like a concession to neoisolationism. But the proposed approach is not by any means a mere restatement of the traditional American preference for capitalistic enterprise or dollar diplomacy. It may not involve foreign investment at all, and it certainly calls for curious new mixtures of public funding and private

[18] John D. Montgomery, "Land Reform as a Means to Political Development in Vietnam," *Orbis*, Vol. 12 (Spring, 1968), pp. 19–38.

leadership. It may even open the way for experiments in controlled corruption—that is in the use of financial incentives to redirect the efforts of civil servants toward more productive activities in the agricultural supports services.

Even more controversial actions are implied in a second suggestion put forth here: that social scientists should find ways to assist political leaders in their efforts to stimulate the national will to develop. But their credentials in this field are not very good, either. They have seldom openly applied analytical techniques to assessing a nation's developmental efforts (as an operational definition of will) in terms of its needs and capacities, or computed these relationships over time in order to identify areas of progress; less still have they tried to compare the efforts of one country with those of another as a means of introducing competitive incentives. Such approaches are now quite possible (and therefore, in all probability, necessary). Once social science works its way into this area of activity there will be the question of how, with propriety, it can help the politicians reach the various groups most closely involved in agricultural development programs. But clearly these participants must at least have access to information on the basis of which to evaluate their own roles and efforts. The information base supplied to the three most immediate action groups would have to include the civil servants, the political leadership at various local levels, and the farmers themselves; and they each require different attitude and information bases in order to make decisions and carry them out. The tasks of designing a communications system and defining its content for these purposes is, of course, one of politics as much as technique, and in politics the social scientist is still an amateur. But it is becoming increasingly clear that the communications sciences have something to contribute to the mobilizing efforts of development-minded leaders.[19]

Finally there comes the task of designing change programs so that their impact will pose the least possible threat, and offer the maximum incentive, to these three action groups. Finding

[19] Ithiel D. Sola Pool presents the need for political organization to supplement communications in "The Mass Media and Politics in the Modernization Process," in Lucian W. Pye, ed., *Communications and Political Development* (Princeton, N.J.: Princeton University Press, 1963).

the optimal design for such purposes involves close collaboration with the political leadership. The calculus of administrative efficiency is only one of the factors to be considered, and experience suggests that it is far from the decisive one. It is in discovering the necessary and permissible areas of compromise along these lines that development administration reaches its climax as an art form.

There are various ways in which social scientists may collaborate to reduce the consequences of their collective ignorance. In the past few years it has become modish to recommend various structural arrangements in development planning and administration that will encourage interdisciplinary cooperation. Recent experiences with team efforts have been somewhat discouraging, but the widespread separation of economists from other social scientists in program planning is surely a disservice to both groups. In dealing with the rural sector, development administration depends upon the knowledge and skills of technical specialists, agricultural economists, and other social scientists. But a fundamental change in the professional conservatism of all these groups is now in order. It is time to restate the operational problems of development in such a way as to challenge the conventional wisdom of the experts.

Challenge can be overdone, too, of course. Social scientists serving in the government have often found themselves confronting problems restated too frequently, and situations calling for new solutions too rapidly. Glib challenge, like glib response, can become a professionally conditioned reflex action. What is needed, institutionally, seems to be something between conventionally structured, exclusively professional approaches to development problems, at one extreme, and, at the opposite pole, direct involvement in action programs, many of which are now so indeterminate that their basic decisions have to be made without much time for reflective thought.

Development administration and agricultural economics both are discovering that they need to be just as experimental and creative in adapting their own scientific roles as they expect central and local governments, the private sector, and the farmers to be in confronting the demands of modernization.

PART IV

SOCIAL SCIENCE
AND DEVELOPMENT

EDITORS' INTRODUCTION

The two principle presentations in Part IV, those of Irwin Sanders and Harry Triandis, are very different in nature, form, and coverage. Sanders makes a valiant effort in support of parsimony of concepts. Triandis uses many concepts ranging across most of social science. Nevertheless, both chapters and especially that of Sanders can easily be related to the change agent–change target system model used in the introductions to the previous parts. Sanders is specific in his use of the conceptualization: "The change agents which seek to carry out the details of the plan are themselves in relationship with persons in a variety of positions and must react accordingly. Mere emphasis upon technical information is not enough, since the new knowledge must be translated into values, roles, and norms." Sanders' disclaiming of the concept, "social system," in favor of the concept, "social relationship," in no way makes for any lack of fit with the change agent–change target system model here used. In several instances, he consciously or unconsciously uses the term "system" in his presentation. Thus, in reviewing Roland Warren's discussion of linkage between the national government and the local community in the person of the subject matter expert, the field consultant, or the inside "village" worker, Sanders states specifically that Warren is "treating the social relationships between the vertical systems." Charles Loomis in his synthesis of social sciences (Chapter 10) shows how Sanders' past work effectively treats social change in terms which we use in our analysis here. Even though Sanders makes an effort to be parsimonious in the use of concepts, mentioning only four (position, role, value, and norm), he does not, and cannot, hold to these. He notes that "fear or lack of fear of sanctions (enforcement of norm)" may have consequences. The content, parsimony, and simplicity of Sanders' chapter so perfectly fits our model that we believe it unnecessary to present more of his thinking here.

Robert Polson in his discussion supported our position that systems analysis has a place in efforts to direct and analyze change. "The general concepts of social relations and social systems lend themselves . . . to what we might call 'snapshots' of a social situation in a given time and place. We need better concepts to systematically analyze development phenomena over time and across national boundaries." Howard Beers commenting on the extent of agreement and disagreement among social scientists' use of concepts noted that, although the vocabularies might vary, there was enough agreement and consensus among the users that the important concepts might be used interchangeably.

The presentation by Harry Triandis mobilizes research on directed social change from pertinent social science fields in many parts of the world. The last part of his chapter specifically designates "the agent of the change" (Figure 1) and, in addition, what we would call the target of change, namely "the farmer, his subjective culture, his personality, and his social systems." The agent of change is also considered in the light of his subjective culture, his personality, and his social system. The manner in which these two are linked is discussed and analyzed in considerable detail by Triandis. Whereas the change agent–change target system orientation of Sanders as a sociologist focuses on social relationships and groups, that of Triandis as a social psychologist tends to give special priority to personality systems. His analysis in general is in terms of microsystems. As indicated by Loomis in Chapter 10, the field of psychology, stressing the personality system; that of sociology, stressing the social system; and that of cultural anthropology stressing cultural systems, all use different frames of reference and basic concepts, but meet on one common ground, namely, the status role. Here we have a special type of systemic linkage. Importantly, Sanders' parsimonious set of four concepts includes what he calls position role, while Triandis' discussion of personality relates especially to what he calls subjective culture or "the totalities of beliefs." Triandis presents an imposing list of components of the "subjective culture," namely, categories, links among categories, affects toward the categories, attitudes, values, aspirations, self-image, behavior to reach goals, norms, customs, and so forth. He states that "the agent of innovation must learn 'the categories of people' and the most important links between the category and a goal which the change agent has in mind." He notes that "the strategy of change in a particular agricultural practice" will vary with the "farmer's basic attitudes about the nature of the universe." Tying C. E. Osgood's consideration of the semantic differential (which focuses attention on such concerns as good or bad, strong or weak, active or passive) with cognitive dissonance developed by L. Festinger, Triandis carries forward his analysis of the strategy of change. "If a man does not experience dissonance, if he is entirely satisfied with himself, he will be most unlikely to change." The man who smokes may be satisfied until he learns that smoking can produce cancer. Although the reader can best see how this social psychology–oriented change strategy can be used through reading the presentation, it is worth noting here that Triandis pays special attention to the importance for strategy of the choice of the change agent as well as the change target in terms of personality. As he notes, more research is required before it will be known exactly what type of personality is best and most effective as a change gaent and likewise how and under what conditions individuals and groups become innovators.

In terms of our change agent–change target model the reader must be impressed with the difference of the microview of Triandis and those broad views presented in parts I, II, and III. Robert MacLeod in his discussion of Triandis' chapter does not disagree with particular items focusing on psychology; he joins the editors in bemoaning our ignorance of what actually happens psychologically when development takes place.

8. Sociology

IRWIN T. SANDERS

Rural sociology is a branch of general sociology and, as such, does not have a distinctive theoretical posture of its own. Its specialization on matters relating to rural life gives it a competence in analyzing such problems; it uses some sociological concepts more frequently than would another branch, such as criminology. But it is the frequency of use and not the idea behind the concept that makes the difference since all concepts used in rural sociology will on some occasions prove useful to other branches, and vice versa. Therefore, the concepts treated here will be drawn from general sociological theory, but their application will be made to topics in which rural sociologists have done special work and have produced a number of findings.

Societal Change as a Part of Social Change

Rural sociologists, like all social scientists, are interested in broad social changes, or those changes which affect man. They run the gamut from alterations in the physical environment, through social consequences of modern technology, demographic growth and decline, threat of war, or possibilities of peace, to complexities of the space age. These challenges need to be studied, understood, and planned for more intelligently. Their study, however, calls for the inputs of economists, geographers, biologists, psychologists, humanists, and the whole range of scholars studying the world in which we live. What influences man is by definition social.

But this is much too broad a context for any single discipline. Instead, we must decide what aspect of the social to treat. Sociologists can contribute best by describing what happens to particular societies, or societal change. This, of course, is influenced by and tends to influence all of the social phenomena listed above, but society rather than any of these other phenomena is the focus. Restricting the inquiry to society rather than to man himself begs the question, however, unless we make quite clear what we mean by society.

Two Approaches to Societal Analysis

Society consists of the arrangements people of any common territory inherit or devise to deal with their mutual problems. They cannot solve these as individuals, but must do so collectively. They develop institutions, some time-honored, as religion and the family, and others on the rise, such as the body of peace-keeping and peace-building international agencies. Every individual performs his daily round as a member of numerous groups; these in turn are reciprocally interrelated. Societies accumulate a history, consisting of a set of recognized values and goals; they have a varying stance toward other societies (in the form of nations) both near and far. They change their leadership from time to time in several divergent ways: national elections to *coups d'état*. They face internal strains as well as outside threats. They also differ in their conceptions of the place of an individual within the society or the way the basic property should be owned. Some societies are predominantly rural, centering around agriculture; others are highly industrialized and urbanized.

Various sociologists use different methods in describing the essential characters of society and place different emphases upon the factors to be analyzed. For our purposes, two approaches will be mentioned: the processual and the social systems types.

Processual Approach

Some sociologists stress the dynamic nature of society by calling attention to and trying to classify the many forms of interaction which they observe. It has been argued that all patterns of interaction can be sorted out into a relatively few types, such as cooperation, competition, conflict, accommodation, or assimilation. As they observe the flow of interaction among persons and groups through time within a society, some sociologists select out one type as being more important than the rest: it may be cooperation or mutual aid; it may be conflict; or it may be accommodation, or ecological competition. Society is therefore viewed in all its rich ramifications as the working out of one or more of these parts (subprocesses) of the total social process.

To others, process may have a different texture. Without stressing the type of interaction which occurs among people or groups, process may be a convenient way of designating certain broad-scale, visible changes which are occurring in the society. These could include the familiar processes of differentiation and stratification, industrialization, mechanization, commercialization, and urbanization. Through the study of these change processes one can, it is argued, get a picture of the nature of society since such a major process tends to involve the entire society before it is finished. One notes old structures that are changing and new ones that are coming into being. One has to look at conflict and tension as well as competition and methods of inducing cooperation. Several social science disciplines observe these processes (e.g., urbanization) but it is the duty of the sociologist to describe their societal effects, as shown in the modifications in social arrangements and intergroup behavior.

And we find another group of sociologists, many of them sociologically trained social psychologists, studying the processes of social control. These describe how an individual is "socialized" into a contributing and satisfied member of a society; why and how alienation occurs; and how society deals with deviance.

Social Systems Approach

For some sociologists, the concentration on processes and their concomitant structures is a bit too haphazard, a little out of context. They admit their importance but urge that they be placed within a society viewed as a social system, made up of component groups and subsystems, and functioning through a series of operations necessary for its survival (recruitment of new members, boundary maintenance, communication, allocation of power, resources, and prestige, etc.). Society as a social system in this view would have certain prerequisites for its existence; it would have to maintain a running equilibrium, adjusting to internal and external change, if it is to keep its identity and its ability to deal with other social systems which might challenge it. Any part would be studied in terms of its relation to other parts, and therefore the system as a whole. Processes, such as conflict or urbanization or alienation, could be studied in terms of their origin within the system and their effects upon the system or as to how external changes introduced into the system become modified in behavior of persons and groups within the system.

In approaching, therefore, the analysis of a developing country, sociologists involved might reflect two different styles of inquiry. One would be that of looking at some major process, trying to relate it to its societal manifestation, and then moving the inquiry to ever-broadening circles. Others who used the social systems approach would do differently: their analysis would posit the fact that certain conditions must be met if a society is to exist (not denied by the processual exponents); that one had better view as much of the whole social terrain as is possible and certainly pertinent, and then concentrate on the particular process (urbanization) in systemic terms.

The layman is confused by the fact that the vocabulary of the two approaches is frequently different. He also learns when talking to the processual sociologist that he has a well-defined picture in his head of what society is (often as a system, but not explicitly so). He finds that the social systems person may talk a great deal about the structural aspects of society but may find his real fascination in analyzing processes. The layman may also come across sociologists who call down a plague on both of these approaches in order to highlight one more congenial to themselves. This is not to imply that there is chaos in the field, but rather that there is rich, fruitful diversity which keeps the field from settling down prematurely into a body of fixed doctrine which has not been fully formulated or sufficiently tested. Given such diversity, one might wonder whether there is any common unit which can be useful whatever the theoretical approach of the sociologist. The *social relationship* is one such analytical unit.

The Social Relationship as an Analytical Unit

Society is based on the fact that people as well as groups develop reciprocal bonds of interaction. They communicate with each other and develop patterns of association continuing through time. To understand these bonds or relationships requires a minimum of four concepts in addition to the concept of the social relationship itself. These are position, role, value, and norm. These are shown in Figure 1.

Position. As society becomes more complex the number of positions (statuses) increases; occupational specialization occurs; formal organizations grow in number. Every individual in his daily life moves in and out of many positions vis-à-vis

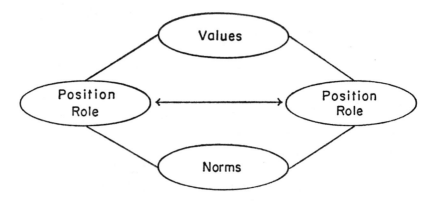

Figure 1. Social relationship concept

other people. He is successively father, motorist, employee, luncheon companion, P.T.A. member, buyer, and neighbor. The person with whom he is reacting at a given time is also occupying a position relevant to the one he is holding. The other person may be a daughter, policeman, employer, luncheon companion, P.T.A. officer, salesman, and neighbor. Groups, too, can be said to occupy positions since they interact with each other.

Role. For each position held, there are a number of behavior patterns (role repertoire) one is supposed to carry out. Fathers are supposed to behave in certain ways toward their daughters and daughters to act correctly toward their fathers; motorists are constantly being reminded of what their role should be.

Employees may have to be trained in order to perform their roles properly, but this goes beyond the mere performance of a technical skill to the way one behaves toward a fellow employee or a superior. Part of growing up consists of learning what the expected role is in a given situation. The deviant does not play the role that others anticipate, which means that they in turn must modify their behavior. Role perception is therefore important. If the partners in a social relationship perceive the roles of each other differently, then there may be role conflict or, at least, faulty communication.

Value. For every activity involved in a social relationship there are some social values attached. These may embody goals toward which the activity should be moving, or priorities as to what is most important and least important in life as viewed by the majority of the members of the society. In a social relationship, one partner is usually in a superordinate position to the other since he embodies in his person or in his possessions more of the dominant values. The father is traditionally superordinate, the daughter subordinate, although this situation may change if the daughter is caring for the father in his old age. The policeman is superordinate, the motorist usually subordinate. And so it goes through employer-employee, buyer-seller, P.T.A. officer–member relationships. The point to be made is the fact that the value system stipulates which partner is superordinate, which subordinate. This is a critical feature in cross-cultural technical assistance, for value systems in two societies may differ in significant details.

Norms. Just as values help determine the relative importance of the positions in a relationship, so the norms help determine the limits within which the roles may be carried out. A father may discipline his daughter (under certain circumstances he is expected to do so), but he cannot use means which violate the norms of the community. A policeman may arrest a motorist, but he must do so within carefully prescribed rules; a salesman may seek to persuade the buyer to purchase, but within well-understood limits. Thus, around all role-playing there are "rules of the game," or norms, which people have to learn as they are learning values, roles, and all the other intricacies of being an adult member of society.

This, then, is a social relationship in its simplest possible presentation. It could be made more complex through the introduction of several other concepts, but these suffice to demonstrate its connection with change and to show its utility in developmental programs.

Social Relationship as Indicator of Change

Societal change does not occur unless there is some change in social relationships. This is self-evident since one defines society as being made up of social relationships, viewed both in their structural and interactional aspects. Thus an increase in the number of positions in a society (increased specialization) is change, for it means that earlier positions have been circumscribed and new ones created to fill some of the activities of the former. Conceivably, a reverse trend might set in—with the density of positions declining—but this is not a very likely occurrence through time.

Also, values may be modified to the point that one position which at one time was superordinate vis-à-vis another position is now subordinate. This happened for a period of time after the communist take-over of Bulgaria where the student from a communist home had the upper hand in a classroom taught by a teacher thought to be unsympathetic to communism. The student embodied the values held by those in power.

Roles change as well. What in one generation was expected behavior for an incumbent in a particular position may no longer seem appropriate. The housewife role, for instance, calls for very different expertise than it did before the newer technology invaded the home and specialized services sprang up outside the home to take over the baking, dry cleaning, and the like. Whether the husband's expectations have shifted to correspond with the new housewife's role is sometimes a moot question, but change has taken place in roles.

Norms also become modified. The Supreme Court rulings about the rights of persons arrested have set up new norms for the police, who may be otherwise carrying out the traditional roles expected of them. Universities are experiencing drastic shifts in norms surrounding the student's role, and unionized public school teachers are questioning the customary norms which have set limits on their behavior in the past.

Utility of Social Relationship Concept

Societal change, a broad concept, can thus be made concrete in the analysis of a specific social relationship. When enough different kinds of these have been studied, and perhaps measured, one can develop and test hypotheses about societal change. To describe a social relationship, therefore, one does not have to delineate the value system for the whole society but rather to list those values which are relevant to that particular relationship. The same goes for norms. So the first evidence of utility is its specificity.

The social relationship concept is useful, too, in that it can be applied by sociologists from various theoretical positions. The processual sociologist who concentrates on urbanization and industrialization can look for impacts of these processes in social relationships. The social systems sociologist recognizes the social relationship as part of the social system. On the other hand, the facts learned from the study of social relationships can find their way back into the theoretical positions with which the sociologists are identified. Thus, one can make the kind of analysis suggested here without having to fight the battle of theoretical approaches all over again.

Further utility lies in the possibility that selected key social relationships may serve as a sample for society. The tendency is to sample through an individual as a general member of society; it would be much more revealing to study him as a partner in a social relationship and make the latter the sampling unit. Experience would have to show which relationships were bellwethers of the kinds of change in which the investigators were interested, and a sample drawn with this in mind.

For purposes of development programs, however, the chief utility is the relative simplicity of the social relationship in introducing the nonsociologist to the rudiments of societal change. It is a heuristic as well as an analytical device. It is complex enough to show the ramifications of one kind of change and the interconnectedness of the elements of a society; it is concrete enough so that a given relationship can be discussed by those from different societies in such a way that their implicit value assumptions can be made explicit, their expected roles can be shown to vary culture by culture in small but important ways, and their fear or lack of fear of sanctions (enforcement of norms) be made evident.

Further utility is found in the fact that the social relationship as outlined here applies to more than two persons in interaction; the scheme can describe interaction between groups, between segments of the society (government-economy), and even between societies where roles, values, and norms apply as much as between individuals. Also, social relationships can be combined in a single analysis of a situation where several connected positions are all in the same field of interaction (or same social system). In this case, the totality can be best approached through a full understanding of the component relationships themselves.

The utility described here is dependent, of course, upon treating the social relationship as *generic* and not that existing between a particular father and his daughter or a particular P.T.A. and a particular school administration. Rather, it is the generally accepted pattern to which individuals are *supposed* to subscribe.

In summary, the concept of social relationship (with its attendant concepts) is the most useful contribution which rural sociology, as a branch of sociology, can make to the understanding of the development process. This case is made on the grounds that it: (1) is sufficiently complex to make useful analysis possible; (2) can be adapted for use by those with different sociological theoretical styles; (3) serves as a heuristic scheme for nonsociologists; and (4) can be built into much more elaborate fields of interaction (or social systems) without losing its utility. It is further suggested that societal change can possibly be better understood if we take a regular sampling of changes occurring within social relationships selected because of their key place in the kinds of changes being studied. The relevance of the social relationship for development programs becomes more evident as we look at the nature of planned change itself.

The Nature of Planned Change

Planned change, no matter what its other trappings may be, always requires a program which must be carried out by people in various capacities. Its formulation is also done by people in social relationship to each other, whether these be a small group of planners at the top or a large number of people from several sectors or different horizontal levels. Even if viewed as a statement of goals and means, a program of planned change inevitably expects these to be made specific in terms of particular positions within the society. It also seeks to assign roles to incumbents of various positions.

Therefore, the concept of social relationship is part and parcel of any attempt to bring about the development of a specific society. It is relevant at the national level in terms of analyzing the part to be played by those in specified positions, but it is also useful as a method of looking at the reciprocal interaction between some of the larger sectors of society which figure in over-all country plans. In looking at the relationship between agriculture and industry, for instance, one immediately confronts the fact that values differ in each case as do the functions or roles each is supposed to contribute to the total effort. Norms which pertain in the case of one may not apply in the case of the other by the very fact that a few industrial firms can be regulated much more efficiently than hundreds of thousands of individual agricultural producers.

At the other extreme, the local level, the change agents who seek to carry out the details of the plan are themselves in relationship with persons in a variety of positions and must react accordingly. Mere emphasis upon technical information is not enough, since the new knowledge must be translated into values, roles, and norms.

It should be clear, then, that planned change involves much more than an increase in the gross national product or the construction of hydroelectric plants or a new highway system; it inevitably has its *societal* overtones. If social arrangements are not modified in some respects, the plan never becomes incorporated in the life of the people. This may occur so gradually that change is almost imperceptible at the time; but it is nevertheless real and can be measured eventually.

The emphasis on the social relationship as an analytical unit in development programs is designed to make the rural sociologist's contribution as meaningful as possible. Another approach we could have taken was that of tallying the concepts

most frequently used in the seven or eight widely used text-
books in rural sociology, sorting these into some kind of meaningful array, and then suggesting that these be used by anyone
wishing to incorporate the sociological approach. The net effect
of this would be to overwhelm rather than help, obfuscate
rather than enlighten, and to fail to differentiate the sociological approach from other approaches to social change.

Anyone is, of course, free to add to the sociological arsenal,
particularly if the problem of interest is not fully encompassed
in the concept of the social relationship. For example, some
might argue that the social system would prove a better single
concept to advocate. This is certainly true for the study of
small groups and even certain change programs, but it becomes
unwieldy for those not trained in its use when applied to a
total society. One then has to resort to partial concepts, of
which social relationship is a good example: it is partial in
that it does not embrace the total social universe surrounding it.

The best way to find out to what extent the social relationship as an analytical concept is useful is to look at actual studies
in the developing countries or the rural sectors of Western
societies.

Selected Studies

The first study deals with changes among French peasants
of the Sundgau in Alsace.[1] Henri Mendras traced many of the
technological changes and how they came about, concluding
that today the role of the social structure in effecting change
is very important. Over half of the farmers who adopted new
practices were influenced by neighbors and parents, and one-
fourth of them had seen the practice elsewhere. In suggesting
future research, Mendras asks for further study of the role
of farm women and how they relate to men in decision-making
for the farm. He also presses for a study of rural ideology, particularly with respect to the farmer's idea of progress. His study
in Alsace leads him to believe that the peasant is not against
progress but that he postpones changing because "he is entrenched in traditional structures which oppose any change."

[1] H. Mendras, *Les Paysans et la modernisation de l'agriculture* (Paris:
Centre National de la Recherche Scientifique, 1958).

Here the peasant is running up against social relationships within the village. But it goes beyond that. He considers his village an in-group in conflict with the out-group and it is within this context that modernization of agriculture must be seen.

Granted that this is only a partial summary of the interesting work by Mendras, it does follow that many of his conclusions and suggestions can be fitted easily into the social relationship paradigm suggested above, particularly through the use of the in-group–out-group relationship. Rural values and urban values differ; the agricultural technician is on a different wave length in his association with the ordinary peasant; and the norms governing work in the field have not been compared to those governing work in a factory, a matter which Mendras thinks needs further exploration if we are to gain deeper insight into modernization and social change.

Arthur R. Jones, M. Lee Taylor, and Alvin L. Bertrand studied human factors in woods-burning in a national forest in Louisiana.[2] Their central problem was to look at the social relationship between the forest service personnel and the local residents. How had contacts affected the residents' behavior? They observe that association with the forest ranger and other forest service personnel does remind forest residents that fires should be regulated. They studied the characteristics of those who occupy the position of "resident" in this relationship, with special attention to the beliefs that they hold about burning practices. The authors make use of a social action model, in which one group or the other must adapt itself to the program and goals of the second group. Within the "action situation" which they select there are three different types of objects: social objects, or the actors; physical objects, or the forest itself, the cattle of residents, etc.; the cultural objects, or the beliefs and ideas which the forest residents and the forest service representatives have about the use of the forests. The authors also assume a set of concepts such as "conservation," "forest," etc.

[2] *Some Human Factors in Woods Burning: A Study of Change in Beliefs in Louisiana,* Bulletin No. 601, August, 1965, Louisiana State University and Agricultural and Mechanical College Agricultural Experiment Station, in cooperation with Southern Forest Experiment Station, Forest Service, U.S. Department of Agriculture.

which makes a communication possible among the partners in the social situation.

This study provides a slightly different approach (social action model) to the social relationship approach. All but the "physical objects" can be fitted into the social relationship scheme, and these can be taken as environmental factors to the social interaction. "Social action" carries a more dynamic connotation than does "social relationship," but if one wishes to know what has changed then one would not say "social action has changed," but one could say that a relationship has changed. When one looks at the social action model, it is the elements in a social relationship as here defined that have changed.

A technical assistance endeavor in Pakistan has been reported on by James W. Green.[3] In an effort to learn more about the effectiveness of the institutes training village AID workers, Green decided to spend several months in villages to study the graduates of the training institutes. His method was that of role analysis, which involved the reconstruction by the worker of what he had done in past weeks. The worker also described his own motivation and that of the peasants with whom he had been working. With this information in mind, the worker was then asked to describe the adequacy of the training received in preparation for the actual roles performed. The reports based on these interviews finally influenced the chief administrator, though at first he rejected them, and led to a different relationship with Green, the foreign adviser.

Role analysis, which proved so productive here, is most useful when it is clearly specified (as it is in the social relationship) just who is on the receiving end of the role being performed. Green assumed most of the time that the worker was dealing with villagers, but there are different kinds of villagers. Did his behavior change as the partner to the relationship changed? Some of the behavior was directed toward supervisors and government officials. This introduces a different set of relationships. In Green's behalf it should be pointed out that his focus was almost solely on the village development worker: how well had he been prepared, what changes should be made in the

[3] "Success and Failure in Technical Assistance: A Case Study," *Human Organization*, 20 (Spring, 1961), 2–10.

training institute? He was interested in the worker's own perception of need as related to tasks which could be recounted. One may conclude that for some purposes it is sufficient to make only a partial analysis of the social relationship of which role analysis represents a case.

Roland Warren has dealt with a similar theme in highlighting the linkage between the national government and the local community in the person of the subject matter "expert," the field consultant, or the "village worker." [4] He is treating the social relationship between the vertical systems, often at the national level but outside the community, which reach down and affect life in the community, and the local or horizontal systems. How do the two establish a satisfactory *modus vivendi?* Although the social relationship paradigm as outlined here is not expressly used by Warren it would cover the chief concepts he presents. Should the external agent of change come in a superordinate position, telling the people what to do, or should he seek a coordinate relationship in which he tries to strengthen the educational process? Warren's article gives rich insight into what makes for community cohesion, both in formal and informal structures, and how this cohesion can keep developments in the vertically organized community units in line. This article would suggest that within the social relationship approach it is at times necessary to state the social characteristics of the incumbents of each position (in this case two social systems) in order to understand the ebb and flow of interaction as values, norms, or roles are modified.

Workers in community development are also the central theme in a paper prepared by Gelia Tagumpay-Castillo and her colleagues in the Philippines.[5] The study gives some details about the relationships between the rural workers and the barrio people, and the rural workers and the key influentials (school teachers, government officials, parish priest). It then describes how the worker gets established in the barrio, develops rapport with the barrio people, and the approaches used to

[4] "Group Autonomy and Community Development," *Autonomous Groups,* 15 (Autumn–Winter, 1959–60), 3–11.

[5] Gelia Tagumpay-Castillo, Conrado M. Dimaano, Jesus C. Calleja, and Shirley F. Parcon, "A Development Program in Action: A Progress Report on a Philippine Case," 1963, unpublished manuscript.

introduce change. What the worker does is part of his role performance and constitutes a full professional repertoire. It includes field trips or educational tours, farm and home management surveys, farmers' and homemakers' classes, answering service calls, use of visiting experts, and a lay leadership institute. This study brings out clearly the importance of the competence of the technical assistance worker, for the barrio people did not object to a young worker if he really knew enough to be of help to them. The implicit frame of reference for this study is the social relationship, and rich insights are provided concerning it.

Among the greatest contributions made by rural sociologists have been their studies of the diffusion of farm and home practices. To try to fit all of the work done in this field into a social relationship framework would do violence both to the intent and the findings. Yet, a great deal is germane. One study by Charles E. Ramsey, Robert A. Polson, and George B. Spencer seeks to understand the connection between values and adoption.[6] Put in terms of the social relationship paradigm, the questions posed dealt with the connection between values held and roles adopted. The values, however, were those held by an individual farmer. The hypotheses were borne out but at a low magnitude. Much more relevant it would seem would be the farmer's perception of values of those people with whom he had regular, important interaction—people who were frequently influencing his decisions. The social relationship approach, although it does not go all the way to a full social systems analysis, does steer one away from the individual-in-isolation syndrome, attractive though this is in neatness of data collection and statistical manipulation.

Morris Asimow, from the engineering school at the University of California at Los Angeles, has spent much time in efforts to start small industries in Latin America with the help of some of his students. He has reported on his experiences in northeast Brazil.[7] Due attention is of course given to the raising of the required capital, but implicit in this approach,

[6] "Values and the Adoption of Farm Practices," *Rural Sociology*, 29 (March, 1959), 35–47.

[7] "Project Brazil: A Case Study in Micro Planning," *International Development Review*, 6 (June, 1964), 26–29.

according to Asimow, is the need for training and education of entrepreneurial groups. Much, though not all, of this entrepreneurship must be devoted to strengthening new kinds of social relationships: with stockholders who own stock for the first time, with boards of directors who never have served on a board which has functions distinct from management, to say nothing of the other relationships involved in managing the internal affairs of the company.

The chances are that a sociologist, using the social relationship paradigm, could provide much-needed insights to those responsible for setting up the new company, although no claim is made that this sociological approach is any substitute for the economic or technological backstopping.

Implications for Work in Development

We have tried to demonstrate that a sociologist who is a member of a development team can, through the use of a relatively few concepts, inject an added dimension. He can deal with the concrete situation by drawing upon the social relationship approach. When he wishes, he can elaborate the model toward a social action or a social systems level, or can introduce more sophisticated treatment of various processes. With the social relationship, however, he does have a starting point that is productive, that is distinctive to his field, and that can be sufficiently grasped by the nonsociologist to become incorporated in team thinking.

For any projected program, the sociologist would list the positions to be involved at various stages and connect those that will be working together. He then, with the help of the paradigm, proceeds to an orderly consideration of each of the concepts as related to the two positions constituting the relationship. Goals and perceptions can be subsumed under values, both with respect to those held by each partner in the relationship as well as the correspondence of what they hold with others involved in the program. One partner may be more "typical" in his beliefs and values than the other. Central to this analysis is the relation of the change agent toward his target group.

Examination of the expected role repertoire would then be in order. What is each expected to do vis-à-vis the other, not only concerning social discourse but concerning demonstration of specialized skill as well? Where there are discrepancies or inadequacies, those in charge of the programs can take proper action. Varying interpretations of norms by the partners in a relationship are important too. How far can one go in pursuing idiosyncratic interests and where do social controls begin to operate?

The net effect of this analysis, which is elementary procedure for any well-trained sociologist, is to move the program planning into behavioral terms and away from sole preoccupation with finances, material results to be achieved, and overelaboration of goals devoid of considerations of those who are expected to carry them out.

After the program has been in operation for a sufficient period of time, efforts can be made to measure change. Patterns of superordination-subordination, and modifications in goals and values can be gauged in the various paired relationships; the increase and decrease in role repertoire can be studied, as can the changes in relevant norms.

But to do this simply on an interpersonal level is not sufficient. Changes which occur in the relationships among groups and among various subsystems of the society, based again on the social relationship paradigm, provide systematic indices of societal change.

Thus the rural sociologist in development is called upon to play a three-fold role: he seeks to educate those with whom he is in association as to the utility of sociological insight; second, he advises different program leaders as to ways in which the program can be planned to take advantage of the human resources by analyzing the social relationships which comprise the program; finally, he uses his skills to measure societal changes brought about by the program (or other concurrent influences). These, then, can be studied for their implications for future programs. In this way, development continues to be viewed as a process, of which societal change is an important ingredient.

Response

ROBERT A. POLSON

Irwin Sanders' chapter is a thoughtful presentation on the use of the social relationship concept as an analytical unit for developing an understanding of the societal setting in which behavioral change takes place. His presentation of societal analysis and change as the context within which sociologists contribute to development is well taken. Much of our sociological research has been concerned with microsocial units as separate entities without relating them to societal settings and trends. This larger dimension is needed to rapidly enhance our understanding of developmental processes.

Social science is entering an era of comparative research that should produce evidence on whether developmental strategies and techniques that are successful in one society are applicable in another or are unique. Until we have the evidence, we have to resort to short cuts and use whatever information we can obtain quickly. Sanders' proposal to use the social relationship concept permits focusing on sensitive areas in implementing developmental problems. It also has the likelihood of a quick pay-off in what can be characterized as snapshots of selected social situations.

A relevant contribution of sociology to behavioral change is knowledge of the social setting in which that change takes place, whether the setting be the rural household, the locality, the market system, or a governmental agency, The social relationship concept has some limitations as an analytical tool if it is the only unit of analysis for the arenas in which behavioral change takes place. Sanders recognizes this limitation when he refers to the social system concept.

I find the social system cluster of concepts particularly help-

ful for training change agents in analyzing the setting of behavioral change in such program units as the household, the
locality, and governmental agencies. I agree with Sanders that
it is difficult to use these concepts in their entirety. However,
the analysis of social relationships in the context of social system analysis seems to be advantageous for at least the following
reasons: it places the relationships being examined in their
structural setting; it permits inventorying related social relationships in a systematic frame of reference that helps avoid
overlooking significant phenomena; and it aids in making judgments about the relative importance of the various relationships involved in making specific behavioral changes.

Whatever well-documented concepts for analysis are used,
the systematic examination of social relationships affecting agricultural development has the potential of contributing useful
information for the formulation of appropriate strategies to
obtain greater food production. It is appropriate in this context to discuss disciplinal contributions to problem-solving.
The evaluation of discipline-oriented concepts in terms of their
value to an applied area points up the dilemma of the acade-
mician who becomes a developmental program trainer, adviser, or evaluator. The objective of his activity turns from producing new knowledge to solving problems. In this latter role
he not only uses the most relevant concepts from his own discipline but also those from other disciplines that may help deal
with the problem at hand. When one is involved in problem
solving, it is doubtful that any single discipline contributes an
adequate number of concepts and insightful information for
a satisfactory solution. In examining a developmental problem
in a specific situation, use is made of concepts from many disciplines on the basis of their perceived helpfulness.

Developmental strategies require a vast amount of information for the planning and implementation of the decisions that
must be made. The demand for helpful information is exceedingly large compared to the amount of it available—especially
the amount available at the point of decision-making. Recent
overseas experience indicates a growing demand for information by decision makers in certain areas of concern where sociological research could contribute materially.

Developmental projects often encounter difficulties because

there are missing inputs or an inappropriate combination of inputs to obtain the desired behavioral response. Research at the applicational level (farm, village, agency) during the early years of a project could help identify the trouble spots and indicate possible needed adjustments in inputs. This is an area of research where the rural sociologist and agricultural economist might well combine talents.

Practice-adoption research has produced much useful information about the diffusion of innovations and is potentially useful to many food programs around the world. Coupled with program evaluation and the input studies suggested above, it has the potential of expanded contributions. To illusrate: The rate of practice adoption is hard data in measuring the behavioral changes resulting from agricultural programs, thus making a contribution to program evaluation. Also, data on the reasons for acceptance or nonacceptance of practices can aid in identifying the appropriate inputs or combinations of inputs to facilitate adoption, whether these be services, physical inputs, knowledge, or attitudes.

Research on developmental agencies and services in terms of their appropriate organization and relationships to effectively promote desired behavioral changes is also needed. It is an area in which sociological research has the potential of large contributions in improving organizational efficiency when measured in terms of the results obtained.

We as Americans have committed numerous errors abroad in the strategies we have recommended. In our society many of the required supporting facilities preceded or developed concurrently with extension programs. They were taken for granted and therefore we took them for granted abroad where they often were missing ingredients. Strategy formation needs improved societal analysis and social accounting to supply a factual basis for decision-making. International and bilateral aid programs should encourage such research by investing in more comprehensive feasibility studies prior to major financial commitments.

We must recognize the continuing efforts of sociologists toward the refinement of old concepts and the testing of new ones that may be more helpful in understanding the phenomena of development. The concepts of social relationships and social systems contribute to understanding a specific social situation in a given time and place. We need better concepts to systematically analyze developmental phenomena over time and across national boundaries. There are promising lines of research underway that may yield more useful concepts and economical styles of research. In the meantime, there are many useful contributions that can be made with the tools at hand. The social relationship concept is one such tool.

9. Social Psychology

HARRY C. TRIANDIS

The production records of farms in the United States and certain other parts of the world reveal disparities: American farms are more productive, extracting more grain per acre, more milk per cow, more meat per head of cattle. These disparities can be traced to certain technological innovations that can be communicated. It is obvious that if these technological changes could be communicated they would be readily introduced in other countries. However, this is not the case. Innovative behavior cannot occur in a social vacuum; it has to be considered within the total context of a particular society. When we examine such social contexts we discover elements that inhibit or impede innovation. Some of these elements are traceable to the kinds of beliefs, basic attitudes, and values held by those engaged in agriculture in developing countries. Our present concern is to examine some of the concepts that are relevant in understanding how human and social factors may impede agricultural innovation and to indicate the implications of this analysis for strategy in introducing innovations in developing countries.

Every human being has a system of beliefs about how the world is structured, the goals or outcomes that are highly desirable or less desirable, and the actions he should undertake in order to reach his more desirable goals. The totality of these beliefs we may call a person's subjective culture. For example, a person may think that by doing a particular dance he will produce conditions conducive to rain; another person associates this dance with the loss of certain "calories" which have to be replaced through increased food intake, but sees no connection with the occurence of rain. It is safe to assume that the former person would have no concept corresponding to that of "calories" and hence could not have the particular connection which occurs in the subjective culture of the latter. If these two individuals were to discuss what to do in order to irrigate a particular field, it is safe to assume that they would disagree.

This example suggests that in creating innovation the change agent has to introduce new concepts, introduce new connections among concepts, and weaken the connections of certain concepts to each other. Not only must the farmer in the developing countries learn new concepts and their relationships to old concepts but he must also *unlearn* the connections among certain concepts. However, as these connections are unlearned they may modify his subjective culture in radical ways. If he is to forget about the existence of good and evil "spirits," he will also change the way he perceives his ancestors, his family, and himself. Thus, the changes may produce an "unhinging" that will result in great anxiety and disorientation. In other words, the successful introduction of a new way of thinking may have unfortunate as well as happy consequences. To the extent that the farmer in the developing countries sees the connection with the unfortunate consequences, he is justified in refusing to be influenced by the agent of change. Many programs of change fail because they are not designed to accommodate the majority of the important consequences of change, in particular, the social and human consequences.

Our first task is to examine some of the major psychological and social concepts that are relevant for the analysis of technological innovation in developing countries. If we understand the network of relationships among the various human and social factors, we will be in a better position to plan the strategies of creating change.

Focus on the Individual

People do not respond to every stimulus in their environment in different ways; they respond to *groups* of similar stimuli in similar ways. This phenomenon is called categorization. In the area of color discrimination, for instance, there are 7,500,000 discriminable colors, but most people utilize about a dozen color categories. Women use more than men, and artists use more color categories than people who have no interest in art. But even women and artists use a very small number of color names and no one uses several million names, though most people are capable of distinguishing that many colors. The language that we use influences very considerably the way we categorize experience. The Arabs have about 6,000 words for camel, of which about 50 describe various stages of camel pregnancy. We have several words we can use to refer to automobiles (Fords, Chevies, etc.) while most people categorize all cars in one large category. Clearly, the frequency of use of a particular object in our environment is related to the number of distinctions we make. Thus, categories can be very refined or very coarse, very abstract (e.g., animal) or rather concrete (e.g., poodle). The content of categories is greatly influenced by culture.[1]

The agent of innovation must begin by learning the major categories of the people he wants to influence. He must learn what events are grouped together, how much differentiation is made among events, how salient are some events as opposed to other events, what is the temporal frame of reference in which the categories are placed, and how much information supports a particular category.

He might have to find out, for example, what particular agricultural practices are seen by his audience as related to each other, what distinctions are made among agricultural practices, which of the practices are considered more effective, which of the practices are considered harmful, and what kinds of "evidence" are employed.

In making such analyses it is important to remember that even very underdeveloped people have a coherent view of the world and have "good reasons" for the way they think about their environment. For example, a Polynesian native who thinks that the earth is still and the sun goes around it gave two bits of "evidence": (1) the sun is cooler in the morning and the evening than during the day, showing that it is cooled by

---

[1] R. W. Brown and E. H. Lenneberg, "A Study of Language and Cognition," *Journal of Abnormal and Social Psychology,* 49 (1954), 454, 462; O. Klineberg, *Social Psychology* (New York: Holt, 1954); H. C. Triandis, "Cultural Influences upon Cognitive Processes," in L. Berkowitz, ed., *Advances in Experimental Social Psychology* (New York: Academic Press, 1964), vol. I, pp. 1–48.

the water as it approaches the sea, and (2) the position of the sun changes in relation to the fixed stars. Since without fixed stars this man would be unable to perform his remarkable navigational exploits, it is not surprising that he relies most heavily on the latter piece of evidence.[2]

When a category is frequently associated with rewards, or pleasant experiences, it acquires the property of eliciting positive affect or pleasurable emotions from the people who have made this association. The more frequently the association has occurred the more reliably does the category elicit positive affect. Conversely, when a category is frequently associated with punishments or unpleasant experiences it elicits negative affect (unpleasant emotions), or anxiety.

Many psychologists define attitudes as the degrees of positive or negative affect associated with a particular psychological object. Others prefer to think of attitudes as involving three components: cognition, affect, and behavioral intention.[3] No matter how this concept is defined, it is clear that it is important to study the categories and their links (cognition), the affect towards the concepts, and the behavioral intentions toward them. Thus, the agent of change might inquire about the connections among a particular agricultural practice and other events or outcomes (cognition), the way a person feels about the practice (does he like or dislike it), and whether he intends to adopt and use it (behavioral intention).

In general the three components of attitude are closely interrelated. However, there are circumstances when they are not. For example, a person may have a strong link between the category "smoking" and the category "cancer", yet may "like to smoke." When this happens there is "cognitive inconsistency," or what can be called "cognitive dissonance." [4] The existence of dissonance gives rise to pressures to reduce it and to avoid

[2] W. H. Goodenough, *Cooperation in Change* (New York: Russell Sage Foundation, 1963).

[3] L. L. Thurstone, "The Measurement of Social Attitudes," *Journal of Abnormal and Social Psychology*, 26 (1931), 249–269; H. C. Triandis, "Exploratory Factor Analyses of the Behavioral Component of Social Attitudes," *Journal of Abnormal and Social Psychology*, 68 (1964), 420–430.

[4] L. Festinger, *A Theory of Cognitive Dissonance* (Stanford: Stanford University Press, 1957).

increases in the dissonance. The manifestations of the operations of such pressures include behavior changes, changes in cognition (ways of thinking and feeling), and circumspect exposure to new information. The magnitude of the dissonance between any two elements depends on the importance of the elements. Furthermore, if the person is "committed" to his cognitions and his likes and dislikes and these are in a dissonant relationship, he will be particularly prone to experience the discomforts of dissonance.

The implications of these concepts for the innovator are widespread. If the innovation that he is trying to introduce involves elements that are dissonant with well-established cognitive elements to which the farmer is firmly committed, the introduction of such elements makes the farmer more and more uncomfortable. He will then avoid these dissonance-producing elements with every strategy that he can adopt. For example, he might avoid being exposed to the agent of change, or he may convince himself that the agent of change is "evil," "unreliable," or "a trouble maker."

Agreement with other people reduces dissonance, and disagreement increases it. The magnitude of dissonance resulting from disagreement is a function of a number of variables: the testability of the point of disagreement through empirical observation, the number of agreeing or disagreeing people, the importance of the issue in dispute, the attractiveness of the disagreeing person, the credibility of the disagreeing person, and the amount of disagreement. Thus, if a proposal by an agent of change leads to testable results, it will produce less dissonance then if it has only indirect implications. If the majority of the farmers in an area have adopted a new method, the fact that one farmer has not adopted it makes little difference to those who have. On the other hand, if the adopters are in a minority, the nonadoption behavior of this very same farmer produces more dissonance. When the agent is attractive and credible he produces more dissonance than if he is unattractive or easily perceived as unreliable.

In thinking about these relationships it should be kept in mind that though dissonance is an unpleasant state of affairs, it is necessary to impose such a state on the farmer in order to change him. If a man does not experience dissonance, if he is entirely satisfied with himself, he will be most unlikely to change.

It is desirable to consider why people have attitudes. It is because attitudes (a) help them understand the world around them, by organizing and simplifying a very complex input from their environment; (b) protect their self-esteem, by making it possible for them to avoid unpleasant truths about themselves; (c) help them adjust in a complex world, by making it more likely that they will react so as to maximize their rewards and minimize the punishments received in the environment; and (d) allow them to express their fundamental values.[5] Individuals have a need to give structure to their universe, to understand it, and to predict events. Furthermore, they tend to maximize rewards and minimize penalties, so they need a "cognitive map" which tells them what kinds of behaviors are likely to lead to what kinds of rewards or punishments. This helps their adjustment. Attitudes also help adjustment by making it easier to get along with people who have similar attitudes. The people who really count in our environment tend to have attitudes similar to ours and often we bring our attitudes "in line" with those held by "important" people.

One of the main points made by those who have presented a "functional analysis of attitudes" [6] is the importance of understanding the functional bases of attitudes in order to change them. Thus, if you know why a person holds a particular attitude you are in a much better position to change it than if you do not know. For example, the strategy of change of a particular agricultural practice may be different depending on the basis of its adoption. If the practice is believed to be the best because it leads to good crops, one might show how another practice leads to even better crops. But, if a practice is derived from the farmer's basic ideas about the nature of the universe,

[5] D. Katz, "The Functional Approach to the Study of Attitudes," *Public Opinion Quarterly*, 24 (1960), 163–204.

[6] *Ibid.*; M. B. Smith, "The Personal Setting of Public Opinions: A Study of Attitudes towards Russia," *Public Opinion Quarterly*, 11 (1947), 507–523; M. B. Smith, J. S. Bruner, and R. W. White, *Opinions and Personality* (New York: Wiley, 1956); and D. Katz and E. Stotland, "A Preliminary Statement to Theory of Attitude Structure and Change," in S. Koch, *Psychology: A Study of a Science* (New York: McGraw-Hill, 1959).

the demonstration that another practice is better may not be as effective. It may be necessary to change many more elements in the farmer's cognitive system before the new practice becomes acceptable.

If the practice is "ego-defensive" it may be even more difficult to change. For example, a farmer may have a view of himself as being exceptionally hard-working, and by using his hands in his farming he validates this view of himself. If he were to use agricultural equipment which requires him to sit comfortably on top of a machine, this may appear dissonant with his concept of being a hard-working farmer. He may thus prefer the hand tools to the machine because the former support his self-image better than the latter. Finally, if the attitude is "value-expressive," it may be extremely hard to change it. For example, one of the fundamental human values is concerned with whether man should change nature or simply adapt to nature.[7] Americans have a strong value that man should change nature and have carried this value to considerable extremes. People in other cultures sometimes have equally strong values that man should adapt to nature. Thus, a particular agricultural practice may be seen by the farmer as adaptive to nature, therefore good, while the practice proposed by the agent might be seen as changing nature, therefore bad. It is clear that if the attitude towards various practices expresses the farmer's values the demonstration by the agent that his method works better is totally irrelevant. The important consideration is that this method changes nature, hence is evil, and the fact that it yields more wheat merely demonstrates that "the evil spirits are helping him." After all, the Dr. Faustus fantasy is one of the most common throughout the world.

Attitudes are organized in hierarchical systems. It is convenient to conceptualize concrete specific attitudes as the leaves of a tree, attitudes towards abstract concepts as branches, and abstract values as the trunk of the tree.

All humans look at the same limited number of problems and propose solutions that are neither limitless nor random. All alternatives to all solutions are present in all societies at all times, but are differently preferred. One can assume the

[7] Florence R. Kluckhohn and F. R. Strodtbeck, *Variations in Value Orientations* (New York: Harper and Row, 1961).

existence of five basic value orientations that underlie all values, at the highest level of abstraction:

1. *Man's nature.* It can be evil, good, or neither. It can be mutable or immutable. It is also possible for man's nature to be conceived as a mixture of good and evil and immutable.

2. *Man versus nature.* Man may be a changer or an adapter to nature. This can be done in relationships in which man is subjugated to nature, in harmony with nature, or master over nature.

3. *Time.* Man may be oriented toward and value mostly the past, the present, or the future.

4. *Activity.* Man might value the intensive experience of the present in which the only consideration is his *being* in a particular state. Or, man might value most his self-actualization, his own development, which is the *being-in-becoming* orientation. Finally, man might adopt the *doing* orientation, so common in America, which values activity for its own sake.

5. *Relations with others.* Man may emphasize the value of the relationship with others which involves continuity of the group. This is the *lineal* orientation which emphasizes the importance of the ancestors, or of aristocratic descent. Another orientation emphasizes the relationship with one's contemporaries, or peers. This is the *collateral* orientation. Finally, a third orientation permits the dominance of individual rather than lineal or collateral goals and may be called the *individualist* orientation.

This system emphasizes seven views about the nature of man, three views about the relationship between man and nature, three views of time, three views of appropriate activity, and three views on appropriate relationships with others. This allows for 2688 different configurations of values. Kluckhohn and Strodtbeck claim that these configurations are sufficient to describe the value patterns of all humans.

People have ideals concerning the states of affairs which are highly desirable; such ideals are aspirations. People differ in their aspirations. The greater the success that they have previously had the higher their aspirations. Conversely, if they experience a series of failures they are likely to reduce their aspirations.

Aspirations also depend on the awareness of what other people have. Thus, when a person is not aware that others have a particular commodity or machine he is not likely to aspire to own it; but once he knows that others have it, he may want to acquire one also. Thus, a farmer's aspirations are dependent on the kinds of people that he aspires to be like.

Related to a person's aspirations are his needs. Needs are dependent on the difference between aspiration and realization. Thus, a farmer who has high aspirations and low realizations will have strong needs to change the situation, while one whose aspirations are quite similar to his realizations will be satisfied with things as they are.

A person's aspirations define a variety of goals, each of which may be very valuable or not. Goals that are consistent with general values, or associated with very positive attitudes, are exceptionally valuable. Behavior directed towards reaching a particular goal depends upon the value of the goal as well as the subjective probability that the goal will be attained if certain behavior is followed. Thus, if adoption of a particular method of farming is seen as very vaguely and unreliably related to the goal of a bumper crop, it is unlikely that the method will be adopted. If having a good crop is not particularly valuable, perhaps because a good life can be had without a good crop, then again adoption of this method is unlikely.

Even more interesting is the fact that every bit of behavior is likely to be seen as having a variety of consequences. For example, the adoption of a new method of farming may be seen disrupting one's relationships with family and friends as well as decreasing the rate of erosion. It may also appear pleasing to the government and to the head of the tribe. Each of these results has a certain subjective probability of occurrence and a certain value. One theoretical model currently popular in social psychology states that the probability of a behavior is proportional to the sum of the products of the above mentioned probabilities and values.[8]

An important characteristic of the individual related to innovation is self-image. Does he see himself as a starter, as a leader, as a person who tries things out and sometimes fails,

[8] M. J. Rosenberg, "Cognitive Structure and Attitudinal Affect," *Journal of Abnormal and Social Psychology*, 53 (1956), 367–372; and V. Vroom, *Work and Motivation* (New York: John Wiley, 1964).

but often succeeds, as a person who teaches others what to do (an opinion leader)? Such considerations are critical.

Most social groups have ideas about what is appropriate behavior, or norms.[9] For example, in America it is appropriate for a man to let a woman go first through a door; in Japan the opposite is true. Such norms of behavior may be very relevant when it comes to adopting innovation. The proposed innovations may be contrary to important norms; they may require people to behave in ways which they consider completely inappropriate.

Customs or habits get established when they gratify needs. This elementary fact is often forgotten by persons visiting a foreign culture. They tend to see customs as an exotic collection of practices rather than as expressions of important values or clues about the existence of certain needs. Admittedly, it is difficult to determine what particular needs are served by each custom. But a careful analysis is often most revealing.

Customs, taboos, moral prescriptions, and legal institutions provide privileges, define rights and duties, and satisfy the needs of at least some people in each culture. An analysis of who is satisfied and in what way can be most helpful in understanding the culture.

Visitors in foreign cultures are often quite ethnocentric; they tend to think of their own culture as superior to the culture of their hosts. Such judgments of superiority are possible only if they forget the undesirable features of their own culture. For example, Americans tend to forget about their high divorce and delinquency rates, their riots, the "anomie" (normlessness) of the large cities and concentrate on their superior standard of living, the number of bathrooms per capita, and similar statistics. Thus, they view the culture of their hosts in accordance with their *own* criteria and naturally conclude with extremely uncomplimentary pictures of their host culture.

An example may be helpful. In most cultures in which there

[9] H. C. Triandis, "Towards an Analysis of the Components of Interpersonal Attitudes," in Carolyn W. Sherif and M. Sherif, eds., *Attitudes, Ego-Involvement, and Change* (New York: Wiley, 1967), pp. 227–270; and H. C. Triandis, Vasso Vassiliou, and Maria Nassiakou, "Three Studies of Subjective Culture," *Journal of Personality and Social Psychology*, Monograph Suppl., 8 (1968), 1–42.

are strong taboos prohibiting brothers and sisters to find themselves together unchaperoned, there is less evidence of sexual inhibition than in cultures where this custom is not present. Of course, it is a lot of trouble to have to provide a chaperon for one's children, so many Western cultures have introduced internal controls (guilt). The Western customs serve the needs of the parents, but not necessarily the long-term adjustment and happiness of their children. The custom of chaperoning seems to an American silly, wasteful, time-consuming, old-fashioned, etc. But he does not realize that he may be paying a price in excessive sexual maladjustment for not having this custom.

Ethnocentrism in judgments of our culture's customs is parallel to high self-esteem in judgments of our own personal characteristics. Most people in the world are unusually well satisfied with themselves, particularly with their own characteristics. This is surprising when we think that most people are quite mediocre, live hungry, miserable, unhealthy lives that most middle class Americans would find quite impossible. Yet not only do most people not commit suicide to deliver themselves from these unpleasant conditions, but they are actually quite content. How is this possible? M. Rosenberg analyzed the self-concepts of thousands of American high school students and found them exceptionally positive.[10] He discovered that this is done by means of certain mechanisms, which involve various forms of selectivity and distortion of perception.

It is important for the agent of change to ask himself: "Is the way I look at this group of people due to my own efforts to maximize my self-esteem, or are they *really* the way I perceive them?" In all probability, if he is honest, he will discover that his own perceptions are distorted by his need to give value to himself. If he cannot work out this problem, which *is* his own problem, he will be handicapped in trying to help his clients.

He must also decide whether the customs of his clients are really incompatible with his innovations, or the innovations can be adopted to fit the customs. Quite often the innovations can be adapted without losing any of their essential efficacy.

[10] M. Rosenberg, "Psychological Selectivity in Self-Esteem Formation," in Sherif and Sherif, eds.

D. C. McClelland presented the argument that the large differences in per capita income that characterize various regions of the world are primarily due to differences in the need for achievement (n-Ach) that characterize those who inhabit these regions.[11] The argument is rather complex and in the present summary it will be over-simplified. Basically, high self-reliance training of the child and high achievement standards used by the mother lead to a personality type characterized by high n-Ach. Marian Winterbottom showed that mothers of high n-Ach boys make more early demands on them (e.g., expect them to learn to put their clothes on earlier), expect greater accomplishment and reward it more frequently than mothers of low n-Ach boys.[12] Those high in n-Ach, according to McClelland, work harder, choose experts over friends as working partners, are more resistant to social pressures, and are more apt to compete with a standard of excellence than those low in n-Ach. His measure of n-Ach utilizes thematic analyses of ambiguous pictures, such as those used in the Thematic Apperception Test (TAT). However, he has also used a variety of content analyses of other materials, such as the literatures of ancient Greece, sixteenth- to nineteenth-century England, and thirteenth- to eighteenth-century Spain. In the latter analyses he showed that the climax of these three civilizations was preceded by high n-Ach themes in their literature. Even if one controls for the availability of natural resources, McClelland reports that countries high in n-Ach have higher standards of living than those whose inhabitants have low n-Ach.

Among the intriguing findings of this book are the following: There is a tendency for countries with moderate mean annual temperature (around 50°F), with large seasonal temperature variations, and with a poor quality of soil to have people with high n-Ach. High n-Ach is more common in those countries where the culture is less tradition-directed, where the authority of the father has been challenged, and where the child-training practices are warm, but firm and demanding of

[11] D. C. McClelland, *The Achieving Society* (Princeton, N.J.: Van Nostrand, 1961).

[12] "The relation of Need for Achievement to Learning Experience in Independence and Mastery," in J. W. Atkinson, ed., *Motives in Fantasy, Action, and Society* (Princeton, N.J.: Van Nostrand, 1958).

excellence. High n-Ach results in moderate and reasonable risk-taking, individual responsibility, and willingness to delay immediate gratifications in order to obtain more rewards in the future. These characteristics, according to McClelland, are associated with entrepreneurial success, upward social mobility, and hence high economic development.

Within American culture some of these statements appear supported by a variety of studies. For example, one study found that fathers of high n-Ach boys are on the average less rejecting, less pushing, and less dominant, while mothers of these boys are more dominant and stress achievement training. They reward success with warmth and punish failure with hostility; they are very involved with their child's achievement. Another showed that high n-Ach is related to upward occupational mobility and low n-Ach to downward occupational mobility.[13]

A number of cross-cultural studies suggest that some of these findings have considerable generality. For example, there is more emphasis on independence training in Indonesian professional families than in working class families. Furthermore, the professional families imposed eating and sleeping schedules at an earlier age than did the working class families.[14]

Just as those high in n-Ach are extremely concerned with achievement, so those high in the need for affiliation (n-Aff) over-emphasize getting along with others and being successful in social relations. However, according to McClelland and others, the n-Aff of an individual impedes rather than helps his entrepreneurial activities, so that n-Aff is negatively related to economic development. We can extrapolate from these statements that those who are over-concerned with getting along with others do not have enough time to engage in experiments, take risks, or work very hard in the accomplishment of a task, so that they are less likely to engage in innovations.

The need for extension (n-Ext) is reflected in "concern for

---

[13] B. C. Rosen and R. D'Andrade, "The Psychological Origins of Achievement Motivation," *Sociometry*, 22 (1959), 185–218; and L. W. Littig and C. A. Yeracaris, "Achievement Motivation and Intergenerational Occupational Mobility," *Journal of Personality and Social Psychology*, 1 (1965), 386–389.

[14] K. Danzinger, "Parental Demands and Social Class in Java, Indonesia," *Journal of Social Psychology*, 51 (1960), 75–86.

the common good." McClelland argues that this is also related to economic development; and U. Pareek proposes that economic development is a positive function of n-Ach and n-Ext and a negative function of the need for dependence.[15] People high in the need for dependence (n-Dep) avoid taking initiative, finding arguing with others most unpleasant, and generally depend on others for guidance and leadership.

In an influential study on the personalities of extreme antisemites, Adorno *et al.* presented evidence for the existence of what they called the "Authoritarian Personality." [16] The authoritarian tends to repress unacceptable tendencies in himself; to idealize his parents (they are wonderful and faultless); to look at the world in terms of black and white rather than shades of grey; to avoid introspection; to refuse sensual enjoyment; to have little liking for art, music, and aesthetics; to be status conscious and mystical; to use sex to improve his social status; to want to have power rather than the love of other people; to accept the values of his family and friends uncritically; to have rigid opinions; and to be intolerant of ambiguity. Literally hundreds of studies have been undertaken to check the hypotheses advanced in that book. Many have attacked the specific findings or the methodology, but on the whole this personality type appears to be real and to have many of the above mentioned characteristics.

One of the critics of the authoritarian personality, M. Rokeach, argued that this type of person is typical of fascist or right-wing dogmatism, but dogmatism is a more general characteristic that can be found in both members of the extreme right and the extreme left.[17] He proposed another way of assessing the "Dogmatic Personality" (the D-Scale) which he also described as "the closed mind." Thus, he argued that the dogmatic is a more general type, of which the authoritarian is a subtype.

Highly dogmatic persons, or highly authoritarian individ-

[15] D. C. McClelland and D. G. Winter, *Motivating Economic Achievement* (New York: The Free Press, 1969); and U. Pareek, "Motivation for Accelerated Development," *Journal of Social Issues,* 24 (1968), 115–123.

[16] T. W. Adorno, Else Frenkel-Brunswik, D. J. Levinson, and R. N. Sanford, *The Authoritarian Personality* (New York: Harper, 1950).

[17] *The Open and Closed Mind* (New York: Basic Books, 1960).

uals, as described above, would not be suitable targets for social change. The agent of change should try to identify them,
and once he identifies them he may do well to leave them
alone. They are least likely to be innovators. He will be wast-
ing his time if he directs his energies at making them adopt
his innovations.

In most traditional societies people believe that the world
is the way it is because some supernatural power has "wanted
it this way." There is no sense in trying to alter the world. In
fact, the supernatural power may get angry at those who try to
change things. This view accepts as natural the low productivity, high rates of accident and disease, and the lack of progress that characterize such societies. It may be described as
fatalism. Those who are fatalists are unlikely to be good targets
for the change agent.

The Mexican psychiatrist R. Diaz-Guerrero has described
two personality orientations that are characteristic of developed
and underdeveloped countries.[18] In developed and highly industrialized countries, such as the United States, the predominant personality type is "active." In many underdeveloped
countries, and he uses Mexico as an example, people are predominantly "passive." By these two terms Diaz-Guerrero means
to describe two approaches to coping with stress. The active
coper who does not like something about his society reacts to
it by doing something to change it; the passive coper who does
not like something about his society adjusts to it by changing
himself. The typical passive coper changes his needs so they
conform to his environment.

This distinction is in many ways similar to the fatalism
dimension, but it is also more specific. Furthermore, Diaz-Guerrero has prepared a questionnaire which asks a variety of
opinion questions. People can be classified on the basis of the
way they answer these questions into active or passive copers.

It is again possible to extrapolate that when the agent of

[18] R. Diaz-Guerrero, "Socio-Cultural Premises, Attitudes, and Cross-
Cultural Research," paper presented at the 17th International Congress
of Psychology, Washington, D.C., 1963; "The Active and the Passive
Syndromes," *Journal of the Interamerican Society of Psychology*, 1 (1967),
263–272; and R. Diaz-Guerrero and R. F. Peck, "Estilo de confrontacion
y aprovechamiento: un program de investigacion," pp. 127–136.

change sees a range of different types of copers among the people who might adopt his innovations, he should concentrate his efforts on the active rather than the passive copers.

Research suggests that there is a general characteristic that can be described as persuasibility.[19] Early adopters of innovations tend to be above average in intelligence and high on communication competence.[20] However, such ability variables are less important predictors of innovative behavior than the previously described personality variables.

Focus on Interpersonal Relations

We have examined characteristics of the individuals that have relevance to acceptance or rejection of innovations. We will now examine simultaneously characteristics of the agent of change and the farmers he is interested in changing. Thus, while the previous analysis was monadic, dealing with *one* individual, the present analysis will be dyadic, dealing with *two* individuals.

We begin by agreeing with Goodenough's argument that change can be viewed from four different perspectives:

a. from the point of view of the agent of change;

b. from the point of view of the farmer;

c. from the point of view of farmer, with respect to the agent's goals;

d. from the point of view of the agent, with respect to the farmer's goals.

It is important to realize that the goals of the agent and the farmer are by no means identical. For example, the farmer's goals may include acceptance by his family, peers, and community, while the agent's goals may not include the farmer's acceptance by significant people in the farmer's social environment. Furthermore, the people "who count" are different for these two people. The farmer wants to be accepted by his family and neighbors, while the agent wants to be accepted by his supervisors and colleagues in a government agency or sim-

[19] C. I. Hovland and I. L. Janis, *Personality and Persuasibility* (New Haven: Yale University Press, 1959).

[20] E. M. Rogers, *Social Change in Rural Society* (New York: Appleton-Century-Crofts, 1960); and "A Conceptual Variable Analysis of Cultural Change," *Rural Sociology*, 23 (1958), 136–145.

ilar institution. In other words, the agent and the farmer do not experience the same sorts of pressures, from the same sorts of people. Although they may both consider high productivity of the farms an important goal, this goal is imbedded in a network of other goals, so that the total pattern of goals may be quite different.

There is a great deal of research showing that the greater the similarity between two people the greater the liking between them. This research may be summarized by saying that in the area of similarities in subjective culture, the greater the proportion of similar views, the greater the number of aspects of subjective culture on which the agent and the farmer are similar, the more they will like each other. Liking is generally related to the prospect that the agent's ideas will be accepted by the farmer.

One of the major variables of importance is similarity of culture. In general, if the agent and the farmer belong to different cultures, they are likely to have very different points of view, customs, and ways of interacting with each other. A good deal of resistance to the ideas of the agricultural expert can be traced to differences in customs.

In each culture, the "Achilles' heel" of the agent of change may be at a different place in his system of social relationships. For example, in Thailand, "saving face" is an important value, and to provide criticism is generally very difficult. Not only is criticism difficult to give, but any "bad news" is avoided. For example, a Thai may not inform his neighbor that his house is on fire, because this would be telling him something unpleasant. Thus, special skills in appropriate interpersonal interaction are required in order to introduce change. Many of these skills are culture-specific, although a certain amount of general sensitivity to the fact that other people are different may provide some help.

The greater the prestige of the agent the more likely it is that his message will be accepted. In addition, the greater the credibility of the agent, the more "unbiased" he appears to be, the more he will be successful in communicating his message. Thus, agents of change who appear to be likely to "make a personal profit" from adoption of their suggestions are less likely to be influential. The past behavior of the agent, the extent to which his suggestions were sound and led to useful improvements will also be important determinants of the acceptance of his suggestions.

Finally, basic characteristics such as the age, sex, and social class of the agent may have important influences. In some cultures men are more believable sources of information than women. For example, in Brazil, Hong Kong, and India male sources of information produce more attitude change than female sources, other things being equal.[21] In some cultures a young person cannot be "an adviser."

While similarity in subjective culture is generally "a blessing," similarity in personality is not necessarily always desirable. This is intuitively easy to see: If A is very talkative, the fact that B is also very talkative is not likely to make A like B. On the contrary, for a trait like talkativeness, the more one has the trait the better it is for the other *not* to have it. A theory of compatibility has been proposed in which there are three basic interpersonal needs and each has an active and passive mode: the need to include (and be included) in the group, the need to dominate (and be dominated), and the need to love (and be loved).[22] Compatibility occurs when a person with a high need to love meets a person with a high need to be loved, a person with a high need to dominate others meets a person who likes being dominated by others, a person who likes being included in groups meets a person who likes to include others in groups, etc.

Focus on the Group

As soon as people begin to interact with each other, they develop ideas about likes and dislikes as well as dominance of one over the others. These ideas can be described by means of the "sociometric structure" and "status structure" of a group. The sociometric structure is the system of relationships between the affective (emotional) bonds found in a group. The status structure reflects the relative status of different mem-

[21] J. O. Whittaker and R. D. Meade, "Sex of the Communicator as a Variable in Source Credibility," *Journal of Social Psychology*, 72 (1967), 27–34.
[22] W. C. Schutz, *FIRO: A Three-Dimensional Theory of Interpersonal Behavior* (New York: Rinehart, 1958).

bers. In addition to these structures, group members develop, through interaction, a number of ideas about correct or appropriate behavior for group members. These ideas are called norms. Finally, each of the positions in a group (e.g., leader, lieutenant, member) is associated with certain ideas about correct behavior; these are called roles.

The agent of change must learn to recognize the important structures, norms, and roles that characterize a group. This is particularly true in traditional societies where roles are sometimes very clearly defined, and behavior according to the proper roles or norms is strictly followed by an individual.

If the agent were to ask each member of the group to tell him whom he likes most, and were then to draw some arrows to indicate the choices that each member makes, he would be drawing a *sociogram*. This diagram would reflect the sociometric structure of the group he is interested in understanding. It would show that some members receive a lot of choices (are overchosen) and some receive few choices (are underchosen). He could also ask a lot of other questions about this group. For example, he might ask who is the most respected person. A diagram showing the direction of choice involving respect judgments could reflect the status structure in the group. In most groups the two structures are likely to be very similar. The important reason for knowing such structures is simply that if the agent of change convinces a person at the top of these structures to change his farming methods he will have less trouble convincing the remaining members, but if he were to convince a person at the bottom of the structures he might actually discover that the innovations he proposes are rejected as "appropriate for only *low* status members."

An interesting study was done concerning the relationship between sociometric structures and the adoption of new drugs.[23] These researchers interviewed all doctors in one location and obtained sociometric ratings. One of the questions was: "Could you name the three or four physicians whom you meet most frequently on social occasions?" Such questions resulted in a variety of sociograms. In addition, the researchers

[23] H. Manzel and E. Katz, "Social Relations and Innovation in the Medical Profession: The Epidemiology of a New Drug," *Public Opinion Quarterly*, 19 (1956), 337–352.

checked the files of the local pharmacies to determine the time of adoption of new drugs by different physicians. The data showed a direct relationship between leadership and adoption of the new drugs. However, the most overchosen (popular) physicians were likely to be late adopters. On the other hand, when they adopted a new drug all the remaining physicians in the sociometric network also adopted it. The pioneer physicians were only moderately popular.

When individuals make decisions they utilize a few groups as "their reference groups," in order to compare themselves with others and in order to develop standards of normative behavior. S. K. Sharman and V. S. S. Potti reviewed several studies in which it was shown that reference groups are influential in the adoption of agricultural innovations.[24] These authors tested the hypothesis that the "greater the positive reference group relationship, the higher the adoption" rates. They found support for this hypothesis. They also found evidence to support three more hypotheses: (a) the attitudes towards innovation of an individual's reference group will correlate with his attitudes towards innovation; (b) the greater the adoption score of an individual's reference group the greater will be his adoption; (c) the greater the closeness of ties between an individual and his reference group, the greater will be the agreement between them on attitudes towards innovations.

In some groups the sociometric choices are reciprocal and include every member of the group. Such groups would be very cohesive. In such groups members are likely to follow group norms quite religiously, so that the only way to change a member is to change the whole group at once.

This approach is illustrated by studies carried out by Kurt Lewin during World War II.[25] The purpose of these studies was to change food preferences. The first study attempted to increase the consumption by groups of housewives of beef hearts, sweetbreads, and kidneys. Two methods were used. In

[24] "Differential Adoption of Improved Farm Practices in Relation to Reference Group Influence," *Indian Journal of Extension Education,* 2 (1966), 51–58.
[25] "Group Decision and Social Change," in G. E. Swanson, T. M. Newcomb, and E. L. Hartley, eds., *Readings in Social Psychology,* 2d ed. (New York: Holt, 1952).

some groups a lecturer who was presented as an expert on diet, gave a most impressive talk in which he covered the nutritional value of the meats, their economy, and provided recipes for their preparation. In other groups the same information was given in a discussion in which the housewives participated. After the discussion the housewives were asked to indicate, with a show of hands, whether they intended to serve such meats. In a follow-up study it was found that only 3 per cent of the housewives in the lecture groups had served the meats, while 32 per cent of the housewives in the discussion groups had served at least one of these meats. In this study the housewives were asked to make individual decisions in a group setting, rather than to develop group norms. The effect would have been even stronger if the housewives had developed group norms and had constituted a cohesive group.

According to follow-up studies designed to determine the reasons the discussion group method is superior to the lecture method, it was shown that the act of making a decision and the degree of perceived consensus in the group, in combination, determine these results. Furthermore, in high cohesion groups there is more homogeneity in the observed behaviors than in low cohesion groups. In the latter a lot of individuals deviate from established norms.[26]

One of the most frequent findings in observations of opinion change in natural settings is that information does not go from the mass media to the individual but from the mass media to opinion leaders, who then influence individuals in face-to-face contacts. This is true in election campaigns as well as for the adoption of new drugs.

✗ Groups norms specify behaviors that are appropriate for members of the group. Some of the innovations proposed by the agent of change may require behaviors that are seen as inappropriate for members of the group.

Roles also specify behaviors that are appropriate for members of the group. But they are associated with certain characteristics of group members, such as age, sex, etc., or certain

[26] Edith B. Bennett, "Discussion, Decision, Commitment, and Consensus in Group Decision," *Human Relations*, 8 (1955), 251–273; and S. E. Seashore, *Group Cohesiveness in the Industrial Work Group* (Ann Arbor: Survey Research Center, 1954).

positions of group members such as leader, father, physician, etc.

In most traditional societies sex roles are very clearly specified. On the other hand, in industrial societies there is overlap among the behaviors that men and women are supposed or allowed to engage in. Some of the innovations proposed by the agent of change may be incompatible with existing sex roles. Similar examples may be given with respect to other types of roles.

Focus on Behavior

Behavior is determined by the interaction of a large number of factors. First, there are internal factors, such as attitudes, values, and habits. Then, there are external pressures exerted by other people, groups, or organizations. The final determination of behavior is dependent on the individual's ideas about (a) what he would like to do, (b) what he should do, according to himself, (c) what he should do, according to other people, (d) what he usually does, and (e) what will be the outcomes of what he does.

The last factor should be described somewhat more specifically. Every behavior is related to some probable outcomes; each of these outcomes has some value for the individual. Thus, adoption of an innovation may lead to better crops, but this is not sure. There is a probabilistic relationship between the behavior and the outcome. Furthermore, each behavior may have several outcomes, each with its own probability of occurrence. Finally, each outcome may vary in its degree of value. Some outcomes may be very valuable and others may be most unpleasant.

In order to assess the effects of his proposed innovations, the agent of change should consider the kinds of outcomes that are likely to be relevant for each of his clients. He should also consider if he can adapt his innovation so that it will not have outcomes that are disruptive to the community and the life of his clients.

Perhaps the first lesson on how to change the behavior of his clients is concerned with how to change his own, i.e., how to adapt his innovations to the particular social situation.

Focus on Innovation Process

It is important for the agent of change to analyze the effects of his innovation. He should examine, for example, not only the technological effects but also the social. In addition, he should know something about the stages of adoption of innovations.

The process of adoption requires several stages. First, the farmer has to become aware that there is such a thing as a particular innovation. At that stage he does not know any of the details. Typically in the United States this phase is carried out through the operation of mass media, e.g., farmer magazines. Second, he goes through a phase of being interested in getting more information about this innovation. Third, he goes through a "mental trial" of the innovation, during which he thinks of such matters as "Can I do it?" "If I do it, what will happen?" "Will I be better off than I am now?" Fourth, he tries the idea, and if it is successful, the final stage is adoption.

In the United States the chief sources of awareness are the mass media, but neighbors and friends are also important. The interest phase is also satisfied mostly by mass media and personal contacts, in that order. However, the mental trial is primarily influenced by neighbors and friends and secondarily by government agencies, such as extension workers, and much less by the mass media. The actual trial of the idea again depends much on neighbors and on government agencies. Finally, the adoption is almost entirely dependent on satisfaction with the trial. There is little outside influence on the adoption decision.

E. M. Rogers described one of his studies in which he categorized adopters into innovators (2.5 per cent), early adopters (13.5 per cent), early majority (34 per cent), late majority (34 per cent), and laggards (16 per cent). The demographic characteristics of these groups were reported. In general, education, status, and number of contacts with others and with government agencies were positively associated with early adoption of an innovation.[27]

Y. P. Singh and U. Pareek reported an analysis of the process

[27] "Conceptual Variable Analysis"; and "Categorizing the Adopters of Agricultural Practices," *Rural Sociology*, 23 (1958), 345–354.

of adoption based on Indian data, which is quite parallel to that proposed by Rogers.[28] They distinguish seven stages: need, adaption, interest, deliberation, trial, evaluation, and adoption. They also report that in those practices which involve substitution of the old product by a new one, the most frequent sources of influence are people who have themselves tried the practice. On the other hand, in practices that involve adoption of completely new technologies, communication is more frequently through the influentials of the community (opinion leaders).

The adoption of innovation also depends on a variety of social and economic factors that have not been discussed because they are outside the major focus of interest of social psychology. To mention but two, the size of the land holdings [29] and the relationship between the farmer and his government are relevant variables. For example, according to Indian informants, the Indian ministry of agriculture has adopted the policy of materially helping early adopters, but giving much less help to those who wait before they adopt an innovation. The result is that certain farmers are seriously motivated by an interest in taking advantage of the facilities offered by the ministry of agriculture. A related observation was that South Dakota farmers were motivated to seek contacts with agricultural extension agents to learn new techniques which would increase their social status.[30] Monetary considerations were secondary.

Focus on Influence Process

It was pointed out above that for different stages of adoption different kinds of communication channels are appropriate or most effective. Thus, the mass media, friends, neighbors, extension agent, etc., each have a different contribution to make, at different points. All of these sources transmit messages.

[28] Y. P. Singh and U. Pareek, "Interpersonal Communication at Different Stages of Adoption," *Indian Journal of Social Work,* 27 (1967), 344–352.

[29] F. C. Fliegel, "A Multiple Correlation Analysis of Factors Associated with Adoption of Farm Practices," *Rural Sociology,* 21, (1956), 284–292; and D. J. Hobbs, "Factors Related to the Use of Agricultural Chemicals in Iowa Farms," M.S. Thesis, Iowa State University, 1960.

[30] J. D. Photiadis, "Motivation of Contacts and Technological Change," *Rural Sociology,* 27 (1963), 316–326.

There is a very considerable literature concerning the characteristics of messages, such as style, structure, and content, that make them most effective.[31]

We have examined the importance of subjective culture, personality, and certain features of the interpersonal process as aids or inhibitors of innovation. We also examined certain group characteristics that are relevant. Behavior was shown to be determined in a complex way by all these factors.

It is fair to conclude this section by pointing out that the values of traditional cultures are sometimes superior to those of Western culture and more conducive to proper behaviors by the farmers. It would be a mistake to assume that Western values and beliefs should always be involved in the introduction of innovation. For example, in colonial countries, the models that farmers have learned to look up to are white colonial administrators who disliked "dirtying their hands" with manual labor. The result is that Asia and Africa now have a problem with primary school educated youth who refuse to do the jobs that are available while their societies are unable to provide enough white collar jobs for them. The old Ceylonese saying, "Dust a peasant and you get a prince," has now been replaced with Western colonial values favoring white collar work, the employment of others in farm work, etc.

In addition, it is fair to remind the agents of innovation that rapid innovation may disturb the stability of the personal and status relationships of a society in such a way that a person may experience "anomie" and normlessness. E. Fromm has analyzed how the stability of medieval society was disturbed by the rapid innovations that accompanied the Renaissance and how Lutheranism represented "an escape from freedom" into a new order where a new set of norms replaced the old and created a new equilibrium for the individual.[32] Rapid social change may create conditions which seriously change the meaning of life, and suicide, divorce, delinquency, and other social manifestations of normlessness become prevalent. One of the important research questions of this century is "What rate of

[31] Summarized in H. C. Triandis, *Attitudes and Attitude Change* (New York: Wiley, 1971).

[32] E. Fromm, *Escape from Freedom* (New York: Farrar and Rinehart, 1941).

change is optimal?" If the rate is too great to be accompanied by proper accommodations in the social processes, it may be seriously disruptive.

Relationships among These Concepts

In the present section we will now review studies which show that there is evidence that the above-mentioned variables and concepts are relevant to the adoption of innovation. The focus will be mostly on empirical studies showing that certain social psychological variables are relevant for adoption of innovation. In addition, a number of generalizations proposed by E. M. Rogers will be introduced to give structure to the presentation.[33]

Subjective Culture and Innovation

Tully, Wilkening, and Presser present a most convincing argument that the major focus in introducing change in farming methods must be directed towards changing the norms, values, and aspirations of the farmers. They show that such factors have a direct influence on the adoption process. Non-adopters put more value on ease and convenience and have lower aspirations and less need for money than adopters. The way the innovation is perceived, for example, its cost, convenience, and risk, are directly related to adoption. "The relative advantage of a new idea, as perceived by members of a social system, affects its rate of adoption" (Rogers, p. 312). "An individual's innovativeness varies directly with the norms of his social system of innovativeness" (Rogers, p. 311). His individual values are good predictors of his innovation behavior.[34]

The attitude towards the proposed innovation is also relevant. Moulik, Hrabovzky, and Rao found that the attitude

[33] E. M. Rogers and A. E. Havens, unpublished paper (1961) mentioned in *Diffusion of Innovations* (New York: The Free Press, 1962) pp. 311–314. All page references given in the text refer to this book.

[34] J. Tully, E. A. Wilkining, and H. A. Presser, "Factors in Decision Making in Farming Problems," *Human Relations*, 17 (1964), 295–320; J. E. Kivlin and F. C. Fliegel, "Differential Perceptions of Innovations and Rate of Adoption," *Rural Sociology*, 32 (1967), 78–91; and R. Cohen, "A Theoretical Model for Consumer Market Prediction," *Sociological Inquiry*, 32 (1962), 43–50.

towards nitrogeneous fertilizers was one of the best predictors of adoption of such fertilizers in Northern India. Similarly, Fliegel found that the attitude towards the innovation was an important predictor of its adoption. The amount of knowledge about the innovation is also relevant.[35]

Personality and Innovation

In our discussion about personality variables we emphasized the importance of n-Ach (need for achievement). There are numerous investigations which support this generalization.

McClelland reports the results of an experiment conducted in Kakinada, a town in Andhra Pradesh, India, with a population of about 100,000, as well as in a "control" town. The businessmen of Kakinada were invited to take a ten-day course offered in Hyderabad, about 350 miles away from their town. Fifty-two participated in this study in 1964. They learned to think in n-Ach terms, they role-played various situations in which they acted as though they were people with high n-Ach. They learned to score their TAT protocols according to the n-Ach scoring manuals. They introspected about their emotions when thinking of "success" and "failure." They formed an association to promote economic development. The results of this experiment indicate that there was a marked increase in the frequency of innovative behavior in Kakinada. About one-third of the businessmen showed unusual innovative behavior: they worked harder; they paid attention to their customers; they invested their money in enterprises involving more risk.

The evidence suggests that high n-Ach is related to innovative behavior not only among businessmen, but also among farmers.[36] Rogers and Neill, in one of the best studies relating personality variables to adoptions of agricultural innovations

[35] T. K. Moulik, J. P. Hrabovzky, and C. S. S. Rao, "Predictive Values of Some Factors of Adoption of Nitrogenous Fertilizers by North Indian Farmers," *Rural Sociology*, 31 (1966), 467–477; Fliegel, "Multiple Correlation Analysis"; L. M. Sizer and W. F. Porter, *The Relation of Knowledge to Adoption of Recommended Practices*, Agricultural Experimental Station, Bulletin No. 446, (Morgantown, West Virginia, 1960).

[36] E. M. Rogers and R. E. Neill, *Achievement Motivation among Colombian Farmers* (East Lansing: Department of Communications, Michigan State University, 1966).

that has ever been done in a cross-cultural setting, measured achievement motivation as follows: Farmers were interviewed and asked to complete sentences such as these: "For a better life on my farm, I need . . . ," "My greatest aspiration in life is . . . ," "Farmers in our country are . . . ." They were also asked: "What are your plans for the next five years?" (Such questions had previously been found to predict farm labor efficiency in Ohio.) [37] The scoring of the answers was done by coding each response in one of three levels of achievement. For example, a response such as "God is Master," to the query about plans for the next five years, was scored zero. Answers indicating some achievement were scored 1, and answers indicating much achievement, e.g., "I plan to get more land, so I can operate more effectively" were scored 2. The study was carried out in six Colombian communities. The major crop grown was either coffee or potatoes. The percentages of respondents that are functionally literate in these communities ranged from 15 per cent to 49 per cent. A total of 302 interviews was completed. They were tape-recorded and a number of internal validity and reliability checks were carried out.

The major hypothesis of the study was that "agricultural innovativeness scores vary directly with achievement motivation scores" (p. 57). Innovativeness was defined as "the degree to which an individual is relatively earlier than his peers in a social system in adopting new ideas" (p. 57). The correlations between these two kinds of scores proved to range between —.19 and +.48 for the six communities. Two of the six correlations were significant, one of the .05 and the other at the .01 level. The authors report that the range of scores on the variables in question was greater in the two most traditional villages, and it is exactly in these two villages that the correlations reached significance. Thus, it appears that there is support for the hypothesis.

The authors also show relationships between (a) "home innovativeness" (adoption of sanitation, health, nutrition, and household equipment innovations), (b) attitude toward innovators, (c) the desire to increase farm size, (d) land ownership, (e) farm production per land unit (yield per hectare), (f) the

[37] R. E. Neill, "Achievement Motivation among Ohio Farmers," M.S. thesis, Ohio State University, 1963.

farmer's status in the social system, and (g) his reputation as a good farmer, and achievement motivation scores.

Consistent with previous findings, the authors report that their measure of independence training of children is related to achievement motivation. Furthermore, the more family power is concentrated in the hands of the father, the less the achievement motivation. Moreover, the greater the wife's role in farm decision-making, the higher the achievement motivation.

It appears that achievement motivation is also related to (a) the amount of exposure to mass media, (b) the amount of political knowledge, (c) the degree of cosmopoliteness (orientation towards external social system), (d) the level of literacy, (e) the years of formal education, (f) the educational aspirations, (g) the occupational aspirations, and (h) a positive attitude towards credit. Finally, achievement motivation is inversely related to age and fatalism (feeling that the individual cannot control his future).

The authors also provide a multiple correlation analysis of the variables that account for achievement motivation scores. The most important, in terms of variance explained, is mass media exposure. However, this varies from community to community. In one community the most important variables were years of formal education and literacy. One might summarize these findings by stating that openness to outside influences (through the mass media, education, or whatever other sources) is related to a high need for achievement. What is cause and effect here cannot be determined from this study.

Finally, the authors review seven other investigations which utilized similar approaches in India, Malaysia, and the Philippines. These studies show a very similar pattern of results. The consistency in the findings is sufficiently striking to allow considerable confidence in the generality of the results reported by Rogers and Neill.

"The innovativeness of individuals is related to a modern rather than a traditional orientation" (Rogers, p. 311). There is a strong evidence to support this generalization. For example, Chattopadhyay and Pareek found fatalism and conservatism to be significantly related to their "adoption quotient." The greater the fatalism and conservatism the lower the adoption rate. The two variables together account for 49 per cent of the variance of adoptions, as computed through a multiple regression analysis. Hoffer and Stagland found that conservatism and a high value for security are related to low adoption of approved practices in corn growing. The opposite of fatalism is "belief in the possibility of efficacious change and control of the environment" and was found to be highly related to adoption behaviors on the part of Pakistani farmers.[38]

A self-rating of innovation proneness was found to be related to the adoption of fertilizers. A related point of view has been called "cosmopoliteness" and has also been found to be related to adoption. Cosmopoliteness is the degree to which an individual's orientation is external to a particular social system.[39] "Opinion leaders are more cosmopolite than their followers" (Rogers, p. 314).

Another personality variable of interest is dogmatism. Jamias and Tordahl have shown that when a group's norms of innovation are favorable, there is no difference in the adoption of new practices recommended by agricultural experts between persons high and low in dogmatism.[40] On the other hand, when the norms for innovation are not too favorable, then the low dogmatism group adopts many innovations and the high dogmatism group adopts few innovations. Thus, there is an "interaction" between social norms and personality in which when the norms are unfavorable and the person is dogmatic the rate of adoption is very low, while in all other conditions it is quite high. In view of the fact that this study was done in Michigan,

---

[38] S. N. Chattopadhyay and U. Pareek, "Prediction of Multipractice Adoption Behavior from Some Psychological Variables," *Rural Sociology*, 32 (1967), 324–333; C. R. Hoffer and D. Stagland, "Farmers' Attitudes and Values in Relation to Adoption of Approved Practices in Corn Growing," *Rural Sociology*, 23 (1958), 112–120; and H. Schuman, *Economic Development and Individual Change: A Social-Psychological Study of the Comilla Experiment in Pakistan* (Cambridge, Mass.: Center for International Affairs, Harvard University, 1967).

[39] Moulik *et al.*, "Predictive Values"; Hobbs, "Factors Related"; and Cohen, "Theoretical Model."

[40] J. F. Jamias and V. C. Troldahl, "Dogmatism, Tradition, and General Innovativeness," a 1965 manuscript described by M. Rokeach, "Attitude Change and Behavioral Change," *Public Opinion Quarterly*, 30 (1967), 529–550.

where there is a generally high acceptance for innovation and therefore the range of scores on this variable is likely to be narrow, the findings are particularly interesting. Unfortunately, the particular measure of dogmatism used, the Rokeach D-scale, is contaminated with "acquiescence response set"; that is, people who tend to agree, no matter what question they are asked, tend to get high scores. Such acquiescence is theoretically related to behavior according to norms. So, when the norms call for innovation the high D-Scale scorer does what the norms call for; when the norms call for little innovation he does again what the norms call for. This interpretation of the findings appears as plausible as the one based on the theory of dogmatism and is somewhat more parsimonious.

A number of characteristics of earlier adopters of innovation are well-established in the literature. They tend to be younger, of higher status, in a better financial position, somewhat more intelligent, and they have more specialized operations than the later adopters (Rogers, p. 313).[41]

Group Characteristics and Innovation

The status of the farmer, both social and economic, and his sociometric position in a sociometric network consisting of the other community farmers, appear to be closely related to this adoption behavior. There is good support for this generalization: "Early adopters and opinion leaders have higher status than later adopters and opinion followers" (Rogers, pp. 313, 314). There is also much evidence that the economic status of the farmer is associated with his adoption behavior. The wealthier farmers are more willing to adopt innovations.[42]

[41] J. H. Copp, *Personal and Social Factors Associated with the Adoption of Recommended Farm Practices among Cattlemen*, Agricultural Experimental Station Technical Bulletin, No. 83 (Manhattan, Kansas, 1956); "Towards Generalization in Farm Practice Research," *Rural Sociology*, 23 (1958), 103–111; and Rogers, "Conceptual Variable Analysis."

[42] T. K. Moulik and U. Pareek, "Group Factors in Participation," *Indian Journal of Social Work*, 24 (1963), 79–84; Rogers, "Conceptual Variable Analysis"; Sizer and Porter, *Relation of Knowledge;* Cohen, "Theoretical Model"; Copp, *Personal and Social Factors* and "Towards Generalization"; Hobbs, "Factors Related"; and Fliegel, "Multiple Correlation Analysis."

The cohesiveness of the group and the feeling of belonging to the group are also related to adoption rates. When the wife is supportive of the farmer's role, there is a higher adoption rate.[43]

"Social system norms on innovativeness seem to determine at least in part, the innovativeness of opinion leaders" (Rogers, p. 314).

Opinion leadership is an important factor in the adoption of innovation. Rogers (p. 314) suggests: "Earlier leaders conform more closely to social system norms than the average member, . . . Opinion leaders use more impersonal, technically accurate, and cosmopolite sources of information than do their followers." Singh and Pareek identified what they called "key communicators" whom they defined as "those who had performed more than average acts of communication at the different stages of adoption of the three farm practices." They used a sociometric procedure to obtain nominations of such persons. However, they discovered that these people do not necessarily exhibit innovative behavior. The proportion of nonadoption was exceptionally low among this group, but not the number of innovative behaviors themselves.[44]

Adoption Process

The discussion about the stages of the adoption process, in which mass media play a bigger role in the early stages, such as in creating awareness, and interpersonal relations play a larger role during the later stages, is also well supported by empirical investigations. For example, Singh and Pareek have broken down the adoption process into seven stages and report that during the early stages the mass media play a role, while during the later stages they do not.[45] Rogers summarizes some of the major findings as follows:

[43] Moulik and Pareek, "Group Factors"; and M. A. Straus, "Family Role Differentiation and Technological Change in Farming," *Rural Sociology*, 25 (1960), 219–228.

[44] Singh and Pareek, "Interpersonal Communication," and "Adoption Behavior of Key Communicators," *Indian Psychological Review*, 2 (1966), 121–124.

[45] "Sources of Communication, Different Stages of Adoption of Farm Practices," *Indian Journal of Social Work*, 26 (1966), 385–391.

Impersonal information sources are most important at the awareness stage and personal sources are most important at the evaluation stage in the adoption process (pp. 311–312). There is little evidence that lack of knowledge about innovations actually delays their adoption (p. 321). Awareness occurs at a more rapid rate than does adoption (p. 321). The awareness-to-trial period is longer than the trial to adoption period (p. 312). Earlier adopters try innovations on a smaller scale than later adopters (p. 312).

Rogers also states that the complexity of the innovation, the divisibility and the communicability of the innovation affect the rate of adoption. Finally, he generalizes: "Personal influence from peers is more important for relatively later adopters than for earlier adopters" (p. 314).

Implication for Strategy

The agent of change, the farmer, and the innovation constitute a system of three elements which are closely interrelated in any situation involving behavioral change. Figure 1 shows the "total system" that is relevant in analyzing change.

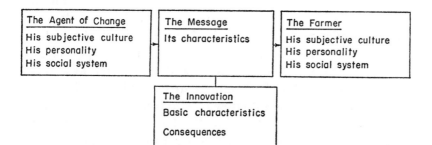

Figure 1. Total system of agricultural innovation

In thinking about the optimal strategy of change, it is important to consider what change will occur in each of these elements, and how change in one of these elements will influence change in the others. It is further desirable to consider two courses of action which are applicable to each of these elements: selection or change.

Thus, there are six strategies that must be combined in an optimal manner: (a) selection of the agent, (b) training of the agent, (c) selection of the farmer, (d) training of the farmer, (e) selection of the correct innovation for the particular condition, and (f) adaptation of the innovation to the existing conditions.

It is most desirable to select the agent who belongs to the same culture as the farmer, or one who can easily become sensitive to the basic features and requirements for behavior that is appropriate to the farmer's culture. The agent's "social skills" should be highly developed. His technical knowledge should be adequate. His personality should be suitable (probably high in n-Ach, n-Ext, and average in n-Aff). Research is needed to determine what agents are most effective.

The agent should learn to identify the basic concepts used by the farmer. He should know how to discover the links between these concepts. He should learn to analyze the attitudes and customs of the farmer in terms of the functions they play and the needs they satisfy. He should be sensitive to differences in values and able to analyze the way his values influence his perceptions and his stereotypes of the farmer. He should learn to diagnose low and high n-Ach in the people he is working with. He should know how to train people to increase their n-Ach, how to train farmers to increase their concern for the common good, their active orientation, and how to decrease their dependence on fatalistic thinking. He should know how to use sociometric procedures in the selection of the best targets for his persuasive messages. He should know how to employ the reference groups of his targets to maximize the influence of his messages. He should know how to construct messages that have optimum effectiveness. Finally, he should know how to adapt the innovations he wants to teach to the particular time and place and to particular farmers.

Certain farmers are more likely to adopt change than others. In the previous sections we reviewed a number of demographic social and personality characteristics that are relevant to the adoption of change. If the agent is aware of the characteristics of his potential clients, he can select his clients so as to maximize the probability that his suggestions will lead to adoptions.

The basic training may have to concentrate on the values and basic attitudes of the farmers concerning innovation. In addition, certain of their concepts, and some of the cognitive links they employ may have to be modified. An appropriately selected set of messages may be able to create these changes.

Training the farmer for achievement, concern for the common good, and reduction in need affiliation and familism may also be needed. Changing the way the farmers perceive the agent may also be highly desirable. For example, it may be highly desirable to increase the prestige, credibility, and attractiveness of the agent.

The selection of the innovation depends most on the influence of technological-economic factors. However, it is well to consider the consequences of the innovation, both real and as perceived by the farmer. It may be the case that such an analysis would suggest that one kind of innovation may be more suitable than another, although both are likely to result in the same degree of economic gain for the farmer.

There is some flexibility in the way an innovation is adapted. It is generally possible to change some features of an innovation, without sacrificing its efficacy. Efforts should be made in the direction of adapting the innovation to the subjective culture, personality, and social system of the farmers.

Response

ROBERT B. MACLEOD

In commenting on the chapter by Harry Triandis I should like to examine some of the broader implications of his thesis rather than quibble about details of his presentation. Triandis asks us to consider the human factors which contribute to or detract from agricultural innovation. He has posed his question within the framework of psychological theory, has marshaled the evidence from empirical research, and has left us, I hope, with the conviction that psychological research is indeed relevant and with a number of questions which invite further inquiry. I should like, at once, to compliment him on the skill and clarity with which he has disentangled an enormously complex problem. Any misgivings I express have to do not with his treatment of the problem but rather with the current state of psychological science.

It used to be said, and not altogether facetiously, that the pattern of Western involvement in the affairs of underdeveloped countries has been: first the missionary, then the capitalist, then the gunboat. The history of the great empires has always been a story of ideological, economic, and military intervention, with ideological concerns steadily yielding to those of profit and power. A more up-to-date formulation of the cliché would include as a fourth agent of intervention the officer of AID or of the philanthropic foundation. Having disrupted a foreign culture—whether for motives of ideology, of profit, or of power—we now find it necessary to send in a team of social surgeons to patch up the wounds. This is an oversimplification, of course, but as we consider methods of introducing change into other cultures we cannot evade the fact that, societies being complex and delicately balanced systems, any alteration of an existing pattern of behavior may have far-reaching consequences which the innovator has not foreseen. Every biologist is familiar with the dangers inherent in an "upset of the balance of nature," and the impending population crisis is a reminder that the principle applies also to man; lowered death rate, however desirable it may seem to be, creates a whole new set of problems. Being an unashamed interventionist, I cannot argue against the deliberate fostering of change in other cultures. Human interaction is going to increase, not decrease, and the proper response to the Malthusian challenge is not to let nature take its course but to study the processes of social change and to control them in accordance with an enlightened plan. I am merely stressing a point which ought to be obvious, namely, that the promotion of agricultural innovation—or, for that matter, of any innovations which lead to social disruption, e.g., in medicine, education, or legal procedure—should be accompanied by an attempt to identify and cope with both the immediate and the remote consequences of the innovation. Triandis is, I believe, in full agreement.

My major misgiving has to do with the adequacy of present-day psychology for programs which involve interaction with people of cultures radically different from our own. My argument is that much of what we call psychology is quite irrelevant, that the information we have which is relevant is meager and culture-bound, and that we still lack the tools necessary for the kind of research that ought to be done. Triandis may consider me unduly pessimistic. May I hasten to add that the very fact that he and a few other capable psychologists are actively engaged in cross-cultural research augurs well for the future. May I, however, make a few points in support of my argument, overstating them somewhat in the hope that they will stimulate controversy.

(1) *Much of contemporary psychological theory is irrelevant to the practical problems of introducing, regulating, and assessing the effects of cultural change.* Psychologists have traditionally been in search of generalizable laws which govern the mental activities of normal, human, adult individuals. From time to time they have been stimulated by challenges from the world of practical affairs, e.g., the connection with education of children, the diagnosis and treatment of mental abnormality, the

selection of personnel for industry—and the payoff has usually been rich; but regularly the psychologists have disengaged themselves from the challenge, have withdrawn from the study of real people in real life situations, and have redefined their problems in language so abstract as to be invulnerable. Thus, for instance, the concept of intelligence became redefined "operationally" as that which is tested by an intelligence test, the "laws of learning" were derived from the behavior of sophomores memorizing nonsense syllables and of rats mastering mazes, and theories of motivation were based on the reactions of animals to food and water deprivation or to electric shock. The models of behavior which have emerged can be generalized to the conduct of real people only with extreme ingenuity or bland fatuity. The *reductio ad absurdum* of this search for elegant miniature models of behavior is the currently popular computer model. The claim that behavior can be described in terms of the input, the processing, and the output of information is as unchallengable as the Freudian concept of the unconscious; it satisfies because it gives us a new set of metaphors, but it leaves the central problems pretty much where they were before. My own feeling is that the building of psychological models, while good fun, should be strictly spare-time activity. For some time to come the main activity of psychologists should be focused on the observation, description, classification, and measurement of phenomena; and among the most sadly neglected of psychological phenomena are those to be found in the behavior of people in other cultures. This is not to disparage psychological theorizing, which happens to be my major preoccupation; it is merely to assert that theories without facts are not very useful, and that theories based on poorly sampled facts can be positively misleading.

(2) *The available psychological information is meager and culture-bound.* This seems to fly in the face of the evidence which Triandis has marshaled so capably. It is true that many of the psychological problems basic to an understanding of people in other cultures are being actively explored within the context of our own culture. Triandis has made an excellent selection of these. I think he would be the first to admit, however, that the neatest and best designed of the empirical studies

he quotes have had the Western, and usually the American, social scene as their focus. To what extent may their findings be legitimately extended to other cultures? This breaks down into two subsidiary questions: (a) How adequate are the conceptual formulations? (b) Even if the concepts are adequate, can they be readily applied in the practical context of another culture?

The first of these questions does not bother me too much at the moment. Although it is true that faulty conceptualization may lead to serious practical errors, we must always work with the available conceptual tools, and the important thing is that we be ready to modify them. I see no harm, consequently, in retaining such established psychological terms as need, goal, value, ingroup, social role, and personality. These are all flexible enough to be open to a variety of interpretations, and there is no point at this stage in proposing a different vocabulary. The difficulties arise when we try to use them concretely in a practical situation. Let me illustrate very briefly. The concept of "need" is an old one in the psychology of motivation, and psychologists usually recognize a hierarchy of needs, ranging from such simple physiologically defined states as hunger and thirst, to complex states, such as security and social acceptance, which are hard to distinguish from values. McClelland and his colleagues have made extensive studies of the need for achievement, measuring it, balancing against other needs, relating it to personality formation, etc.[1] In spite of the fact that most of these studies have involved the familiar population of college sophomores I agree with Triandis that they are theoretically significant, and I applaud McClelland's attempt to extend his theorizing to include people of other cultures and of other periods in history. But if there ever was a culture-bound concept it is the concept of "achievement." "To achieve" is as open-ended a concept as "to go." Within a given culture we can make a moderately meaningful distinction between high achievers and low achievers, although even this distinction may break down when we shift from the context of the classroom to the

[1] D. C. McClelland, *The Achieving Society* (Princeton, N.J.: Van Nostrand, 1961); and J. W. Atkinson, *An Introduction to Motivation* (Princeton, N.J.: Van Nostrand, 1964).

context of the playing field. In both cases, however, we know approximately what is considered as worth achieving and can make some sort of stab at measuring the intensity of the need. In a culture with values different from our own the term can have little meaning until we know something about the values of the culture and the goals of the individuals whose motivation we are attempting to assess. To say that a particular society or a particular person is low in achievement motivation is consequently to say nothing at all, or else it is to say merely that this society or person does not share our concept of achievement.

It may or may not turn out that a theory of achievement motivation based on observations in one culture will hold true for all other cultures, whatever meaning the term achievement may have. If so, it will be a useful theory. In the meantime, however, our urgent task is to understand the *content* of the cultures with which we have to deal, what Triandis terms "subjective culture." How do we go about the study of subjective culture?

(3) *We still lack the necessary tools.* But, I hasten to add, the situation is by no means hopeless. The simple fact is, as I have pointed out above, that until recently psychologists have shown very little interest in the psychological content of other cultures. This has, for the most part, been left to the anthropologists; and, indeed, in this country the behaviorist movement in psychology has represented a profound disinterest in psychological content of any sort. The traditional alternatives have been, on the one hand, a psychology which stresses the prediction and control of behavior, and on the other hand, a psychology, often philosophically or clinically oriented, which stresses understanding. Too often, as in the German *Verstehends Psychologie*,[2] the "understanding" psychology has been only nominally empirical and has made little use of methods of controlled observation of properly sampled populations. Since World War II the picture has been steadily changing, and these two alternatives no longer seem irreconcilable. In animal psychology, for instance, pioneers like E. C. Tolman

[2] H. W. Gruhle, *Verstehends Psychologie* (Stuttgart: Georg Thieme Verlag, 1956).

had been arguing that if one is to predict the behavior of an animal one must understand the kind of world it is living in;[3] and now, sparked by the ethologists, students of animal behavior have been adopting what might almost be called an "understanding" approach. In child psychology, Piaget and his associates have been prying into the structure of the world *as it appears to the child;* and there is a similar trend in clinical psychology.[4] In social psychology there is still what seems to me to be a premature and not particularly profitable preoccupation with miniature models of social interaction which bear almost as little relation to the everyday behavior of people in society as mathematical learning theory bears to the problems of education. Nevertheless, particularly since World War II, which revealed our social psychology as not only culture-bound but class-bound, there has been an encourageing awareness of the fact that a mere plotting of the patterns and frequencies of behavior is useless without an understanding of its psychological content. This has led, for instance, to an enrichment of the studies of social attitudes. The failure of the 1948 election polls made it clear that without an understanding of the "why" of a person's choice a prediction of his voting behavior might go sadly wrong.

What is needed now is an extension of this liberalized social psychology to the study of behavior in other cultures. It is easy to ask the general question: What is the nature of the world as the individual apprehends it? His world includes not only the things and persons which surrounds him, but also the institutions, the symbols, and the values of his culture. We frequently speak of the "internalization" of culture. This is an unfortunate expression, but it points to the fact that if we are to deal intelligently with people different from ourselves we must somehow get "inside" their world, look out upon it as it were through their eyes. If we are to be successful in introducing change in agricultural methods, even something as appar-

[3] E. C. Tolman, *Purposive Behavior in Animals and Men* (New York: Century, 1932).

[4] J. Piaget, *The Construction of Reality in the Child* (New York: Basic Books, 1961); see also J. H. Flavel, *The Developmental Psychology of Jean Piaget* (Princeton, N.J.: Van Nostrand, 1963).

ently simple as contour plowing, we must appreciate the fact that we are not merely changing practices, we are changing people.

Triandis has given us an excellent analysis of the psychological factors which must be considered if agricultural innovation is to succeed, and his own research augurs well for the future. If I sound somewhat dismal in my comments about cross-cultural research in psychology, perhaps all I am saying is that there are not yet enough men like Harry Triandis.

Synthesis Response to
Sanders and Triandis

One problem common to professionals and scholars in the various disciplines is to cast themselves as change agents among colleague-clients and to make personal application of the strategies they have devised for others to use in developmental change (strategy meaning planned action to accomplish a purpose). One of the concepts contributed to behavioral change from a discipline is the self-concept of the discipline, and the concept of its functionaries: sociology and the sociologists; social psychology and the social psychologists. Some participation in developmental change will be within the conceptual limits of the discipline; perhaps even more will be ancillary or supplemental—hence nondisciplinary or nonprofessional (which does not mean unprofessional). The professional man who knows his discipline thoroughly, who continues to try to enlarge its scientific competence, and who continues to seek appropriate ways to apply it, becomes a broad-guage general practitioner in problem-solving, situation-analysis, *ad hoc* interpretation, and *ad hoc* organization. He acquires a wisdom which reaches beyond the formal limits of his discipline, so that much of his participation in developmental change uses the discipline and its concepts as points of departure rather than as tools for direct and precise attack. His work language will convey the meanings of the concepts, but often without their names.

The law of parsimony is of some use in transfering discipline concepts to developmental-change practice. It's better to use the least number essential to make the most relevant input. Elaboration of conceptual schemes, and differentiation of specialized concepts is essential to discipline building, but probably not to developmental change. Sanders and Triandis have made overlapping lists of concepts from sociology and social psychology. Probably those they present in common, although in different order and of different description are most immediately relevant to strategy for developmental change. (Starting with these we may now take the role of change agent and see what to do about their proffered concepts and suggested applications.)

What we are seeking is not sociological or social psychological concepts, but developmental change concepts contributed by sociology or social psychology, and which a change agent may incorporate, perhaps namelessly, into his developmental skill. He may never pause to attribute a term or its meaning to the mother discipline, but may draw it into application when needed, as the driver of a vehicle with his destination in mind will keep to his own side, accelerate or decelerate, and signal turns never thinking of the principles of engineering or even the (hopefully well-internalized!) laws of traffic control.

The objective of knowing concepts from the disciplines is to enhance the change agent's creativity. He may never aspire to a kit of concepts like the plumber's tools, with a wrench for every type of awkward reach; a change agent on the job is a tool maker—and not just a tool user. He'll shape the tools—or devise the strategies, in cooperative association with his clients, from his ingenuity at play among the concepts—but only to the extent that he really knows their meanings and their flexibilities for application.

It is unlikely that many change agents will be in a position to exploit formal sociometric, psychometric, anthropometric, or econometric tests during their analyses of predevelopmental and developmental situations. It will, however, be exceedingly helpful to them to have included study of and practice with tests and research techniques during their formal preservice or in-service education, in order to better ingest and assimilate these concepts into their general comprehension and their general strategy-planning skill. Wherever feasible, of course, the application of testing procedures will be useful.

The concept of "need to achieve" (n-Ach) was ingeniously studied, and it is reasonable to believe. No doubt there is a plus or minus loading of n-Ach in every person, a distribution in every society of persons according to n-Ach, and an average n-Ach for every group. But what will be the object of achievement? Will not n-Ach be met by different objects in different groups and societies, as defined by tradition there, and as prescribed by value and norm? And will not the role of the seeker-to-achieve vary from person to person and society to society?

It may be that the values and norms directing the effort to achieve in a given society (structure of relationship) will be more important for a change agent to understand in a given case than the statistics on n-Ach, even if they could be had! And what if there is, in a client community, a shortage of persons with n-Ach, or a low level of n-Ach pervading the group? Do we walk away and say "no chance for developmental change here?" If so, probably we would be sent back by our sponsoring agencies, so it will be wise to have strategies in mind even for the case of low n-Ach. Some of us find the concept of n-Ach interesting but of uncertain applicability in some given situations.

This kind of doubt about the implications of n-Ach may be expressed also about other and parallel conceptions of need. However, it makes sense to acknowledge the probable existence of distributions of n-Ach and n-Aff and other n's as well as dependence, dogmatism, etc., and assist clients to devise activities and programs to enhance their possibility of realizing these needs—as reflected in their values and norms.

The core of agreement between the Sanders presentation from rural sociology and the Triandis presentation from social psychology seems to be in the concept of social relationship. Sanders gives it central importance; Triandis doesn't designate any one concept as of central importance, but he does list relationships. He gives *interpersonal relations* coordinate position with the individual, (some of us would prefer to say person than individual—only the socialized person has subjective culture)—and the *group*—listing other coordinates as *behavior, innovation process,* and *influence process.* Both Sanders and Triandis include position, role, value, and norm.

With some juggling and telescoping, larger areas of identity could be established. For example, one might merge (for developmental change purposes) attitudes, aspirations, and goals into values, or at least treat them as synonymous. One could merge dogmatism, authoritarianism, fatalism, and customs into norms (granted that for specific and not developmental-change purposes they may be required to have their separate conceptual specificity). In other words, one could slip over or around the items in a textbook table of contents, for social psychology as well as sociology. Sanders did this rather facilely, by the way. Did he dispense with too many concepts too fast?

So as a first approximation I would accept the concepts (drawn from both lists) of relationship, position, role, value, and norm, and I would explore further than either Sanders or Triandis have done to seek implications for developmental change. In particular I would want to expand the illustration of the use of the relationship concept to more than one agent, one farmer, and one innovation. Actually, the need is not as simple as that—as indicated by Mosher's inventory of the variety of participants and practices in farming, agri-supportive activities, and agri-climates in Chapter 1. There are many and varied change agents—and each is also a client to someone else in the system.

For our present interest, the authors have rendered timely and appropriate service in directing attention to social relationships as a nexus of the sociological and social psychological concepts that are useful in developmental change. There is sanction in theory from many sources on the side of sociology—and social psychologists generally focus on social relationships. The format of the concept as here advanced by Sanders, however, has innovative features in the particular configurations of position, role, value, and norm.

Each author has helpfully contributed cases and anecdotes which encourage us to seek the joint application of the two disciplines. In the process of preparing these comments, another case was studied. Taken from the community development program in India, it seemed to be of possible use in considering further the application of the social-relationship concept as a point of merger for sociology, social psychology, and perhaps other disciplines in the prosecution of developmental behavioral change.[1]

The study was undertaken as a device for consultation rather

[1] Howard W. Beers, *Relationships among Workers in C.D. Blocks* (Hyderabad: National Institute of Community Development, 1962).

than research, or perhaps more accurately as consultation via study. It was conducted by reconnaissance-observation, with Indian associates, in four selected development blocks, and by discussion-consultation with development officials at all levels: national, state, district, block, and village.

Had the Sanders model of the social relationship, reinforced by the Triandis discussion, been explicitly at hand when the study was planned, this case might have been a better exhibit of its application. Even so, the case seems retrospectively (as in each of the others cited by the authors) to confirm the judgment that the sociologist, social psychologist, and anthropologist can promote developmental (behavioral) change by introduction of the concept of social relationship and its vocabularistic kinfolk.

Without requiring different data and without changes in meaning, the language of the report could be supplemented, or replaced, by insertions of or substitutions by the proposed concepts from sociology and psychology. The chances are that similar insertions or substitutions could be taken from the concepts of cultural anthropology, education (including extension education), and political science, but probably not those from economics or agricultural technology.

An exercise in the relevance of sociological and social psychological concepts was conducted by the compilation of four lists, not here reproduced: (1) sociological or sociopsychological concepts that appear in the report of the "C.D." study in India; (2) other "nonconcept" terms appearing in the excerpts; (3) sociological concepts treated either peripherally or centrally by Sanders; (4) social psychological concepts presented, with definitions (and illustrations) by Triandis.

Presentation of the lists would be space-consuming and tedious here—any interested game-player may replicate the exercise; but the results are of interest. (1) There were no concepts offered from the two disciplines which could not have been slipped into the report at various points (a) without altering the meanings, (b) but occasionally offering the possibility of a better explanation. (2) There is no essential sociological or social psychological material in the excerpts which could not have been presented within the framework of the social relationship and its component concepts.

PART V

SYNTHESIS: CONCEPTS
AND STRATEGIES

EDITORS' INTRODUCTION

In the Preface it was stated that an effort was made to build into the design of this volume a continuity ranging from concept identification in the various subjects considered, across a continuum of analysis and specificity, to a synthesis of strategy implications for decision-making about problems and approaches to agricultural modernization. Part V is especially focused on synthesizing major concepts developed in the previous parts and their implications for strategy in their applications to practice. There are four focal points of the synthesis: (1) social sciences, (2) agricultural sciences, (3) administrative policy, and (4) the résumé.

In Chapter 10 Charles Loomis attempts to provide a full range of social science concepts which may assist in furnishing specifics for the study of the strategy of change involved in the change agent–change target model used in the editors' introductions to each part. Both the elements of social structure and the processes involved in function and change are briefly specified and illustrated. Their relevance for the volume is evident and should require no further elaboration. Those in quest of means of conceptualizing agricultural development may, we hope, find assistance by reading Chapter 1, the editors' introductions which precede each part, and Chapter 10.

Although primarily a summarization of previous presentations, many of the contributions of the noted agricultural scientist A. H. Bunting, in Chapter 11, are important for understanding agricultural development and were not stressed by others. Thus he compares the rate of change achieved either with or without a specific change agent to an electric current or energy transfer and notes that the rate of agricultural development may vary proportionally with the change potential (for example, market demand) and vary inversely with the resistance manifest by social, economic, political, legal, and other hindrances. He makes a plea for quantifiable methods of analysis of change. He maintains that specific and rigorously defined concepts must be employed so that inputs by the change agent may be measured by study of results in the change agent–change target model (he does not use these terms but they are implied) through cost-benefit and systems analysis, etc. He stresses the greater need and importance of applied science over pure science. Noting that applied science may be placed lower in the "pecking order" of scientists, he mentions the fact that in agricultural research in Great Britain the ratio of financial support for applied to that for pure science is about nine to one. We take it that this applied research would be, in part at least, directed toward making more effective the link between knowledge centers and farmers, and between change agents and change targets as we have used these terms.

For the training of change agents and agricultural scientists who are to work in various regions and cultures where traditional agriculture prevails, he stresses the importance of the fundamentals and universals rather than empirical specifics of one locale, though he is careful to point out that agricultural technology is location-specific. Most important for scientists and change agents in agricultural development is that basic scientific orientation by which all dogma is questioned. Among transferable universals in which change agents and scientists should be grounded are those of cell molecular biology, the biology of agriculturally important organisms, and environmental sciences. These are related to local specialties through the comparative study, on a social ecological/economic basis, of actual systems of agriculture. From these foundation subjects the training of change agents may move to physiology, breeding, health and pathology, and economics, leading on to the final task of synthesis of system-building.

In Bunting's judgment science has not made the contribu-

tion to agricultural development in the poorer countries that
it could. He stresses both the lack of production of viable scientific knowledge in the knowledge centers and the ineffective
linkage of these centers to traditional agricultural societies.
These failures result in "bellies remaining unfilled and farmers poor." He notes that in most developing countries even the
available knowledge is ineffectively "packaged" for local use
and there is relatively too much attention to export crops. He,
like Kenneth Parsons, stresses the need for introducing labor-
intensive methods rather than those based upon the large-scale
farm machinery of advanced societies. He thus supports a
rather general consensus of the authors in this volume that agricultural development, at least in its early stages, should seek
to minimize the extent to which subsistence agriculturists are
uprooted to create and fill ghettos in the cities.

As would be expected, James Heaphey as a social scientist
presents his summary statement in terms that are easily articulated to the change agent–change target model. In fact, many
of the concepts employed in the previous editors' introductions
and in Chapter 10 are used. Thus, in discussing the need for
and the nature of decentralization he notes that "organizations
of power . . . link at one end a role such as that of an agricultural extension agent, and at the other end a role such as the
minister of agriculture." He makes a strong plea for training
programs designed to make change agents more effective, stressing the importance of including in this training what he calls
the development of "value integration" or what in Chapter 10
is described as consensus on the ends and norms of action.

Heaphey makes a strong plea for the importance of stability
and order in societies which are to move from the traditional
to the more differentiated and industrial configuration: "To
emphasize change without [these considerations of order] is less
than reasonable." No advocate of free-wheeling freedom for
freedom's sake, he states that "increased creativity requires increases in control." He reviews the nature of power employed
by change agents as discussed by Deutsch, Frey, Montgomery,
and others. All the considerations involved in the use of power
including decision-making and initiation of action come up for
consideration as Heaphey reviews the presentations of these
outstanding social scientists. Thus in relating the change agent

to target system Deutsch would stress the need for flexibility in control and call for a "self-transforming organizational system" with two-way interaction. Frey would also stress flexibility but through "feedback administration." Heaphey emphasizes the need for "order" whether derived from these or other models. His differentiation of development administration from public administration is not unlike that of John Montgomery but we as social scientists consider both as importantly related to power, decision-making, and initiation of action. We, like Frey and Deutsch, find bureaucracy not only in public administration. We, like Max Weber, find it everywhere that "rational" organizations operate. There seems to be agreement that there must be present in a society the "will" to develop, whether spoken of in these or other terms, before people can be lead or forced to become modern.

In Chapter 13 John Holt pulls together the salient themes and issues which emerged from previous chapters. All of these have relevance for our change agent–change target model. Most of them stress the fact that agricultural development when effectively achieved never comes from simplistic models and plans.

The strategy of optimum complementarity for instance, not only argues that the successful change agent should advance suitable "packages" of such items as improved seeds, appropriate fertilizers, tillage, etc. Optimum complementarity as a strategy may also require that the change agent either seek out areas for his work in which needed transportation, marketing, and other facilities are available or set about providing these and other requirements. With such a strategy as "optimum complementarity," as in complicated game theory or in cost benefit and highest profit analyses, there are many options and it is up to the change agent to make decisions which bring success according to some criterion such as the highest profit combination. Many factors, not to be detailed here, enter in such decisions: costs of inputs and their resulting contribution not only separately but especially in "optimum combination and complementarity." Sometimes the highest profit combination may be obtained by inaction on the part of the change agent but usually it is derived from complicated calculations and actions. Here we may mention a type of combination several authors warned against. Optimum complementarity seldom allows a change agent to play simultaneously the conflicting roles of teacher, policeman, tax collector, or other traditional bureaucrat often found in peasant societies.

The themes of multidisciplinary science and transcultural technology are predominant throughout the book. As just noted, Bunting stresses the crucial importance, in broad agricultural development in many societies and cultures, of highly generalized foundation knowledge. Multidisciplinary transcultural diffusion can best be achieved when change agents and scientists know universal principles derived from science. Of course, such science must be adapted to the localities and cultures in which it is to be used. To accomplish this adaption multidisciplinary applied science is recommended. The difficulties of change agents from one environment and culture attempting to understand another environment and culture and carry out programs for modernization can scarcely be overemphasized.

A general theme of systems analysis snythesis, and of conceptualization also prevails. This is not to say that the terms of reference in the "system" which are most important for the botanist are easily articulated to those of the soil scientist or are the same as those employed by the sociologist. In Chapter 10 Loomis attempts to indicate how change agents trained in sociology, anthropology, biology, and psychology can find common ground in one concept, that of status role. This recognition of common ground has grown up in social science as effort has been made to develop a "general" social theory. That a general systems theory which encompasses all knowledge which a change agent needs exists now would be maintained by no knowledgable person. Nevertheless, progress toward "general" theory is being made.

The issue of "multifocal–cross-cultural education" like "multidisciplinary science" pleads for nonsimplistic models. The many reasons for success and failure of change agents and their strategies as employed in directed change are reviewed by Holt in Chapter 13. There is remarkable agreement among the various contributors to the volume but complete agreement on strategy is too much to expect even if it were desirable. Thus, whereas the economist Kenneth Parsons puts his faith in "free choice [for actors in the target system including peasant farmers] with minimal control from government," his colleague Chandler Morse expresses grave doubts that the "new order" would allow development of peasant agriculture without help from both within the agricultural system and control and protection measures from outside.

Under the theme of administrative development the very important factors of social power and control come into the spotlight. When peasants have for generations learned that survival depends on avoiding bureaucracies which so far as they know have done little else than police and control for tax collection, how can development bureaucracies come to be trusted in rural areas? Holt summarizes the political scientists' and others' efforts to deal with this and other problems of administration. Here the linkages between citizen and government and between change agent and change target become crucial.

10. Social Sciences

CHARLES P. LOOMIS

The change agent–change target model, used as it is in the introductory parts of this book, provides a common conceptualization for the various chapters. Even though its use serves to stress the convergences among the chapters, the reader cannot but be aware of the great differences, both in emphases and in levels of abstraction, among the subjects treated by the various scientists. The most notable difference, perhaps, is the one which marks the doer from the theorizer. The former tells in straightforward terms how changes have been wrought or have been tried in specific situations under specific conditions. He usually makes no attempt to ponder the question of how applicable the same techniques would be to different problems in different locales. This latter is more in line with what the theorizer does. He typically examines dozens or hundreds of such changes or change attempts and out of the welter of detail notes similarities which allow him to generalize. He deduces principles which, if carefully and correctly drawn, permit the trial-and-error methods of the many doers to be refined to principles.

The two types of scientists, the applied and the theoretical, are reminiscent in a way of the two types of prophet identified by Max Weber. The exemplary prophet, of the religions either having no Gods or only imminent Gods, influence others by their deeds, somewhat as the "doers" exert an influence by the example of their works. The ethical prophets of the transcendental religions influence others by their "truths," by the principles they expound, somewhat as the theoreticians influence others by the abstracting they do from their multitudinous observations. Ethical prophets claim special qualities, not from science as in the case of the pure scientists, but from God which gives them charisma. Woods Thomas (Synthesis Response, Part II) notes the two types of change agents and the need for the works of both. The conceptualizations of the scientists and their generalizations which constitute our small body of scientific truth are needed as much as are the educational actions carried on by agricultural extension workers. Both are change agents.

Change Agent–Change Target Systems and the PAS Model

The distinction between the change agent and the change target systems is basic to analyzing the process of change. But it is not enough. Whether the analysis be applied to an in-process change, or whether it be applied to reports about changes as is the case in the chapters of this book, an analytical tool that provides the basic concepts for each system and the interrelation of both is needed. One such analytical tool has been provided by the PAS model—the processually articulated structural model.[1] Table 1 gives the essence of the PAS model. It will be noted that the model incorporates both social structure and process or change. Wilbert Moore metaphorized about the PAS model: It "made a notable advance by inviting in . . . the strangers [process and change] to put the house on rollers and permit it to move, while furnishing the interior with flexible and movable partitions and occasionally discordant inhabitants." [2] The PAS model will furnish the means of organization for the bulk of this chapter. It will be relied upon to perform the same function as it has elsewhere: to furnish a basis for possible comparisons among the presentations, to organize certain findings which are relevant for agricultural development from the Michigan State University Five-Nation Study,[3] and to

[1] One of the groups at the conference used the model in its work. That document is available as a report on cross-cultural transfer by Linwood Hodgdon. Mimeographed copies and the reports of other work groups may be had at cost by writing the senior editor.

[2] "Editorial Introduction" in Charles P. and Zona K. Loomis, *Modern Social Theories* (Princeton, N.J.: Van Nostrand, 1965), p. xxiii.

[3] The study was planned and/or carried through by Hideya Kumata, Charles Loomis, Robert Stewart, Frederick Waisanen, and associates. The study is based upon modified probability samples drawn from among persons aged 21 and over in Costa Rica, Mexico, Japan, Finland, and the United States. (All figures as given in the text refer to the countries

furnish an integration of parts written by a number of authors. One further step needs to be taken before putting the model to work here. We need to spell out the fundamentals of "system."

Systemic Analysis of Change

The core datum of sociology is human interaction. Interaction has been defined as "any event by which one party tangibly influences the overt actions or the states of minds of the other." [4] It is a reciprocal and interdependent activity, designated as having the quality of complementarity or double contingency.[5] The reciprocal activity or interaction that is repeated and persists comprises social relations. Social relations exist

---

in this order.) It was financed by the Carnegie Corporation, the Ford Foundation, the National Institutes of Health, and the Michigan Agricultural Experiment Station. The useable interviews numbered 1,040 from Costa Rica, 1,414 from Mexico (1,126 from places 2,500 and over and 288 from rural areas), 990 from Japan, 893 from Finland, and 1,528 from the United States.

Readers who need details concerning sampling procedures may procure them by writing the author of this chapter and paying the cost of xeroxing and mailing. Also, standard deviations and other measures will be furnished upon demand under the above conditions.

Writings based upon data from this study authored and/or coauthored by the present writer include the following: Charles P. Loomis, Zona K. Loomis, and Jeanne E. Gullahorn, *Linkages of Mexico and the United States*, Michigan Agricultural Experiment Station Research Bulletin 14 (East Lansing, 1966). In this bulletin residents of rural Michigan, rural and urban Mexico, the Spanish-speaking Chicanos of the U.S. Southwest, and the U.S. general public are compared on various dimensions. Jeanne E. Gullahorn and Charles P. Loomis, "A Comparison of Social Distance Attitudes in the United States and Mexico," *Studies in Comparative International Development*, vol. 11, no. 6 (1966). Charles P. Loomis, "In Praise of Conflict and Its Revolution," *American Sociological Review*, vol. 32, no. 6 (December, 1967). Charles P. Loomis, "In Defense of Integration," *Centennial Review*, vol. 14, no. 2 (Spring, 1970). In this publication U.S. blacks at varying levels of education are compared with categories mentioned in Loomis, Loomis, and Gullahorn.

[4] Pitirim A. Sorokin, *Society, Culture, and Personality* (New York: Harper and Brothers, 1947), p. 40.

[5] Talcott Parsons, "The Social System: A General Theory of Action," in *Toward a Unified Theory of Human Behavior*, Roy R. Ginker, ed. (New York: Basic Books, 1956), pp. 55–56. Here Talcott Parsons, who frequently uses the concept "double contingency," gives Robert R. Sears credit for originating it.

between or among incumbents of status roles such as those of mother-father and buyer-seller. Here we will be mostly concerned with social relations between the change agent and the change target considered as systems, and providing the basic aspects needed to explain the inner action within each system and the interelations of both systems. Those social systems between or among actors who are intimate, affective, and/or have a common goal are defined as bonds. The range of the phenomenon of interaction is wide. It may be as simple as the personal interaction of two actors of the same or different social systems up to the indirect, enormously interlinked interaction of subsystems of "society." The concept of the social system enables the analytical observer to move from a given subsystem to a larger system and back again, whether these systems be change agent, change target, or any other system. The analyst may be examining something as complicated as American society and its subsystems, or he may be limiting himself to the relationship of Dr. Jones and his patient Mr. Brown. Both are social systems which are interlinked.

An investigator can delineate a social system by observing the interaction among members; a more intense and frequent occurrence of specific types of interaction takes place among members than among nonmembers within a situation having both physical and symbolic aspects. This simplified means of delineating social systems requires accurate use, however. Actors from a given family whose members are scattered about in an industrial society may retain solidarity as a family but interact less frequently with family members than with nonfamily members on the job and in other places. Because there is a difference in the type of interaction and resulting bonds among the family and nonfamily members, the phrase "specific types of interaction" in the definition is important. Among the dimensions that determine the type of interaction are intensity, extensity, duration, direction (i.e., whether solidary or antagonistic), and nature and extent of interaction.[6]

Because an example seems the best means by which the abstractions of social change can be conveyed, I propose to deviate from the rather nonfocused use of the term "system" and treat

[6] Pitirim A. Sorokin, *Social and Cultural Dynamics* (Boston: Porter Sargent, 1957), p. 444.

social change by means of discussing the social relationships
studied in two rural farming villages in the Turrialba area in
Costa Rica not far from the Inter-American Institute of Agricultural Sciences, one of the eight Organizations of American
States (see Figures 1 and 2).

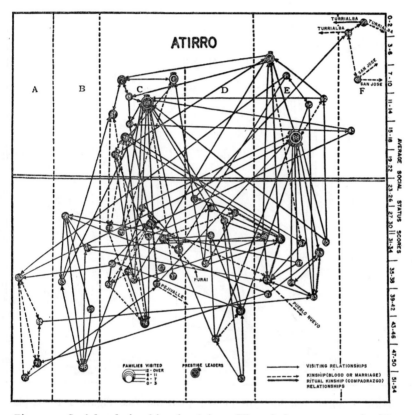

Figure 1. Social relationships in Atirro. The circles represent families.
The size of a circle is determined by the number of visits to the family.
Arrows on the lines which connect circles indicate the direction of the
visiting. Broken lines indicate visiting between kin; crosshatching, ritual
kinship, e.g., godfather. The families depicted by the larger circles hold
key positions in the network of visiting and are popular leaders. Those
depicted by circles with blocks above are prestige leaders. The family-
friendship groups are separated by vertical broken lines and identified
by letters. Social status is indicated by the position of the circles on the
vertical axis—high status families are at the top, as indicated by the
scale of average status scores at the right margin of the chart.

An Effort to Modernize Agriculture: A Case of Near Failure

That Costa Rica's education system is one of the most effective and advanced in Latin America is the frequent claim of both the Costa Ricans and others who write about this country.

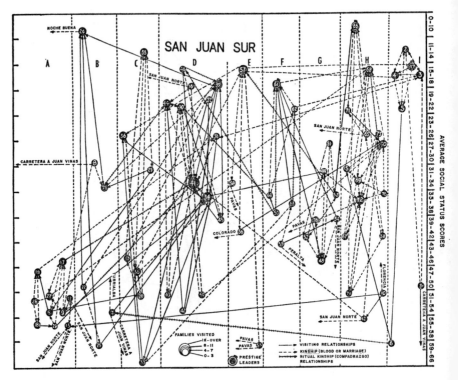

Figure 2. Social relationships in San Juan Sur (see Figure 1 for explanation)

"We have more teachers than soldiers" is a slogan not outmoded by war.[7] Less than 20 per cent of the general population and less than 30 per cent of the rural population is illiterate. In Latin America, only Argentina, Uruguay, and Chile have such

[7] John and Mavis Biesanz, *Costa Rican Life* (New York: Columbia University Press, 1946), p. 10. Also see Eduardo Arze Louriera and Roy A. Clifford, "Educational Systems," in Charles P. Loomis *et al.*, eds., *Turrialba: Social Systems and the Introduction of Change* (Glencoe, Ill.,: The Free Press, 1953), p. 172.

small percentages of illiterates. In 1965, 20 per cent of tax funds in Costa Rica went for education.[8]

Rural Teacher as Out-of-School Change Agent

The goal of the proposed program was the improvement of agriculture and health in the area. Although fairly broad in its aims, the ends and activities were reasonably specific. Two of them will be used here as illustrations: that of providing and using chlordane for the elimination of field ants which cause great damage to crops of the area, and that of building privies to cut down the incidence of hookworm. The Inter-American Institute of Agricultural Sciences at Turrialba enlisted the help of the national ministry of education and the teachers of the thirty-two villages surrounding Turrialba to carry out the program. At about the same time that this program was launched, early in the 1950's, a broadside effort was being made to vitalize the national agricultural service. So as not to interfere with that effort and to try out another approach, the decision was made to use change agents other than the extension workers. The presence of a school in every village of any size and the services of one or more teachers in each of the schools made the rural school teacher a natural choice. During the school vacation period special workshops and courses in simple agricultural and health procedures which would improve life in the area were conducted for these elementary teachers from the villages. The program was begun with considerable enthusiasm and it was reasonably well financed.

At the outset it would seem that the teachers as change agents had some valuable advantages. Most of the teachers were men, their level of knowledgability over that of the ordinary village dweller was recognized, and they were held in high esteem.[9] Careful studies based on probability samples of specific areas

[8] F. B. Waisanen and J. T. Durlak, *The Impact of Communication on Rural Development: An Investigation in Costa Rica,* A Final Report submitted to UNESCO/NS/2516/65, Article 1.4, December, 1967, Paris, France, p. 13.

[9] One report implies that in Costa Rica teachers are "natural" change agents who in an area comparable to that in Turrialba "by their high credibility, expertise, developmental concern and continued presence in the village, . . . are the principal change agents of this [San Isidro del General] and other rural areas of Costa Rica," *ibid.,* p. 17.

and likewise of the whole country demonstrate that scarcely any professionals, *if known personally to the informant,* are accorded so much confidence and considered to be as reliable in the advice or information they impart, as are teachers.[10] However, when teachers were "not known personally" they were accorded relatively low reliability and credibility as compared with priests and medical doctors who were likewise "not known personally" to the informant. Sociologists who specialize in the study of the professions have noted this phenomenon with respect to groups other than teachers. When incumbents of status roles are evaluated as inferior in reliability and accorded low confidence because of not being known personally, we may assume that the professionalization of the status role leaves something to be desired.

One is tempted to say that the teacher is more like the ethical prophet mentioned above. He tends to be evaluated for his personal magnetism and his skill in personal relations. The medical doctor does not necessarily have to exhibit these personal characteristics to rate a high evaluation, and in this way he is more like the exemplary prophet. Let us turn to a discussion of this and other aspects of status role as used in the PAS model (Table 1). We shall be watching for evidence which might throw light on reasons for the failure of the rural teachers as change agents.

[10] Waisanen and Durlak used the "self-anchoring" scale to study the reputed reliability and credibility of various professionals and mass media especially for change agents. After introducing the notion of the ten-step ladder the informant was told "Let's suppose at the *top* of the ladder stand all those things in which you have *complete confidence* and which you are *ready to believe* with little doubt. At the *bottom* of the ladder are those things which are unreliable, unbelievable, and in which you have no *confidence.* On which step would you place [the following; each presented with a separate discussion] 'School teachers whom you know personally,' 'School teachers whom you do not know personally,' 'Medical doctors whom you know personally,' 'Medical doctors you do not know personally'? [etc.]." Teachers "known personally" were more highly evaluated in reliability and credibility than medical doctors, priests, nurses, and midwives who were likewise "known personally." How important the condition "known personally" turns out to be is given in the text of the present volume. F. B. Waisanen and J. T. Durlak, *A Survey of Attitudes Related to Costa Rican Population Dynamics* (San José, Costa Rica: American International Association for Economic and Social Development, 1966), pp. 132–139.

Table 1. Elements, processes, and conditions of action of social systems: The processually articulated structural (PAS) model

Processes (elemental)	Social action categories *	Elements
(1) Cognitive mapping and validation	Knowing	Belief (knowledge)
§ (2) (a) Tension management and (b) communication of sentiment	Feeling	Sentiment
‡ (3) (a) Goal attaining activity and (b) concomitant "latent" activity as process	Achieving	End, goal, or objective
(4) Evaluation	Norming,* standardizing, patterning	Norm Status role (position)
(5) Status-role performance †	Dividing the functions	
§ (6) (a) Evaluation of actors and (b) allocation of status roles	Ranking	Rank
‡ (7) (a) Decision-making and (b) its initiation into action	Controlling	Power
(8) Application of sanctions	Sanctioning	Sanction
(9) Utilization of facilities	Facilitating	Facility

Comprehensive or master process

(1) Communication	(3) Systemic linkage	(5) Socialization
(2) Boundary maintenance	(4) Institutionalization	(6) Social control

Conditions of social action

(1) Territoriality	(2) Size	(3) Time

Source: Charles P. Loomis, *Social Systems: Essays on Their Persistence and Change* (Princeton, New Jersey: D. Van Nostrand, 1960), p. 8.
* These categories have by some writers been called processes. Thus Howard Becker writes that "it would be quite proper always to speak of human activities as essentially 'knowing-desiring-norming.'" H. Becker, "Current Sacred-Secular Theory and Its Development," in H. Becker and A. Boskoff, *Modern Sociological Theory in Continuity and Change* (New

Dividing the Functions

Status Role as a Unit Incorporating Both
Element and Process

The two-term entity, status role, contains the concept of a status, a cultural element implying position, and the concept of role or functional process. Both are important determinants of what is to be expected from an incumbent. Although in both industrialized and traditional societies the size of communities is correlated positively with the number and variety of status roles available to members, it is well to remember that a high level of living has never been attained by a society without a considerable division of labor; i.e., differentiation of status roles. "A nation can be wealthy only if few of its resources are required to produce food for subsistence," [11] and there are many status roles for its citizens. As traditional societies are modernized and the proliferation of status roles is extended, "economic development of various primitive and agrarian economies will produce greater similarity among world cultures." [12]

In modern cultures, societies are dynamic because high eval-

York: Dryden Press, 1957), p. 140. Elsewhere Becker calls these categories processes, p. 165. They are also used as activities, pp. 141 and 175.

† Status role, alone of the concepts, includes both element and process.

‡ The social action categories of achieving and controlling have primacy in the kind of pattern which may be designated as external, to use that term somewhat in the sense attributed to it by G. C. Homans and others. Likewise the elements of end and power and their respective articulating processes, goal-attaining activity as process and decision making and its initiation into action have primacy in the external pattern. This in the present author's conceptualization constitutes a more *Gesellschaft*-like aspect of the social system than the internal pattern.

§ The social action category of feeling has primacy in the kind of pattern which may be designated as internal, to use that term somewhat in the sense attributed to it by G. C. Homans and others. Likewise the elements of sentiment and its articulating process, the communication of sentiment, have primacy in the internal pattern. This in the present author's conceptualization constitutes a more *Gemeinschaft*-like aspect of the social system than the external pattern.

[11] E. O. Heady and J. Ackerman, "Farm Adjustment Problems and Their Importance to Sociologists," *Rural Sociology*, 24, no. 4 (December, 1959), 315ff.

[12] Wilbert E. Moore, "Creation of a Common Culture," *Confluence*, 4, no. 2, 232–233.

uation is placed upon the quest for knowledge. The scientists and philosophers, likened unto Max Weber's ethical prophets, see to it that change is omnipresent. No successful scientist can differ much from his fellow scientist in his fulfillment of his status role; and this holds whether he is in the "hard" sciences or in the social sciences, and quite irrespective of his other attributes such as nationality. In peasant cultures there is considerably more room for an individualized interpretation of the status role from society to society. In nontraditional societies the range of status roles available to an individual is wide, but there is not much variation within the playing of any given selection. A Norwegian physicist is going to be doing pretty much the same thing as an Italian or Japanese physicist. Whether we consider the scientist who is responsive to the world arena of science or the peasant of traditional society, culture through the status role determines in large measure what is expected locally. The following oversimplified description may serve to illustrate how culture in traditional society is important in the status role of the farmer or herdsman.

To draw an analogy . . . assume that a social scientist, upon returning from summer vacation, finds on his desk invitations to lecture before various women's clubs, to join an administrative committee of his university, and to run for political office in his community. These invitations draw him away from what he had been before—a research worker. In this situation the Yaqui Indian would accept every invitation but would also continue his research; each activity [or what a Yaqui farmer or herdsman actually does] would be well organized. . . . The Pueblo would probably refuse all invitations so as to remain a pure scientist [i.e., farmer], but even if he did accept just one he would never lose his research perspective. . . . The Navaho would not understand the invitations and would leave at the first opportunity for another vacation.[13]

Presumably the Yaquis, Pueblos, and Navahos manifest concensus on expectancy patterns within their separate societies. If a given Pueblo farmer would start behaving as a Navaho farmer in the above mentioned respects, he would appear as a

[13] Edward M. Bruner, "Differential Cultural Changes: Report on the Inter-University Summer Research Seminar, 1956," *Social Science Research Council Items,* vol. 11, no. 1 (March, 1957).

deviant and sanctions would be applied. In a sense this is what happened with our effort to use school teachers as change agents in the Turrialba area. Popular expectations of what could and should be done within the status role of teacher were violated. From the villagers' point of view this is what happened.

The teachers had to be concerned with the installation of privies. The villagers who respected the teacher's knowledge in the classroom and who were willing to be influenced by the teacher's opinions about nonschool matters, nevertheless found themselves uneasy when they talked about privies with the teacher. They felt it was not an easy subject to talk about with someone to whom you normally show a certain amount of deference. Privies were not properly a concern of teachers. The school inspectors felt very uncomfortable about the new work of the teachers. Ordinarily it was their task to supervise the teachers and to rate them on their classroom activity. They had no standards for rating them on this new task, and so there was ambiguity in both status roles, that of the supervisors and that of the supervised. From all points of importance, pressure was exerted within the village toward the end of pushing the teacher out of this new agricultural extension status role and back into the familiar teaching status role. Even though the teachers could ordinarily muster considerable influence, they could not resist this solidary and sustained pressure.

In sociological terms the filling of the new status roles by incumbents of other and different roles had never been legitimized. Although the process of legitimation is not elaborated here since it more clearly is a part of norming which is treated below, suffice it to say that by this process, change is made rightful in the eyes of the members of the change agent–change target system. Even after legitimation has been achieved the change agents must "deliver the goods"; that is, they must act to achieve their objectives. This will be discussed below under achieving.

The term "status role," whether or not it is used in connection with other elements and processes of the PAS model, represents such a basic sociological concept that it or its equivalent is used liberally by most of our authors. Sanders, for example, uses the terms "position" and "role." Mosher examines the feasibility of an "agricultural ambassador" in capital cities where the incumbent of this status role would promote the infrastructure required for a given country's agricultural development. Problems not unrelated to those met by the Costa Rican school teachers would almost certainly attend such a program. Such an ambassador who would function in a capital city with some of the same characteristics of a charismatic ethical prophet could readily be successful with a given change target. The continuation of the program, however, as he succeeded himself with different change targets, or as he might be succeeded by replacements, would require what Max Weber called the "routinization of charisma." Status roles of such charismatic figures must be legitimized in the target system and in the change system and a certain specificity of pattern must be developed and maintained.

Leagans advocates improving the efficiency of agricultural extension organizations. This, of course, requires that organizational skills and knowledge on the part of what some would call "organization men" be developed within the power structure of the extension system as a change agent system. Also he notes that extension personnel as change agents must become more effective as both teachers and scientists. They must learn how to evaluate their own work. The first of the three routes to modernization he specifies as "creating a macroenvironment . . . that makes possible and encourages the ultimate decision makers (farmers) to modify farming patterns." The other two include "building a body of useful technology" and "optimizing . . . extension education . . . [to] stimulate innovations" for the modernization of agriculture. This is no small order and may change the existing status roles of extension administrators and workers.

Parsons talks about espousing programs that would lead farmers and peasants who, like most humans, tend to engage in rational and efficient use of scarce resources, to become more rational and efficient. His program for agricultural development would remove restraints on rational action so that peasants and all others important for agriculture would become "economic men."

Deutsch warns against making the "entreprenurial type" central to agricultural development programs. He and other authors disapprove of advancing the most efficient actors and thereby increasing the relief loads in the cities and ghettos by displacement of the inefficient. This theme seems to have the general support of other authors who over and over emphasize the fact that their objectives are to further the free enterprise system. I find it inconsistent to condemn out of hand the principle of "let the devil take the hindmost" (presumably the most inefficient). Rather I would agree with Marx that to create capital, efficient capitalists of the "entreprenurial type" are needed. In the future, hardship will be a part of development and change just as it has been in the past. However, the strategy of change must be so planned that hardship is minimized. If the status role "displaced peasant or subsistence farmer" is a part of planned change, or results without planning, plans must be created whereby these displaced people find new or old status roles which fulfill their own personal needs and advance the society.

Frey, in focusing upon the intermediary status roles of those bureaucrats who are expected to link the seats of power in government to the peasant, deals with the rather general expectancy patterns which peasants in traditional society have for government officials. After a history of thousands of years of venal exploitation by a government with which the peasants had no connection except to pay excessive taxes, they view with deep suspicion these new government bureaucrats who try to win their confidence and who encourage them to let them know the strengths and weaknesses of agricultural programs. The expectation on the peasant's part that "all government men are bad men" does not die easily. Lele notes a similar difficulty in which regulatory and administrative officers attempt to use authoritarian power on the one hand, while with the other they seek to get a high level of popular support by various manipulations of symbols. There is an inconsistency, of course, in vesting in a single status role the regulatory function (such as the revenue officer or the police officer) and the consultant-teacher function (such as the extension worker). There is also an inconsistency in vesting in a single governmental bureau, even though under different status roles, the policeman and teacher function. The peasant cannot always be sure which status role he is encountering in the person of the bureau official. Lele suggests that a new status role of "committee member" be used in these anomolous cases, and that the committee member or members have built into their status roles the responsibility for representing the many-faceted government points of view as well as the peasants' point of view.

The term "status role" or its equivalent is used extensively by Triandis. Its connotation in the hands of a psychologist, however, is quite different from that which we have so far encountered. It seems appropriate here to discuss briefly the problems of conceptualization for social scientists who contribute to volumes such as this one. Any concept—status role, for example —represents a distillation of a number of interrelated thoughts. It says something to another scientist only if it stands to both of them for the same interrelated thoughts. It sometimes happens that terms are used which convey somewhat different meanings to different readers. A. H. Bunting mentions our need to put everyday language into some "functional mix" with technical talk; "frames of reference" get in the way of understanding. To a degree, student insistence upon relevance is aimed at this same problem. I cannot solve this problem, but I should like to try to give it focus by using status role as employed in the PAS model to relate the various social sciences to one another in one aspect of each.

In this discussion I maintain that the field of psychology specializes in the system known as the personality system, that the fields of sociology and political science specialize in the phenomena studied through the use of the concept of the social system, and that the cultural anthropologist specializes in that field conceptualized in the cultural system. Each field has its own conceptual scheme, and not all of the concepts used in explanation and prediction in one specialty are applicable in another. This, of course, may seem obvious, but the frequency with which psychologists, for instance, describe social systems using psychological concepts often surprises sociologists. This problem was raised not by a sociologist or a psychologist or an anthropologist in this volume but rather by an economist. Chandler Morse makes a plea, which enconomists understand, for noting the difference between what some call welfare economics and the classical economics which some of us learned while studying John Stuart Mill and Alfred Marshall. In his discussion of Kenneth Parsons' chapter, his use of the distinction between "will to economize" and "will to develop" as comparable terms, touches on the problem I wish to stress now. "Moreover the notion of a 'will' to develop, which 'must somehow be a national will' seems to imply the existence of a 'group mind' to apply to a psychological concept at the social level." The problem here becomes that of how power (Table 1, Item 7) may result in decision-making and action for both individuals and pluralities. How to relate needs and value orientation of individuals to those of pluralities so that needs and values of both

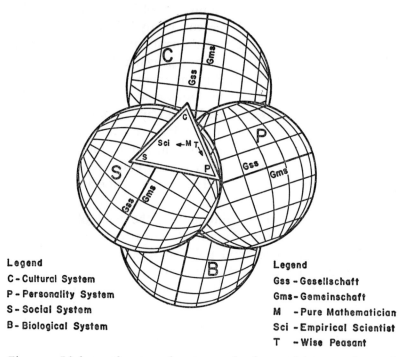

Legend
C - Cultural System
P - Personality System
S - Social System
B - Biological System

Legend
Gss - Gesellschaft
Gms - Gemeinschaft
M - Pure Mathematician
Sci - Empirical Scientist
T - Wise Peasant

Figure 3. Linkage of systems by status roles in cognitive mapping and validation—a tentative model

individuals and plurality are maximized has perplexed the greatest of thinkers. However, a goodly number of social psychologists believe that in articulating the relationships between the social system, the personality system, and the cultural system the one common term used by all is that of status role.

In Figure 3, I attempt to indicate how the three systems may be interrelated with the status role forming the interlinking triangle using the terms which Ferdinand Toennies developed along the line coming at least in part out of status and contract as used by Sir Henry Maine. I have indicated how the three systems may be divided into these two forms of orientation. For another purpose, I attempted to show how the status role of the pure mathematician might be more influenced by the personality system than that of the empirical scientist. "T" on the chart indicates a tentative location of the status role of the traditional men of knowledge in a peasant village. As will be noted, he is heavily influenced by social and cultural factors which place him in the status of *Gemeinschaft*-like value orientation. The empirical scientist, of course, falls in the contractual or *Gesellschaft*-like orientation and would, in Toennies' thinking be governed by the societal components of rationality derived from *Gesellschaft* or contractual relations.

The personality system is of course influenced by "energy" from the biological system. Beliefs, values, and expressive symbols contribute to the "actor" in role and these come from the cultural system. The status role of the social system influences this "actor" in various ways determining in part what is expected from him.

The considerations which Triandis treated as "status role" are chiefly those of the cognitive and affective aspects of a given individual's personality. Using Festinger's concepts of "cognitive dissonance," and following Osgood and others interested in the semantic differential as these relate to the personality system, he develops part of his theory of change. In oversimplified terms we may summarize by saying that a change agent interested in improving the health of a patient who fears cancer but enjoys smoking may create cognitive dissonance by teaching this patient that smoking produces cancer, which would be a step toward the desired change. In these examples, as well as the literature dealing with McClelland's "achievement motivation" and with his attempts to change fatalistic thinking into a more active orientation, the change target is always an individual personality. The circumstance leads sometimes to interpretations which are very different from those emerging from group-focused thinking. For example, Triandis maintains that "in cultures . . . in Western societies the needs of the parents 'have introduced internal controls (guilt) into the child's personality.' " He writes, "The custom of chaperoning [practiced in various cultures], with strong taboos prohibiting brothers and sisters to find themselves together unchaperoned, . . . seems to an American silly, wasteful, time-consuming, old-fashioned . . . but he does not realize that he may be paying a price in excessive sexual maladjustment for not having this custom." This line of thinking brings me back to the earlier reference to cultures with transcendental gods with their ethical prophets. The existence of a transcendental god provides a built-in support for father figures who may help inculcate the superego. Probably the actors in such cultures have more internalized guilt than others; Max Weber might have observed that the honesty of the Puritan Boston and Quaker Philadelphia bankers was based upon the guilt they might feel if they filched funds. I believe it is important that this "social psychological consideration" be given attention in developing status roles of change agents in developing societies. Business and trading might not be very profitable if it were necessary in every business transaction to have the equivalent of a chaperone stand by. One of Max Weber's important theses, often ignored, is that the Protestants, especially the Calvinists, Methodists, Baptists, and Pietists, internalized norms of brotherhood and honesty which were supposed to be applicable to all mankind, thus being effective far beyond the family and religious sect, and in this way different from those of the Jews, Parsees, Jains, and similar groups.

Ranking

Rank as an Element

Rank as used here is equivalent to "standing" and always has reference to a specific act, or system, or subsystem. Rank thus represents the value an actor has for a system in which the rank is accorded. The position of the spheres ranging from bottom to top of Figures 1 and 2 is determined by the ranking the family received when judges who were knowledgeables living in the villages evaluated the family in terms of their "importance for the community." It is not difficult to perceive that in the large estate community Atirro (Figure 1) a type of "proletariat" or work group holds the positions at the bottom. Above this "proletariat" are the intermediary supervisors and professionals who form a sort of "middle class," and then above them are the owners of the hacienda, the commissary, and the coffee mill noted in the upper right side of Figure 1. The location of the horizontal line would show on any such chart at what point interaction decreases up and down the social class structure. If the figure represented a social system in which a very few members formed an "upper crust" who interacted almost exclusively with each other, and everyone else in the social system formed the *hoi polloi* among whom there was no significant difference in rank, the horizontal line would be very close to the top of the figure. The ranking system of Atirro shown in Figure 1 is a modified version of such a pattern. Statistical procedures determine the location of the line which figuratively demarks the lower from the upper classes. By such a device one can "see" three classes in Figure 1.

The stratification structure in the family-sized farming community of San Juan Sur (Figure 2) is far less obvious. In fact, there is no point at which interaction from the bottom to the top is significantly less than that which prevails among the members at the top and among the members at the bottom. Although differential ranking is assigned to the members of this social system, the rate and frequency of interaction is apparently not a function of ranking. Figure 2 portrays a much more unitary social system than does Figure 1. It is not possible from charts such as Figure 2 to find points at which interaction was "class or caste structured" as was possible in Figure 1. In this respect description of the stratification structure in the relationships of the family-sized farming community presented in Figure 2 is not so simple as that in Figure 1.

It should be obvious that such ranking patterns in target systems are of great importance in plans made by change agents. They should be taken into account in both tactics and strategy as developed by change agents interested in modernizing agriculture. Thus in the large estate community of Atirro it would be quite easy for the administrator to change the facilities and processes of some agricultural operations such as pruning the coffee trees. All he would have to do would be to provide the facilities and order the *jornaleros* through their supervisor to carry out the required instruction and to initiate the change.

At most, simple demonstrations would be needed. It would be quite a different matter to accomplish this objective in the family-sized farming community, the relationships of which are depicted in Figure 2. This will be discussed further under the concept of controlling and boundary maintenance.

Evaluation of Actors and Allocation of Status Roles as Process

In the communities depicted in Figures 1 and 2, rank is accorded as is usual in Costa Rica. Rank comes from various qualities such as (1) authority and power, the legitimized and non-legitimized ability to influence others, (2) kinship relations, (3) personal attributes and achievements such as age, sex, beauty, skill, and ability, and (4) property holdings and wealth. These latter may function as symbols of social status and/or means of initiating action by which authority or power over others is established. However, as noted in Chapter 1, rank does not necessarily derive alone from wealth and power. Each of the judges here who ranked the families in Figures 1 and 2 gave reasons for their placements. Often they said the man whom they had placed high was *"muy honorado,"* very honorable. In a way this could be thought of as comparable to the Brahmin in India who might be without wealth and power and yet have high prestige. The owner of the hacienda Atirro derives his social rank mostly from the first and last criteria mentioned above. The principal leader in San Juan Sur (number 66, Figure 2) derives his social rank mostly from the third criterion. He is a very clever and effective speaker and although possessing only two years of education has many human relations skills.

Controlling

Power as an Element

Power as defined here is the capacity to control others. It has many components which may be classified as authoritative and nonauthoritative control. Authority is the right to control as determined and legitimized by the members of the social system and built into status roles as discussed above. Unlegitimized coercion and voluntary influence are nonauthoritative. In Figures 1 and 2, two somewhat different manifestations of the power structure in the villages may be noted. On the one hand there are so-called "grass-roots" or popular leaders with many visiting relationships and on the other, there are leaders called "prestige leaders" who are those individuals who would be chosen to make representations for the village to the governor of the state. Power as derived from social relationships described on the charts comes largely from clique groups or what some call congeniality groupings. These groupings are delineated by the vertical lines on the charts and are determined by the answers of all informants to the question, "In case of a death in the family, whom would you notify first?" The rank of the cliques descends from right to left on the charts. In each of the communities these systems of relationships are important for change agents who may wish to reach all members of a given clique through one or more leaders. As will be noted on the charts, most of the so-called prestige leaders are in the upper classes in the large estate communities and occupy higher positions of rank in both communities than most other members. It is obvious that grass-roots or congeniality leaders as well as the prestige leaders have power. Of course, the large estate community is so organized that the most powerful individual is the owner and usually he has made the administrator the second most important person. The owners of haciendas in the area do not all live on the haciendas. Some spend considerable time abroad and/or in San José. It is of interest to those change agents advancing improved agricultural practices and stocks that very often the ordinary worker manifests more antagonism toward the manager than toward the owner who is generally called the *patron*. Not infrequently the *patron* and the administrator play a sort of game by which the *patron* retains both his power and prestige and even esteem. Generally the manager cannot be both loved and in control. When he takes his position as administrator he may well know or actually even be informed that he will be "hated." Workers frequently told our interviewers that some of the things about which they were most bitter and complained most would be corrected if only the *patron* knew about them. Often a large fiesta takes place when the *patron* who has been away visits the hacienda. At this time the *patron* plays the game of overriding the administrator and granting certain small favors in order to retain prestige and esteem and even quite often appears to be affectionate.

Decision-Making and Its Initiation of Action as Process

Since charts such as Figure 1 and Figure 2 were available for the other thirty villages in the municipality of Turrialba, all of which are in the sphere of influence of the Inter-American Institute of Agricultural Sciences, some rather interesting consequences developed. As a sort of experiment the director of the Institute invited all of the prestige and clique or popular leaders to a demonstration at which chlordane was used to eliminate ants which infest the area and greatly reduce crop production. The next day after the demonstration hundreds of villagers appeared at the Institute requesting the chlordane. Another example of the power of influence and informal leadership occurred when interviewing began in the village represented by Figure 2. Villagers were hesitant to provide the data which the interviewers requested. Some refused to be interviewed. We noted that Maximino Torres, number 66, at the top of the clique H, left in a hurry on foot to walk five miles to the trade center in Turrialba. We learned later that he went directly to the *Jefe Politico,* the most powerful representative of the government in the municipality, to find out what we were doing. Fortunately, we had previously visited the *Jefe Politico* and explained the purpose of the study and its connection with the Institute. After Maximino Torres returned to the village, in a matter of hours, people young and old, men and women began coming to the interviewers from all parts of the village inviting them to come and interview them. Often refreshments were served.

Two years after the interviewing I had occasion to walk into the village again which was the only way to get there during the rainy season. I was surprised to find a substantial new concrete bridge across the small river which had been previously covered by a flimsy narrow bridge. Upon inquiry I found another manifestation of how decisions are made and initiated into action in the village. On her way home from school during the rainy season a small girl fell in this river and was drowned. This created a crisis situation in the village. All that could walk gathered and marched behind Maximino Torres the five miles through the mud to the office of *Jefe Politico* where they demanded a bridge which was installed as soon as the dry season came and materials could be hauled in.

Those familiar with the village culture of Latin America will recognize that in the family-sized farming villages this type of action is very common. The informal leaders usually rise to prominence both because of personal characteristics and other qualities such as wealth and education. In the case of Maximino Torres he does not own the largest farm in the community and his education is little more than two years. However, no one could talk with him long without noting that he had true qualities of leadership including some of that quality mentioned above in connection with ethical prophets, namely, charisma. When Maximino delivers an oration, his command of the language is superb. Certainly he is influential and nonauthoritarian. His power does not derive from formal office. Such informal leadership crops up in most social systems, and no doubt it exists on the large estate as well as in the community of small, family-owned farms. But its manifestation in the hacienda community is quite different. In a power-centered situation such as exists on the hacienda, where the power is concentrated in the hands of the owner, the manager, and the various supervisors, it would be unthinkable that nonformal power such as that held by Maximino Torres could be articulated toward community endeavors such as bridge-building. In neither type of community was the teacher mentioned as a prestige leader unless he or she was a member of a village farm family. Although the local priest has high prestige and, of course, considerable power, he likewise is not mentioned as a prestige leader. In the networks of relations designated on Figures 1 and 2, neither the teacher nor the priest appears as prominent in either the visiting patterns among the villagers or among those who would be chosen to represent the village before the governor, namely the prestige leaders.

Of course, the effort of the Institute to use the teacher as a change agent met with very different results in villages with family-sized farming units and in hacienda villages. In point of fact the project was designed more for the family-sized villages. On the large estates many changes such as disposal of refuse, for which privies were built on family-sized farms, could be handled as an expenditure of the hacienda. On large estates how ants are to be killed and defecation disposed of can be determined by the *patron,* the administrator, and other similar power figures. Likewise if these actors were to oppose the changes advocated by the teacher as change agent, the teacher's position would be in jeopardy.

The editors' introductions have carried much of the thinking of the authors on the subject of power, decision-making, and their application to action. Parsons' design for establishing enough order and an optimum-type infrastructure in order to permit and motivate peasants and others to behave rationally has been reviewed. Here it may be noted that Chandler Morse reacts to this in what I would call a sociological interpretation of power, stating that the order which Parsons wants for the operation of free choice and markets may not come without a stage characterized by disorder and violence.

Deutsch's ideal, the "self-transforming organizational system" is remarked in the editors' introduction as are his other models for viewing power in systems. He challenges the statement "that the government that governs best governs least." Frey demonstrates how both "amount" and "concentration" of power is important and his treatment of power focuses upon its articulation through relating the seats of government to the people, including agriculturists. He outlines the various organizational components that provide the systemic linkage between rulers and ruled and the forms they have taken at various stages of development. The possibility of the power figures "in between" rulers and ruled who may side either with local power in revolt or with the rulers in exploitation of the localities is well presented as is his entire analysis of power. I note that the various ways of creating trustworthy linking systems such as "civil service" training do not include using eunuchs, reported by Louis Coser as being prevalent in early Moslem nations.[14] Eunuchs with no family, community, and friendship ties proved to be the most loyal intermediaries for Moslem rulers.

We may close this section on power and its articulation with

[14] Louis A. Coser, "Political Functions of Eunuchism," *American Sociological Review,* 29, no. 6 (December, 1964), 880–885.

reference to Sanders' omission of the concept. In his parsimonious use of concepts he employs only position, role, norm, and value. He justifies his omission of power by arguing that an actor has power only to the extent that the individual or the office is highly evaluated by the group. I am sure that he would agree that the hijacker on a passenger plane has power but I doubt that he would claim that this power is the result of positive evaluation by those over whom he holds it. It seems to me best to include power, a concept used by most of the authors, somewhat as discussed above. Power in the form of authority exists because of positive evaluation. However, mobsters who through use of firearms and other facilities take over government and exercise great power are not generally so evaluated. Only after the new personnel and order is "legitimized" or evaluated as right does it become authoritative and have positive value. This brings us to the concepts of norm and evaluation.

Norming, Standardizing, Patterning

Norm as an Element

The rules which prescribe what is acceptable or unacceptable are the norms of the social system (Item 4, Table 1). Among the most important norms for the change agent to understand are those by which the three most generalized values of society are allocated: power, wealth, and prestige and/or esteem. Force is often used to obtain wealth and power but prestige and/or esteem or general ranking accorded by an actor's fellows and peers is less often so achieved. Max Weber noted that the ethical prophet might, because of his charisma, be highly evaluated by immediate followers but if he were to establish an organization meant to bridge generations and fit himself and followers into status roles, the charisma must be routinized. The high evaluation formerly accorded the personal qualities of the individual must be transferred to qualifications attached to position, the elemental component of the status role. This is not the place to discuss in detail the norms for legitimizing the possession of power, wealth, prestige, and other values but we may note that in all societies such norms do exist. For the legitimizing of power of public officials in democratic societies, the nomination and election norms or laws including rules on voting are crucial.

Of course, incumbency in other status roles such as those of medical doctor and teacher involves various certification procedures.

Norms for Change Agents

In Chapter 3, Deutsch dramatized the restraints peasants in traditional societies place on innovative behavior. He noted that "in traditional cultures that have moved up to the very limit of subsistence, further innovations promise very modest and marginal rewards, but swift and terrible risks which are intensely salient. To this degree, a traditional agriculture that fills up its Malthusian process to the limits of subsistence becomes an engine for teaching its people to fear and distrust innovations. It becomes a Pavlovian conditioning mechanism against innovation." Thus, from experience, members of traditional society learn to fear innovators who, unless they have charisma, will be negatively sanctioned as deviants. As Durkheim observed, the traditional society is anchored in stable consensus which he called "mechanical solidarity" supported by repressive norms.

George Foster, an anthropologist, presents a somewhat different explanation for the conservative nature of traditional society.[15] He maintains that the members of traditional society explain achieving in economic activities in accordance with "pure conflict" conditions of the zero-sum type. This form of explanation is more generally used for political activities by conflict theorists (Karl Marx, Max Weber, and others). According to Foster, norms for activity in peasant and traditional societies restrict individuals from achievement because, as in the zero-sum-type game, the total that all actors considered together can achieve is given. Under these circumstances any achiever who adds to his original portion has done so in the view of himself and others only at the expense of taking it away from other actors. (This basic way of viewing the world would be more correctly treated below under "knowing," but here we are interested in the norms which result from this type of cognitive mapping.) In societies in which it is believed that all

[15] George M. Foster, "Peasant Society and Image of Limited Good," *American Anthropologist*, 67 (April, 1965), 293–315, and 68 (Fall, 1966), 210–214. See also *Human Organization* (Winter, 1970), 303–323.

may gain from individual attainment of wealth, the norms or rules of the game do not prohibit competitive striving as much as in traditional societies. This is true whether acquisition of wealth is considered as a zero-sum game or not.

In the case of the effort to make teachers into change agents in the Turrialba area, the inspectors' norms did not lead them to approve the extra income the teachers might earn by engaging in the project. Likewise villagers were opposed if not indignant when teachers advised them on agricultural and sanitation matters. It was as if they might say: "Let them stick to doing what they know something about. Let them teach our children as best they can, but don't let them try to teach me what to do."

What is identified as norm and evaluation in the PAS model receives heavy emphasis at the hands of several authors of this volume. Parsons, for example, considers that as traditional societies become modern the old norms (called *status* by Sir Henry Maine) must yield to those more suited to modernization. Those new norms (called *contract* by Sir Henry Maine) are Parsons' crucial "rules of the game." Once *contract* becomes the model for action, *Gesellschaft* (or societal norms) replaces *Gemeinschaft* (or community norms). Rational action becomes prevalent and the model of the economic man begins to become a viable concept. Then as Parsons notes, "The term rationality is . . . a 'personification' of acts of choice—in a 'free-choice' system. Honoring 'free choice' . . . this is the shift 'from status to contact.' " For Parsons it is up to the change agents who want to modernize agriculture to accomplish those things which release the peasant and all others from restraints so that they have freedom of choice in buying and selling in almost all realms. "In modern agriculture such a farmer becomes, in varying degrees, the proprietor of a firm in which investment, business, and managerial decisions become of strategic importance." Nothing could be farther removed from that of the laborer and worker on the traditional manor of the Middle Ages or on the modern collective farms under communism. Triandis stresses that the change agent must know the norms of the members of the target system, so that in selecting a given innovation for dissemination, "the consciousness of the innovation, both real and as perceived by the farmer" is considered. Of his three main broad categories of "activities and influences," Mosher makes the norm component central. "For agri-climate influences and 'rules of the game' within which both farming and all agri-support activities must operate [including such things as] social values and forms of social organization that flow from the central culture of the country . . . or region [and of course including such things as] legislation, . . . ownership, . . . tenancy, . . . taxation [etc.]" are of crucial importance.

Evaluation as a Process

The process through which positive and negative priorities or values are assigned to concepts, objects, actors, or collectivities, or to events and activities, either past, present, or future is identified as evaluation in the PAS model. If the values of individuals and pluralities result from the process of evaluation defined in this manner, all of the nine elements in Table 1 can, under certain conditions, be values; likewise the social action categories can also be thought of as values. Activities such as birth control or family planning, mentioned by several authors, especially Cummings, can be evaluated.

In the Michigan State University Five-Nation Study, informants from probability samples drawn from among those twenty-one years of age and older in Costa Rica, Mexico, Japan, Finland, and the United States were questioned to ascertain their evaluations of birth control as an activity.[16] It was considered wrong for married couples in Costa Rica, rural Mexico, urban Mexico, Japan, Finland, and the United States respectively by the following percentages of informants: 55.2, 49.1, 43.4, 24.5, 11.7, and 23.9. In few nations is population increasing so rapidly as in Costa Rica and Mexico, but obviously these figures indicate that birth control is evaluated much more negatively there than in the United States, Japan, and Finland. Obvious also

---

[16] See Note 3 above; see also Loomis, Loomis, and Gullahorn. The manner in which questions are stated is, of course, important in such research. Our birth control question was stated as follows: "Family planning or birth control has been discussed by many people. What is your feeling about a married couple practicing birth control? If you had to decide which one of these statements best expresses your point of view: It is always right; It is usually right; It is usually wrong; It is always wrong." Of course, provision was made for, No answer, Don't know, etc. Readers who want copies of the questionnaire used may have it under the same provisions as indicated in Note 3.

is the importance of this evaluation of change agents who are attempting to reduce the birth rate. If the teachers who were attempting to change health and agricultural practices in the Turrialba area of Costa Rica had attempted to advance birth control, which they did not, disapproval of their activities would have been greater than it was.

Evaluation and Legitimation of Change and Change Agents

Elsewhere I have attempted to specify the processes which are crucial for the change agent as he attempts to bring about directed change.[17] Here only the crucial part evaluation plays will be mentioned. The processes of initiation, legitimation, and execution are important to directed change but it is the process of legitimation which is most akin to evaluation. Legitimation is the process whereby the proposed change is made "rightful" to the target system. Prestigeful sponsors, rituals, prayers, and other legitimizing procedures are used in this aspect of the strategy of change. Of course, those actors with legitimizing authority vary from culture to culture. In cultures such as that of the United States they may be prestigeful personalities from the scientific, literary, sports, entertainment, and military worlds and from the judiciary and religion. For some programs in India, Brahmins or other priests may be helpful. In Russia, outstanding Communist party members may be important.

In this connection it is pertinent to report a case of belated legitimation which I had occasion to observe as I attended a workshop for agricultural workers held at the Inter-American Institute of Agricultural Sciences in Costa Rica. Monsignor L. G. Ligutti, the executive director of the National Catholic Rural Life Conference, in his formal address to the extension agents and other administrative personnel from all parts of Latin America, advised them to call upon local Catholic priests to help with important agricultural and health programs. His words came too late to save the efforts of the teachers in the Turrialba experiment discussed above, but having seen how this effective Catholic leader works, I believe that if he had advised the village teachers of the area to have the local priests support the program, and if he had himself helped with the

[17] Charles P. Loomis and J. Allan Beegle, *Rural Sociology: The Strategy of Change* (Englewood Cliffs, N.J.: Prentice-Hall, 1957), p. 19.

legitimation in the local Catholic system, the program would have succeeded. He told the extension agents from the Latin American countries that if in any case a priest refused to help, to let him know and he would see that the reluctant priest would change his mind. He implied that the priest would hear from him and/or Rome.

Achieving

End, Goal, or Objective as an Element

The end, goal, or objective is the change (or in some cases the retention of the status quo) that members of a social system expect to accomplish through appropriate interaction. In Marxist thought, interests or what we here call ends, are of central importance, but norms and evaluation, and beliefs and sentiments (and the relevant articulating processes) are considered to be epiphenomena. It is, of course, true that in acts actually executed or experienced, there is a merging of ends, norms, beliefs, and sentiments. Students of change and change agents however, can achieve a precision of thought not otherwise possible if these various elements are separated for analytical purposes. There is a degree of actual separation in real life too as societies become increasingly differentiated. For example, those agencies responsible for cognitive, cathectic, and moral activities such as schools, cultural and recreational centers, law courts, and churches are differentiated.

One of the problems common to areas in the process of development is that of rising but unfulfillable expectations. In a probability sample drawn from Costa Rica, 1,500 informants twenty years of age or older were asked: "How many years of school would you like your son(s) to complete?" (or: "If you had sons of school age . . . ?"). The percentages who want university, high school, and completion of elementary schooling for their sons were as follows: 43.6, 23.3, and 20.2. Informants were then asked, "Do you consider this to be possible?" Percentages of those answering yes, no, don't know, or giving no information were respectively as follows: 65.1, 23.6, 10.1, and 1.1.[18] Of course, in Costa Rica and elsewhere outside of the communist world, educational achievement of children is

[18] F. B. Waisanen and J. T. Durlak, *A Survey of Attitudes*, pp. 166–167.

highly related to the income of parents. About the same proportion of informants want university training for their children as have family incomes of less than $1,000 per year. With only about 3 per cent of the population having family incomes of $4,000 and above there seems to be plenty of evidence here of rising unfulfillable aspirations.

In an effort to discover how people regard their conditions of life in relation to where they want to be, the so-called "self-anchoring" scale was used.[19] Informants in our Five-Nation Study were told: "Now here is a picture of a ladder. Suppose we say that at the *top* of the ladder stands a person who is living under the best possible conditions of life, and at the *bottom* stands a person who is living under the worst possible conditions of life. On what step would you say you are at present?" The percentages of informants who placed themselves on the bottom three steps of the ten-step ladder for the general public of Costa Rica, urban Mexico, rural Mexico, Japan, Finland, and the United States were respectively as follows: 20.2, 22.7, 26.4, 9.0, 6.1, and 2.6. Looked at another way, the average step placement on the ladder for Costa Rica, Mexico, Japan, Finland, and the United States was respectively as follows: 4.6, 4.4, 4.7, 5.5, and 6.8.

The pressures of rising expectations in Mexico, Japan, and Costa Rica may be noted from the manner in which the same informants responded when asked to place themselves on this hypothetical ladder as they thought they would stand five years hence. The average step placement on the ladder respectively as above was: 6.0, 6.1, 6.0, 6.3, and 7.8. Only about half as many of the Costa Ricans, Mexicans, and Japanese placed themselves on the bottom three rungs as they anticipated their situation five years from then. For the U.S. Americans and Finns on the three bottom steps, the change, although in the same direction, was negligible in absolute numbers. Obviously, relatively large proportions of Costa Ricans and Mexicans are not satisfied with life as it is. The belief that people in traditional societies are "happily poor" is nonsense. The programs which the change agents initiate, legitimize, and execute must be those which of-

[19] For a discussion of the scale see F. P. Kilpatrick and Hadley Cantril, *Self-Anchoring Scaling: A Measure of Individuals' Unique Reality Worlds* (Washington, D.C.: The Brookings Institution, 1960).

fer improved conditions of life for the members of the change target system. Apparently the rural people in the thirty-two villages in the Turrialba area were not convinced that the agricultural and health programs advanced by the village teachers would make a substantially better life for them.

Few of our authors failed to discuss ends, objectives, and interests, but Mosher and Parsons present what might be the primary goals for development. Parsons notes that "the primary objective of agricultural development policy is the achievement of a system of agricultural economy which has the capacity of carrying the burdens of development." Counterposed to this target are "the traditional systems of agriculture, by whatever name [which] lack the capacity for growth." Mosher's eight "elements" of agricultural development include the goals to be achieved by the change agent system as linked to the target system; that is, upgrading the quality of land, developing an optimum of farm supplies correctly distributed in time and space, increasing agricultural growth per capita, bringing into being and strengthening a progressive rural structure, and providing adequate research and extension. The goal for Cummings is production of useable knowledge developed for specific regions. The importance of ends comes out forcefully in Leagans' distinction between what ought to be and what is. Ends must become motivating forces within the change targets so that the actors there more effectively than at the present satisfy their physiological, social, and moral needs, thus activating self-fulfillment.

Goal Attaining and Concomitant "Latent" Activity as Process

There is frequent reference in the preceding chapters to what is called rational action. Usually rational action is manifest and not latent. It is manifest because its relation to the goal is both recognized and intended by the actor. Of a different order is action which produces results which are either not intended by the actor or come about without his knowing it. As an example of manifest activity, the Inter-American Institute of Agricultural Sciences gave a demonstration on the use of chlordane in the control of ants to the leaders of the thirty-two villages in their immediate sphere of influence. The calculated objective was to induce the villagers to wish to adopt the use of chlordane for ant control. The objective was realized very much as anticipated. If the villagers had, as the result of the demonstration, pronounced the director of the Institute a God or even a prophet, it would have been latent activity because the result would not have been intended. Very often the unintended results do strengthen the target system by providing it integration. An example is the rain dance of the Hopi Indians which unifies the society even though it does not bring rain.

A latent result of various types of directed change discussed by several authors is the flight of peasants to the ghettos of the cities as modernization and development shuffles people about and relocates them. Cummings notes that "innovation is most likely to begin with the best and most progressive farmers." Students of diffusion have shown that early adopters of improved practices in agriculture gain more than late adopters. The early increases in yield usually take place while the product is relatively scarce and prices are consequently high. Later adopters contribute to a plentiful supply and consequently market their wares when prices are not at a peak. Such events are characteristic of competition in the free enterprise system. Those who are able and lucky dispossess others. Often such results are latent and not intended by change agents, but I cannot join Deutsch in his condemnation of them and in fear of the entrepreneurial type. As Clark Kerr and associates note, "The middle class once in full control of the industrialization process has never in history lost its authority for internal reasons . . . [A manifest function of communist action is to see to it that the 'over-ripe' capitalistic order is displaced but] it is communism that withers away [and] even agriculture becomes an industry . . . [as] France still attests." [20]

Knowing

Belief (Knowledge) as an Element

A belief is any proposition about the universe which is thought to be true. The present section deals with the cognitive

[20] Clark Kerr *et al., Industrialism and Industrial Man: The Problems of Labor and Management in Economic Growth* (Cambridge, Mass.: Harvard University Press, 1960), pp. 276–283.

aspect of an actor's behavior. For Triandis, the totality of beliefs [is] a person's "subjective culture," which appears to be
composed of cathetic elements or sentiment, of moral and
evaluative elements, and of cognitive elements. Whereas he
views these as a totality, each of these is a separate entity for
analytic purposes, as treated in the PAS model.

In our Five-Nation Study, beliefs were probed using a
Lickert-type question to find the extent of belief in the following proposition: "I believe the world would really be a better place if more people had the same religious beliefs which
I have." The percentages of informants for the general public
of Costa Rica, urban Mexico, rural Mexico, Japan, Finland,
and the United States who agreed with the statement are as
follows: 73.4, 82.6, 93.4, 27.3, 52.4, and 48.5. Obviously the
responses reported here did not come from scientists, who subscribe to the following norms as identified by Merton: uni-
versalism, communism (in the sense that the substantive findings of science are a product of social collaboration and are assigned to the community, constituting a common heritage from
which the discoverer's equity is limited or removed), disinterestedness, and organized skepticism.[21] Skepticism, criticism,
and disinterestedness, of course, cannot exist in the minds of
those who know that only they are always right. Even for those
who are not scientists the application of scientific norms to
what one will and will not believe would appreciably change
the task of the change agent and the nature of the change
target. It is appropriate here to cite Mosher's advice to the
change agents: get the farmers to "learn to shift from the reliance for validity on who tells them something to increased
reliance on 'probabilistic' knowledge from research reports,
production and price projections, and other statistical information." This brings us to the process of cognitive mapping and
validation.

Cognitive Mapping and Validation as Process

Cognitive mapping and validation may be defined as the
activity by which knowledge, or what is considered true and

[21] Robert K. Merton, *Social Theory and Social Structure* (Glencoe, Ill.: The Free Press, 1957), p. 553.

what false, is developed. In the national probability samples from our Five-Nation Study, another difference in cognitive mapping emerges. Informants were asked to indicate whether they agreed or disagreed and to what extent with the following statement: "Everyone should think the same about what is right and what is wrong." The percentages agreeing for Costa Rica, Mexico, Japan, Finland, and the United States were respectively 90.0, 94.9, 65.5, 86.9, and 49.0.

When the proportions agreeing to this proposition for different levels of education are studied, the part the teacher may play in developing the scientific attitude may be contemplated. In the United States, the higher the level of education the less likely the informant was to agree with the above dogmatic statement. However, the informants in urban Mexico who disagreed with the above statement were not better educated than those who agreed. We hypothesize that teachers and education in Costa Rica and in Mexico do not reduce dogmatism to the same extent that they appear to in the United States. We have no proof of a connection, but we speculate that this may be another reason for the failure of the effort of the teachers in the Turrialba area as change agents in health and agriculture. We are led further to speculate that open-mindedness, tolerance, and flexibility, are not only functions of the number of years of exposure to the educational process, but are also functions of the content of the educational program. An understanding of the many guises with which "truth" has been viewed through the ages by the peoples of the world is of special importance in this regard.

One of the most important contributions to the subject under discussion appears in Cummings' chapter, and focuses on what he calls the "backlog fallacy." After noting that world population may increase by over 50 per cent by 1985 he states that "in terms of providing the increases required to meet future needs—two to three times the present yields will be necessary, and available information [to achieve this] is completely inadequate." Leagans anchors this thrust for new knowledge and observes that extension education "is the provision by which knowledge may be disseminated . . . thereby bringing together new knowledge and helping farmers in their natural setting." He notes that in cognitive mapping the "effective change agent is neither an abstract thinker nor a user of 'tricks.' He is both."

Feeling

Sentiment as an Element

Whereas beliefs embody thoughts, sentiments embody feelings about the world. Some change agents appeal to the patriotism of decision makers in the change target. In general, as traditional and new nations begin to modernize, nationalism and patriotism increase. In the Five-Nation Study, we obtained answers to the following "self-anchoring" question: "Imagine that you are on the middle step of a 10-step ladder. On the top steps of the ladder are things which, in your judgment, are more important than you as an individual. And on the bottom steps are things less important than you as an individual. On what step would you put your country?" The respective average step placement for Costa Rica, Mexico, Japan, Finland, and the United States was as follows: 9.00, 9.35, 5.84, 7.92, and 8.47. It is obvious that if this approach measures the loyalty people might have for their countries, both Costa Ricans and Mexicans are highly imbued with this sentiment.

In an effort to ascertain some measure of the attachment respondents have for their countries these same persons were asked, "Can you imagine that conditions could get to the point that you would consider moving to another country?" The percentages of informants answering this question in the negative for Costa Rica was 82.4, and for whites and blacks respectively in the United States, 85.4 and 77.5.[22] For Mexicans, Japanese, and Finns the percentages were 83.6, 88.3, and 74.4. These differences are not great and my hypothesis that the percentage for Costa Rica would be higher than for the United States was not validated.

In the study from which these data come, another hypothesis was not validated, namely, that "the family [as evaluated] in terms of the amount of interaction taking place among its members and in terms of its members' evaluation [of it in comparison with other organizations] is more important in

[22] Loomis, "In Praise of Conflict," p. 890.

both Costa Rica and Mexico than in the United States." [23] The directors of the study were surprised that these data indicate that appeals to family sentiments would be no stronger in Costa Rica and Mexico than in the United States.

To what extent could one use loyalty to one's community for motivational purposes? We do not have the data mentioned in the preceding paragraph for the Turrialba community, but we have comparable data (substituting community for nation in the question as it appears above) in general for Costa Rica, Mexico, Japan, Finland, and the United States. The percentages of persons stating that the community was more important than they were as individuals were respectively: 77.5, 90.1, 39.9, 65.2, 73.2. As in the previous paragraph the average placement on the ladder follows the same pattern as do these percentages. To ascertain to what extent the community of residence was a true home base and not just a way station the same respondents were asked, "Have you ever considered moving from this town or community?" The proportions answering, "No," were 69.0, 72.7, 67.7, 51.4, and 51.7. From this we may judge that if Turrialba is typical of Costa Rica, the sentiment of community loyalty may be used for motivation purposes by change agents.

Deutsch stresses the importance for the change agent of the loyalty of citizens to government and he specifically advises governments to develop loyalty. Thus a government may gain confidence and loyalty of citizens through a health program and thereby be able to launch an unpopular food program. But the health program may have the latent function of increasing population replacement rates and lead to famine. Elsewhere Deutsch notes that loyalty is "credit . . . to be earned," and calls it "a gold reserve" which may inhibit "incipient panic." Since most of the directed change in the world today is carried on by governments there is no denying the importance of loyalty of members of the change target to government.

[23] Loomis, Loomis, and Gullahorn; and the Five-Nation Study. For the following frequency categories of relatives getting together outside the home; namely, never; 1-few times a year; 2-once a month; 3-few times a month; 4-once a week, for Costa Rica were: 13.9, 22.0, 12.6, 19.9 and 31.6; for Mexico 10.8, 18.7, 13.8, 14.4 and 42.2; for Japan 3.8, 37.1, 23.7, 17.7, and 17.7; for Finland .6, 24.6, 33.8, 14.8 and 26.2; for the United States 3.7, 10.2, 17.1, 11.7, and 57.4

Tension Management as Process

This process may be defined as action by which elements of the social system are articulated in such a manner as to (1) prevent sentiments from obstructing goal-directed activity, and (2) avail the system of their motivating force in achieving goals. Prayer is among the many such tension-managing activities, and the only one to be discussed here. For the probability samples mentioned above drawn in the United States and Mexico informants were asked "When you have a decision to make in your everyday life do you ask yourself what GOD would want you to do?" [24] For urban Mexico, rural Mexico, and the United States the proportions answering in the affirmative were respectively 90.2, 89.2, and 70.4. The frequency with which this prayerful activity was engaged in is indicated by the percentages of informants who answered "Always" when questioned. For these same samples the percentages were respectively 56.4, 65.8, and 18.4. Assuming that the same proportions as reported for Mexico would hold for Costa Rica, for which I do not have comparable data, we could assume a high level of religiosity in Costa Rica. This impression is reinforced by the religiosity manifested in the Costa Rican villages in which I worked. It reinforces the impression that had the church legitimized and supported the efforts of the teachers in the Turrialba area, the attempts to effect change might have been more successful.

Communication of Sentiment as Process

Action is taken by the members of a social system which leads to motivation to achieve goals, conform to norms, and carry out systemic action through transfer of feeling by symbols. Elsewhere I have attempted to demonstrate how the two processes, tension management and communication of sentiment, are utilized in the promotion of change by communists after social systems are torn by disruption, and how they may be used as communities are disabled by disasters.[25] Triandis discusses a similar problem. He states that "if a man does not experience [the pain of] dissonance, if he is entirely satisfied with himself, he will be most unlikely to change." The skillful

[24] Loomis, Loomis, and Gullahorn, p. 57.
[25] Loomis, "In Praise of Conflict."

change agent will recognize the euphoria attending a satisfying communication of sentiment following relief from disruption and be able to channel it toward the change he wishes to effect, much as the communists do. Usually democratic norms do not permit the manipulation of sentiments in the manner used by communist agitators. But there is no doubt that within the realm of sentiment communication much dynamic force exists which, if understood more, could be harnessed.

Facilitating

Facility as an Element

A facility is a means which, except for slaves, is nonhuman, and used within the system to attain the members' ends. Mass media is one such facility that often is used effectively to help change agents attain goals. In the effort of the teachers in the Turrialba area to advance agricultural and health practices little use was made of mass media, and radio and television were not used at all. Radios, purchased by the Institute, and placed in each village, might have increased the chances for success, if pertinent radio programs and forums on the subject had been planned.

Another facility prominent in this particular attempt at change was the demonstration of the use of chlordane. Village leaders saw it and were enthusiastic. They communicated their enthusiasm to the villagers who came in unprecedented numbers to stock up. The quantity held by the Institute was insufficient, and most went away empty-handed.

Utilization of Facilities

From the point of view of the change target, how members use their facilities presupposes some surplus over subsistence and some choice among facilities. Concerning the first supposition of surplus, the informants in the Five-Nation Study provide some information. "Property is something which should be shared" was the statement to which informants in Costa Rica, Mexico, Japan, Finland, and the United States agreed by the following percentages: 62.5, 63.5, 52.6, 18.0, and 40.2. It is tempting to speculate that the remarkably lower number agreeing with the statement in Finland is connected with Finland's proximity to Russia and its unhappy experiences with that country. A related statement: "Some people have too much property and others don't have enough" elicited the following percentages respectively: 84.3, 82.3, 56.8, 80.8, and 61.2. From these figures may we argue that countries in Latin America could easily go the route of Cuba so far as the relation of facilities and private property is concerned?

I must admit that the ideological and political skies do not appear bright. However, an American who hopes the free enterprise system will develop in neighboring countries may find bright spots. We asked the informants in our Five-Nation Study, "Do you own stock or any other shares in any private enterprise?" The percentages responding "Yes," were as follows: 3.3, 12.4, 18.1, 15.9, and 24.1. Although these answers may be no great cause for optimism for the American, our next question put to the same informants was: "Have you ever thought about buying stock or other shares in any private enterprise?" The percentages responding "Yes," were as follows: 13.9, 42.4, 26.1, 35.4, and 59.7. It is interesting to compare the Costa Rican and Mexican responses with those of the Finns here and especially above on the matter of "sharing property" and giving consideration to leaving the home land. One is tempted to speculate that Finland's closeness to Russia and experience with her affects these answers. Will Cuba produce the same results for our neighbors?

An important question for the change agent is "How does the change target use its surplus?" In the Turrialba area, for example, would a farmer be more likely to buy a votive candle or a bag of chlordane? If the farmer is already attempting to exterminate ants by some means the change agent's job (to switch him to a more effective ant control) is far different than if the farmer protects ants because they are the friends of the monkey-god as in India. Many times the utilization of facilities is not done as effectively as it might be simply because the members of the change target do not know what is available. They use the facilities with which they are familiar because they have not seen and do not know about improved models. It can be something as simple as substituting a fly swatter for a piece of paper, or something as complicated as installing electricity to replace candles. Media devoted to description and sale of facilities are of invaluable aid in extending the horizons of the change target. Mail-order catalogs and county fairs are examples of media which fill this function. Of course the availability of a facility does not insure that it will be extensively used. Credit offices offering loans at low rates of interest and easily understood methods of saving such as postal savings accounts are examples of facilities which require considerably more than availability to insure use.

The Master Processes

Of the six master processes of the PAS model, communication, boundary maintenance, systemic linkage, socialization, institutionalization, and social control, there is only space to discuss briefly the first four which are, I believe, the most important in the analysis and discussion of the strategy of change.

Communication

Communication is the process by which information, decisions, and directives pass through the system and by which knowledge is transmitted and sentiment is formed or modified. In addition to the numberless ramifications of communication through personal means, other means such as mass media, mail service, telephone lines, highways, and advertising devices should be included.

In the efforts of the officials of the Inter-American Institute of Agricultural Sciences to reach people, the interrelationships which are described in Figures 1 and 2 and sociograms here represented were of assistance. How the complete network of personal communications was achieved by one demonstration to a few leaders substantiated to the Institute adminstrators the value of the sociogram. Likewise the teachers studied such charts in the courses they took on the strategy of change at the Institute.

Leagans lays great stress on the quality of the communication of agents of change. "Extension educators need to demonstrate competence, humility, persistence, empathy, integrity, and flexibility. . . . [A] speaker . . . must be sure of the values held by his audience so that he can summon the reaction he desires to his message." Turning from the change agent to the change target, Mosher observes that "a progressive rural structure is composed of an identifiable set of facilities and services.

. . . Roads should come first [but the actors in the change agent system must facilitate the] strengthening (or creation where necessary) of market towns." As revealed by our Five-Nation Study, communication via the various mass media reaches the most people in Finland and the United States and the least in Costa Rica and Mexico.[26]

We may terminate our consideration of communication as a process by reference to Frey's inclination elsewhere to give the condition of access to the change target system and communication with and among its actors more primacy than achievement motivation as the latter concept is used by McClelland. Relying heavily on empirical studies, Frey advances what he calls "a communication hypothesis." He believes that certain adoptions (such as the plow, for example) are brought about, not so much by a man's change in receptiveness or by an increase in his psychological motivation, as by his seeing that the tool exists, is available, and is used by others with whom he has a chance to interact. According to this hypothesis, travel to a city might make people adopters of many things seen there. This is remindful of Ralph Beals who observes that in potential for producing change "one road is worth about three schools and about 50 administrators." [27] Various diffusion studies have found urban contact, urban pull, mass media contact, etc., very important in the adoption of agricultural and health practices. The available evidence indicates that any society which becomes isolated from the activities that take place in the world's major routes of transport, cities, and knowledge centers will be disadvantaged by a lower level of living than would otherwise be the case. Iron curtains, bamboo curtains, and high tariffs exact their penalty in lack of opportunity to develop.

Boundary Maintenance

Through boundary maintenance the solidarity, identity, and interaction patterns within social systems are maintained. If

[26] The percentages of informants respectively reporting not viewing television were as follows: 90.0, 63.9, 14.1, 43.3, and 11.5. The percentages not listening to radio as reported were: 36.3, 23.3, 53.5, 7.8, and 20.5; those reporting not reading newspapers were: 45.1, 64.7, 9.7, .7, and 18.2; and those reporting not reading magazines were: 76.3, 42.9, 48.2, 7.4, and 5.6.

[27] "Notes on Acculturation," in Sol Tax *et al., Heritage of Conquest* (Glencoe, Ill.: The Free Press, 1952), p. 232.

one is thinking of the change agent working on the problems of a small village, the boundaries which might prove difficult between him and the change target could be the resistance to change by a hacienda owner who sees no advantage to himself in improvements for his laborers as long as labor is cheap. Or it could be the resistance to a poultry program if the change agent is a man and poultry tending is viewed as "women's work." [28] Another type of boundary would be encountered if the proposed change espoused by the change agent were to be directly in conflict with cherished beliefs and sentiments of the change target as might be an ant extermination in parts of India or birth control in a traditional Catholic country.

On a larger front it might be fear of institutional innovation which provides the change target with a boundary which might be a formidable one for a change agent. Chandler Morse points out that one of the frequent results of a successful economic change is the creation of a surplus. While the local power structure might not be opposed *ipso facto* to more goods, only a little projection would reveal that in the wake of modernization such institutions as company stores or company credit would be drastically altered; that people could move about more freely and that the local reservoir of cheap labor may dry up; that extensive small land-holdings might be possible which would change the relation of the big estate to the government. Many of the feared consequences would be vaguely visualized but not the less threatening for their vagueness.

On a still larger front is the barrier posed by free trade or restricted trade, depending on which side of the argument one finds himself. Morse argues against compulsively worshipping at the altar of free trade and he questions "dependence on export agriculture" for developing societies. He notes that "dependence on agricultural and other exports makes a country so dependent on external decisions and problem handling process, so subject to externally oriented innovated behavior, that it never succeeds in developing its own problem handling capacity." He cites Mexico and South Africa as countries which followed "inward-looking policies" which manifest considerable advantages over "export economy."

Of course boundary maintenance affects the extent of inter-

[28] Thomas L. Norris, "Economic Systems: Large and Small Land Holdings," in Loomis *et al.*, *Turrialba*, pp. 102–103.

national collaboration which is possible. Informants in our Five-Nation Study responded to the following statement indicating whether and to what extent they agreed with it: "It is a good thing for companies and business firms from other countries to do business and have factories in our country." For Costa Rica, Mexico, Japan, Finland, and the United States the percentages respectively agreeing were: 68.7, 68.1, 35.6, 41.0, and 57.2. It is interesting to speculate whether or not Cuba before Castro would not have responded as did Costa Rica and Mexico. Although we tend to think of underdeveloped economies as exercising high boundary maintenance, here is an instance where the more modernized societies express a greater desire for boundaries than do the less developed ones.

Irwin Sanders cites Henri Mendras' excellent study of peasantry,[29] saying that the peasant is "entrenched in traditional structure" and the modern agricultural change agent is often on a different wave length. Deutsch describes a special type of boundary maintenance by noting that in the case of a revolution "governments function . . . as bankers do. . . . A revolution is to a government as a run is to a bank." Not unrelated to this is his claim that "modernization . . . generally makes countries harder to govern." In this connection I should note that various studies have shown that revolutions and revolts do not come as frequently when suffering and depression is highest but rather when conditions are improving.

Systemic Linkage

This is the process whereby the elements of at least two social systems come to be articulated so that in some ways and on some occasions they may be viewed as a single system. Whereas the processes previously discussed deal chiefly with interaction within a system, systemic linkage relates members of at least two systems.

Several linking processes were involved in the Inter-American

[29] Henri Mendras, *Les Paysans et la modernisation de l'agriculture* (Paris: Centre National de la Recherche Scientifique, 1958). Mendras notes that over half of the peasants who adopted new practices were influenced by neighbors and parents and one-fourth of them had seen the practice in use elsewhere. He wants a study of the influence of peasant women and rural ideology on agricultural change.

Institute of Agricultural Sciences' effort to use the local village teachers as agricultural and health change agents. First the Institute involved and obtained agreement on the part of the National Ministry of Education for the experiment and in effect the two agencies became the change agent system. Of course, the change target systems to which the change agent system was to be linked were each of the thirty-two villages. This latter linkage, for reasons discussed above, was never finalized to a significant extent. The linkage which was most productive and of greatest duration was that between teacher and such groups as athletic clubs, especially soccer clubs.

Leagans' definition of extension gives a good example of systemic linkage without using that term: "[Extension is] how to effectively transmit useful information from the centers of creative thought to those who can use it . . . [thus] making provision for an instrument through which wisdom may be disseminated. [Its] primary . . . and its potential ability to continuously bring together new knowledge and help people in their natural setting to learn to apply it in solution to their problems" is its long suit. The level of inclusiveness at which systemic linkage is most effective in developing societies was a subject to which Woods Thomas addressed himself: " 'Pay-offs' . . . in developing societies would be greater [if focused on a wide area including the relevant infrastructure] than from similar efforts at the farm decision levels."

Ralph Cummings sees the development of regional seats of knowledge and science which stand behind agricultural development as most important. He describes a type of linkage which keeps the action close to science and the knowledge centers: "These village agents in contact with farmers need to be backed up with a group of subject matter extension specialists who have a still higher level of scientific training and competence . . . [then these] extension specialists need to be backed up with a group of well-trained research scientists. . . . Trained people [with scientific backgrounds] are more important initially in stimulating innovation than is a large number of demonstrations." Other linkages mentioned as essential by various writers are those between government and sectors of society and those between peasants and markets. Desirable as might be the links between society's subsystems and government, there are also dangers. Parsons, for example, notes that "the use of powers of government for private purposes is endemic in Latin America."

Depending upon the objective only a few people may have to comprise the change target for the attempt to be successful, or a very high percentage may have to be involved. A community's drinking water, for example, may be chlorinated with a relatively few people linking with the change agent prior to the decision. Deutsch gives an example of the opposite situation, where a great number have to be involved. Literacy and birth rate are negatively correlated, for example. It is not enough that a few people become literate for the birth rate to show a change. Even when literacy is extended from 10 per cent of the population to 60 per cent, there is no correlation. But by the time literacy reaches 80 per cent of the population the birth rate begins to drop. His idea of the "threshold" at which point changes can be observed because of a wider and wider linkage should be of interest to change agents.

The so-called "package program" of Indian agriculture is an illustration of a systemic linkage which is designed to insure an input from all relevant facilities and services in such a way that there will be an optimal or "highest profit combination" output. A system of interrelated parts described by Mosher as a "multiple complementarity" is systemic linkage par excellence. It seems to include what is in the "package program" plus a provision by which all various pertinent agencies involved in producing, marketing, transportation, education, and research would engage in a team effort so that the optimal "mix" for the highest level of living would result for a whole region. Nations which are unabashedly planners, such as India and Russia, seem so far to encounter considerable difficulty in effectively linking so many systems. Nonetheless, nations which are only occasionally planners, and then go about planning a bit furtively, as the United States, link a good many subsystems not ordinarily thought of as compatible bedfellows (such as the private and public sector) when an otherwise unobtainable goal is important. Reflectors and molders of public opinion who ordinarily denounce "socialistic" tendencies if there is any deviation from private enterprise were peculiarly silent about criticism, and noticeably jubilant about results when the race for leadership in the space program led to the moon landings. If it is just as imperative in the eyes of Guatemala or Kenya or Pakistan to increase their food supply and to modernize as it seemed to be in the eyes of Americans to maintain space leadership, perhaps their motives in systemically linking the government with the private industrial sectors should appear to us to be no more threatening than our own motives in our recent space adventure. That we still view any such alliance with deep suspicion is shown by the Five-Nation Study. Informants were asked whether and to what extent they agreed with the following statement: "The only way to provide good medical care for all of the people is through some program of governmental health insurance." The percentages respectively agreeing for Costa Rica, Mexico, Japan, Finland, and the United States were as follows: 84.9, 84.1, 90.3, 83.9, and 57.2.

Socialization

Socialization is the process whereby the social and cultural heritage is transmitted. In primitive and developing societies the family is of crucial importance for socialization. In industrialized societies specialized institutions of various types emerge which carry on socializaton in addition to that which the child receives in the family and from friends and neighbors. The high evaluation which Costa Ricans place on schools and education has been mentioned. In an effort to ascertain how people generally feel about socialization for agricultural development, informants included in our Five-Nation Study were asked the following question: "Some people believe that the government should play a bigger part in training rural youth in agricultural practices. What is your feeling on this statement: 'Rural youth who remain on the farm should be given more training to make them better farmers, even if we have to pay more taxes.'?" Proportions of informants from the various countries who agreed with this statement are respectively as follows: 82.6, 93.3, 42.7, 78.1, and 59. 4. There seems to be no question about the readiness of Costa Ricans and Mexicans for agricultural development. Such answers might indicate that the Costa Rican Ministry of Education and the Inter-American Institute of Agricultural Sciences might well have trained vocational agricultural teachers to give this type of training directly to Costa Rican rural youth.

Other findings from the Five-Nation Study indicate that both in Costa Rica and Mexico the people have been socialized to accept thoroughly the society in which they were reared. The informants were asked to indicate whether and to what extent they agreed with the following statement from the well-known F-Scale used by Leo Srole to measure authoritarianism: "Children should be taught that there is only one correct way to do things." The percentages respectively agreeing are as follows: 78.3, 94.8, 58.8, 63.9, and 60.2. These data substantiate the contention that industrialization, urbanization, and other processes involved in modernization change people; such a milieu seems to exert a socializing process of its own.

Conditions of Social Interaction

The elements and processes constitute the working components, i.e., the parts and articulating processes, of the social system. Not all aspects of social action are encompassed in these concepts but the remaining components are only partly systemic, that is, partly structured and partly under the control of the actors of the system. Space, time, and size are such components.

Territoriality

The setting of the social system in space is called its territoriality, and it determines within limits how much space each person or group may have, the frequency and intensity of interaction within the group, and probabilities of systemic linkages between groups and between change agent and change target systems. In the Turrialba area a rather simple consideration involving the change agent–change target relation was studied. A study was made in one of the communities to ascertain a location where most people could see a poster display. On the large estate of Aquiares it was found that the greatest number of contacts are made at the butcher shop. Since no local refrigeration exists, a steer or hog is butchered almost every day and the people come to buy fresh meat as it is needed. It was recommended that certain posters developed by change agents be displayed in the butcher shop.

How services of farmers are related in space and the relation of prices to markets has been the concern of agricultural social scientists at least from von Thuenen's time to the time of

Galpin, Christaller, Loesch, Berry and others.[30] Mosher's concern for organizational activities in space is mentioned in the Editors' Introduction to Part I.

In Figure 4, the physical location and interaction patterns of

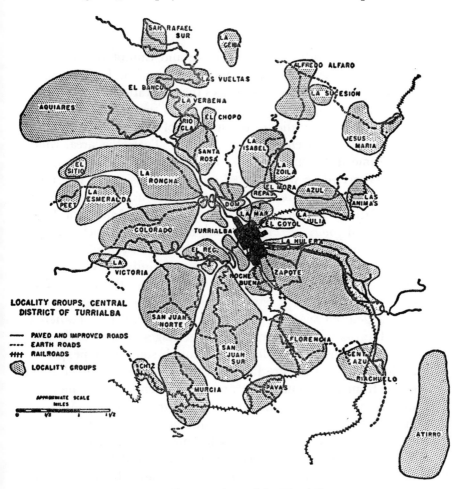

Figure 4. Locality groupings of the Turrialba area

[30] Johann Heinrich von Thuenen, *Der isolierte Staat in Beziehung auf Landwirtschaft und Nationaloekonomie* (Jena: Fischer, 1930); Charles J. Galpin, *The Social Anatomy of an Agricultural Community*, Wisconsin Agricultural Experiment Station Research Bulletin No. 34, (Madison, 1915); Walter Christaller, *Die zentralen Orte in Sueddeutschland* (Jena: Fischer, 1933); August Loesch, *Die räumliche Ordnung der Wirtschaft* (Jena: Fischer, 1941); and Brian J. L. Berry, *Geography of Market Centers and Retail Distribution* (Englewood Cliffs, N.J.: Prentice-Hall, 1967).

the villages in the Turrialba area are presented. Lines around the villages considered as social systems are drawn at those points at which there is minimal travel and interaction either toward the village or away from it.

Time

Time as a condition is inexorable and cannot be made to stand still or be completely controlled by man. Even though man is the only animal that bridges the generations through the transmission of culture, he is nonetheless time-bound and this is reflected in all studies of the strategy of change. In the effort to use teachers as change agents in the Turrialba area, time often came into consideration. Training for the change agent role was carried on when school was not in session. In the Turrialba area people are not as "time conscious" as they are in industrialized societies. *Hora española* and *mañana,* not *hora englesa* and *today,* describe timing of events to which change agents either already are or must become accustomed.

Matthews mentions the importance of timing: "When . . . inputs other than extension [are not available] the wise course may be not to attempt agricultural development." In terms of timing Deutsch raises an important problem which has bothered the Marxists who may argue whether stages such as early and ripe capitalism can be "leaped." Deutsch states that people in traditional societies "are far more likely to need a direct transition from traditional government to essentials of a modern welfare state. . . . Asia, Africa, and parts of Latin America may have to accomplish . . . within a few decades [what it took] Western Europe and North America . . . many generations." However, as Deutsch discusses the model of the Japanese political scientist Maruyama, he is not sure about the nature of the "leap forward." He gives the approach his unqualified praises as "one of the most economical, powerful, and indeed elegant ways of generating new questions and hypotheses." Such a classification as Maruyama's (see Chapter 3), according to Deutsch, generates the question as to whether traditional societies which are highly decentralized with many "privatized" actors must "go through a stage of atomization and authorianism" to modernize. Can they move directly into "centralized or federalized government?" Deutsch does not answer this. He presents evidence to prove that at least for the noncommunist world the larger the percentage of the GNP spent for government services the more innovative and progressive the society may be. However, he proves elsewhere that the manner in which power is articulated by change agents and the resulting linkage is very important in determining the results regardless of the timing by stages.

Size

Insofar as size of social systems is not controlled by the actors, it may be discussed as a condition of social action. Although inventions which improve man's efficiency in the use of energy tend to increase the size of certain systems, various systems in different organizations, societies, and epochs are remarkably similar. It is interesting to note how frequently eight and twelve persons are the supervisory unit in various organizations. The original squad in armies is an example. Another aspect of size as a condition is numbers of people per unit of space. Some think this is a condition and uncontrolled because of man's inability to manage reproduction; others, such as many catholics, consider the matter a moral issue. The extent to which beliefs in countries such as Costa Rica and Mexico affect the evaluation of birth control was discussed above. Cummings thinks the present "runaway" growth of population will continue so that if famine is to be avoided food production per year must be doubled or tripled. At the present time concern about the rapid pollution of man's environment has made the problem of population size more than one of famine. Lung cancer from smog, hearing damage from noise, and many other dangers seem to lurk in the future and to be directly related to man's reproduction and replacement rates.

Summary

Agricultural development is no simple process to be achieved by the separate contributions of a society's economy, polity, or its research and educational establishments. Neither can one academic discipline alone, as Leagans points out, claim success in predicting or explaining the course of agricultural development. In reality it depends on favorable conditions not only in rural institutions but in the sectors of "agri-support" and "agri-climate," which supply, transport, market, finance, purchase, and provide the technical advantages and incentives as well as a stable governmental administration for agricultural production. The complexity and magnitude of the processes involved are so great that many scientific disciplines must be brought to bear on them if they are to be predicted, understood, and furthered. This being true, it is necessary to assist specialists in the various scientific disciplines involved to understand one anothers' frames of reference and concepts.

Often in the past, disproportionate efforts have been made to "educate" the agricultural producer. The enlightenment of the peasant is important but too little attention has been given to improving his environment of incentives, technology, and facilities, which would encourage and enable him to respond as desired. Policy and strategy must deal with all sectors of the total system and its subsystems which affect the producer. Most sectors of the whole society must change. The approach must be "macroeconomic" in order to permit and encourage "microeconomic" change.

As agriculture in developing societies becomes increasingly dependent upon the development of other sectors, the coordinating and service roles of government become increasingly complex, extensive, and important. Moreover, the traditional agriculturist, exploited and neglected by representatives of the larger society for many generations, distrusts governmental and educational officials. Also governmental and other administrative officials may lack the required administrative capabilities. Their traditional origins may foster corruption and nepotism. Changes in incentives of government and organizational structure may be required to get results. Often a government's use of political power to attain development objectives involves political costs exceeding immediate inherent political gains. Nevertheless, societies must develop governmental strategies for the economical and effective use of their power. Professionally trained, socially minded, adequately supported, effectively organized, and properly facilitated educational, scientific, and administrative personnel is the *sine qua non* of agricultural development.

If traditional agricultural societies are to modernize, hinderances which prevent freedom of effective human action and use of resources for human betterment must be removed. Land tenure systems, marketing arrangements, and human relations generally must not only permit but facilitate efficient action and economical use of both human and nonhuman resources. The concepts and tools developed in fields such as agricultural economics and rural sociology are applicable. However, the optimum combinations of labor, capital, land, entrepreneurship, and other "inputs" will be different in developing countries than in industrialized societies. Developing societies are universally burdened with underemployment of labor and heavy farm-family food requirements. The prescriptions carried over to developing societies by agricultural economists from industrial societies may be more pertinent to the commercial pockets of agriculture generally found in developing countries than to subsistence farming. Nevertheless, the potential rationality and desire for an improved life on the part of the traditional agriculturalists should not be underestimated.

Science applied to the control of disease has resulted in such decreasing death and increasing population rates that the world faces critical food and other shortages on a scale never before known. Unless agricultural science produces disease-resistant and otherwise regionally suitable plants and animal stocks and improves cultural practices and agricultural knowledge generally, famine is inevitable. If famine is to be avoided and agricultural development attained throughout the world, all scientific disciplines must team up on the problem. Control of environmental pollution requires a similar approach. This holds whether the sciences focus on nature in general, scarce resources in particular, the personality, human power or politics, culture, health, education, or other arenas.

There is not sufficient "stored knowledge" available to save us, but much knowledge now available is ineffectively used. It is in the arena of the behavioral sciences that knowledge necessary for agricultural development is most lacking. The very fact that effective and economically feasible birth control procedures are now available to prevent famine, if the knowledge and organizational facilities were available to motivate people to use them, proves the need for the behavioral sciences. Likewise their development and contribution should make it possible to speed up agricultural and societal development generally without undue application of force, violence, and cruelty. To avoid famine and secure the future, all scientific disciplines must be employed.

11. *Agricultural Sciences*

A. H. BUNTING

Chapter 4 of this book is an excellent review by Ralph Cummings on agricultural science. His presentation has received little comment or criticism, but the facts of food and population in the world today and the evident poverty of most farm people suggest that in fact agricultural science and technology (though they have much to offer), are not being sufficiently applied in practice by the vast majority of farmers. From the point of view of agricultural science I think there are three reasons for this: in many regions agricultural science and technology are not appropriately developed; many of the most significant obstacles to change lie in other parts of the system; and for lack of understanding of this system agricultural scientists and technologists do not sufficiently understand their role in the process of change.

Underlying the third of these reasons are some fundamental problems of definition, mode of thought, and action which I wish to discuss first.

I take behavioral change to mean "change in the way people or systems behave." Change is a neutral term, but it is tacitly accepted that the changes we would wish our strategies to achieve are of a positive kind, leading to increased yields or profits. Put in a way which lies more comfortably on the back of an applied scientist, the central question then is not, "What strategies lead to behavioral change in agriculture?" but, "How can we induce farmers and others connected with agriculture to act in ways that will increase *yield* (in, say, kilograms per hectare per year or litres per cow per lactation), or *profit* (in say dollars per man-hour, dollars per year per $100 of capital employed, or dollars per acre per year)?" Thus stated, the question still contains two abstract nouns, it is true, but they are abstracts which (like work, force, energy, and power) can be precisely defined and measured in specific units. Abstract nouns which are not rigorously defined in such a way too often become Humpty Dumpty words, which mean precisely what each speaker intends them to mean, no more and no less. They are a major reason why communication between "natural" or "agricultural" scientists on the one hand and economists, sociologists, and other "human" scientists on the other so often fails. Agricultural scientists must eschew such words themselves (because they too are far from blameless, as a brief consideration of the word "infertility" will show) and must also insist on rigorous definitions of the abstract terms used by their colleagues from the human sciences. Indeed, where undefined or undefinable abstracts imply (as they so often do) general statements or interpretations which cannot be tested experimentally, it may be better to avoid them altogether, and to speak strictly in terms of the facts of observation. In these dialogues, the agricultural scientist will usually reject primarily intuitive and deductive arguments of the "I think or believe, therefore" variety in favor of those more predominantly objective and inductive kinds which say "the facts are . . . , therefore it may be that . . . , and I propose to test this hypothesis by . . . ." Deduction and induction are after all two dialectically opposed modes of thought, and their uncontrolled mating, though often spectacular, may well be infertile.

Strengths and Weaknesses of Agricultural Science and Technology

The main defect of agricultural science in the developing countries is that there is not enough of it. Insofar as this is a "behavioral" question, it arises from the behavior of administrators rather than of farmers or scientists, and so falls outside the bounds of my submission. Not all of what there is, however, is of the most useful kind.

The successes of agricultural research, coupled with education and extension, in developed countries, have given it a reputation and a status which on the whole it has not fully earned in the less developed ones. In many developing countries we have discovered, and proudly demonstrate on our experiment stations, means by which considerable increases of yield may be obtained, and our research tools for extending this knowledge are both appropriate and powerful. Far too often, however, the yields of the local farmers outside the station fence are quite unaffected by this demonstration. Bellies remain unfilled and farmers poor.

The reasons for this are largely historical. The roots of agricultural science and technology are of course more ancient than agriculture itself. Preagricultural peoples have wide practical knowledge of the nature, management, and uses of plants and animals, and of weather and other biologically significant features of their environment. About 9,000 years ago the deliberate sowing and tending of plants began, at about the same time, apparently independently, in both the Old World and the New. Agricultural animals began to be domesticated, at least in the Old World, at about the same time. Agriculture led to settlement, and, when irrigation had been invented, to cities, civilization, and the emergence of organized states, writing, and money. This major evolution of social organization was directly based on the new modes of production of food. It was accompanied by a great increase in practical biological knowledge, and led to the rapid development of many other sciences, including mathematics, hydraulics, and calendrical science. In the hands of the early farmers of the Old World, the new methods spread gradually into the tropics by way of India and of southern Arabia and Ethiopia, into the Mediterranean basin, and into the northern temperate regions and across Asia to China, in the wake of the retreating ice. Similarly, agriculture in the Americas spread both north and south from its ancestral hearth in Mexico. The inventions of ironworking and of the use of animal power (in the Old World only) added greatly to the technical efficiency of agriculture and increased the range of conditions in which it could be carried on.

Up to about the end of the eighteenth century the technical methods of agriculture everywhere were essentially those of the Iron Age. In northwestern Europe, however, the economic relations of agriculture had already begun to change, and new cultural methods (based in part on the deliberate growing of legumes) not only increased yield but made it possible to overwinter animals. (In the seasonally arid Mediterranean, subtropical, and tropical regions, the corresponding problem posed by the dry season was only partially solved by nomadism or transhumance).

The growth of knowledge was accompanied by centuries of effort to systematize and explain it, but it was not until the seventeenth century that what we can today recognize as scientific method became clearly distinguished from magic, religion, philosophy, and art. In its earlier stages, all science had practical purposes: only in the nineteenth century did the concept of pure science emerge as an offshoot from the parent trunk.

Today, in most countries, pure science, which is immensely exciting and satisfying intellectually, stands considerably higher in the pecking order than applied science, and this has had some unfortunate consequences for agriculture. The methods of pure science developed of necessity in an essentially analytical way, by breaking down complex situations and phenomena and classifying their components into more easily comprehensible categories and systems. This has led naturally to ever-increasing refinement of method and to ever-greater fragmentation and specialization. The converse process of synthesis, the attempt to use the results of analysis to make acceptable statements about more complex situations, though not, of course, absent from pure science, becomes increasingly difficult as specialization proceeds, which is why Sir Daniel Hall, in the first decade of this century, had deliberately to foster the cousin-marriage of pure and agricultural science when he founded the new Rothamsted. This is also why what it is fashionable to call an "interdisciplinary approach" has become increasingly important in pure science. By contrast, to be effective, applied science must always be interdisciplinary, particularly in agriculture, since it has to study systems as a whole and is often unable to proceed in a purely analytical way; and where it analyzes or uses the results of analysis, it has always to put the pieces together again in order to produce practically useful answers.

Methodological Defects in Agricultural Science

Nevertheless specialization in many parts of agricultural science has in the past prevented many of its exponents from seeing the practical problems whole. Hence the prominence of single-factor experimentation and single-factor panaceas—fertilizers, animal nutrition, improved varieties or breeds, control of disease, insect pests, or of weeds—and the tardy recognition that it is often necessary to experiment with several factors at once, and to introduce simultaneously a whole package of innovations, in order to maximize the effect of each. Thus, for example, in the improvement of cotton production the (British) Cotton Research Corporation has devoted a great deal of effort for many years to breeding for yield, quality, and disease resistance, and has produced varieties which have greatly extended the area of cotton grown by peasant cultivators in many parts of the tropics. Recently the prospects of cotton-growing in all the areas in which the Corporation works have been transformed, because cotton pests can now be controlled effectively with insecticides, and new methods of soil mangement, including the use of fertilizers, have been developed. All these measures applied together have made it possible to attain unprecedentedly large yields, and the way is now open for a new cycle of breeding to produce new varieties which can best take advantage of the new environment we can now provide for them.

Similarly the great increases in wheat and rice output during the past twenty-five years in Mexico, the Philippines, the Indian subcontinent, Turkey, and elsewhere depend essentially on varieties of improved morphology and disease resistance which respond outstandingly to fertilizers. The importance of such "packages" of innovations was very correctly stressed by Cummings, but it is salutary to reflect that it is over forty years since Fisher pointed out the importance of multifactorial experimental methods, and since Gregory and Crowther demonstrated that varieties within a crop species may respond very differently to nitrogen fertilizers, and made the first physiological analysis of the reasons for this extremely important phenomenon.

This factorial approach leads directly to an additional tool in practical agricultural research—the "maximum yield" approach. The theoretical maximum conversion of light energy to chemical energy is 20 per cent. The best experimental figure so far recorded is about 12 per cent, over a short period, but the most efficient crops actually harvested seldom represent a conversion better than 2 per cent. In most undeveloped agricultures the conversion is a fraction only of 1 per cent. If these figures could be increased by 0.5 per cent the world food problem would be under control for a considerable time to come. Agricultural technologists should devote part of their time to the deliberate attempt to maximize this conversion on small areas, using all the means they can beg, borrow, or steal, and regardless of normal agricultural costs, or of whether the local farmer is likely to use the means in the near future or not. (Everywhere today farmers are using methods no one would have expected them to use thirty years ago.) "Maximum yield" trials, particularly if they are factorially designed, will indicate the principal technical limiting factors of the agricultural environment, and by showing what is technically feasible, they will encourage the search for the combination of measures which is most profitable and for cheaper ways of attaining the effects which are shown to be possible. In this type of research the sky—or at least 20 per cent energy conversion—is the limit.

The exalted status of pure science may also seduce the agricultural scientist from the empirical solution of practical problems, which is often the most effective way of tackling them, and lead him to prefer to study fundamental problems. We have recently concluded in Britain that nine-tenth of our agricultural research effort (measured in support cost) should be in projects which are intended, however indirectly, to solve some practical problem; all such projects should be able to give more or less plausible answers to the question, "And how would that increase the yield?" To answer this question sensibly, it is necessary to base research priorities, at least in part, on economic criteria. The objectives of research may correctly have to be assessed by some form of cost-benefit analysis which can forecast the comparative advantages of different patterns of deployment of the human and financial resources likely to be available for scientific endeavor.

Another important difficulty arises from the geography of agricultural change. The agricultural changes which began in Europe with the enclosures, and were accelerated by the new methods of production introduced in the eighteenth century, released manpower and provided part of the capital for the Industrial Revolution. Instead of being based primarily on agriculture and trade in agricultural products, the economy of societies came to rest on the industrial production of vast quantities of new commodities. The progress of agriculture itself has become closely tied to industry and cities, often at a great distance, which provide many of the inputs of modern farming and consume the vast bulk of the products. Particularly was this true in North America, where the great expansion and transformation of agriculture after the abolition of slavery and the settlement of the prairies has been based upon machinery and in particular on the internal combustion engine and the electric motor, and in more recent times on the extensive use of fertilizers and chemical and biological materials for crop and animal protection. The new agriculture, and so inevitably agricultural science, developed first in temperate regions and (except for certain industrial and other export crops) have made considerably less progress in other regions, particularly in the tropics.

Now though the broad generalizations of climatology, soil science, plant and animal physiology, and microbiology appear to be universally applicable, the ways in which they can best be fitted together to maximize the exploitation of a particular environment depend on the specific nature of that environment. In the temperate regions, the growing season is limited by the cold of winter; it starts with the soil profile fully or partially charged with water (accumulated from the rain or snow of the winter months) and crops are harvested as temperatures fall and humidities rise. In the seasonally arid tropics the start and end of the cropping season are determined by heat and drought, the whole of the soil profile is usually effectively dry when the rains start, and crops are gathered in when temperatures are rising and humidity falling. In the wet tropics it is hot and wet all the year round, and the profile is always full of water. In Mediterranean regions, the winter is cold and wet but the summer is hot and dry. In equatorial regions, the seasonal march of the pressure systems gives a bimodal distribution of rainfall, with two wet seasons per calendar year. The seasonal course of day length varies enormously with latitude. All these differences mean that the practical recipes of successful temperate agriculture almost always fail if they are exported unmodified to the majority of less developed countries. Set down in this way this seems obvious, but vast sums have been spent in the past on costly and humiliating failures whose authors attempted to copy in the tropics the methods with which they had succeeded back home.

This process may also work in reverse: a method which is impossible back home, or in one part of the tropics, may be condemned without trial even though it could well be satisfactory elsewhere. My favorite example is the use of small tractors. Agricultural engineers in the west have tended to condemn these machines on both technical and economic grounds, using for example a graph of cost against horse power which can be made to show that a tractor with no horse power at all will nevertheless still cost $1,000. Yet the Japanese agricultural revolution depends on over three million small tractors used by peasant farmers.

A further deficiency of agricultural science in many developing areas has arisen from the leading role which export commodities, destined for markets in the developed world, have had in their economies. In the past, the great bulk of agricultural research in the poorer countries has been applied to cotton, rubber, coffee, tea, cocoa, sugar cane, and exportable fruits and until about twenty years ago very little attention was given to food crops, except insofar as the results of general studies of soils and climate provided "fallout" benefits for them. In many instances, the export crops were or are produced mainly on foreign-financed plantations, where the total system was or is under expatriate control; but in others, they are "cash crops" produced by indigenous farmers alongside their traditional crops, and therefore often introduced, perhaps even with legal sanctions, into systems of farming to which they are foreign and which are often unable to accept them without great difficulty. For example it has proved extremely hard, in most parts of Africa, to persuade subsistence peasant farmers to sow cotton early enough for satisfactory yields, because their first priority is inevitably given to the sowing and weeding of the food crops on which they and their families depend absolutely for their survival.

Some Implications for Agricultural Education

All this has important implications for those agricultural scientists and technologists who educate and train the agricultural scientists and technologists of the future. Their students must be equipped not only to comprehend the diversity of agricultural systems as they exist today, but also to generate change in them during the forty years of working life that lie ahead of them. For this purpose, an old-fashioned course based on the current practice of agriculture in the vicinity of the teaching institution (or even worse, an idealized representation of that practice thirty years before, when the professors were young), thinly disguised as the "principles of agriculture" and embellished with a glamorous selection of in-topics such as molecular biology, biochemistry, biophysics, and quantitative genetics, will not do. A viable course in agricultural science is founded on four main components—cell and molecular biology; the biology of agriculturally important organisms; environment sciences; and the comparative study, on a social ecological/economic basis, of systems of agriculture, particularly those within reach. From these topics the student progress to the physiology, breeding, health, and protection of agricultural plants and animals, and to economics; and so equipped he is at last ready to tackle the analysis and synthesis of the methods and systems of production. A general foundation course of this sort is intended to explain how the more or less universally valid generalizations of the pure and applied sciences and of economics are put together in different ways to form technologies which can maximize output in particular ecological and economic circumstances, so that the student will understand not only how to adapt the technology as circumstances change over time, but how to apply himself to new countries and climates. He is trained, moreover, from the start to question all dogma and received opinion, to innovate, and to test his innovations by rigorous analytical procedures. New courses of this sort are already emerging in some schools, but many mouldering skeletons still rattle hollowly in academic cupboards in spite of the bright new labels attached to the doors.

To summarize, there is not enough agricultural science and technology in developing countries, and what there is has been relatively ineffective in meeting the needs of farmers for the following technical reasons: the subject has been fragmented among a series of specialist disciplines, so that technical systems or packages of innovations have generally not been designed as a whole; some of the practitioners are too readily tempted from their primary purpose by the professional and intellectual attractions of "pure" science; the methods of advanced agricultural technology have generally developed in temperate regions, and usually cannot be exported to ecologically different regions; and finally agricultural science and technology in the poorer countries have been too largely concentrated on export crops, which do not always fit well into the indigenous farming system, and they have hitherto given very little direct attention to food crops.

Consequently, in many developing regions, agricultural science, in spite of its technical excellence in certain areas, and the profound effect it has often had on the economies of emerging nations, has generally had very little effect on the indigenous traditional systems of agriculture or on the life and health of the majority of country people. Only during the past twenty-five years, largely as a result of the cooperative programs in many countries of the Rockefeller and Ford Foundations, has this situation begun to change to any marked extent. All this carries with it some important implications for agricultural education in its various forms.

Agricultural Science and Change

In general, the great majority of agricultural scientists and technologists do not yet understand the profound social significance of agricultural change. Here again history can come to our aid. At an early stage of development, when the great majority of the people are directly involved in agriculture, the technical methods are simple, and the capital involved is small, the structure of society is built around agricultural production in ways which tend to ensure the survival of the community, at the expense of the individual if necessary. Consequently, we must expect to find, and indeed we do, that many customary social and legal constraints, and the personal attitudes which they engender, are opposed to change in agriculture. As agriculture changes and industry develops, an ever-diminishing fraction of the people work on farms, and more and more live in towns and cities and earn their living in other ways. In Britain today, comfortably more than half the food of over 50 million people is produced by fewer than 485,000 full or part-time workers (less than 3 per cent of the labor force); and the subsidized industry is capital-intensive, yet flexible and amenable to change. In the history of Britain, the transformation of agriculture was associated with vast and often violent and painful social changes, many of whose consequences are yet unresolved. In the United States, the replacement of men by machines as prime movers appears to have left the nation, a century later, with many millions of individuals for whom society has yet to find a fully productive place. Parallel problems of poverty and destitution exist throughout the Caribbean, though it has taken a century for massive immigration to bring them home to us in Britain, in spite of the Commonwealth Sugar Agreements, which have tended to stave off the problem by maintaining an artificial price for sugar in the British Commonwealth.

These are specific and perhaps extreme examples. A practical and topical one is offered by the social relations of traditional agriculture, in many tropical regions, which often depends on the shifting cultivation of annual crops. It is often not technically difficult to devise a permanent system of farming suited to the region; but any such system will require a complete change in the relation between the community and the land it uses, particularly if perennial crops are to be introduced. It may even require private ownership of land in the western sense, a concept which is not only foreign but perhaps even incomprehensible or repugnant to many traditional farming societies. The general point is that in planned and directed agricultural change the package of innovations which the technologist must strive to introduce has to be supported by change in the economic, social, legal, and political fields as well. Research, education, and extension, which may suffice when the rest of the agricultural environment is already on the move, must be buttressed in less developed societies by such devices as the provision of cheap credit and of new marketing systems, reform of land tenure, consolidation of fragmented holdings, and often by much more far-reaching changes, including the development of transport, storage, and processing facilities, and the supply of new inputs. In some instances large-scale agrarian reform and political change may even be necessary. Of these matters the agricultural scientist is usually ignorant and often unaware, but as components of the change he is dedicated to producing, they should be very much his concern.

What Sort of Farmers?

Most agricultural change has come about in the past as a result of the initiative, drive, ambition, and technical managerial ability of individuals—whether they were invading conquerors, feudal lords, landowners, entrepreneurial industrialists, or enlightened farmers producing for the growing market. In those agricultural revolutions which have begun or are beginning in our times in many of the poorer countries, the same emphasis on individual enterprise and initiative is evident. Most, if not all, of the efforts to base major agricultural change on communal organization and cooperation (which are the basis of traditional agriculture) have found their objectives extremely difficult to achieve, even where (as in irrigation settlements) one of the principal means of production demands some form of large-scale organization. Perhaps this is because the production process itself, at our present level of technical development, depends for its success on the experience and judgment of competent individuals, who can handle and forecast the movement of the continuously changing variables of soil conditions, weather, and prices, while at our present levels of social development these personal qualities are most readily mobilized for personal profit.

However, this may be, we must recognize that the agricultural revolution in many developing countries includes forces which are likely to destroy the preceding communal basis of society, with its built-in communal social security; to produce, or increase the predominance of, a class of larger farmers; and perhaps even to decrease the relative prosperity of the other farmers. It may at the same time do little or nothing to help the landless rural poor who have nothing but their labor to sell, and who in many of the poor and hungry countries include a very important fraction of the rural population. When this happens, we have the raw material for future social and political conflicts, particularly as the facts of demography and the conditions of world trade are not such as to encourage development of off-farm employment (for example in industry and public services) with sufficient rapidity to absorb the new potential proletarians. If this could not be done in the past in the rapidly expanding economies of some of the now advanced countries, how much less is it likely to be possible in the less developed ones at the present time? These are serious questions for technologists and agricultural scientists as well as for social scientists and politicians, since part of the solution may rest on the development of labor-intensive rather than highly mechanized methods, of perennial rather than annual cultures, and of industries based on agricultural products, which will need particular types and qualities of produce as well as appropriate types of technology.

Essentially then I am suggesting that since change in agriculture is a many-sided business, the agricultural scientist and technologist must be aware not only of the technical limitations on the rate of change, but also of the many economic, human, and social constraints which must be modified before change can occur. In changing agriculture in less developed countries, we shall often be changing the very structure of society itself; and we can do this better, and with less human and social damage, if we understand what we are doing and plan the changes and their consequences in as scientific and rational a way as possible.

Process of Change

This leads one back naturally to where we started, with Mosher's agricultural wheel (Chapter 2). His valuable model is essentially descriptive and indicative rather than dynamic: it classifies the forces bearing on farming, and so can be used to indicate areas in which these forces are too small, or the resistances to change too large, to permit sufficiently rapid progress. But to be effective in handling the phenomena of change any model must include time as a dimension (see Leagans' model, Chapter 5). I have come to think of the rate of change in the same way as one thinks of electrical current (rate of transfer of energy)—as being proportional to potential (e.g., technical possibilities and market demand) and inversely proportional to resistance (social, economic, political, and legal constraints), but to determine the system of units in which rate of change, potential, and resistance are to be measured is a task for an econometrician rather than for an applied botanist. Whatever units are appropriate, the analysis must evidently be of a network type with feedbacks of many kinds; and the circuitry is plainly such that some at least of the components of potential are affected by changes in the resistance— for example, a land reform may increase the potential of a particular innovation. Other features of the model must include (perhaps in the dimensional systems used) cost-benefit relations, so that the effects on change of different levels of expenditure can be compared and the efficiency of expenditure maximized. This is "think-tank" stuff, but I do not believe the task is more complex in kind than many which systems analysts and synthesizers have tackled successfully in the past, provided enough empirical data are available to define those parts of the system which cannot be handled "theoretically" or on the basis of past experience.

Indeed the immediate need is to evaluate, in terms of models like Mosher's, our current and recent empirical experience, of failures as well as successes. Much material of this sort is reflected in the sixty-seven cases studies analyzed by the International Seminar on Change in Agriculture at Reading in September, 1968.[1] Such work will not only assemble information: it will test hypotheses and improve them, and it will also develop the communication and understanding between "natural" and "human" scientists.

[1] A. H. Bunting, ed., *Change in Agriculture* (New York: Praeger, 1970).

12. *Administrative Policy*

JAMES J. HEAPHEY

The previous chapters and discussions contain a vast and complicated array of implications for administration. My intention is to discuss, unexhaustively, three matters: (1) Is development administration different from public administration, and is it the case that the problem for agricultural or any kind of development is an inability of public administration systems to manage development programs effectively? (2) Is there a serious dichotomy between the needs of development and the needs of national order, one which tends to be overlooked as we engage our passion for development with the institutional obstacles found in developing countries? (3) What are some implications for administrative policy?

Public Administration,
Development Administration, and Control

Frederick Frey (Chapter 7) analogizes administration with control; therefore, he concludes, public administration and development administration are not different. John Montgomery in his synthesis response to Frey and Parsons, says that public administration is concerned with control, whereas development administration is concerned with releasing individual and social initiative and energy with a minimum of government interference. I would suggest that both public and development administration are involved with control, but just as men and women are different despite generic similarity, so are the two forms of administration. However, I am more concerned with a distinction of public administration from bureaucracy. It is a common oversight to refer to all agencies of government, to all government bureaucracies, as public administration. But public administration is a particular exercise of government bureaucracy, one which originated in the Western nation-state and is now only emerging in bits and pieces in the non-Western world.[1]

This is not the place to detail the history of public administration. Generally and oversimply, the bureaucracies of the Western states which emerged in the sixteenth and seventeenth centuries were originally conceived as instruments of the crown. Then movements to curtail arbitrary discretionary uses of power, such as, most notably, attempts to establish constitutions, led to the idea that government administration should be done in the service of "the public." There occurred throughout the Western world a depersonalization of the state and its agencies. Different doctrines envisioned different approaches—in some countries the state was conceived as being equivalent with the public, although the state was depersonalized; in other countries the public was conceived as existing separately from the state, with its own interests and rights which are not always consistent with the interests and rights of the state; but throughout the different doctrines ran the theme that there is something public to be recognized and honored by the government bureaucracy.

One of the clearest articulations of public administration came from L. Duguit, a jurist, who maintained that the notion of the state, the public power, being able to impose sovereignly its will because it has a nature superior to that of its subjects, is imaginary. Duguit argued that the state is the result of a natural differentiation between men of the same social group, and from this there comes the concept of public power, which

[1] An example of the problem is found in a study by Glenn D. Paige and Doo Bum Shin. They report on what they claim to be a study of attitudes toward public administration and say that they asked thirteen Korean administrators what the words "public administration" meant to them. The authors say they used the Korean term *haengjong* for "public administration." Then they explain that literally this term means "the conduct of government," a term widely used to designate the executive branch of government. If the purpose was to inquire into attitudes towards "government," then the study should have been so designated. "Aspirations and Obstacles in Korean Development Administration," *Public Policy* (Harvard University Press, 1967), p. 7.

cannot be made legitimate by reference to its legal origins, but only to the services it renders according to the rule of law. *"La loi,"* he wrote, *"est avant tout la loi d'un service public."* [2] The essence of public administration, as a type of government administration, is the idea that governors and agents do not constitute an imperium over their subjects, nor are they instruments of a corporate personality which commands; rather, they are administrators of the affairs of the public.

In most of the countries that have a tragic food shortage there is very little public administration, though there is, in some, a fairly effective government bureaucracy. The reasons for this (the colonial tradition, the Spanish approach to administration, and so on) are fascinating, but not of immediate relevance. What is important here is that values traditionally associated with public administration and values associated with development administration are intertwined, for we have talked about agricultural development in a context of treating bureaucracy as a public service. We have emphasized the need to regard agricultural development as something to be valued by the people, to be pursued by the people, with the continuing support and assistance of the government. We have, therefore, assumed the desirability of both public and development administration, neither of which is currently an overworked concept in the developing countries.

Control and Creativity

The contention by Frey that all administrative systems are control systems is nonetheless true, just as Montgomery's contention that public administration is different from development administration is true. Furthermore, whatever the philosophy of government, any state requires a bureaucratic control system. As Louis Dupree comments about King Amanullah's frustrated attempts to modernize Afghanistan in the late 1920's, which led to revolt among the Pushtuns of the south, desertion by the army, religious resistance, and a takeover of the capital city and the throne by an illiterate Tajik folk hero–bandit: "Amanullah, in his zeal to reform, had failed to realize that or-

[2] Duguit, as quoted in Brian Chapman, *The Profession of Government* (New York: Humanities Press, 1966), p. 36.

ganized power is essential to effective reform." [3] Mr. P. T.
Odumosu, Secretary to the Military Government of the Western State of Nigeria, has said: "Here in Nigeria, the activities
of the governments are most pervasive. We expect the governments to provide social and economic services, develop industries and agriculture, and *ensure the maintenance of law and
order.*" [4] The tendency in this volume has been to view the
control system aspect of government as an undesirable obstacle
to the exercise of creativity. As is common when we express our
hopes for development, the bureaucratic control system looms
large and unfriendly. Nonetheless, a simple truth remains: development programs depend upon the bureaucratic control
system for success.

Ralph Cummings (Chapter 4) says that agricultural development cannot take place on the basis of existing knowledge. We need new knowledge, we need to do research, he
advises. Karl Deutsch (Chapter 3) calls our attention to the need
for flexibility, which could be achieved if we were able to design
self-transforming organizational systems. Fred Frey presented
a difference between "programmed administration" and "feedback administration," suggesting that agricultural development
may need "feedback administration." But "feedback" is a concept that is derivative from "program." There is no way of
evaluating feedback if you do not have a program in terms of
which you can make the evaluations. If a "self-transforming
organization" is one in which the control system overthrows
itself, then I question the concept. My position is that to emphasize change without indicating how it will interrelate with
the need for order is less than reasonable. A hypothetical story
about "the law of sunk commitment" may exemplify this point.
On Monday morning, October 23, 1969, Robert Sterling, agricultural expert, advises Gorb Favorab, a high level bureaucrat
in the country of Dif, that his scientific knowledge indicates a
need for increased government encouragement of subsistence-
level farmers. Sterling is persuasive. Favorab proceeds to use

[3] "Tribalism, Regionalism, and National Oligarchy: Afghanistan," in
Expectant Peoples, K. H. Silvert, ed. (New York: Random House, 1967),
pp. 45–46.
[4] "Leadership in the Public Service of Nigeria," *Administration*, 2
(January, 1968), 65. Italics added.

his influence in the bureaucracy to establish programs along the lines prescribed by Sterling. He must present the program at his own. He can give Sterling credit, but he must accept responsibility for the program. His bureaucratic world is such that he cannot present himself as Sterling's supporter. Favorab pounds a few desks, spends some of the power he has built up over the years, and goes out on a few limbs in his bureaucracy. Favorab is successful. He gets the program, is named administrator of it, and the budget is handsome. In the meantime, which has been eighteen months, Sterling has changed his mind. Agricultural science has shifted to a belief that support of subsistence-level farmers is a mistake in agricultural development programs. This has been demonstrated in countries where subsistence-level farming has been encouraged. Poor Favorab. What does he do now? Is the new and completely different advice "feedback?" How can he be the link with the environment that tells the organization to countermand its previous decision? And what about him as an individual human being who finds himself running the hundred yard dash on the advice of a friend and being told by the friend as he runs that the advice was faulty, that he should be running the hurdles which is taking place at the same time.

I think that creativity and learning are excellent concepts for development; but I also think that they are meaningless if they are not related to the need for, and problem of, control. As pitifully anti-rational as it may sound, there is a time we must try to win the hundred yard dash, though it may not be the best race. A reasonable social strategy does not put unbearable strains on social structures which are crucial to performance of the strategy. So long as we talk about learning and adaptation without questioning the capacity of control systems in developing countries to learn and adapt, we are toying with unrealizable notions. Indeed, implementation of change appears to require more control than implementation of routine. On the larger scale we see that nation-states increase control systems as they attempt change. This has been the case in Western democracies as they have moved from peacetime to wartime systems, and in countries that are undergoing rapid development programs today. On a smaller scale, we see an increase in control as organizations undergo change. What this suggests is that our yearnings for change need foundation in the mechanisms and social reality of control.

Some Implications for Administration

There is a need for a national development vision in which agricultural development will have a specific place. At certain times—and these are the crucial times for agricultural development programs—allocations of scarce resources are made at the national level. The claims for agricultural development are weighed against many other claims. It is not just that a good case need be made for agricultural development; in addition, agricultural development must be related to other development goals in the country. Increasingly, it appears, developing countries are using central planning and budgeting offices to prescribe allocations to specific sectors according to a total view of the country and its development problems. To say that it is the job of those who think in such total terms to decide how agriculture fits in with other sectors would be a mistake, I submit; better, anyway better for agricultural development, if those concerned with agricultural development formulate for planners ways in which agriculture relates to the rest of the development picture.

Unfortunately, there is a notion that technology harbors no social or economic vision, and should not. The result of this is that we often separate technique from socio-economic consequences in our thinking and acting. For example, as two USAID officers have noted, "Technical experts in production tend to feel that problems related to distribution are the problems of other people, i.e., of economists and social scientists as well as political leaders. However, these 'others' may also lack the skills or the feeling of priority in this field." The deeper problem, they go on to say, is that technicians have biases which they act upon, though claiming to be dealing entirely with technique. Most modern technicians "do not really believe that small, labor-intensive farms are a feasible solution for any country's rural development. Despite statements to the contrary and support of some important programs aimed at small farmers, Western advisors by and large welcome and are happy to support agricultural development programs that strengthen large mechanized commercialized holdings vis-à-vis small family ones; support concentrating innovative practices on the larger farms; and generally oppose land redistribution as a central element of agrarian reform." [5]

I do not mean to suggest that no agriculturalists have concerned themselves with broader implications of agricultural technology. There have been too many thoughtful essays on the subject such as Clifton R. Wharton, Jr.'s "The Green Revolution: Cornucopia or Pandora's Box" to make such a suggestion.[6] Rather, my point is that these truths will have to become more operational in the field of action, as programs are actually being devised, than they now appear to be. There was a day when technologists, and the rest of us, could hide, at least in the United States, behind the principle that our foreign aid was concerned strictly with technique; that we were, as a matter of policy, quite deliberately avoiding questions of socio-economic effects, such as alterations in the balance of economic and political power between small and large farmers. Now that Title IX of the Foreign Assistance Act says that American aid, as a matter of policy, should be concerned with such effects, we can no longer retreat to that hiding place.

Another implication is that within the total development picture of which agriculture is a part, those concerned with agricultural development will need to have spatial location abilities. Arthur Mosher points out in his paper that the key to agricultural development is establishment of *localities,* which involves the necessary roads, markets, and so forth. Where will the first five agricultural localities for development be located? I do not think that technical knowledge of agriculture alone will provide a workable answer to that question. If agricultural development specialists learn to think in terms of total country development, they may get many helpful clues from those total pictures regarding where to place localities. Borrowing logic from what may appear to be nonagricultural questions may improve possibilities of agricultural development. This, and the first implication stated above, brings out the fact that agricultural development must *engage* with the

[5] Jerome T. French and Princeton N. Lyman, "Social and Political Implications of the New Cereal Varieties," *Development Digest,* 7, no. 4 (October, 1969), 117.

[6] *Foreign Affairs,* 47, no. 3 (April, 1969), 464–476.

total administrative machinery of the country, and that it must find paths to follow that, while they need not be identical to those of other sectors and national felt needs for order and control, are not complete detours from paths along which the national bureaucracy feels comfortable to travel.

Another important administrative consideration is that the control system must adapt to requirements of developmental programs, for agricultural and all development programs. For example, an agricultural experimental program must be evaluated in ways different from evaluation of police work. At certain stages agricultural development "work units" are far less tangible and measurable than are "work units" of a police department. Ultimately, of course, an increase in agricultural yield is the goal, and that is measurable; at least, we can talk about it in numerical terms and see differences in numbers. But along the way many administrative decisions—such as mundane matters of promotion and pay raise—must be made without numerical symbols of agricultural growth to guide the decision makers.

Bureaucrats, for example, will have to learn how to evaluate agricultural extension agents. Agricultural development requires organization. Organizations require systems of evaluating performance by persons working in that organization. Some may regard these as unimportant nuts and bolts; I submit that to do so is the first step toward ensuring failure of the development program. As much care must be lavished on the organizational needs of the machinery established to carry out the program as on the program itself. One of the critical differences between developed and underdeveloped countries is that in the former you do not have to concern yourself so much with organizational questions as you do in the latter. A great deal of organizational experience has already been built up in developed countries; indeed, they are, in a sense, organizational cultures; the people fall easily into organizational roles. Kenneth Parsons notes that agricultural economics is a product of modern economies, and by the time it emerged in American thought this country was far beyond the stage of agricultural development confronted in the underdeveloped world. I would like to add that by the time we began consciously pursuing agricultural development in this country our people had organizational skills, as a total population, considerably more sophisticated than one finds in developing countries.

I am troubled by the suggestion that we must think about agricultural development as a highly complex activity involving many imponderables, as in Solon Barraclough's response. Surely no one would deny the importance of searching for complexity, but I think it is just as appropriate for us to remember that when we design administrative systems we must be modest regarding the amount of complexity that can be managed. Organizations need simple and concretely stated purposes.

Another important implication is the need for commitment to agricultural development in a country as part of the development vision of the country's elite. No matter how adequately the administrative structure learns to locate and give emphasis to agricultural development within its total vision, no matter how well those who try to improve agriculture come to a *modus vivendi* with the style of control systems, no matter how sufficiently standards of evaluation are formulated, if commitment of political elites is missing then there is an ever-hovering doubt whether the programs can succeed. I list this under "administrative implications" because the existing bureaucracy can play an important role in encouraging political elites to have the necessary visions. In some countries the bureaucracy is the only means of communication political elites have with the masses. Such a situation places the bureaucracy in the critical position of affecting the premises of the elite's viewpoint. It is conceivable, in some situations, that he who is bent upon agricultural development should work first, and most seriously, with the bureaucracy, attempting to influence the bureaucratic viewpoint.

How can these implications be articulated in a model enabling us to begin designing action imperatives? What is the goal we should seek that is, at least theoretically, promising with regard to what we have said thus far? I would like to suggest a concept that Karl Deutsch introduced some years ago. Just as I am troubled by his suggestion of the "self-transforming system," I have always found his concept of "strength" to be most useful. Strength is the ability of a system to preserve only a few essentials of its structure while being capable of change in a wide variety of other aspects, if it is to be the basis of development in agriculture or anything else. Deutsch has noted that steel has strength and cast iron does not. The molecules in a steel bar will flow into new patterns when under stress. Cast iron molecules do not move until the bar collapses. What I prefer about the concept of strength, as opposed to the concept of a self-transforming system, is its allowance for consideration of the essentials of control and order, without which a developmental strategy suffers.[7]

In terms of administrative theory, the decentralization system has the most capacity for this kind of strength. A decentralized system, as I use the term here, is a type of centralized system. The concept of decentralization is meaningless outside of the context of centralization. What is meant by a decentralized system is that central authorities (say, high level bureaucrats in ministries in the capital city) allow discretion in decision-making to their subordinates in the field without divesting themselves of responsibility for what their subordinates do. Thus, responsibility remains at a high administrative level, while some freedom to exercise discretion is allowed at a lower level. The need for discretion at the lower levels is probably quite clear, that is, the need for a capacity in the decision-making process to respond to the local situation. There is an equal need for responsibility remaining at the highest levels of the administrative hierarchy. Any number of times, in the preceding chapters, the point has been made that agricultural development requires a "commitment from above." People in high places must view agricultural programs as relevant to development in general and as a responsibility. I assume a person with program responsibility for something is more likely to take an interest in it than is a person who at one time indicated support but is no longer officially responsible.

Decentralized systems are very difficult to maintain, mostly because those who hold responsibility are not eager to allow another to act for them, so long as they are being held accountable. Probably the most effective basis for a decentralized system is value-integration of those who are being held re-

[7] Deutsch's ideas on these points are found in two of his books: *Nationalism and Social Communication* (Cambridge: M.I.T. Press, 1953); and *The Nerves of Government* (Glencoe: The Free Press, 1963).

sponsible and those who are acting as their agents in the field. If both parties see the job to be done in similar terms, when what the agent in the field does tends to be similar to what the administrator back in the capital city would do were he in the field and confronted with the same problems as the agent, then there is a sound basis for a decentralized system.

There is an established organizational strategy for building value-integration. Training programs and development of administrative language are examples. A training program not only conveys certain skills; more importantly, it conveys values about how work should be done, reported, and evaluated. The development of administrative language is a way of establishing the culture of administration. I use culture here as a set of norms for identifying and handling problems; it has the function of preventing "truly uninterpretable situations from occurring." [8] Without meaning to stir up the McLuhan controversy here, I think the idea that "the medium is the message" has relevance. The technologies—personnel classification by task, budget by program, and so forth—which are taught to bureaucrats encompass a value system about how things ought to be done, just as teaching children mathematics through the use of examples from a free market instills a belief in the free market system as *the way* to have a market.

The purpose of a decentralized system is not to allow free-wheeling freedom of decision in the field. We are considering here organizations of power which link at one end a role such as that of an agricultural extension agent, and at the other end a role such as the minister of agriculture; when trying to think through many administrative problems such a separation is misplaced. The purpose of decentralization, as we are presenting it here, is to enhance the viability of organizations of power by increasing their ability to receive, assimilate, and learn from information which administrators come upon in their work.

A final point is that some of the frustrations suffered by agents of agricultural development vis-à-vis bureaucracy are results of inappropriate laws rather than stubborn bureaucrats. We have learned a great deal from the sociologists' theories of

[8] W. T. Jones, *The Sciences and the Humanities* (Berkeley: University of California Press, 1965), p. 7.

bureaucracy and its structural dysfunctions, but we have also misled ourselves somewhat. Some of the stupidity practiced by bureaucrats in developing countries results from the fact that the laws they administer are stupid rather than from the alleged incorrigible capacity bureaucrat structures have to act irrationally. Richard Nunez has pointed out how ex-colonial states adopt the laws that were in effect when they were colonies. These laws were "made" by the colonial powers to serve colonial power purposes. In many cases they are contradictory to the purposes of the new state.[9] The American expert in high-yielding grain varieties is irritated watching the Asian bureaucrat measure each and every bag of grain before it is used, and he blames it on "bureaucracy." Sometimes this blame should be placed on law, which is changeable, though there is an incredible tendency to assume that law is not a variable in the developmental process. Try to find articles, books, reports, etc. on relationships of law to development. They simply do not exist. Look for the words "law," "legal," or "administrative law" in the indexes of books on development. You will not find them except for a few, very isolated, cases.

[9] Nunez has recently completed a one-year study in Cyprus on this phenomenon. His reports are available from the Comparative Development Studies Center, State University of New York at Albany.

13. Résumé

JOHN B. HOLT

This volume on strategies for behavioral change in modernizing agriculture brings together an array of concepts and vocabularies, a wealth of hypotheses, major points of general agreement and controversy, and a considerable amount of mutual education among the contributors. This résumé is designed to crystallize the major points of agreement and disagreement, bringing into common focus the wide range of issues and strategies.

Strategy of Optimum Complementarity

Broadest in scope and widely accepted are the concept and strategy of "optimum complementarity." As Paul Leagans emphasizes in Chapter 5, promoting planned agricultural change that results in progress is a timeless process of skillfully manipulating critical elements, including customs, traditions, ideologies, technologies, physical resources, education, opportunity, and a sense of purpose. Leagans lists no priorities but specifies three "routes" as most promising:

1. Creating a macroenvironment that makes possible and encourages the ultimate decision makers on the farms to modify farm practices.

2. Building a body of science and technology that fills requirements for achieving modernization.

3. Creating and implementing an extension education system that will relate these conditions to each other and match them with current farmer behavior in ways that stimulate innovation and progressively overcome achievement disparities common to countries dominated by traditional agriculture.

Arthur Mosher (Chapter 2) makes more explicit some of

the elements in Leagans' points. He accepts for the farmer the role of assembling the inputs and turning out the product. He also ascribes to farmers all over the world a capability of some measure of autonomous innovations and development. It is his thesis, however, that it is not farmers alone who must change the ways in which they think and act. The task is to stimulate and encourage the broad spectrum of behavioral changes that are essential to agricultural development, a task of providing what he has aptly termed the "agri-support" activities of industry, mining, commerce, transportation, storage, credit, research, and extension education necessary for farm production, and the "agri-climate" within which farmers and the agri-support activities must operate—the politically based and encouraged institutional freedoms, conditions of tenure, taxation, administration, policies, and price and consumer goods incentives, terms of trade, etc., to which agricultural production largely responds and by which it is controlled.

Highest among Mosher's eight priorities he lists (1) infrastructure, including agricultural extension education and credit, (2) research and technology, and (3) supplies and equipment. But he comments that farm and agri-support activities will prosper only in the presence of an appropriately favorable agri-climate. He suggests that probably the first thing to do in endeavoring to assist a country in modernizing its agriculture would be to send a good ambassador of agricultural development to persuade the political leadership of its importance and to create thereby the political climate to make it not only possible but a political necessity. The priority of a favorable political agri-climate is without doubt, along with the concept of "optimum complementarity," the most accepted theme of the book.

Multidisciplinary Science and Transcultural Technology

"It is difficult," says Ralph Cummings (Chapter 4), to find examples anywhere in which substantial and rapid changes in agricultural practice and agricultural productivity have been achieved without a base of new or newly introduced technology and, in recent years, this has usually been a product of application of modern science." He agrees on the necessity for "multiple complementaries." Certain basic conditions must be met if changes resulting in accelerating agricultural productivity are to be brought about. Together with technology of a high degree of dependability and a risk of a predictable order, Cummings lists as basic requisites technically trained persons who understand the technology and are in a position to demonstrate it, an economic climate which makes innovation profitable, the necessary physical inputs, consumer goods as market incentives, programs socially, culturally, and politically acceptable and desirable to the people concerned, and a direction of development consonant with the national and local interest.

Cummings and his colleagues also agree that there is a widespread fallacy in the belief that a large backlog of technology exists either blocked by cultural and institutional barriers or lack of channels of information to eager farmers. Certainly there is a lag in the adoption of the newest technical practices which needs to be reduced, but A. H. Bunting, in summarizing the views of the agricultural sciences (Chapter 11), concludes that:

a. The available science and technology is not enough,

b. It is not sufficiently adapted to the situations of developing countries, predominantly located in the tropics,

c. It is insufficiently "packaged" for use, and

d. There is insufficient reading of the facts and inductive reason.

Finally, they agree on still another point: Unadapted technology is usually not applicable to conditions in developing countries; for the most part only universalistic scientific method and basic scientific knowledge are "exportable." Geographical and cultural differences require new selective syntheses of generally applicable facts and new syntheses of applied technology. There has been until the last several years an overemphasis in applied research on export crops—cotton, rubber, coffee, tea, cocoa, sugar cane, and too little on food crops for local consumption.

Implications of all this for the curriculum and direction of higher education in agricultural science are summarized by A. H. Bunting: The complexity of adapting new developments to the infinite peculiarities of different climates, soils, and economic situations requires that students be taught how universally valid generalizations are put together in different ways to form technologies to maximize outputs in particular ecological and economic circumstances. Students must, therefore, be trained to question dogma, to innovate, and to test innovation by rigorous analytical procedures. They must be equipped not only to comprehend the diversity of agricultural systems as they exist today, but also to generate change in them during the forty years of working life that lie ahead of them.

It is therefore pertinent to ask, says Marlin Cline, whether the institutions of higher learning have consciously designed a strategy of training adequate for development of interdisciplinary understanding on the part of those who will be responsible for programs of behavior change in developing regions.

The deficiencies in agricultural science and technology are paralleled by a similar lack of social science research and techniques. This limits the change agent's ability to spot and to analyze the critical barriers, supports, and interrelationships among elements in the social system (values, beliefs, practices and roles or norms, sanctions, power, etc.) which might impede or accelerate the efforts of the change agent. This would apply to sociology, anthropology, social psychology, public administration, and the science and techniques of politics and power. Work in these fields is largely dependent on government support and therefore on public or elite attitudes and policies.

Social System Strategy

Mosher's sense of a need for a "systems approach" to apply to the "multiple complementarities" is indicative of a general recognition of the need to comprehend the functional interrelationships of the many prerequisites for agricultural development. But social scientists point out that the inducement of change requires more than the formula for the combination of inputs required on the farm assembly line, as Mosher expresses it. A conceptual framework adequate for the difficult task of analyzing and mapping strategy for social change requires, as Linwood Hodgdon says, a systems approach which permits the analysis of the basic elements and patterns of institutionalized relationships. The social system approach of Loomis' PAS model provides for the analysis of goals, beliefs, sentiments, norms, status roles, sanctions, power, and such basic processes as communication, linkage, conflict, and boundary maintenance, in short for the important interdependent aspects of social interaction which characterize all forms of human relationships.

Loomis points out that the cultural anthropologist has developed his conceptual framework for cultural analysis and the social psychologist his conceptualization of the personality system, similarly the sociologists and political scientists their own models; but there is at least one concept of relationship common to all, that of status role, a point of linkage among the personality, cultural, and social systems. This enables all to contribute to the analyses of behavioral change, for changes required in the farmer or of any other actor affecting the farmer's behavior can be understood in terms of changes of roles within the social structure, always attended by changes in their supporting and guiding norms, beliefs, and sanctions.

Sympathetic to but avoiding a commitment to the social systems approach, Irwin Sanders (Chapter 8) proposes instead the concept of "social relationship," described and measured in terms of position-role, values, and norms. He recommends it as the simplest, most flexible conceptual framework for understanding system changes required by new practices (roles) and capable of bridging the gap between the system and process approaches. Recommending the systems approach as particularly useful in a simplified form for training change agents in detecting barriers and weaknesses in programs for social change, Robert Polson nevertheless warns against the danger of oversimplification and, in cross-cultural comparisons and analyses, against easy misconceptions. Social systems proponents agree that the dynamics require major research before prediction for purposes of planned change becomes reliable. It is one thing to be certain that, in systemic language, a change in an agricultural subsystem requires changes in roles, norms, beliefs, values, facilities, sanctions, and power as well as a change in the environment of policy, but it is another to know the sequence and consequences in trying to effect changes in traditional subsistence agriculture. However, Howard Beers, after an inquiry into the extent of agreement among social scientists on the substance if not the vocabulary of systemic analysis, reports reassuringly that few of the terms of the separate disciplinary vocabularies are not interchangeable, although he grants that many of their users might not agree with him.

Multifocal and Cross-Cultural Education

Granting the indispensability of new and well-adapted technology for agricultural development, Leagans underlines the similarly essential role of extension education. To expect a traditional subsistence farmer, generally illiterate and hemmed in by habit and tradition, to hear about, perceive the advantages of, and learn by himself how to apply modern technology in agriculture approaches sheer romance. Hence, an extension education system is needed to reduce delays and errors in translating research findings into action.

It is easy to say that, given the generally lacking multiple prerequisite complementarities, educational strategy becomes essentially a task of information and persuasion, or, as some would conceive of it, a task simply of cognitive mapping. However, when Harry Triandis (Chapter 9) states that the major focus in introducing change in farming methods must be towards changing the norms (roles), values, and aspirations of the farmers, he is pointing out that in cultures in which authority lies in the traditional, in which goals are communal subsistence and survival, and in which a premium is placed on preservation of the traditional, with sanctions supporting both, agricultural innovations will be rejected so long as the norms, roles, values, and aspirations remain unchanged.

There is little quarrel with Triandis' portrayal of the general theoretical solution of the problem through the conditioning of responses—a task of inducing an association between new knowledge and practices with favorably regarded "categories" of the farmers' experience, creating often temporarily uncomfortable "dissonances" between new and old conceptions and attitudes, often necessary in the learning process. To cope with and to exploit cultural and personality differences and capabilities, one could exercise selectivity in choice of agents, "targets," innovations, and messages. But Robert MacLeod, accepting the model as a theoretical mechanism, throws a big doubt into its applicability to overseas situations, set in completely alien cultural systems. He questions not only the relevance of our present concepts in psychology, heavily culture-biased, but also of our techniques of psychological measurement and investigation in the alien complex of values, goals, beliefs, and sanctions underlining Beers' skepticism about the significance of "achievement" and other "needs" as criteria of probability of development.

Woods Thomas points out that since the strategy of optimum

complementarity among multiple complementarities requires the involvement of all other sectors affecting agricultural production, the education process must be focused on them as much as on the farmer, and that intergroup, as well as interpersonal education and persuasion must be undertaken accordingly. Triandis comments that the principles of interpersonal influence would apply equally to intergroup persuasion through mass media, as in advertising.

Thus, in cross-cultural educational efforts to transplant successful U.S. technical innovations to traditional subsistence agriculture of underdeveloped countries of quite different ecological and cultural character, the problem of cognitive linkage encounters all the realities of systemic incompatibility—sharp cognitive dissonances, fundamentally different values and aspirations, absence or inappropriateness of facilities, and contrary or inadequate power structure and sanctions.

Paul Leagans spells out some of the problems in referring to the reasons for failure of traditional extension education to operate effectively abroad: (1) lack of adequate supplies of inputs related to the level of technology to be applied, (2) failure to adapt the U.S. pattern to accommodate cultural norms, physical conditions, and manpower resources, (3) involvement of the local change agents in other work incompatible with promotion of technological change (such as political or ideological campaigning, distribution of requisites, regulatory and multipurpose work), with consequent dilution of focus, (4) lack of staff able to establish the credibility among farmers which is necessary to influence behavior and lack of supporting staff at state and national levels, (5) inadequate functional coordination with research centers and colleges of agriculture.

At times, as Joseph Matthews comments, progress may be practically impossible in a developing country. The situation may exist because of cultural, economic, political, or other conditions prevailing at the time. It may be the strength of forces opposing change, the unavailability of the resources needed for the educational effort, or it may be the lack of other inputs required for success. Solon Barraclough gives this case a fundamental political character by asking whether an extension service based on the premise of an individual agricultural entrepreneurial class would perform any useful function in countries where the cultivators, the mass of population employed in agriculture, could make few if any meaningful economic decisions, having little ownership and disposition over land, credit, supplies, equipment, and other facilities, apart from their submersion in norms and values contradictory to the needs of entrepreneurial development. Wage workers and small subsistence level farmers in countries dominated by latifundia, as in many Latin American countries, are caught up in an intricate net of institutional arrangements and resource limitations that would make the best extension service in the world ineffective, he concludes.

What Kind of Farmer?—
The Multilevel Decision-Making Model

Economists and anthropologists have debated whether the concepts systematized as bodies of theory which now shape the intellectual climate and modes of thought in agricultural economics are relevant to the analysis of the issues in agricultural development in underdeveloped countries. Kenneth Parsons says that there is no simple answer. Modern economics has assumed an investment-exchange (market) oriented farmer, institutionally free and supported to make effective decisions, to acquire, combine, and dispose of available resources with the objective of maximizing income in the market. The traditional subsistence peasant lacks many of these institutional freedoms and supports found in modern societies, being limited in his freedom of decision by the scarcity of his resources, facilities, and restrictions and obligations imposed on him by tradition-bound institutions of the family and the community.

Nevertheless, Parsons and his economist colleagues at the conference tended to agree that within that institutional framework the traditional subsistence farmer is rationally sensitive to the dimensions of his alternatives and does make rational choices. This permits the economist to concentrate on relationships among the elements with reference to which the farmer "economizes," though this may not be calculable in terms of modern price theory. Therefore, there is common ground for a single system of analysis to the extent that economic analysis and policy analysis both function within systems of interrelationships, focusing on behavior as a function of the alternatives which are confronted at moments of creative choice and decision.

Parsons notes in nearly all the less developed countries the existence of a dual system of traditional subsistence agriculture interspersed with enclaves of modernized export agriculture. This he thinks poses policy alternatives—whether to extend modernized export agriculture, usually of a larger scale and more highly capitalized character, displacing by "assimilation" (absorption) traditional subsistence agriculture, or to transform the latter into more highly capitalized, market-oriented managerial units of smaller size. A policy to follow the former course would tend to be politically infeasible in newly independent countries, where everyone "counts" in political policy, Parsons believes, and it would moreover result in swamping urban centers with human problems of the un- and underemployed. Chandler Morse comments that such a course would also deprive a country permanently of its real independence through its loss of independence in its domestic food supply, which has in the past been produced largely by subsistence farmers with a marketable surplus beyond family requirements. Parsons assumes and Morse recommends, therefore, that national policies in underdeveloped countries will and should be to "transform," rather than to displace traditional subsistence agriculture and that it will require economic policies and corresponding action to accomplish it.

Lacking the capacity for growth, traditional subsistence agriculture requires the establishment of an institutional environment conducive to behavioral patterns creative of growth. In terms of behavioral functions this is basically, according to Parsons, the transformation of man's struggle to wrest his subsistence from nature (an exploitation of natural fertility) into efforts toward investment, specialization, and exchange. The functions are combined and institutionalized in different patterns in different national systems of agricultural economy. But in every case a new system must be created which permits and encourages these functions. In nonsocialist societies, observes Parsons, it will require the creation of "secure and objective opportunities for free choice" in investment and specialization —essentially therefore the complex institutional environment of property rights, credit structure, markets, and infrastructure, including transportation, communication, and education, which maximize the security of opportunity of the free enterprise system.

The corollary is the minimization of administrative direction by government of farm activities. In feudal, communal, tribal, familistic societies the policy, insofar as it exists, sanctions and enforces working rules, defined largely by tradition, which maximize behavioral patterns insuring local group survival by subsistence agriculture. In contrast the norms imposed by a free enterprise society are in terms of avoidances—guaranties of individual freedom from government and other group intervention. In a free enterprise society, government norms and sanctions do not require performance. It is through the norms and sanctions imposed by the price system that the farmers are given the opportunity and forced to share in the decision process. The new, vital function or role of the state in the modern system is to provide infrastructure and optimal exchange relationships for access to capital and commodities through the sale of products.

Parsons notes that in most of the underdeveloped world, authoritarian systems, whether military or Marxist, are easier to design and institute in the earlier stages of development. In such systems the behavior of the cultivator is a matter of command and obedience; the working rules of the system do not constitute property relations which provide opportunities. Decision and control of the process are with the government. Competition between the two developmental systems—one in which operational decisions and opportunities lie with the state and one in which they lie with the entrepreneur—is present in most developing societies and simply characterizes our time; it's the fundamental economic-political issue of the day.

In adopting the entrepreneurial farm model for modernization with its complementing, supporting, regulating, but minimally directing government, Parsons intentionally accepts as a value judgment that this is agricultural development through maximizing the potentialities of the free choice system in the behavior of peasant farmers. Chandler Morse, however, challenges in part the organizational rationale of this model for modern agriculture. If, he observes, we adopt a policy of transforming, not liquidating, peasant farmers, small farms will be faced with a multitude of potential problems beyond their innovative and initiating capacities. He believes that innovative decisions must be provided at two levels: (1) inside the producing enterprise, and (2) in the institutional environment of all the enterprises taken together. He suggests organizational forms which combine private incentives with public powers, to different degrees at different levels of decision, distributing incentives accordingly.

Karl Deutsch also questions the appropriateness of a farmer-entrepreneurial model which concentrates a maximum of decision-making in the farmer as a satisfactory solution to the task of modernization under all circumstances. He suggests that present urban slums and political upheavals have resulted in some countries in part from the creation of politically powerful entrepreneurial elites in agriculture, whose interests and power lie in monopolizing the decision process and the fruits of labor, with resultant displacement or discouragement and elimination of smaller farmers and farm labor from the modernization process. This raises questions of policy for U.S. government economic assistance and academic development programs which support national policies furthering such displacement. It might, he suggests, be wise to explore development alternatives which have been adopted with less disruptive effect—combinations of rural progress with greater community collaboration, or cooperatives, and appropriate national educational, monetary, and foreign trade policies, as observable in Denmark, Switzerland, Tanzania, and, others might add, Japan.

Administration for Development

In underdeveloped countries the vastly increased and vital role expected of government in supporting and coordinating development is generally recognized, whether in the all-pervasive, directing role of government in totalitarian states (Marxist or non-Marxist) or in the limited regulatory and supportive role of government in free enterprise countries. In the predominantly agricultural, less developed countries, which lack the requisite "agri-support" and "agri-climate"—infrastructure and political-economic conditions required for modernization—the modernization task, its planning, organization, coordination, and stimulation, falls primarily on the shoulders of the political and administrative elite.

The first administrative problem of a government faced with an urgent need for agricultural development is, Montgomery observes, to find mechanisms for dealing in volitional terms with a relatively inaccessible portion of the public, the rural majority, often not fully assimilated into the national political system. As Frey points out, force and authority may have been an adequate base of power for the traditional regulative and exploitive functions of government, but the fact that the farmers are at the furthest end of the line of communication and make an infinite number of decisions which can help or hinder development, places a premium on what Frey calls "feedback" administration and Jayant Lele terms simply "responsible government."

In modern countries government is characteristically conducted more in the interest of the governed, although the governing classes or individuals tend to benefit in terms of their own values. The power of those who govern, as Jayant Lele points out, is contingent on effective performance in support of welfare and development programs. It is open to challenge on grounds of efficiency in problem-solving to which, mainly, institutionalized power mechanisms are oriented. The "responsive" power, as Lele terms it, is dependent upon "feedback" not only for a continuous evaluation of its performance in terms of its goals but also to maintain its power and to permit flexible, rapid adjustment to fit local conditions or central changes.

The most common mechanisms for "feedback," to sensitize the governing elite or administrators to the degree of effectiveness of their administrative efforts, are: (1) direct and informal inquiries, (2) the bureaucratic flow of information or reporting (perhaps normally distorted by fear of consequences of unpleasant reports), (3) independent public media, (4) public advisory committees, (5) interest group representation, (6) political party organizations, and (7) elections. In development, extensive use has been made of public, especially local, advisory committees, for these have been thought to possess the advantages of economy, directness, less bias, two-way feedback, and educational value. But experience has indicated that, depending on their composition and attending circumstances, they may hinder modernization. The effective constitution and use of committees is a critical art of government in developing countries. They can form citadels for conservative "boundary maintenance" to obstruct as well as to build effective bridges for the promotion of innovation.

As Lele notes, the problem with many administrative structures in developing societies lies in the fact that they are regulative structures charged with incompatible development functions and goals. Actors in a regulatory structure of administration will attempt to use authoritarian power to implement development goals and will endeavor to manipulate symbols expressing the authority of the government to obtain the "cooperation" of farmers who would normally respond best to opportunities, facilities, and incentives. Civil servants imbued with a regulatory and tax-collecting tradition, viewing themselves as faithful agents of a government interested primarily in extracting and regulating, make poor development officials. By contrast, the developmental mission requires values, norms, and sanctions which meet the farmers' needs and aspirations and thereby induce them to respond to developmental opportunities. Both Jayant Lele and John Montgomery conclude that it is best to transfer functions of development from old line civil services to development ministries, since reform of the traditional civil service mentality is problematic.

Fred Frey warns of the long time required for changes in the attitudes of the rural governed toward the government, since the traditional exploitation by government and the hostility toward government may be replaced soon by a benevolence on the side of the government but not by an early appreciative response on the part of the rural public. Montgomery supports the point by reporting studies which indicate that peasants' subsequent encounters with government have tended in fact to confirm their long-justified prejudices against government as primarily exploitive in nature—a policeman and tax collector, despite efforts on the part of policy makers and administrators to promote the new image of a benevolent developer.

Nevertheless, Deutsch reminds us that among the agricultural as well as the general populations of the developing countries a differential and favorable response exists which can be developed. Deutsch reviews the physical, socio-economic, cultural, and class characteristics which may well account for much of the differential response of population groups to environmental opportunities and efforts toward modernization. He draws particular attention to the importance of health and vigor, to the rates of mortality and morbidity of the population, both basic. He asks whether it might not be better for the long-run interests of the free world not to keep developing countries on short rations but let them, through more food, assistance, better health, and strength, become more responsive to opportunities and alternatives in development and politically more stable. Cultural factors, he observes, are no less significant in determining response to environmental opportunities and political leadership. "Favorable technological and economic habits" are part of the institutional heritage which makes some groups more apt and responsive than others. In some cultures a resistance against innovation has been developed in self-protection for survival. Deutsch theorizes that when population pressure on land resources in a certain region is so great that an unsuccessful innovation would threaten starvation, innovation is actively discouraged by group sanctions. By reducing the risks and increasing the rewards, it might be possible, he reasons, to accelerate innovation. Finally, Deutsch parallels and supplements the institutionalists' stress on an all-important role of the institutional system in creating change-minded farmers by providing opportunities and rewards for change-mindedness.

As a matter of importance in administrative institutional development, Montgomery reminds us that executive and managerial talent is scarce in developing countries. He agrees with Parsons, Morse, Leagans, and Deutsch that there would be a substantial economy in substituting market and budget controls for bureaucratic regulations, operations, and personnel. This is, in other words, an argument for optimum use of the free enterprise system for the sake of economical development administration, with government exercising only those controls necessary to support and guide the economy through maximum use of the market and free choice of individuals responding to opportunities.

James Heaphey warns, however, that a developing country can afford decentralized control, presumably in this or other forms, only to the extent compatible with the government's power to preserve the essentials of its structure and policy. Administrative control and supporting political strength are necessary, he argues, if the government is to undertake development, regardless of the field. On this, Deutsch and others who stress the priority of a national policy and power to develop are entirely in agreement. Heaphey adds that the control of agricultural development must be integrated with the control of development of other sectors, often accomplished through use of central planning and budgeting offices in the developing countries.

Mobilization of Political Power for Development

In the early part of this chapter it was suggested that priority of a favorable political "agri-climate" was, undoubtedly, along with the concept of "optimum complementarity," the most accepted theme of the conference. According to the concept of complementarity, agricultural modernization requires societal change and, as several of the authors have emphasized, this requires a "national will to develop"—a high order of value placed on development among the governing elite, not merely, as Montgomery points out, among the immediate target groups of development.

Political changes of the order suggested, observes Montgomery, are almost revolutionary in character. They include using government policy to balance off the claims of the privileged elite against incentives to the rural poor, finding substitutes in private or associational institutions for government action, and decentralizing decision-making from capital city to provincial towns and villages. Changes of this magnitude, he comments, cannot be expected to emerge anywhere in the absence of a powerful will to develop the country.

Faced with the task of massive institutional reconstruction it would seem, observes Deutsch, that governments, politics, and ideologies are the most powerful devices known to change the characteristics of a population. They cannot always do so, but political regimes, particularly if united with religious or ideological movements, have brought about some spectacular changes, both violent and peaceful in process. Governments and ideologies can command and exhort, but social and economic institutions can provide more continuous and ubiquitous organizations and rewards for developmental endeavor.

Political mobilization is required at all levels. Barraclough quotes Deutsch's own definition of social mobilization as "the process in which major clusters of old societal, economic, and psychological commitments are eroded or broken and people become available for new patterns of socialization and behavior." It involves first a stage of uprooting or breaking away from old settings, habits, and commitments, and secondly a stage of inducting the mobilized persons into some relatively stable new patterns of group membership, organization, and commitment. As Barraclough maintains, this must be as much a part of agricultural development as of any general development.

That development can occur within and despite an "establishment" has been amply demonstrated, though there are ample cases of failure. Heaphey suggests that in some situations he who is bent upon agricultural development should work first, and most seriously, with the bureaucracy in attempting to influence the bureaucratic viewpoint and that the existing bureaucracy can play an important role in encouraging political elites to have the necessary vision. Clearly the advisability or prospect of success of this course would depend upon the character of the bureaucracy, its personnel and its situation in the power and interest structure. For working within the established order, Woods Thomas advises that the most promising avenue to right decisions and appropriate behavior would be about the same as for farm-level decisions and behavior—an educational process directed at the particular order of problems and at the responsible sets of individuals within the society, despite greater difficulties in the complexity of the network, an absence of scientific guidelines, and a lack of decision-maker identification.

But Barraclough, reflecting his experience in certain Latin American countries, comments that social mobilization may require rather drastic social, economic, cultural, and political changes. It is then an integral part of what is substantially a revolutionary process of social change. For this reason it is unlikely to be peaceful and orderly. Relations among groups will change, especially those regulating the distribution of wealth, power, and status. It would be folly, he thinks, to expect those benefiting from the traditional order to relinquish their position without struggle. Effective power in his thinking is that which governs the relationships among persons, groups, and institutions, in a zero-sum game. If the government accumulates power within a country, it will be at the expense of other groups. Hence the bitter resistance. The shifting power relationships explain why development is such a tumultuous process.

Linwood Hodgdon provides a fitting summary of this problem of mobilizing the national will and power to develop: (1) in most developing nations the role of central government is all-powerful in establishing through legislation or other means the basic agricultural policies and conditions favorable to the agricultural sector and increasing and sustaining a network of supportive services without which agriculture cannot emerge from its generally static situation, (2) institutional loyalties in developing countries are severely circumscribed, making it difficult or impossible for actors in existing indigenous institutions to mobilize farmers toward the attainment of new social goals, (3) experience supports the basic hypothesis that modernization is politization and that its progress depends in substantial measure on political inputs and services, as agricultural development depends upon the infusion of the new factors of production.

However, whether these inputs will more often have to be revolutionary than peaceful, though turbulent, and whether, in order to increase the likelihood of the latter, Morse's "crisis-solving mechanism" and Deutsch's process of "self-transformation" can be built into the existing social system remains for further exploration. Certainly Frey's and Heaphey's suggestions for measuring feedback and Deutsch's proposed instruments for measuring government capability, public compliance, and degrees of opposition and support would usefully bear elaboration.

In summary, we have produced a comprehensive outline of problems and strategies of modernizing agriculture. Most generally accepted is the broad concept of the problem—that of inducing change not only in the agricultural subsystem of the society but in all those subsystems or sectors of the entire society which affect the availability of prerequisite technology, supplies, facilities, and incentives that limit or stimulate the farmer's ability and interest in adopting more progressive methods. The problem is a society-wide psychological, social, and cultural task of inducing changes in institutionalized behavior, in attitudes, goals and values, beliefs and knowledge, in roles, status, and identification, in norms, techniques, and skills, in sanctions, both legal and informal, coercive and competitive, and of creating the facilities and artifacts which provide the technical potential for agricultural development. Finally it is a problem of changing national political, administrative, and free market coordinating institutions.

As for strategy, it is generally accepted (1) that without substantial innovations in technology, modernization would be impossible, and (2) that science is still far from having produced or adapted technology adequate to meet the highly differentiated conditions of food production in tropical or subtropical climates, where most underdeveloped agriculture is found. An effective strategy must therefore include an expansion of research and teaching programs developed and coordinated for this purpose. This would require the necessary political, administrative, and financial support.

Recognized also are the inadequacies of institutions for "educating", i.e., disseminating new technology to farmers and to those who provide supplies, facilities, and incentives—a problem of linking rapidly the centers of knowledge with centers of decision and action. This is seen partly as a psychological-educational task of creating "cognitive and value dissonance" and of linking new practices with established values by conditioning responses effectively with the help of well-selected agents, targets, media, and messages, a difficult feat of transcultural communication with cultural differences at their extreme. But it is assessed also as a problem of socio-economic-political conflict, between those who would defend and those who would extend the boundaries of their status and economic interests. An effective strategy must therefore include not only expanded psychological, sociological, and political research into the problem of multifocal and transcultural education. It must provide also for conflict resolution in directions favorable to modernization.

Traditional subsistence agriculture usually lacks not only an effective mechanism for distributing the supplies and facilities required by modernized agriculture but also the institutionalized legal and economic sanctions which would reward, i.e., provide the incentives for, investment and effort toward increased agricultural production. Hence the importance of a strategy not only to provide the needed infrastructure of technology, transportation, credit, and marketing facilities, but also the constitutional-legal changes necessary to provide opportunities and rewards for choices conducive to agricultural modernization.

Given the characteristic absence in traditional societies of built-in mechanisms for creating new technology and for adjusting institutions rationally to achieve social goals through a new technology, the decisive role of the elites and of governments in initiating and pursuing change policies and programs are recognized. Two basic problems emerge: (1) the administrative—how effectively to devise and administer change, and (2) the political—how to muster the political power to support the effort with the necessary authority, funds, and force.

The authors tend to favor a strategy of centralized administrative power and direction over a developmental administrative apparatus sufficient to set and to coordinate effective courses of action but otherwise restricted to establishing the rules-of-the-game, fixing the handicaps favorable to development, and to providing services, facilities, and resources through an administrative apparatus dissociated as far as possible from the government's tax and policing functions and personnel. This is in recognition of the necessity for a strong coordinating government in times of rapid change, of the dependence of government developmental effectiveness on the cooperation of the agricultural population, which the government usually can ill command, however draconic the coercion, and of the wealth of initiative latent in the agricultural population which could be released by a loose rein and stimulated by opportunities promising advantageous returns at acceptable risks.

The emerging consensus seems to favor a strategy which provides an administrative apparatus that would make available information, supplies, and facilities, including both infrastructure and access to land, credit, and the consumer, leaving maximum freedom of decision in agricultural matters to those at various levels of organization, public or private, best informed, most capable of acting, and most motivated to combine resources and opportunities for optimal results.

Finally, the crux of the problem and strategy of agricultural modernization seems in consensus to be that of political mobilization, the mobilization of political support necessary to overcome resistance to the reallocations of power, of political and economic position and status, including rights to benefits (the sanctioning incentives) needed to induce individual choices favorable to economic growth. A strategy including the economizing of political power through prudent political selection of government programs, kept responsive by "feed-back" measurement of public acceptance and in tolerable relationship to government capability to handle change, has been suggested.

But there are strong doubts about the technical and social regenerative capacity of governments in some countries where the appropriation of government powers for the private ends of the governing elite comprises a constitutionally and militarily protected vested interest, which the elite would tend not to relinquish voluntarily, and where therefore the only effective, though usually infeasible, strategy left open to foreign agents of change would seem to be that of identification with the aspirations and movements of normally nationalistic and leftist dissidents.

Contributors

A. H. BUNTING is Dean of Agriculture at the University of Reading in England. He is a member of the Council for Scientific Policy (U.K. Department of Education and Science) and of various committees concerned with agricultural research and education in Britain and in developing countries, particularly in Africa. He is a Foundation Trustee, and Chairman of the Research Committee, of the International Institute of Tropical Agriculture, Ibadan, Nigeria. He was educated at the University of the Witwatersrand in Johannesburg, South Africa, and holds the D. Phil. degree of Oxford University and the honorary LL.D. degree of Ahmadu Bello University, Nigeria.

RALPH W. CUMMINGS is Administrative Dean of Research, North Carolina State University. Prior to his present position he was Associate Director for Agricultural Sciences, Rockefeller Foundation, with responsibility for the Foundation's agricultural programs in Asia and the Middle East. He has served on the Cornell University Faculty, and as Head of the Agronomy Department and Director of Agricultural Research at North Carolina State University. He holds the Ph.D. degree in Soil Science from Ohio State University.

KARL W. DEUTSCH is Professor of Government at Harvard University. Earlier, he was Professor of Political Science at the Massachusetts Institute of Technology and at Yale University. He has served as consultant to the University of Michigan, and as an American Specialist for the U.S. Department of State in India. He is the author of several books, including *The Nerves of Government* (1966), *Nationalism and Its Alternatives* (1969), and

Politics and Government (1970). His current interests include the study of large-scale political communities and the testing of political theories with the aid of quantitative data. He holds Ph.D. degrees from Charles University, Prague, and Harvard University. He served as President of the American Political Science Association in 1969–1970 and is currently Vice-President of the International Political Science Association.

FREDERICK W. FREY is Professor of Political Science, Massachusetts Institute of Technology, and is senior staff member of the Center for International Studies. He has done extensive field research in Turkey, Venezuela, and Chile and has published widely. He holds the Ph.D. degree from Princeton University.

JAMES J. HEAPHEY is Director of the Comparative Development Studies Center and Professor of Public Administration at the State University of New York at Albany. He has published various articles on development administration and has served in a number of consulting capacities with USAID and the U.S. Bureau of Cultural and Educational Affairs. He has edited a book entitled *Development Administration: Spatial Aspects*. He holds the Ph.D. degree in Political Science from the University of California at Berkeley.

JOHN B. HOLT is Research Associate of the Fletcher School of Law and Diplomacy, and Professor of Sociology at James Madison College of Social Sciences, Michigan State University. With an interdisciplinary Ph.D. degree from the University of Heidelberg, Germany, in Sociology and Economics, and an M.A. degree from Columbia University in International Administration, he has served as State Department Foreign Service Economic and Political Officer, coordinating diplomatic and development programs in Asia and the Near East.

J. PAUL LEAGANS is Professor and Chairman of the Graduate Program in Extension and Continuing Education, Cornell University. He holds a Professorship in the Colleges of Agriculture and Human Ecology, Graduate Faculty and University Faculty. Previously, he was on the staff of North Carolina State University and the Federal Extension Service, USDA. While at Cornell, more than 200 graduate students from the U.S. and 40 countries abroad have earned the M.S. or Doctoral degree under his direction. He has served widely as visiting professor and has presented numerous invited research papers at state, national, and international conferences. He has contributed extensively to the published literature related to the extension education process, within the U.S. and in other countries. Internationally, he has been Ford Foundation and USAID consultant on extension systems to several governments in Latin America, Africa, and Asia. He holds the Ph.D. degree from the University of Chicago, where he was a Rockefeller Foundation Graduate Fellow.

CHARLES P. LOOMIS occupies the M. D. Anderson Professorship in Sociology at the University of Houston. Prior to this appointment he was Research Professor in Sociology and Head of the Department of Sociology and Anthropology at Michigan State University, at which he is now Emeritus Professor. He is past President of the American Sociological Association, the Rural Sociological Society, and the Society for Applied Anthropology. Over a period of two decades, he has carried on research in Latin America where he was staff member and member of the Advisory Council of the Inter-American Institute of Agricultural Sciences at Turrialba, Costa Rica. He headed the United Nations Refugee Organization's mission to the Andean countries after World War II and was recently named as the representative from the U.S.A. on the Permanent Panel for the Evaluation of Experimental Literacy Projects for UNESCO. His most recent research experience on social change was in India where he worked two and one half years as Ford Foundation consultant to the Indian government. He has also carried on research in Central Europe, Pakistan, and Iran. His B.S., M.S., and Ph.D. degrees were respectively from New Mexico State University, North Carolina State University, and Harvard University.

ARTHUR T. MOSHER is President of the Agricultural Development Council and has worked in the field of technical assistance since 1933. Before joining the Council, he was principal of the Allahabad Agricultural Institute in India, visiting research professor of economic development and cultural change at the University of Chicago, and professor of Extension Education at Cornell University. He was a member of the World Food Supply Panel, organized by the President's Science Advisory Committee, and has served as Chairman of the Research Advisory Committee of the Agency for International Development (AID). He received his Ph.D. degree from the University of Chicago.

KENNETH H. PARSONS is Professor of Agricultural Economics at the University of Wisconsin, College of Agriculture. He is a frequent contributor to research and has traveled extensively throughout Europe, the Middle East, Central America, and Asia as consultant for the Ford Foundation and USAID. He is the author of numerous articles in his field, many of which relate to international agricultural development. He holds the Ph.D. degree from the University of Wisconsin.

IRWIN T. SANDERS, Professor and Chairman of the Department of Sociology, Boston University, has served as Vice-President of Education and World Affairs in New York and before that as Associate Director for the International Training and Research Program, Ford Foundation, and Social Science Analyst for the Bureau of Agricultural Economics, USDA. His published writings are extensive. He received the Ph.D. degree from Cornell University.

HARRY C. TRIANDIS is Professor of Psychology at the University of Illinois. During the last ten years he has been particularly interested in interpersonal communication, interpersonal attitudes, job satisfaction in industry and cross-cultural studies testing social phychological hypotheses. For the last seven years, he has served as a Consulting Editor of the *Journal of Personality and Social Psychology* and is currently Chairman of the Foreign Grants Committee of the American Psychological Foundation. He is a member and past Chairman of the Scientific Affairs Committee of the Division of Industrial Psychology of the American Psychological Association. He received his Ph.D. degree from Cornell University.

Respondents

SOLON L. BARRACLOUGH, Project Manager, ICIRA, Oficina Reginal de la FAO Castilla, Santiago, Chile

HOWARD W. BEERS, Director, Center for Developmental Change, University of Kentucky

MARLIN G. CLINE, Professor, Department of Agronomy, Cornell University

LINWOOD L. HODGDON, Director, International Programs, Colorado State University

JAYANT LELE, Professor and Head, Department of Sociology, Queens University, Kingston, Ontario, Canada

ROBERT B. MACLEOD, Professor, Psychology, Cornell University

JOSEPH L. MATTHEWS, Assistant Administrator, International Programs, Federal Extension Service, USDA, Washington, D.C.

JOHN D. MONTGOMERY, Professor, Graduate School of Public Administration, Harvard University

CHANDLER MORSE, Professor, Economics, Cornell University

ROBERT A. POLSON, Professor, Rural Sociology, Cornell University

D. WOODS THOMAS, Director, International Programs in Agriculture, Purdue University

Supplemental Readings

The following bibliography is designed to extend the scope of readings listed throughout this volume. In general, the items are current issues, broad-based, and present significant concepts and methodological approaches to agricultural transition and related nation-building problems. In no sense is the list intended to be exhaustive.

Anderson, C. A. and M. J. Bowman, eds. *Education and Economic Development*. Chicago: Aldine, 1965.

Baldwin, Robert E. *Economic Development and Growth*. New York: John Wiley, 1966.

Barrenger, Herbert R., George I. Blanksten, and Raymond W. Mack, eds. *Social Change in Developing Areas*. Cambridge, Mass.: Schenkman, 1965.

Belshaw, Cyril S. *Traditional Exchange and Modern Markets*. Englewood Cliffs, N.J.: Prentice-Hall, 1966.

Bennis, Benne and Chin, eds. *The Planning of Change*. New York: Holt, Rinehart and Winston, 1961.

Berelson, Bernard and Gary A. Steiner, eds. *Human Behavior: An Inventory of Scientific Findings*. New York: Harcourt, Brace and World, 1964.

Berlo, David K., ed. *The Process of Communication*. New York: Holt, Rinehart and Winston, 1960.

Brooks, Harvey, ed. *The Government of Science*. Cambridge, Mass.: M.I.T. Press, 1968.

Brown, Lester R., ed. *Seeds of Change: The Green Revolution and Development in the 1970's*. New York: Praeger, 1970.

Buckley, Walter, ed. *Modern Systems Research for the Behavioral*

Scientist. A source book for the application of general systems theory to the study of human behavior. Chicago: Aldine, 1968.

Building Institutions to Serve Agriculture. LaFayette, Ind.: Purdue University Committee on Institutional Cooperation, current, but no publication date given.

Burke, John G., ed. *The New Technology and Human Values.* Belmont, Cal.: Wadsworth, 1966.

Carneiro, Robert L., ed. *The Evolution of Society.* Chicago: University of Chicago Press, 1967.

Davis, Russell C., ed. *Planning Human Resource Development: Educational Models and Schemata.* Chicago: Rand McNally, 1967.

Eisenstadt, S. N. *Modernization: Protest and Change.* Englewood Cliffs, N.J.: Prentice-Hall, 1966.

Ettinger, Karl E., ed. *International Handbook of Management* New York: McGraw-Hill, 1965.

Faunce, William A. and Herbert Garfinkel. *Cross-Cultural Research in Developing Areas.* New York: The Free Press, Crowell, Collier and Macmillan, 1970.

Finkle, Jason L. and Richard W. Gable, eds. *Political Development and Social Change.* New York: Wiley, 1966.

Foster, George M., ed. *Traditional Cultures and the Impact of Technological Change.* New York: Harper and Row, 1962.

Gabriel, Peter, ed. *The International Transfer of Corporate Skills.* New Haven: Yale University, Division of Research, 1967.

Galbraith, John Kenneth. *Economic Development.* Boston: Houghton Mifflin, 1962.

Hagan, Everett E. *On the Theory of Social Change: How Economic Growth Begins.* Homewood, Ill.: The Dorsey Press, 1962.

Harris, Dale B., ed. *The Concept of Development.* Minneapolis: University of Minnesota Press, 1967.

Hembidge, G., ed. *Dynamics of Development: An International Development Reader.* New York: Praeger, 1964.

Horowitz, Irving. *Three Worlds of Development.* New York: Oxford University Press, 1966.

Hunter, Guy. *Modernizing Peasant Societies.* New York: Oxford University Press, 1970.

Inkeles, A. "The Modernization of Man," in M. Weiner, ed., *Modernization.* New York: Basic Books, 1966.

Institution Building and Technical Assistance, Woods Thomas and Judith G. Fender eds. Washington, D.C.: Proceedings, Conference on Institutional Building and Technical Assistance. Dec. 1969.

Jurian, F. and S. Henry. *Can Primitive Farming Be Modernized?* Brussels: National Institute for Agricultural Studies in the Congo, 1969. Translated from the French.

Kerr, Clark, John T. Cunlop, F. H. Harrison, and Charles A. Myers. *Industrialism and Industrial Man.* Cambridge, Mass.: Harvard University Press, 1960.

Le Breton, Preston P. and Dale A. Heming, eds. *Planning Theory.* Englewood Cliffs, N.J.: Prentice-Hall, Inc., 1961.

Lerner, Daniel. *The Passing of Traditional Society: Modernizing the Middle East.* Glencoe, Ill.: The Free Press, 1958.

—— and W. Schramm, eds. *Communication and Change.* Honolulu: East-West Center Press, 1967.

Lewis, W. Arthur, ed. *Development Planning: The Essentials of Economic Planning.* New York: Harper and Row, 1966.

Loomis, Charles P. *Social Systems: Essays on Their Persistence and Change.* Princeton, N.J.: D. Van Nostrand, 1960.

McClelland, David C., ed. *The Achieving Society.* New York: The Free Press, 1967.

Mellor, John W. *The Economics of Agricultural Development.* Ithaca, New York: Cornell University Press, 1966.

Millikan, Max E. and David Hapgood, eds. *No Easy Harvest: The Dilemma of Agriculture in Underdeveloped Countries.* Boston: Little, Brown, 1967.

Montgomery, John D. and William J. Siffin, eds. *Approaches to Development: Politics, Administration, and Change.* New York: McGraw-Hill, 1966.

Moore, Wilbert E. and Robert M. Cook. *Readings on Social Change.* Englewood Cliffs, N.J.: Prentice-Hall, 1967.

Morse, C., D. Ashford, F. Bent, D. Friedland, W. Lewis, and D. Macklin. *Modernization by Design: Social Change in the Twentieth Century.* Ithaca, New York: Cornell University Press, 1969.

Moseman, Albert H., ed. *Building Agricultural Research Systems in the Developing Nations.* New York: Agricultural Development Council, 1970.

Mosher, A. T., ed. *Creating a Progressive Rural Structure.* New York: Agricultural Development Council, 1969.

——, ed. *Getting Agriculture Moving.* New York: Frederick A. Praeger, 1966.

Myrdal, Gunnar. *Asian Drama: An Inquiry into the Poverty of Nations.* New York: Pantheon, 1968.

Nader, Claire and A. B. Zahlan, eds. *Science and Technology In Developing Countries.* London: Cambridge University Press, 1969.

Novak, David E. and Robert Lekachman, eds. *Development and Society: The Dynamics of Economic Change.* New York: St. Martin's Press, 1968.

Peter, Hollis, ed. *Comparative Theories of Social Change.* Ann Arbor, Michigan: Foundation for Research on Human Behavior, 1966.

Polanyi, Karl, Conrad M. Arensberg, and Harry W. Pearson, eds. *Trade and Market in Early Empires.* Glencoe, Ill.: The Free Press, 1957.

Rogers, E. M. and L. Svenning, eds. *Modernization among Peasants: The Impact of Communication.* New York: Holt, Rinehart and Winston, 1969.

Rostow, W. W. *The Stages of Economic Growth: A Non-Communist Manifesto.* London: Cambridge University Press, 1960.

Schickele, Rainer. *Agrarian Revolution and Economic Progress: A Primer for Development.* New York: Praeger, 1969.

Schon, Donald A., ed. *Technology and Change: The New Heraclitus.* New York: Delacorte Press, 1967.

Schramm, Wilbur, ed. *Mass Media and National Development: The Role of Information in the Developing Countries.* Stanford, Cal.: Stanford University Press, 1964.

Schultz, T. W., ed. *Economic Value of Education.* New York: Columbia University Press, 1964.

———, ed. *Transforming Traditional Agriculture.* New Haven, Conn.: Yale University Press, 1964.

Smelser, Neil J. and Seymour M. Lipset, eds. *Social Structure and Mobility in Economic Development.* Chicago: Aldine, 1966.

Smith, Alfred G., ed. *Communication and Culture: Readings in the Codes of Human Interaction.* New York: Holt, Rinehart and Winston, 1966.

Southworth, Herman M. and Bruce F. Johnson. *Agricultural Development and Economic Growth.* Ithaca, N.Y.: Cornell University Press, 1967.

Spencer, Daniel L. and Alexander Woroniak, eds. *The Transfer of Technology to Developing Countries.* New York, Washington, and London: Praeger, 1967.

Thayer, Lee, ed. *Communication, Theory and Research: Proceedings of the First International Symposium.* Springfield, Ill.: Charles C Thomas, 1967.

Turner, Merle B., ed. *Philosophy and the Science of Behavior.* New York: Appleton-Century-Crofts, 1967.

Walinsky, Lewis J., ed. *The Planning and Execution of Economic Development: A Non-Technical Guide for Policy Makers and Administrators.* New York: McGraw-Hill, 1963.

Ward, Richard J., ed. *The Challenge of Development: Theory and Practice.* Chicago: Aldine, 1967.

Watterson, Albert, ed. *Development Planning: Lessons of Experience.* Baltimore: Johns Hopkins Press, 1967.

Wharton, Clifton R., Jr., ed. *Subsistence Agriculture and Economic Development.* Chicago: Aldine, 1969.

Wolf, Erick R. *Peasants.* Englewood Cliffs, N.J.: Prentice-Hall, 1966.

The World Food Problem: A Report of the President's Science Advisory Committee. Vols. I, II, and III. Washington, D.C.: U.S. Govt. Printing Office: Vols. I and II, May, 1967; Vol. III, Sept., 1967.

Worsley, Peter. *The Third World.* Chicago: University of Chicago Press, 1964.

Index

Academic imperialism, 293
Access, 293
Accounting systems, 173
Achievement: culture-bound, 369; orientation, 169
Ackerman, J., 394
Action: concomitant, 416; cross-disciplinary, 95; initiation, 381, 382; rational, 168; structured, 124
Actors, 388
Adjust vs. revolt; *see* Maladjustments
Administration, 169, 297; administrators, 75; advisory committees, 476; centralized, 216; comparative, 453; decentralized, 34, 479; goals, 225, 226; implications, 458; manpower shortage, 302; policy, 453; private, 219; problems, 300-302; strategy, 483; systems, 228, 462, 463, 479; theory, 219; *see also* Government *and* Public administration
Administrative control systems, 460, 463, 479; based on ideology and socialization, 224; exploitative, 298; feedback, 169, 224, 228, 241, 279, 283, 286, 298, 382, 456, 476; programmed, 223, 224, 228, 240, 279, 286, 456; regulative, 252, 285, 298, 477; supervisory, 286; venal, 223-229, 279, 286, 398; *see also* Government
Administrative development, 170, 219, 251, 289, 296, 303, 305, 384, 455, 475; approaches, 302; definition, 296; economist vs. administrator, 300; educational, 290; implications, 303;

reform goals, 297; status, 288; technological transition, 297
Adoption, 134, 139, 145; behavior, 361; communicability, 363; practices, 138; process, 78, 362; stages, 138-139, 354, 362, 363; types, 329, 353, 361; *see also* Change *and* Innovation
Adorno, T. W., 343
Afghanistan, 46, 455
Africa, 70, 97, 118, 191, 201, 206; colonial, 191; equatorial, 182, 186, 187, 192; states, 190; tribal, 193
Agri-climate, 8, 9, 66, 67, 265, 466, 479; elements, 13; lack, 475
Agricultural administration: development, 290; private, 23; public, 23; *see also* Agri-support
Agricultural development, 5, 12, 14, 18, 29, 69, 76, 109, 173, 435, 458, 459, 460, 480; acceleration, 17, 19; ambassador, 8, 9, 397, 466; central planning, 479; concepts, 14-15, 51-52; concerned groups, 296; definition, 5; institutional factors, 179; international, 95, 159; policy, 167; spatial location, 459; technical knowledge, 459
Agricultural districts, 82, 92
Agricultural economics, 171, 173, 181, 289, 305, 437; *see also* Economics
Agricultural economists, 173, 174, 329; *see also* Economists
Agricultural economy, 177; dualism, 174; export, 174; investment based, 200; traditional subsistence, 174, 200; underdevelopment, 173-176; *see also* Economy

495

Behavioral Change in Agriculture

Designed by R. E. Rosenbaum
Composed by Vail-Ballou Press, Inc.
in 11 point linotype Baskerville, 3 points leaded,
with display lines in monotype Bulmer.
Printed letterpress from type by Vail-Ballou,
on Warren's Sebago Antique, 50 pound basis.
Bound by Vail-Ballou Press
in Columbia Bayside Linen
and stamped in All Purpose foil.